ROMANCING *the* REVOLUTION

IAN BULLOCK

ROMANCING THE REVOLUTION

THE MYTH OF SOVIET DEMOCRACY

and the British Left

AU PRESS

Published by AU Press, Athabasca University
1200, 10011 – 109 Street, Edmonton, Alberta T5J 3S6

ISBN 978-1-926836-12-6 (print)
ISBN 978-1-926836-13-3 (PDF)
ISBN 978-1-926836-37-9 (epub)

Library and Archives Canada Cataloguing in Publication

Bullock, Ian, 1941–
Romancing the revolution : the myth of Soviet democracy
and the British left / Ian Bullock.

Includes index.

1. Socialist parties — Great Britain — History — 20th century.
2. Soviet Union — Foreign public opinion, British.
3. Socialism — Great Britain — History — 20th century.
4. Soviet Union — Politics and government — 1917–1936.
I. Title.

JN1129.L32B85 2011   324.241'09709041   C2011-900884-X

Cover and interior design by Natalie Olsen, Kisscut Design.
Printed and bound in Canada by Marquis Book Printers.

We acknowledge the financial support of the Government of Canada through
the Canada Book Fund (CBF) for our publishing activities.

 Canada Council   Conseil des Arts
for the Arts   du Canada

Assistance provided by the Government of Alberta, Alberta Multimedia
Development Fund.

**Government
of Alberta** ■

For Sue and Chloe,
James and Rob, Andrew and Pat

and in memory of Walter Kendall

CONTENTS

ACKNOWLEDGEMENTS

I have many people to thank for help and encouragement in many forms during the long gestation of this book. There are the participants of the History Research in Progress seminar at the University of Sussex, with whom I tried out the idea of this book in a paper presented in 2002 and, three years later, much of what is now the chapter on the ILP. The support of many other individuals, some of whom will be unaware of their contribution, has been vital. Not least these include Hazel Ainsley, Peter Campbell, Keith Cowell, John Gurney, Tim Haillay, Rachel Hammersley, Roger Hinton, Alun Howkins, Pam Kendall, Siàn Reynolds, Gareth Stedman Jones, Beryl Williams, and the late Walter Kendall. And it was for my birthday in 1974 that Victor Rabinovitch gave me a copy of Macpherson's *The Real World of Democracy* — suitably annotated — thus inadvertently planting one of the seeds of this project. I have tested almost to breaking point the friendship of Logie Barrow and Tony Carew by trying out many attempts at draft chapters over the years. More recently, Kevin Morgan gave me thoughtful feedback on a draft of the penultimate chapter. Their help has been invaluable and I thank them — while absolving them, of course, of any responsibility for the final product. I must also thank all those at AU Press, including Tiffany Regaudie, Megan Hall, Natalie Olsen, and Renata Jass, and, above all, Alvin Finkel and Pamela Holway. More than anyone, I thank my wife, Sue Bullock, for keeping me from giving up on so many occasions and for everything else.

ABBREVIATIONS

BSP	British Socialist Party
Cadets	(Russian) Constitutional Democrats
CLP	Communist Labour Party
Comintern	Communist International (the Third International)
CP	Communist Party
CP (BSTI)	Communist Party (British Section of the Third International)
CPGB	Communist Party of Great Britain
CUG	Communist Unity Group
CWP	Communist Workers' Party
DORA	Defence of the Realm Act
ELFS	East London Federation of Suffragettes
ILP	Independent Labour Party
IWW	Industrial Workers of the World
KAPD	Kommunistische Arbeiter-Partei Deutschlands (Communist Workers' Party of Germany)
LRC	Labour Representation Committee
NAC	National Administrative Council
NEC	National Executive Committee
NGL	National Guilds League
NIGFTLU	National and International General Federation of Trade and Labour Unions
RILU	Red International of Labour Unions
SDF	Social-Democratic Federation
SLP	Socialist Labour Party
SRs	(Russian) Social Revolutionary Party
TUC	Trades Union Congress
WIIU	Workers' International Industrial Union
WSF	Workers' Suffrage Federation; after May 1918, the Workers' Socialist Federation

Timeline MAY 1916 TO JANUARY 1925

THE UK	THE BRITISH LEFT
1916	**MAY** BSP split
	NOVEMBER First national conference of the National Shop Stewards' and Workers' Committee movement
1917	**31 MARCH** Albert Hall meeting
	MAY Strike wave, centred on the engineering industry
	3 JUNE Leeds "Soviet" Convention
	28 JULY *Woman's Dreadnought* becomes *Workers' Dreadnought*
OCTOBER British cabinet calls for special report on danger of revolution	
1918	**JANUARY** Labour Party conference in Nottingham; new constitution adopted
FEBRUARY Representation of the People Act is passed, enfranchising all adult men and women over the age of thirty	
	JUNE Labour Party conference
SEPTEMBER Litvinov deported	**SEPTEMBER** Rothstein becomes chief representative of the Bolshevik government in Britain
DECEMBER British general election	

INTERNATIONAL	RUSSIA/THE COMINTERN
	1–2 MARCH February Revolution in Russia
	25–30 AUGUST Failure of Kornilov "coup"
	7 NOVEMBER Bolsheviks seize power
	25 NOVEMBER Elections for Constituent Assembly
	JANUARY Constituent Assembly meets and is forcibly suppressed
3 MARCH Brest-Litovsk Treaty; Russia makes peace with Germany	**6–8 MARCH** Bolsheviks become the Communist Party
6 MARCH Allied intervention; British troops at Murmansk	
21 MARCH German spring offensive on the Western Front	
	9 APRIL Allied troops land at Murmansk
	MAY–JUNE Russian civil war begins
8 AUGUST The "Black Day of the German army"; the war turns decisively towards an Allied victory	
11 NOVEMBER First World War ends	

THE UK	THE BRITISH LEFT

1919

JUNE WSF conference declares itself the Communist Party but on Comintern advice postpones implementation of the new name

1920

EASTER (EARLY APRIL) ILP annual conference agrees to explore possibility of Third International affiliation

MAY London dockers refuse to load munitions on *Jolly George*

11 MAY British Labour Party / TUC delegation in Russia for six weeks

19 JUNE WSF and others form the Communist Party (British Section of the Third International)

31 JULY AND 1 AUGUST Communist Unity Conference; CPGB formed

16 OCTOBER *Workers' Dreadnought* publishes "Discontent on the Lower Deck"

19 OCTOBER Pankhurst arrested for sedition

EARLY DECEMBER Cardiff Conference of CP (BSTI)

1921

5 JANUARY Pankhurst begins six-month prison sentence under DORA

16 JANUARY CP (BSTI) executive declares the *Dreadnought* no longer official organ of party

29–30 JANUARY Second CP Unity Conference, in Leeds

INTERNATIONAL	RUSSIA/THE COMINTERN
	JANUARY Petrograd radio announces formation of the Comintern
21 MARCH Proclamation of Hungarian Soviet Republic	**2–6 MARCH** Comintern foundation conference
28 JUNE Treaty of Versailles signed	
1 AUGUST Meeting of Socialist International in Lucerne	
	DECEMBER First meeting of Western Sub-Bureau of the Comintern
JANUARY Allied Supreme Council ends economic blockade of Russia	
	3–7 FEBRUARY Amsterdam Sub-Bureau Conference
13–17 MARCH Kapp putsch defeated in Germany by general strike	**MARCH** Denikin evacuates last White army from Crimea
	SPRING Lenin's *"Left-Wing" Communism: An Infantile Disorder* published
AUGUST Battle of Warsaw; Poles defeat the Russians	**17 JULY TO 7 AUGUST** Second Comintern Congress
	FEBRUARY–MARCH Red Army invades Georgia

THE UK	THE BRITISH LEFT
1921 (cont'd)	**MARCH** National Shop Stewards' conference in Sheffield; group renamed the National Workers' Committee movement
	EASTER (LATE MARCH) ILP annual conference rejects Third International affiliation; many of the party's "Left Wing" withdraw
15 APRIL Black Friday	**23–24 APRIL** Third CPGB Congress meets in Manchester to ratify constitution and rules
	13 MAY Final issue of *Solidarity*
	30 MAY Pankhurst released from prison
	10 SEPTEMBER Pankhurst expelled by CPGB executive
1922	**18–19 MARCH** Fourth CPGB Congress in London; Commission on Organisation appointed
15 NOVEMBER British general election	
1923	**JANUARY** Building Guild in receivership
	MAY National Guilds League winds up
	AUGUST Final issue of *The Guild Socialist*
6 DECEMBER British general election; conservatives lose majority	
1924 **22 JANUARY** Ramsay MacDonald heads first (minority) Labour government	
	FEBRUARY Final issue of *The Socialist*
	16 JUNE Final issue of the *Workers' Dreadnought*
	OCTOBER Final issue of *New Standards*
1925	**22 JANUARY** Final issue of *Justice*

INTERNATIONAL	RUSSIA/THE COMINTERN
	7–19 MARCH Kronstadt revolt crushed
	18 MARCH Treaty of Riga and end of Russian civil war
	21 MARCH New Economic Policy (NEP) promulgated by tenth congress of Russian Communist Party
	22 JUNE TO 12 JULY Third Comintern Congress
	JULY Russian famine widely reported
27–29 OCTOBER March on Rome; Mussolini comes into power in Italy	
	DECEMBER Creation of USSR
	21 JANUARY Lenin dies

Romancing the Revolution

n the mid-1960s, C.B. Macpherson, a professor of political economy at the University of Toronto who had just become famous for rethinking the history of seventeenth-century liberalism,[1] broadcast a series of six lectures on democracy for the Canadian Broadcasting Corporation, published in Britain in 1966 under the title *The Real World of Democracy*. The book jacket summarized his general approach: "Professor Macpherson here examines what he considers to be three legitimate forms of democracy: the liberal democracy of the West, the kind of democracy practised in the Soviet block countries, and the mass democracy of the newly independent states of Africa and Asia."

In the second lecture, "Non-Liberal Democracy: The Communist Variant," Macpherson argued that democracy had, in its original meaning, been "a class affair." Marx's "humanistic vision" implied that capitalism would need to be abolished and that the "Dictatorship of the Proletariat would replace dictatorship of the capitalists." Lenin's contribution was to argue that the proletarian revolution would be the work of "what he called a vanguard, a fully class-conscious minority."

Lenin seized the opportunity in 1917. "So," Macpherson noted, "the first communist revolution was made by a vanguard in the name of a whole class. And the Soviet state was from the beginning run by the vanguard, that is, the tightly-knit centrally-controlled Communist Party."

Macpherson then went on to consider the democratic credentials of the "vanguard state," concluding that, although it could not be called a democratic system of *government*, it might still be seen as democratic in "the broader sense" of aiming to eliminate class rule and establish equality. But though Macpherson uses the terms "the Soviet state" and "the Soviet system," he makes not even a passing reference to the *original* usage of "soviet" — a workers' (and peasants' and soldiers') council.[2] Long before the collapse of the USSR, the word *soviet* had lost all such associations even for those such as Macpherson who accepted the broadly democratic legitimacy of the USSR. Now always written with an uppercase *S*, it was simply part of the noun "Soviet Union" or a related adjective. Yet the soviets constitute the only clear example during the twentieth century of a claim to have established — as an alternative to Macpherson's liberal democracy — a distinctively different functioning form of democratic government. As the *New Statesman* put it in March 1920, the soviet system "is the only practical democratic alternative to Parliamentary government which has yet appeared."[3] By the "myth" of soviet democracy I mean the naïve — or, more charitably, over-optimistic — beliefs about its reality and future prospects that were prominent in the thinking of early supporters of the Russian Revolution and of a wider spectrum of sympathizers on the Left.

Enthusiasm for the soviet system played an important role in generating support for the Bolsheviks in Britain — and, of course, elsewhere. Lenin and company themselves clearly believed that at least the appearance of a functioning system of soviets operated and controlled from the grassroots was vital. The Bolshevik seizure of power had, after all, taken place under the slogan of "All Power to the Soviets," and in 1922 it was a Union of *Soviet* Socialist Republics that was set up. A Communist version of soviet democracy — which had entirely lost credibility except among the most faithful supporters of the USSR by the time Macpherson wrote — was propagated with some success in the interwar period. Yet we rarely now pause to consider the significance of all this.

Consequently, there is now a danger that all but specialist historians may lose any sense that there ever was a perception of a "soviet system" that was different — in the minds of its supporters, at least — from the single-party, top-down autocracy that the words came to signify. And without this sense it is very difficult to understand the enthusiastic support that the Bolshevik revolution generated across much of the Left. This is particularly so in a country like Britain, where opposition to dictatorial rule, suspicion of "leadership" within the Labour movement and beyond, and commitment to the most apparently "real" forms of democracy had become deeply embedded in the culture of the Left — if not without ambiguities, inconsistencies, and co-existence with attitudes sometimes difficult to reconcile with such democratic and egalitarian values.[4]

In the twenty-first century it is too easy to assume that vanguardism, as defined by Macpherson, had characterized support for the Bolsheviks from the first hour. By contrast, this book re-emphasizes the part played by the myth of soviet democracy in the early appeal of the Russian Revolution. This is not to claim that soviet democracy was the sole feature of that revolution that attracted left-wing support. Nor is it to deny that there were authoritarian aspects to pre-Leninist socialist thought in Britain. The Fabians had always been suspected, by those to their left, of being lukewarm democrats at best and of subscribing to a "weak" version of democracy.[5] Among the Fabians, George Bernard Shaw became well known as a vehement critic, indeed adversary, of democracy.[6] A more surprising example is offered in Kevin Morgan's detailed exploration of the influence of the US Army Corps of Engineers and its instrumental role in the building of the Panama Canal during the decade preceding the Great War on the thinking of that founder of guild socialism, S.G. Hobson.[7] Although military hierarchy may seem an unlikely model for an advocate of workers' democracy, we should not be surprised to find instances of authoritarian thinking in the statements of even the most ardent supporters of soviet democracy.

Indeed, such ambivalence helps us to understand the later shifts in the direction of support for the notion of the vanguard party and for the version of the dictatorship of the proletariat that legitimized it. The possibility that conflicting ideas — ultra-democratic and dictatorial — could co-exist in the same head is perhaps suggested by the two quotations towards the end of this introduction. But, whatever our own sympathies, we cannot understand the attraction of communism in its earliest days if we imagine that those who experienced it had the remotest notion of the imminent emergence of, in the words of Robert Service, "a social nightmare worse than anything endured under capitalism." When Arthur Ransome, in the introduction to his *Six Weeks in Russia in 1919*, called the revolution "the greatest convulsion in the history of our civilisation," we can be confident that the future author of *Swallows and Amazons* believed this convulsion to be one in which the positive — current and especially future — greatly outweighed the negative.[8]

In part, then, this is a study of the establishment of a legitimacy in the minds of a significant spectrum of socialist opinion in Britain. Right up to its collapse, the USSR could rely on significant groups of people in all parts of the world who, with whatever reservations about its actual policies and practices, regarded the Soviet Union as a — or as *the* — legitimate embodiment of socialist theory. For them, the USSR and other communist countries were the only "actually existing" alternative to capitalism and represented, however imperfectly, a new and higher form of civilization. There were many on the Left — and sometimes elsewhere — who accepted, to varying degrees, the legitimacy of Soviet communism without committing themselves to Communist Party membership. The myth of soviet democracy played a key role in establishing this legitimacy in the earliest years of Bolshevik rule.

If we ask why, in spite of everything that happened, such a stance was quite commonplace throughout the period of Soviet communism, we come back to the wide legitimacy it enjoyed in the minds of so many on the Left, a legitimacy that seemed at times to be almost infinitely flexible: police states, show trials, the gulags, Stalin's pact with the Nazis, the invasions of Hungary and Czechoslovakia could all be explained away, minimized, forgiven, and even justified. This further underlines the importance of the question of how that legitimacy was established in the first place. Why did so many people whose own proclaimed values were those of equality, freedom, and democracy — and who, in many cases, had very honourable records of promoting these values in social and political struggles at home — come to take the vital step of accepting the socialist legitimacy of the Bolsheviks in the early days of their rule?

After all, there was never a shortage of socialist critics of Bolshevism such as, well to the left of the movement, Rosa Luxemburg. In the West, the socialist mainstream, represented in Britain by the Independent Labour Party (ILP) and the Labour Party, officially rejected Bolshevism, notwithstanding degrees of sympathy on the part of many individual members and supporters. So did the generally acknowledged intellectual leader of Second International Marxism, Karl Kautsky. He was not alone, but socialist critics too often tended, like Kautsky or like Henry Hyndman, a leading figure in the Social-Democratic Federation/British Socialist Party from the early 1880s until the "split" of 1916, to be from an older generation — yesterday's men and women. For F.J. Gould, speaking at the Hyndman Memorial Committee's commemoration in 1924, his subject might be a "Prophet of Socialism," but this second such annual event seems to have been the last.[9]

The degree of legitimacy established by communism can be sensed by the extent to which the collapse of the Soviet and Eastern European "experiment" has since been seen as totally discrediting *all* versions of socialism. Long before this, it had been widely perceived that, especially when the Cold War was at it height, the spectacle of "actually existing socialism" greatly inhibited the development of democratic socialism "since all socialist initiatives became suspect and were tarnished by association" with it.[10] Unfortunately, for those favouring such a development, the damage continued after the fall of communism. Tony Judt refers to the "residual belief system" based on nineteenth-century socialist thought and concludes, in *Ill Fares the Land*: "However perverted the Moscovite variation, its sudden and complete disappearance could not but have a disruptive impact on any party or movement calling itself 'social democratic.'"[11] How communism came to be accepted as at least *a* legitimate version of socialism is therefore a question that has contemporary as well as historical importance.

It is the argument of this book that the myth of Soviet democracy — the belief that Russia was embarking on a brave experiment in a form of popular government more genuine and more advanced than even the best forms of "bourgeois" democracy — played a key role in this acceptance. It was part of a complex of perceptions that included the belief that social and economic equality were simultaneously being advanced by means of this higher form of political equality. As we shall see, even some of the most determined anti-Communists of later years were, to begin with, anxious to give the Bolsheviks and their revolution the benefit of the doubt — in some cases for a surprisingly long time. Even those who dismissed any notion of adhering to a Communist Party in Britain often seem to have retained, well into the 1920s and sometimes considerably beyond, at least a "residual belief" in the reality of soviet democracy in Russia. Much of this can be traced in the pages, including the correspondence columns, of the ILP's weekly, *Labour Leader*, and, perhaps more surprisingly, in the Fabian-oriented *New Statesman*.

Initially, in 1920, the Communist Party of Great Britain (CPGB) was little more than the British Socialist Party (BSP) — founded originally, in the 1880s, as the Social-Democratic Federation (SDF) — writ large.[12] At the founding conference, the only other really significant group comprised some prominent members of the Socialist Labour Party (SLP) who had left that party to form the Communist Unity Group (CUG). At this stage, Sylvia Pankhurst's group of

"Left Communists," under attack from no less than Lenin himself in *"Left-Wing" Communism: An Infantile Disorder*, stood aside from the "unity" process and set up their own Communist Party (British Section of the Third International). Only Britain and Germany were awarded entire chapters in Lenin's extended diatribe against the Communist "Left," and the section on Britain consisted of a critique of a single issue (that of 21 February 1920) of the *Workers' Dreadnought*, the weekly paper edited by Pankhurst. In the face of tremendous pressure from the Third, or Communist, International (Comintern) for all the groups it considered eligible for membership to unite to form a single Communist Party, the following year saw the shop stewards' movement and the CP (BSTI), in spite of its hostility to "parliamentarism," brought within the fold.

The CPGB also gained adherents from the "Left Wing" of the ILP and from the guild socialist movement. Apart from the Labour Party itself, of which it was a part, the ILP was the largest of the British socialist organizations. Its "Left Wing" originally consisted of party members who favoured affiliation to the Third International and who sought to move the ILP in this direction. But in all these cases there remained those who rejected the communism of the CPGB. Perceptions of the reality, or otherwise, of soviet democracy in Russia and of the role that this supposedly higher form of democracy ought to play in the coming socialist transformation was crucial in determining the positions that organizations and individuals were to take.

More, perhaps, than any other individual, Sylvia Pankhurst exemplifies the appeal of soviet democracy in its purest form. Pankhurst's small but very active group originated as the East London Federation of the Women's Social and Political Union. When the socialist commitments and working-class orientation of Pankhurst's group led to its expulsion from the union at the beginning of 1914, it reconstituted itself as the East London Federation of Suffragettes (ELFS). During the war years, the ELFS was transformed first into the Workers' Suffrage Federation and then into the Workers' Socialist Federation (WSF). Then, in June 1919, the WSF proclaimed itself to be the "Communist

Party," only to drop the new title for the time being in the interests of promoting wider unity. A year later it became, with the adherence of groups even smaller than the WSF, the ambitiously but not entirely accurately named Communist Party (British Section of the Third International). Overcoming its "Left Communist" misgivings, and with many defections, the CP (BSTI) merged with the "orthodox" Communist Party early in 1921. Pankhurst herself was formally expelled by the CPGB executive in September 1921, and subsequently she and her paper, the *Workers' Dreadnought,* became the promoters of the tiny Communist Workers' Party.[13]

Sylvia Pankhurst figures prominently in Mark Shipway's *Anti-Parliamentary Communism* (1988), which traces the story of the — mainly libertarian or anarchist — advocates of "soviet democracy" (most notably the indefatigable Guy Aldred) in Britain up to the end of the Second World War. The aim of the present book is different. It seeks to show the impact of the "myth" on a much wider and more varied range of opinion than is represented by these "true believers." It concentrates, with a focus on the period from 1917 to 1924, on that part of the ideological spectrum stretching from those on the left of the Labour Party in the ILP, through the early constituents of the British Communist Party, to those organizations — Pankhurst's group, the syndicalist shop stewards associated with *Solidarity,* and the Socialist Labour Party (SLP) — that were early candidates for inclusion in a British Communist Party but later formed a chorus of dissenting would-be revolutionaries who stood to the left of the CPGB — what orthodox Communists came to label the "ultra-Left."

If Pankhurst exemplified the appeal of soviet democracy in its most authentic form, those who *did* accept the tutelage of the new Communist International and join the CPGB are in some ways the most interesting group on the British Left. It is entirely understandable that many who had invested so much in the hopes generated by the revolution, including the myth of soviet democracy, should find it hard to abandon their allegiance to Communism — though many were to do just this. The key question is how those who remained in the CPGB negotiated the change from seeing themselves as promoters of grassroots working-class democracy on a heroic scale to advocating centralized rule by a self-defining vanguard. It is true that Britain already boasted a tiny "vanguard party," of a sort, in the shape of the SLP, although, as we shall see, it is wrong to see the SLP's form of vanguardism as *identical* with that developed by the Communists. But, however one looks at it, this was a dramatic and significant shift.

The scale of the change in outlook can be illustrated by juxtaposing two quotations from the writings of J.T. Murphy, which can be taken as examples of attitudes to democracy before and after the Bolshevization of part of the Left — and of Murphy. A Sheffield engineer who graduated from membership in the pre-war *Daily Herald* League to the wartime shop stewards' movement, Murphy joined the SLP in the autumn of 1917, served as a leading member of the CPGB until his resignation in 1932, and, for a period, sat on the Comintern executive committee. The first quotation below is from his pamphlet, *The Workers' Committee: An Outline of Its Principles and Structure* (1917), an important landmark in the wartime shop stewards' movement:

Real democratic practice demands that every member of an organisation shall participate actively in the conduct of the business of the society. We need, therefore, to reverse the present situation, and instead of leaders and officials being in the forefront of our thoughts the questions of the day which have to be answered should occupy that position. It matters little to us whether leaders be official or unofficial, so long as they sway the mass, little thinking is done by the mass. If one man can sway the crowd in one direction, another man can move them in the opposite direction. We desire the mass of men and women to think for themselves, and until they do this no real progress is made, democracy becomes a farce. . . .

The functions of an elected committee, therefore, should be such that instead of arriving at decisions *for* the rank and file they would provide the means whereby full information relative to any question of policy should receive the attention and consideration *of* the rank and file, the results to be expressed by ballot.* The more responsibility rests upon every member of an organisation the greater is the tendency for thought to be more general, and the more truly will elected officials be able to reflect the thoughts and feelings of the members of the various organisations.[14]

It is easy to see how the Russian soviets initially appeared to exemplify the grassroots, rank-and-file democracy that Murphy advocated. How startlingly different was to be his view in *Preparing for Power: A Critical Study of the History of the British Working-Class Movement*, published in 1934: "The idea that a spontaneous movement of the masses will 'spontaneously throw up' a leadership and a policy is moonshine. Leaders who come to the front in the hour of crisis have invariably years of preparation behind them however obscure it may be."

Now Murphy was dismissive of *The Miners' Next Step* — a once-famous syndicalist-inspired work of 1912 that had much in common with the views Murphy expressed in *The Workers' Committee*. According to the later Murphy, it had "created an anti-official outlook of a character which stultified any real organised effort to replace reactionary leaders with revolutionary leaders." The conference of Workers' Committees in November 1916, in which Murphy had in fact played a not insignificant part, had failed to "define its attitude to political parties":

> This is not peculiar to this conference in that the shop stewards' movement throughout its existence never discussed the question until in its closing days, after the formation of the Communist Party in 1920. In this it was really carrying on the traditions of the syndicalist conferences. At the same time it shows how little the revolutionary socialists understood the role of a revolutionary party. Although the leading shop stewards were also leaders of the S.L.P. and the B.S.P. the parties did not discuss their responsibilities for directing the movement.[15]

---

*   Unless otherwise noted, emphasis is in the original.

One would hardly guess from this that Murphy had ever had any sympathy with such attitudes — let alone that he had been one of the main advocates of a now-heretical position.

While it can be argued that what Ralph Darlington calls Murphy's "political trajectory" was to be characterized by such sharp changes of view, moving "from syndicalism to communism to left reformism to popular frontism to anti-Marxism,"[16] the juxtaposition of the statements quoted above illustrates quite neatly the beginning of the shift of emphasis from what we might call "sovietism" to "vanguardism." Yet even in the latter there was, as we shall see in the penultimate chapter, *some* sort of role for the idea of soviet democracy.

Four decades ago, there was considerable interest in the British Left of the early twentieth century. Among the work whose interest has endured may be mentioned L.J. Macfarlane's book on the early years of the British Communist Party, that of James Hinton on the shop stewards' movement, and that of Bob Holton on British syndicalism. But, more than by any other single work, my own interest was sparked by Walter Kendall's groundbreaking *The Revolutionary Movement in Britain*.[17]

Although Kendall's work centred on the formation of the CPGB, initially my own interest was directed to the very different world of the pre-1914 British Left (to which Kendall's work introduced me), particularly as regards its notions about the relationship between socialism and democracy and its interpretations of the latter. My interest in the pre-war Left was reinforced by Logie Barrow's work on the *Clarion* movement.[18] Later, though, my interest moved on to the period of the Russian Revolution. This book is the main outcome, having been preceded, back in 1992, by an effort to trace Sylvia Pankhurst's route to "Left-Wing Communism."

Interest in the early years of the British Left declined in the 1980s, but a modest revival began with the opening of the Russian archives, which stimulated and informed work on both national Communist parties and the Comintern, based on evidence previously beyond reach. In the case of the British Communist Party, this has included Andrew Thorpe's re-evaluation of its origins, as well as Kevin Morgan's biography of its long-time leader, Harry Pollitt, and his *Bolshevism and the British Left* trilogy.[19] One sign of the renewed interest in the worldwide Communist movement was the appearance in 2009 of the new journal, *Twentieth-Century Communism*.

But by no means has all of the more recent work on the early twentieth century Left in Britain focused on the CPGB. There has been Sheila Rowbotham's definitive biography of Edward Carpenter, while David Howell's contributions have thrown a great deal of much-needed light on the Labour Party and the ILP in the early decades of the last century.[20] And for the period some years beyond those that are the main focus of the present work, there is Gidon Cohen's thought-provoking and stimulating work on the post-disaffiliation ILP.[21]

With some notable exceptions, such as Karen Hunt's enquiry into the feminist credentials of the SDF,[22] for the most part the concentration has either been largely biographical or has centred on the strategies, tactics, and organizational trajectory of various parties and movements rather than on the ideas and beliefs that inspired their adherents. There has been no sustained examination of the ideas about "soviet democracy" that motivated both those who eventually formed the CPGB and those who widely expected, or at least hoped, to be part of this new venture on the Left but who in the end declined to be signed up for that enterprise. This is the gap that the present book seeks to make a contribution to filling.

This is not, in the usual sense, a contribution to the history of ideas or to intellectual history as normally understood. Many of the debates that are presented here concern not the carefully composed texts of recognized theorists but editorial comments, polemical articles, and letters found in the main socialist papers of the period. Sometimes a single strand of argument from an otherwise unknown correspondent in fact serves to crystallize a particular argument, attitude, or belief.

The structure of the book is neither entirely chronological nor consistently thematic. The first chapters follow the reaction to the revolutionary events in Russia on the British Left as those events unfolded. Most of the later chapters focus on what a range of specific left-wing organizations made of the notion of soviet democracy and how they reacted to the different interpretations of it, with some regard to chronology but inevitably with overlaps in terms of time. Interspersed are two chapters that attempt to make sense, first, of the ideas about soviet democracy itself that were initially current and, second, of the hopelessly ambiguous notion of the "dictatorship of the proletariat" that, in some versions at least, came to be associated with these ideas. Ambiguity, though, had its advantages for would-be British Bolsheviks, as we shall see.

1

WELL-PREPARED GROUND
The British Left on the Eve of the Russian Revolution

The Main Constituents of the British Left

Prior to the events of 1917, the shape and contours of the British Left were significantly different from the pattern that was subsequently to emerge. The Labour Party had existed since 1900, until 1906 under the official title of the Labour Representation Committee (LRC). But there was no individual membership until the introduction of the new constitution in 1918, the effects of which took some time to work through. Prior to this, one joined the party either by being a member of one of the affiliated unions (which, essentially, provided the cash) and paying the political levy or by becoming a member of the Independent Labour Party (ILP), which saw itself with some justification as its parent: the Labour Party was Keir Hardie's "Labour Alliance" idea of the 1890s made flesh. The ILP aspired to provide the Labour Party's socialist ethos and policies.

As a Bristol ILP leaflet seeking to explain the difference between the two parties put it: "The I.L.P supplies the driving force."[1] This was in 1919, when Labour's new constitution seemed to put in question the role — even the existence — of the ILP.

Membership statistics for political organizations are notoriously unreliable — and even if they were accurate there would still be questions about how large a proportion of the membership was in some sense "active" and how many were simply "book members." But certainly, by British standards at least, the ILP was large for a socialist organization. It was by far the largest of the parties and groupings we shall be focusing on in this study. Gidon Cohen begins his book on the ILP, *The Failure of a Dream,* by pointing out that, though its membership had declined from a peak in the mid-1920s, at the time of its ill-fated disaffiliation from Labour in 1932 it "was over five times the size of the Communist Party."[2] In the years immediately following World War I, the ILP had about thirty thousand members.[3] The ILP's radical appeal was at this time largely based on its opposition to the war.

The next largest socialist organization was the British Socialist Party. Its origins went back to the 1881 foundation, by Henry Hyndman and others, of the Democratic Federation, which changed its name to the Social-Democratic Federation (SDF) in 1884. Renamed the Social-Democratic Party in 1907, it became the core of the British Socialist Party (BSP) in 1911. Although the leadership of the ILP discouraged the idea, there had long been a desire among at least some British socialists to form a single, united socialist party. In the 1890s and 1900s, this effort could count on the support of Robert Blatchford's popular (for a left-wing publication) weekly, *The Clarion.* The Unity Conference of 1911 failed to bring about the unity sought by many British socialists, but it did bring over to the new BSP a small number of ILP branches and some other, largely local, socialist organizations. The war tore the BSP apart, however, with the party as a whole refusing to support the war and a minority of "Hyndmanites," who saw themselves as the "Old Guard of the S.D.F." and who regarded the war as legitimate "national defence," walking out of the party's 1916 conference.

The SDF had participated in the setting up of the LRC in 1900 but had left the following year. A substantial section of the membership continued to favour returning to the Labour fold, and, during the war, the BSP affiliated to the Labour Party. In 1920, the party affiliated on the basis of a membership of ten thousand.[4] The SDF-BSP is normally regarded as Marxist, which is accurate enough provided that later, more assertive and dogmatic, forms of Marxist thought are not read back into the party's early years. Or at least not as far as the mainstream of the pre-1917 organization was concerned.

The failure of the SDF to adopt a sufficiently "rigorous" Marxist identity had led to the "impossibilist" split in the early years of the twentieth century. The main result of this ideological schism was the formation of the Socialist Labour Party (SLP), composed predominantly, to begin with, of former SDF branches in Scotland that espoused the variety of uncompromisingly purist Marxism advocated by the American socialist Daniel De Leon.[5] One of the SLP's founders and an early editor of its paper, *The Socialist,* was James Connolly, later to be executed for his part in the 1916 Easter Rising of the Irish republican movement in Dublin. The SLP's membership was always small, which SLPers tended to see as a sign of revolutionary vigour and rectitude. Walter Kendall notes that the party's 1920 conference report listed 1,258 members and estimates that by 1924 this had fallen to not more than a hundred.[6] But for a few years either side of the war, the SLP exercised a disproportionate influence on British socialism generally, largely through its press's provision of otherwise unavailable Marxist "classics."

The complicated provenance of Sylvia Pankhurst's organizations has already been summarized. Their stronghold — if that is the right word — was in the East End of London. We can assume that, whatever the name at the time, Pankhurst's groups were always even smaller than the SLP. Kendall gives the membership of the CP (BSTI) as six hundred when it merged with the Communist Party of Great Britain (CPGB) early in 1921, although this is based on the party's own report and is probably on the generous side. Pankhurst's "Left Communist" organization, the Communist Workers' Party, subsequent to her expulsion from the CPGB must have been tiny. But, as with the SLP, the small size of these bodies did not prevent them — and, above all, Pankhurst herself — from playing a prominent role in the years following 1917.

The shop stewards' movement flourished in the exceptional wartime circumstances and its main organ, *Solidarity,* will feature quite frequently in this exploration of left-wing reactions to the notion of soviet democracy. The early ideas and attitudes of the shop stewards' movement can be traced most immediately to the wave of strikes and union amalgamation campaigns that preceded the war and to the Industrial Syndicalist Educational League and other broadly syndicalist or "industrial unionist" initiatives and influences. In wartime, the crucial importance, on the one hand, of industry, especially such industries as engineering, and, on the other, the government's desperate need to conscript more and more men despite the exemption promised to skilled workers, led to intense industrial conflict, including major strikes, and, from November 1916 onwards, to attempts to create a co-ordinated national shop stewards' movement.

The origins of guild socialism, which was also to play its part in the story of soviet democracy in Britain, also went back to the years before the war. It is usual to begin an account of its origins with A.J. Penty's 1906 book, *The Restoration of the Guild System,* and the writings of A.R. Orage, editor of *The New Age.* But much more decisive in attracting people from the Left seems to have been S.G. Hobson's *National Guilds: An Inquiry into the Wage System and the Way Out,* published in 1914, and the adhesion of younger Fabian intellectuals — most notably G.D.H. Cole — in the last couple of years of peace. The National Guilds League was created in 1915, after a policy document advocating guild socialism, written by Cole and William Mellor, a former secretary of the Fabian Research Department, was rejected at the Fabians' annual meeting.

There were of course other socialist organizations such as the *Daily Herald* League and the Plebs League, which will be mentioned from time to time but have not been investigated in depth. Between them, the ILP, the BSP, the SLP, and the Pankhurst groups, plus the shop stewards who gathered around *Solidarity* and the guild socialists, provide a sufficiently wide and varied spectrum of opinion for the purposes of this enquiry. Members of these organizations would not usually have regarded the Fabian Society as part of the "real" Left. Much criticized for being a small, London-based group of intellectuals, the Fabian Society was more like what today would be called a "think tank" than a political faction. Its most prominent members were Sidney and Beatrice Webb and George Bernard Shaw, who in 1913 had taken the lead in founding the *New Statesman*. This journal's changing views on soviet democracy will also feature in later chapters, to give an indication of just how far beyond the Left as generally conceived the influence of the idea of soviet democracy had penetrated.

Radical Plebeian Democracy in British Socialism

From as early as the 1880s, versions of what the Fabians dismissed as "primitive democracy" had flourished in some parts of the British socialist movement. As the *New Statesman* reviewer of the Webbs' *Constitution for the Socialist Commonwealth of Great Britain* noted in 1920, the authors' "central thesis" concerned the "proved inadequacy of the present machinery of democracy . . . to express and enforce the will of the people." The reviewer went on to comment: "Years before the Bolsheviks came forward with their demand for a 'dictatorship' of the proletariat, the 'extreme left' in this country, as well as in America and France, had learned to speak of 'Parliamentary' institutions with open scorn."[7]

Such attitudes went beyond what would normally be understood as the "extreme left." In 1917, the masthead of George Lansbury's *Herald* proclaimed the paper to be "The National Labour Weekly." After the war, when it was able to resume daily publication, the paper expressed the hope that "what the *Manchester Guardian* is to the Liberal Party, so will be the *Daily Herald* to the Parliamentary Labour Party."[8] It is worth noting in relation to this declaration that Lansbury was to become leader of the Labour Party between 1932 and 1935, albeit in unique circumstances following Ramsay MacDonald's formation of a "National" government. In July 1917, *The Herald* attributed to the effects of the war "the degradation of the House of Commons to a mere submissive tool of the Executive, its preoccupation with trivial matters, its deviation by catchwords and empty phrases, its control by vested interests, its indifference to human freedom and human life." The paper called for fundamental reform of the parliamentary system, including demands that had frequently featured in the advocacy of what Fabians had termed "primitive democracy."[9]

The Fabian Society had come close to defining itself in opposition to "primitive democracy" on more than one occasion. "Anti-leadership" attitudes and support for direct democracy in the form of the referendum and initiative were sufficiently widespread on the British Left in 1896 for the Fabians to insist, in a report aimed at that year's Socialist International congress, that "democracy, as understood by the Fabian Society, means simply the control of administration by the freely elected representatives of the people" and to reject any notion that "the technical work of government administration" or the appointment of officials should "be carried out by referendum or any other form of popular decision."[10] And ten years later, in a Special Committee report, the Fabians were even more explicit: "Democracy is a word with a double meaning. To the bulk of Trade Unionists and labourers it means an intense jealousy and mistrust of all authority, and a resolute reduction of both representatives and officials to the position of mere delegates and agents of the majority." Between this and the Fabians' conception of democracy as "government by consent of the people" was a "gulf" that, the report said, "unfortunately cuts the Labour movement right down the middle."[11]

On the far side of this "gulf" was the Social-Democratic Federation (SDF), whose program from 1884 demanded, in its first three points, the election of all "officers and administrators" by "Equal Adult Suffrage" and ratification of all legislation or decisions on "Peace or War" by referendum.[12] In the 1890s, the SDF and its paper, *Justice*, continued to support "a system of pure democracy by means of the 'Initiative' and 'Referendum,' "[13] as did Blatchford's influential socialist weekly, *The Clarion*. Blatchford's colleague, Alex Thompson, also advocated these methods in three *Clarion* pamphlets.[14] This was accompanied by attacks on "leadership," whether in mainstream politics, in the ILP, or, as the episode of the ill-fated *Clarion* federation in the late 1890s demonstrated, in the trade unions.[15] The essence of this approach to democracy was the implementation of all means whereby real power would be put into the hands of the citizen — or member, in the case of the unions — rather than an elected representative. The referendum and initiative was the key demand. Enthusiasm for the referendum and initiative tended to be episodic in early twentieth-century Britain, but it was nearly always to be found in the most "anti-establishment" sections of the Left. This version of "real democracy" by no means disappeared in what we may call the "early soviet" era — even among some of the most fervent advocates of the soviet system.

Soon to become a fervent supporter of soviet democracy and the Bolsheviks, in September 1916 J.B. Askew, a prominent member of the BSP, contributed an article to its paper, *The Call*, titled "Socialists and the Referendum." "One reform to which, it seems to me, Socialists have paid far too little attention," he wrote, "is that all measures passed by Parliament should be submitted, on demand of a certain percentage of the voters, to the verdict of a popular vote, and similarly, that the electorate should have the right in the same way to initiate legislation." Although the system was not a panacea, Askew concluded, the referendum and initiative could provide a way by which class-conscious workers could "make their influence felt in a most effective manner."[16]

This was not an issue that divided Askew from his former comrades in the "pro-war" faction that had left the BSP and whose weekly organ was *Justice*. "Robert Arch" — the pen name of a regular contributor, Archibald Robertson — believed that avoiding future wars presupposed "that peace or war is to be decided by referendum, or by the vote of an

Assembly so accurately reflecting the opinions of the people that its votes are the virtual equivalent of referenda." Achievement of "perfect political democracy" was the key to peace. This meant "the referendum, or at least proportional representation reinforced by the power of recall. But it admits of degrees of approximation." Similarly, a few weeks later, Hyndman demanded that "the initiative, referendum and proportional representation be constituted [as] the bases of political legislation and confirmation of social action." [17]

While "Arch"/Robertson and Hyndman were ferociously anti-Bolshevik, this was hardly a charge that could be levelled at Sylvia Pankhurst. And as we shall see in later chapters, no one was to embrace the idea of soviets with greater fervour. Before the February Revolution, she had advocated the referendum, and she was to continue to do so long after her adhesion to the soviet cause. For Pankhurst, both the referendum and a system of soviets could be part of a drive towards democracy that would truly produce government by the people.

In February 1917, when the report of the Speaker's Electoral Reform Conference was published, Pankhurst argued that Britain should "take rank with the new democracies," Australia, New Zealand, Canada, and many of the American states, by adopting "such innovations as the Initiative, Referendum and Recall." [18] A little later that month, at a conference called by the London Council for Adult Suffrage, whose agenda included adult suffrage, rules for the conduct of elections, proportional representation, and the initiative, referendum and recall, Pankhurst seconded a motion by Liberal Party member J.A. Hobson, the well-known economist and journalist who was to abandon radical liberalism and join the ILP in 1919. The motion demanded the insertion, in the forthcoming Reform Bill, of the referendum, initiative, and recall. [19]

At the beginning of June 1917, the day before the Leeds "Soviet Convention" (to be examined in the next chapter) opened, the *Woman's Dreadnought* reported on the annual conference of the Workers' Suffrage Federation (WSF). The referendum had been adopted for use within the organization, and the conference "urged" the enactment of referendum, initiative, and recall, as well as "the election of Ministers and Judges by referendum vote" for national government.[20] Meanwhile, the WSF was busy in its stronghold of Bow, conducting a "straw ballot on Adult Suffrage for women, Adult Suffrage for men, Proportional Representation and the Referendum."[21]

In July, with the conferences of the British Workers' and Soldiers' Council called for at Leeds due to meet, the *Dreadnought* announced that the WSF hoped to move a number of amendments to what it called the "official resolutions." To the demand for an end to the war without annexations or indemnities, it wished to add the proviso that the right of self-determination should be exercised by means of "an adult suffrage referendum vote." This was to apply to "the British Empire as elsewhere." A second amendment, proposed to the "charter of liberties establishing complete political and social rights for all men and women," specified the inclusion of six "Political Reforms," including "the Initiative and Referendum and Recall." "On the industrial side," the paper also called for the "creation of an industrial Parliament."[22] These demands may seem to belong to different radical democratic traditions, but such a mixture was not peculiar to Pankhurst and the *Dreadnought*. In August 1917, in an article titled "The Next Step in Political Reform," *The Herald* argued for "proportional representation and the alternative vote" and "short term parliaments." But, among other radical changes, the paper also called for the referendum, initiative, and recall, along with the replacement of the House of Lords by "an Industrial Chamber."[23]

In September 1917, Pankhurst's editorial, "The Franchise Situation," ended by urging adult suffragists to campaign for "a genuine Reform Bill which will make Parliament obedient to the people's will" and listed among its demands "the Initiative and Referendum and Recall."[24] A few weeks later the Bolsheviks seized power in the name of the soviets. In her editorial welcoming "the Lenin Revolution," Pankhurst included the following:

> In the political field we believe we are right in saying that neither a Labour Party, Trade Union or ILP Conference has discussed, at any rate within recent years, such essential democratic institutions as the Initiative, Referendum and Recall, institutions which are all actually in being in the Western States of the USA, and which are partially established elsewhere. A Russian socialist woman said to us: "People here are actually discussing whether the Referendum is democratic; why, I realised the democratic importance of the Referendum when I was fifteen years of age." The following evening we heard Mr Bernard Shaw assuming, in addressing a Fabian audience, that our populace is too ignorant to be trusted to use the Referendum and declaring if it were established in this Country, legislation would be held up altogether."[25]

After the October Revolution and even after the — retrospectively proclaimed — break with "bourgeois democracy" following the dissolution of the Constituent Assembly at the beginning of 1918, advocacy of the referendum continued in the pages of the *Dreadnought* (recently renamed the *Workers' Dreadnought*). But soviet democracy was very much centre stage. Thus, in January 1918, we find Pankhurst demanding a referendum in Britain on the question of ending the war on a no annexations, no indemnity basis. In the same issue it was reported that, in Lithuania and other areas of the old Russian Empire, "the Russians insisted on the decision of the matter by a referendum vote of the peoples concerned to be taken under conditions ensuring that there should be no domination or restraint." The issue contained yet a third appearance of the referendum, this time in the context of the forthcoming Labour Party conference. Here, Pankhurst noted: "The proposition to establish the Initiative, Referendum and Recall is new to the Labour Party Agenda, and therefore, in spite of its importance, may not be taken seriously as yet." The very next week brought her apologia for the dissolution of the Constituent Assembly as well as claims for the democratic superiority of the soviet system — which itself contained a passing reference to the "still unswerving demand" of the Bolsheviks for territorial referendums in the German-occupied areas.[26]

And in the spring of 1918, while the last great German offensive seriously threatened the Allies across the Channel, a motion demanding a referendum calling for "an immediate general armistice on all fronts," which had been passed at the National Workers' Committee conference in Manchester, was reported in the *Dreadnought* by W.F. Watson, a pre-war syndicalist in the engineering industry. Pankhurst was meanwhile criticizing the new Labour Party program, "Labour and the New Social Order." There was no shortage of criticisms to make about all its aspects, including its constitutional timorousness. "And why not the Initiative, Referendum and Recall?" she asked.[27]

This was followed in May 1918, in an editorial on House of Lords reform, by further support for the referendum as at least an interim measure, pending the advent of soviet-style democracy:

> As long as the House of Commons exists (it will give place at last no doubt to an Industrial Parliament) the only check upon the decisions which we could countenance would be one furnished by the rank and file of the people from whom the elected Chamber is supposed to derive its powers. The Referendum is, of course, the most direct and democratic means of popular expression and we desire to see the Referendum established without delay.[28]

The same week, writing in the "May Day — Marx Centenary Number" of *The Call,* Pankhurst attributed both the Reform Act and the parliamentary committee on House of Lords Reform to the "wave of fear" that had swept through the "ruling classes" following the Russian Revolution. "Representative Government" was inadequate, she argued, but continued: "Nevertheless, every effort should be made to remove all obstacles that stand in the way of the direct expression of the people's will. The House of Lords is a very serious obstacle and should long ago have been totally abolished." The only argument in its favour "with a shadow of reason" was that it acted as a check on the House of Commons. But that could be accomplished democratically "by the Referendum, accompanied by the Initiative and the Right of Recall."[29]

Pankhurst even took that tireless advocate of guild socialism, G.D.H. Cole, to task for (among many other things) making no mention "of the Initiative, Referendum and Recall, without which no system of representative Government can be genuinely Democratic." Guild organization should include a delegate body, "of which the authority should be second only to that to the Referendum."[30] It is clear — and significant — that some of those who, like Pankhurst, were to become deeply committed to soviet democracy, believing it to be the most genuinely participatory form of democracy, also supported the referendum, initiative, and recall for very similar, if not identical, reasons and continued to do so for at least some time after 1917.

Though Pankhurst's *Dreadnought* featured more advocacy of these methods than any other socialist organ during the early years of the Russian Revolution, it was not alone in combining support for this form of direct democracy and for the soviet system. For example, as late as the beginning of 1920, Joseph Southall, a Birmingham Quaker who would continue to play a prominent role in the ILP for many years, joined the *Labour Leader* debates on parliamentary democracy versus "sovietism," urging that "there must be a change of some sort if the people are to be masters in their own house." "I am inclined to favour the Referendum," he added, "but whether it be this or a Soviet or Syndicalist institution, some modification is necessary."[31]

Also in January 1920, J.B. Askew, now well established as a supporter of soviet democracy and the Bolsheviks and a fairly regular contributor to *The Call*, was still persistently advocating the referendum and initiative. By that time there had been, as we shall see, considerable debate in the BSP paper about the soviet system, the "dictatorship of the proletariat," and their presumed role in replacing parliamentary rule when the revolution finally reached Britain. Askew concluded: "I would like further to point out that both the two most important champions of Democracy, against the Soviet system, J.R. MacDonald and Karl Kautsky, have written against the referendum and initiative, which, together with the right to withdraw or recall mandates, are surely indispensable to a complete democracy."[32]

Shop Stewards, Syndicalism, and Guild Socialism

A crucial new element in left-wing thinking had appeared in the years immediately preceding the First World War. For many, there was a shift to the workplace as the "real" locus of both class struggle and — potentially — democracy. Syndicalism proposed to dispense entirely with political parties and "politics." There was no need for politicians — not even revolutionary ones. Many on the British Left, not prepared to go all the way with the syndicalists, were attracted to guild socialism, which seemed to reconcile the claims of "politics" and workplace democracy. The De Leonists of the Socialist Labour Party (SLP) were dismissive of syndicalism per se but shared the belief that the industrial battle was what counted most. Politics, though still important, merely reflected that battle.

None of this was especially new, but the emphasis on the industrial struggle and the belief in the superior reality of the role of "worker" to that of "citizen" was *experienced* as new, even liberating, by many at the time. Several of the early leaders of the CPGB — Tom Bell, Willie Gallacher, Arthur MacManus, and J.T. Murphy — came from the syndicalist-influenced shop stewards' movement, which had reached its height during the war. As James Hinton says at the beginning of his chapter "The Soviet Idea" in *The First Shop Stewards' Movement:* "The wartime practice of the shop-stewards' movement was an important source of that ideological development in the British revolutionary movement that made possible the formation of a united Communist Party." But its influence was much wider than that. And, as Kendall notes: "A quite disproportionate number of intellectuals who joined the Communist Party at its foundation came from the ranks of the Guild Socialist movement."[33]

The Guildsman, the guild movement's monthly journal, may have been overstating the case in February 1917 when it began an article titled "Workshop Control" by claiming: "The proposal that workmen shall be given a share in the government of workshops is being discussed at the present time by men of all parties and all classes. Schools of thought from the most Capitalist to the most Socialist have recommended it in one form or another."[34] But that the article should make such a claim is indicative of how widespread ideas of workplace democracy were at this time.

The February 1917 edition of *Solidarity* ("A Journal of Modern Trade Unionism") carried an "Open Letter" from Murphy addressed to the forthcoming "Rank and File Conference" of the shop stewards' movement, urging that workshop committees be set up and linked together. The same issue also included his letter "The Illusion of Leaders," which attacked the tendency to depend on such figures. *The Guildsman*, self-consciously an organ of left-wing middle-class intellectuals, was impressed with Murphy's pamphlet *The Workers' Committee*: "Every active trade unionist," wrote its reviewer, "should make it his business to see it obtains a wide circulation."

Published in late 1917, Murphy's pamphlet had sold 25,000 copies by the following March.[35] *Solidarity*, now designating itself as the "Rank and File Fighting Paper," greeted its publication with enthusiasm: "At last! A Pamphlet explanatory of the Shop Stewards' Movement."[36] Strangely, for the modern reader, the pamphlet makes only passing references to the war and — even more surprisingly for something published in *late* 1917 — no mention at all of soviets or the Russian Revolution. This may, in part at least, explain its sympathetic review in the pro-war, and anti-Bolshevik, *Justice,* which described *The Workers' Committee* as "one of the best and cleverest little things that has been written on this subject," while stressing that "political action is absolutely necessary."[37]

Murphy argued for "the Great Industrial Union," which he believed the social nature of modern methods of production and the undermining of the monopoly position of the skilled were together promoting. Unity was to be achieved first at the level of the individual workplace, or workshop: "The procedure to adopt is to form in every workshop a workshop committee, composed of shop stewards, elected by the workers in the workshops. Skilled, semi-skilled, and unskilled workers should have their shop stewards, and due regard be given also to the particular union to which each worker belongs."[38] Shop stewards should then form local industrial committees for "educating and co-ordinating the efforts of the rank and file." These committees should put maximum power into the workers' hands. They should "not have any governing power, but should exist to render service to the rank and file, by providing means for them to arrive at decisions and to unite their forces."[39] "Works or plant committees," elected from among the shop stewards in order to link up the shop committees, and local workers' committees were to be "similar in form to a trades council, with this essential difference — the trades council is only indirectly related to the workshops, whereas the workers' committee is directly related."[40]

Murphy made light of the tricky question of setting up a national organization: "In the initial stages of the movement it will be apparent that a ballot for the election of the first national committee would be impossible, and as we, the workers, are not investing these committees with executive power there is little to worry about." Therefore, rather than wait until it was possible to hold an election in which all members would participate, to get things underway the national industrial committee should be composed of those elected from a conference of delegates from local industrial committees. The committees would be "working with the true spirit of democracy," and the structure was to be topped by a national workers' committee, a sort of counterpart of the Trades Union Congress (TUC), with, Murphy suggested, two delegates from each national industrial committee. He concluded by re-emphasizing the need for "working always from the bottom upwards."[41]

The similarity of Murphy's proposals to the accounts of the structure and functioning of Russian soviets published over the next few years in the socialist press is very clear. Indeed, it is not unreasonable to suspect that the notions prevalent on the British Left about the processes of soviet democracy owed much to this widely read pamphlet. The ostensible purpose of Murphy's committees was not — or at least not immediately — to take over state power. Even so, *The Workers' Committee* and other syndicalist-inspired material — such as the literature of the pre-war Industrial Syndicalist Educational League, the publications of the *Daily Herald* League, *The Miners' Next Step,* and the study classes of the Plebs League — ensured that when power was nominally transferred to the soviets in Russia, the ground for their enthusiastic acceptance had been well prepared.[42]

During these years guild socialism also exerted a considerable influence on many on the British Left. "It will be agreed that more and more, for a variety of reasons, Socialists and Trade Unionists are coming round to a position which is largely that of the National Guilds," wrote G.D.H. Cole at the beginning of 1917, in an article for the I L P's *Labour Leader.* More and more they were "coming to realise the need for self-government in industry, or rather for the direct government by those who work in it in conjunction with the State."[43]

Around the same time — between February and May 1917 — *The Herald* carried a series of articles by S.G. Hobson titled "Labour's Industrial Policy," which culminated in several instalments devoted to explaining the national guilds.[44] By that August, the paper was calling for the "reorganisation of industry upon the basis of State Ownership and Trade Union, or Guild, control." Arguing that "only by the division of function and a balance of power can we guard ourselves against the 'never-ending audacity of elected persons,'" it proposed a "twin democratic structure" comprising a radically reformed House of Commons and an "Industrial Chamber" elected on the basis of occupation. Though a joint assembly might be necessary on some occasions, it was vital that ultimate power remained divided so that the danger of "recreating that very sovereignty we have set about to destroy" and of such an assembly becoming "heir to the Leviathan that we have slain" could be averted.[45]

For Bertrand Russell, in a March 1917 interview in *Labour Leader,* a compromise was needed between state action designed to control "the material distribution of goods" and "the greatest possible liberty in regard to mental and spiritual things" for individuals. "The best compromise I know is Guild Socialism," concluded Russell.[46] Quite how far the influence of guild socialism had penetrated is evident in Ramsay MacDonald's book *Parliament and Revolution* (1919), which, in the words of J. Bruce Glasier, who reviewed it in *Labour Leader,* proposed "a sort of Soviet Second Chamber of Parliament." [47]

Another example of the wider influence that guild socialist and similar ideas had in these years is the Webbs' *Constitution for the Socialist Commonwealth of Great Britain,* which was published in 1920. The Webbs proposed the creation of a separate "Social Parliament" — still to be elected on a geographical basis — in addition to the "Political Parliament," which would continue to deal with such matters as foreign policy and defence. An anonymous reviewer in the *Daily Herald* thought it "not easy to explain the prejudice that exists against the Webbs" but was far from ready to endorse their proposals. The authors seemed preoccupied with "efficiency," but was this the real problem?

> To dispense with the National Parliaments altogether and begin construction from the bottom with the workshop committees in the producers' world and functional municipal authorities elected for the performance of special jobs in the consumers', [with] both committees and authorities sending delegates to National Guilds and National Consumers' Councils, might diminish efficiency by multiplying committees, but would at least provide the common man with a chance of political and industrial expression giving him the feeling that he mattered and that his will counted which would, one fears, still be denied under the Webbs' reorganisation. [48]

Decades later, G.D.H. Cole was to characterize the book as "an attempt to meet the attacks of Syndicalists and Guild Socialists on orthodox Fabian Collectivism without sacrificing the ultimate supremacy of the consumers in economic affairs." [49]

Yet at work in the Webbs' vision was certainly some notion of "functional democracy"— the idea that industries, along with areas of policy such as education and the provision of health services, should be democratically controlled as separate social functions, rather than being subject to centralized state control. And Lisanne Radice is surely right to conclude that "the *Socialist Commonwealth* is far more optimistic about the possibilities of wider participation than *Industrial Democracy* written twenty years earlier."[50] When Philip Snowden published *Labour and the New World* in 1921, the new order *he* proposed similarly retained Parliament, this time with a national economic council based on workshop and district committees subordinated to it. Sylvia Pankhurst basically saw Snowden's proposal as a halfway house between "Parliamentary Social Democracy and a Communist industrial organisation of society."[51] These examples demonstrate that even people like MacDonald and Snowden, and even the Webbs, felt it important to make some kind of response to the problems perceived by the guild socialists. It is clear that guild socialism and the syndicalism of the shop stewards' movement, which were so prominent in the years immediately before 1917, were crucial in lending credibility on the Left to the idea of soviet democracy.

De Leonism and the Socialist Labour Party

An important role in preparing the way for soviet democracy was also played — in spite of its tiny membership even by the standards of the British Left — by the Socialist Labour Party. The SLP platform, as published in January 1915 issue of *The Socialist,* centred on "belief in Industrial Unionism as opposed to Trade Unionism." Inspired by the American socialist theorist Daniel De Leon — who, until his death just before the war, led the SLP's American namesake and the "Detroit" Industrial Workers of the World — the SLP platform differed from that of "pure" syndicalists in allowing political parties a definite, though subordinate, role. Centred on its headquarters in Glasgow, where its paper, *The Socialist,* was published, the SLP had originated in a split from the SDF in 1903.[52]

The SLP was, and usually still is, seen as dogmatic, intolerant of dissent, and "biblically" Marxist. It was certainly more adamant and unyielding than most in its claim to "correctness" and doctrinal purity. "The strength and vigour of the S.L.P. in this country," *The Socialist* confidently asserted in its issue of February 1918, "is due to its being the only party that has assimilated the theories of Marx and sought to apply them to the problems confronting us." The usual verdict therefore seems amply justified. But this judgment is misleading if overemphasized. SLPers certainly saw themselves — and in their early days were seen by Lenin, among others — as the "British Bolsheviks." But how far was this identification predicated on assumptions about the vanguard role of the Bolsheviks in Russia? These suppositions were to become increasingly questionable as time went on — particularly those regarding the Russian commitment to a form of genuine, industrially based working-class democracy. That, however, would become apparent only later and will be examined in detail in chapter 10. Certainly, the Communist Unity Group, which broke with the SLP when the latter refused to continue with the negotiations that led to the formation of the CPGB, as well as subsequent defectors to the British Communist Party, had little trouble in translating their belief in a "vanguard" role into faithful support for the Third International, with its stringent "21 conditions" that would-be affiliates were required to accept. But, as we shall see in chapter 10, for those who remained with the SLP, criticism of the orthodox Communist approach — especially as far as Britain was concerned — became increasingly adamant and at times extraordinarily hostile and shrill. But none of this was apparent in 1917, when the SLP's early support was important in promoting "soviet democracy."

For a few years, the SLP exercised an influence on the Left in Britain that went far beyond its own membership. Indeed, in March 1918, one letter to *The Socialist* — whose author explicitly signed himself "A non-S.L.Per" — claimed: "Generally speaking the Socialist Labour Press is not looked upon as a party concern at all, but as a valuable asset of the Working Class movement."[53] Kendall has stressed the role of the SLP's press as "the most important distributor of Marxist literature in Great Britain." There could, he concluded, "have been scarcely a single person involved in the foundation of the Communist Party of Great Britain who was not, at some time, influenced by the SLP and its literature."[54] Although as an organization it refused to dissolve itself into the CPGB, the SLP did provide a quite disproportionate number of the CP's earliest leaders, including its first chairman, Arthur MacManus.

As the one authentic revolutionary party — as the SLP saw itself — it was to put "correctness" of doctrine before membership numbers and to police this doctrinal purity rigorously. The party's function was to be available as a vanguard when the working class turned to it for guidance. As Kendall observes:

> The party, by achieving victory at the ballot box, would legitimise the conquest of power by the working class. The industrial union, which included the whole of the working class within its ranks . . . would back up the party's victory at the polls by the threat of a general strike or the "General Lockout of the Capitalist Class."
>
> On election to office in all the supreme positions of state and municipality, the representatives would *adjourn themselves on the spot sine die.* Their work would be done by disbanding, for "the political organisation of Labour intended to capture a Congressional District is wholly unfit to 'take and hold' the plants of industry." [55]

The SLP saw the path to socialism via the creation of industrial unionism by the working class, which would

> palpitate with the daily and hourly pulsations of the class struggle as it manifests itself in the workshop. And when it forms its own political party and moves into the political field as it surely will, in that act superseding or absorbing the Socialist Labour Party and all other socialist or labour parties, its campaign will indeed be the expression of the needs, the hopes, the aspirations, and the will of the working classes, and not the dreams and theories of a few unselfish enthusiasts or the ambitions of political schemers. . . . Finally, having overthrown the class state, the united Industrial Unions will furnish the administrative machinery for directing industry in the Socialist Commonwealth. [56]

Seen through the prism of these ideas, Russia in the later part of 1917 seemed to be pursuing a course very like what the SLP was striving for at home. The soviets — at least those of the workers, if not of the peasants and soldiers — were industrially based, or so they seemed, while the Bolsheviks, with their demand for "All Power to the Soviets," seemed to epitomize the "correct" role for the party as perceived by the SLP. As Kendall says: "In the Soviet system of government, the SLP saw before their eyes the living incarnation of the 'Industrial Republic of Labour' advocated by Connolly and De Leon. The Russian Revolution appeared a triumphant vindication of the whole SLP system of ideas. At Easter 1918, Tom Bell, in the chair at the SLP conference, claimed Bolshevism to be the 'Russian wing of the S.L.P.'"[57]

Many parts of the Left — the SLP, the syndicalist shop stewards, the guild socialists, and more general currents in favour of "functional democracy" — helped prepare the ground for soviet democracy, as, in other ways, did the older radical commitment to "real democracy" that looked for ways to make the people "masters in their own house." The referendum and initiative and soviet democracy were both seen as more "direct" approaches to empowering the majority than representative, parliamentary-style democracy ever could be.

This may seem extremely odd. The soviet system, after all, involved a pyramid of councils before it arrived at the All-Russia level. Those operating at that level were only very indirectly elected by the people at the base. This was a structure very similar to that of most British trade unions and of the "workers' committees" advocated by Murphy and others. Supporters of soviet democracy assumed an ideal delegate system, with issues decided and policies formulated by the membership at the base. Unlike the *representative,* who presented his or her policies — or, more likely, those of the party — as a general basis for attracting the suffrage of the voter and then had a free hand to proceed, with no further reference to constituents until the term of office had elapsed and re-election had to be sought, delegation allowed policy to be continually initiated and determined at the base level. A system of mandates ensured that delegates took forward the decisions of their constituents. In this respect, delegation could be seen to resemble the initiative and referendum.[58]

The major difference among those who supported these "direct" forms of democracy concerned the basis on which democratic participation was to take place. Supporters of "soviet democracy" saw soviets as fundamentally "industrial" or "occupational" and therefore more "real" than the "geographical" systems of representative government. This meant in turn that, in the eyes of a large part of the Left, the soviets had the merit of representing *workers* (perceived as "concrete") in contrast to *citizens* (perceived as "abstract"). Given that workers were seen as the oppressed and exploited and, potentially, as the class destined to play the major role in the overthrow of capitalism and the construction of socialism, this industrial or occupation-based approach had a powerful "class" appeal. All those influenced by syndicalism, and even guild socialists to a very large degree, shared the belief that the real struggle was the industrial one. All also shared, to varying extents, the belief that established leaderships, whether trade union or political, were highly suspect, if not totally counterproductive, and needed to be countered by "bottom-up" democracy founded on the "rank and file." In this respect, the new "syndicalist" radicalism was the heir to the older traditions. The National and International General Federation of Trade and Labour Unions (NIGFTLU), launched in the late 1890s — which embraced the use of the initiative and referendum for its policy making — is only one example of the anti-leadership tendency among the Left in Britain.[59] The perceived connection between direct democracy and distrust of leadership is evident for example, in a comment of P.J. King, the originator and promoter of NIGFTLU: "The initiative and referendum will do much to check the abuses of irresponsible persons. We shall no longer see a few well-paid and well-groomed officials thwarting the wishes of the overwhelming majority of men who give them their salaries and look after their interests."[60]

Many individual unions did make use of membership referendums. A suspicion of trade union officials — worthy of P.J. King — and a concern with grassroots control through the use of the referendum, among other means, are apparent in J.T. Murphy's *The Workers' Committee*. In addition to the comments about "real democratic practice" quoted

in the introduction, Murphy's pamphlet contains the following observation on the lack of democracy in British trade unions:

> The constitutions invest elected officials with certain powers of decision
> which involve the members of the organisations in obedience to their
> rulings. It is true to say that certain questions have been referred to the
> ballot box ere decisions have been arrived at; but it is unquestionably
> true also that important matters have not been so referred, and increas-
> ingly insistent has been the progress towards *government by officials*.
>
> The need of the hour is a drastic revision of this constitutional
> procedure which demands that the function of the rank and file shall
> be simply that of obedience.[61]

Presumably, then, according to Murphy, at least at this point on his
political trajectory, all important issues should be put to a referendum
vote ("the ballot box") of the members of the union.

The British Left in 1917 had been well prepared for being enthused
by the idea of soviet democracy. There had been the preparation af-
forded by the very long tradition of radical ideas of democracy. Its
critiques of parliamentary politics and of established leaderships and
its demands for "direct democracy" helped predispose many on the
Left to look kindly — not to say optimistically — at any mechanism or
procedure that claimed to make democracy more real by increasing the
accountability of the elected, transferring real power to "the people,"
and, in Murphy's words, "working always from the bottom upwards."

Industrial unionist and syndicalist ideas privileged the occupational basis of democracy over the territorial and put forward ideas of
structure and process that could be seen as foreshadowing the working
(or supposed working) of the Russian soviets. Finally, as a sort of top
dressing of preparation — very thin but potent — was the De Leonist
ideology of the SLP, which helped not only to legitimize the soviets
but also to provide a rationale for the role of the party. In the context
of Russia, that meant the Bolshevik Party.

2

INITIAL RESPONSES TO THE RUSSIAN REVOLUTION
The British Left in 1917 and the Leeds "Soviet" Convention

The "Marvellous Revolution"

I t is difficult now to appreciate fully the initial impact of the Russian Revolution — that is, of the "February Revolution" (which, in the Western calendar, took place at the start of March). In the midst of an increasingly bleak and horrific war, the events in Russia appeared to many as a ray of hope — the promise of an eventual bright dawn. Well beyond the socialist movement, the revolution was in fact welcomed by all who found the alliance with autocratic tsarist Russia embarrassing, viewing it as something that undermined the political and moral standing of the Allied cause.

"The revolution in Russia is the biggest event of the war. If it succeeds in establishing a Social Democratic Republic it will be the most momentous event in the history of our time," George Lansbury declared in *The Herald*. And the following week, in a *Dreadnought* editorial on adult suffrage, Sylvia Pankhurst wrote that "the marvellous revolution in Russia fills the minds of all men and women."[1] But expectations about what would follow diverged wildly. In its April issue, *The Socialist* began by noting skeptically the general welcome of the mainstream press and the cheers in the House of Commons when "the news arrived that the Russian middle class revolution had at last been accomplished." It did conclude, however, that "the Russian Revolution may be the first step to bring us nearer to the end of this war."

For many others on the Left, the revolution was inseparable from the hope of a speedy and just ending to the terrible war. It inspired Ethel Snowden, for example, to launch the Women's Peace Crusade in the summer of 1917, which built on local initiatives by the Women's International League and the Women's Labour League and brought thousands onto the streets of Glasgow, Nelson, and Leicester in demonstrations in July and August.[2] Even the pro-war *Justice* regarded the revolution as an inspiration for radical change in Britain, where "we too have been thwarted by corruption and treachery." "Is it not high time we followed the Russian example?" it asked. Soon after, a front-page article by Hyndman, titled "The Need for a British Republic," spelled out what the answer to this question might mean. He was "bitterly opposed" to "State Socialism," but the war had made it possible to "transform this Bureaucratic Collectivism, detestable as it is, into the Democratic Socialism of an educated, free and self-disciplined people."[3]

In the BSP, Hyndman's former comrades, now opponents, were among the first to rally enthusiastically to the support of Russia. Under the banner "Long Live the Revolution!" *The Call* proclaimed on the front page of its issue of 8 March: "A political earthquake has shaken the foundations of the material and moral order of things created by the war." An air of disbelief was also evident in some of the earliest comments in the socialist press. On 22 March, for example, Philip Snowden wrote in *Labour Leader* that it was "hardly credible that such a great and powerful autocracy as Czarism, with its organisation of every department of Russian life, administration, and religion, can be completely overthrown by a *coup d'état*."

Meanwhile, meetings were being hastily organized. Seven thousand people reportedly celebrated revolutionary Russia at the Great Assembly Hall, Mile End Road, while "A Great Mass Meeting" for the same purpose was advertised in *Labour Leader* for Saturday, 31 March, at the Albert Hall. The paper subsequently reported that more than 25,000 people applied for tickets and "over 5,000 sorrowful men and women were turned away by the police."[4] *The Herald,* whose editor, George Lansbury, had chaired the Albert Hall meeting, added that people had been standing "three deep in the gallery." It used its whole front page to celebrate the "REVOLT AT THE ALBERT HALL" and gave a six-page report of the proceedings. The following month, *The Herald* reported that *Russia Free!* — the report in booklet form — had already sold out the 6,000 copies of its first printing and that a new edition was being prepared.[5] It was a meeting that would long be remembered. In 1941, Maurice Reckitt recalled what a thrilling, and utterly unrepeatable, experience it had been to participate in the gathering, while Lansbury would remember the warmth and intensity of the atmosphere.[6]

By early May, demonstrations and rallies were taking place in Glasgow, Belfast, Manchester, Huddersfield, Leicester, and other towns, and there were more in London as well. A Brighton meeting of 17 May was billed as a "Mass Meeting" to "celebrate Russian Freedom." Held in the Congress Hall of the Salvation Army — whose band provided music — the meeting was chaired by a local councillor and addressed by a variety of local and national speakers mainly from labour and socialist movement organizations, including Brighton's trades and labour council and the local co-operative society. Slightly incongruously, a collection was to be made for the "Polish Refugees fund."[7] The organizers claimed that sixteen hundred people attended, and the local press reported "some very outspoken speeches." The greatest stir was caused by the fiercely anti-war speech of Sylvia Pankhurst, who was listed first among the main speakers. Correspondents wrote in to the local papers to protest against this "Anti-Patriotic Meeting."[8]

The role in the revolution of the soviets, or the "Council of Work-men's and Soldiers' Delegates," in the words of *The Call,* was soon noted and was generally supported on the British Left. Workplace-based (in principle, at least), the soviets were well placed to assert the dominant role of the direct producer that socialism sought in the economy. In relative terms, compared to the self-appointed govern-ments of the Duma parties, whose elected representatives had pre-war mandates based on a restrictive franchise, the soviets had a credible claim to being the most democratically legitimate source of authority. As Victor Chernov, prominent in the Russian Social Revolutionary Party, put it in *Labour Leader* (in an article originally published in the Italian socialist paper *Avanti!*), the Duma was "the product of one of the most monstrous electoral systems that existed in Europe — the product of reactionary State legislation." The fear among "revo-lutionary Socialists" at this time, he argued, was that they would be "outmanoeuvred by the bourgeoisie," who were determined to prevent an early election of a constituent assembly.[9]

Labour Leader welcomed what it called "the Workmen's Council" and reported that in the Russian Army "the soldiers have taken com-plete control through management committees elected by themselves of . . . everything not connected with the actual fighting."[10] A few days later, Philip Snowden, who was to be elected chairman at the end of the proceedings, told delegates to the ILP's annual conference in Leeds that "the epoch-making event in Russia had revived their faith in inter-nationalism." MacDonald and Glasier moved and seconded a motion congratulating "fellow workers in Russia," but the conference remit-ted to the ILP's National Administrative Council the demand of the Burton-on-Trent branch that "the workers in each and every industry secure complete control over the conditions and management of their industry in order to establish freedom and democracy."[11] Much more forthright was the SLP's *The Socialist*, which explained in its April issue that the "Council of Workman's Delegates" was "a revolutionary body" that resembled the Clyde Workers' Committee rather than the "stable organisations" of French or British trade unionism.

Meanwhile, the "dual power" situation in Russia was identified. Asking "Whose Russian Revolution?" an editorial in the *Woman's Dreadnought* explained that "at present there are virtually two Governments in Russia — the Provisional Government appointed by the Duma and the Council of Labour Deputies which is responsible to the elected representatives of the workers and soldiers." Kerensky was described as "the Socialist Minister of Justice," and the "Council of Workers' and Soldiers' delegates" was commended for its commitment to freedom of the press: "In their desire not to imitate the tyrants they have overthrown, the workers decided to allow even the reactionary newspapers to appear as of old."[12] By May, *The Herald* was sure that the "Council of Workmen's and Soldiers' Delegates leave no one in any doubt who are the real rulers in Russia."[13]

This was at a time when the very existence of the Bolsheviks was only just beginning to register. Among the vast majority of British socialists, enthusiasm for the soviets preceded any real knowledge of Lenin and his associates. The best indication of the breadth and depth of left-wing support in Britain for the revolution in general and the soviets in particular, prior to the Bolshevik takeover, is what took place at Leeds at the beginning of June 1917.

The Origins of the Leeds Convention: Anticipations and Preparations

The "Leeds Soviet Convention" was quickly to become mythologized. By 1921, even the dour John Maclean — the formidable Clydeside socialist theoretician, revolutionary, and teacher — was referring to the "great Leeds Convention of 1917."[14] The convention introduced the idea that soviets were something that might, and indeed should, be introduced into Britain. And this happened at a time when Lenin and the Bolsheviks were barely known to British socialists, still less particularly associated with soviet democracy. So it is worth retracing the sequence of events that brought the convention about.

On 10 May 1917, *Labour Leader* announced that the British socialist movement had to respond to the revolution in Russia and "to endeavour to secure a response to the declaration of the Workmen's and Soldiers' Council in favour of a peace without annexations and indemnities." The "informal committee" that had organized the Albert Hall meeting was, the paper said, co-operating with the United Socialist Council to arrange "a Conference-Demonstration of a national character at an early date." It invited trades councils, trade unions, branches of the ILP and BSP, the Women's Labour League, the Women's Co-operative Guild, and the Women's International League to send delegates to Leeds on Sunday, 3 June. A similar statement appeared in *The Call* the same day. Little had previously been heard of the United Socialist Council, a body formed by the ILP and the BSP the previous year under pressure from the International Socialist Bureau.[15] *The Herald* found it necessary to explain that it was "not a new body . . . but the outcome of a resolution passed by the last International Congress." The following week, *The Call* predicted that what it still called the "Leeds Conference" would "consolidate the forces of Internationalism."[16]

The Herald declared that the main purpose of the Leeds conference was to bring "Great Britain into line with our Russian comrades. We must secure in this country control of the Government by the people." It attacked "the incompetent muddlers," the "grasping, selfish monopolists," and the "Government of business men" that had failed to "control either supplies or prices." There was emphasis on securing better treatment for discharged soldiers, their dependents, and the wives and children of servicemen still on active duty. "The Bureaucracy modelled on Prussia" had "robbed the workers of every vestige of independence and power of organisation." All this, *The Herald* declared, "must be won back, and can only be won back by organised effort."[17] At the end of May, *The Call* anticipated that "the Conference at Leeds on Sunday next . . . will be the most truly representative working class assembly ever held in this country. The overwhelming mass of the delegates will come straight from the factories, mills and mines."

To the initial emphasis on demonstrating in favour of peace had been added a further element. "A call is to go forth from Leeds on Sunday next the like of which has not been heard in this country since the glorious days of Chartism," proclaimed *The Call*. "At Leeds the workers' Magna Charta [*sic*] will be formulated and decided on." Workers, it went on, would "gladly co-operate in forming Workmen's and Soldiers' Councils, but the initiating work, the organising and leading, must be done by Social-Democrats." Broad-based councils could "soon become strong enough to dominate the towns and districts and determine their political future. Then the cause will be won."[18] Readers of *Labour Leader* were told to contact Albert Inkpin or Francis Johnson, the United Socialist Council's joint secretaries, to obtain delegate credentials, on the basis of one delegate for every five hundred, at a cost of two shillings and sixpence per delegate. Major stress was placed on the significance of trade union participation.[19]

Just over a week before the conference, Robert Williams — a member of the organizing committee, secretary of the Workers' Transport Federation, and a member of the BSP — announced in *Labour Leader* that "Leeds is to mark an epoch. Leeds is to reconstitute the International. Leeds is to do for Britain what the Council of Workmen's and Soldiers' Delegates is doing for Russia." He went on to declare: "The conference will certainly mark a turning point in the holocaust of war. We shall send representatives to Russia. These representatives require a mandate from the working class."[20]

By the end of May, the conference had become "The Great Convention," replete with Chartist overtones, a theme made explicit by the BSP's E.C. Fairchild at Leeds when he proclaimed the convention to be "the very greatest we have had in this country since the days of Chartism."[21] Meanwhile, on the eve of the meeting, Philip Snowden, writing on behalf of the United Socialist Council, which he chaired, was presenting the convention as a "call to the democracy of this and all the other belligerent countries to take matters into their own hands as the people of Russia have already done. That is the only way the war can be brought to an end." But the war would leave immense industrial and social problems that could only be dealt with "by organised democratic forces." Labour and "British Democracy" were "without a policy and without direction," Snowden argued. But the convention would provide this: "We must follow Russia and enthrone Democracy in this country. The Leeds Convention will devise the plan of campaign. All Labour, Socialist and Democratic bodies must get ready to play their part." These sentiments were echoed in a letter signed by all the members of the council.[22]

The Herald spread "How Britain Must Answer Russia" across its middle pages, with articles by Lansbury and Williams as well as an introduction to the conference, including the texts of the motions that were to be debated. The "primary object" was to achieve "a peace based on equity and justice," without annexations. Lansbury's contribution was almost entirely about the war and its consequences and about the restoration to the British people of "the rights and liberties which they have been robbed of by Lord Milner and his colleagues in the War Cabinet." Williams's article, rather strangely in light of the speech he was to make at the conference, included no mention of the "dictatorship of the proletariat" or even of the soviets. The nearest it came was in posing the question, "Are you content with an effete Parliament and a self-elected Cabinet?"[23] For its part, the *Woman's Dreadnought* stressed the demand for peace, the priority of which was emphasized by an anti-war cartoon on that week's front page.[24]

Predictably, the pro-war *Justice* was hostile, referring to "The Leeds 'Convention'" and only rarely using the final word without quotation marks. It criticized the lack of real representativeness and warned of the misleading impression that would be given abroad, where the event might be judged "by the number of delegates present without any idea as to the influence those delegates carry."[25]

On the eve of the conference, *The Herald* reviewed the motions to be debated, concluding that the "most important" was the resolution to set up Workers' and Soldiers' Councils. It envisaged that these would form a national body and advocated that "such a Council should meet daily in London to deal with industrial, political and social matters, and to work for a speedy people's peace."[26]

The Convention Meets

The convention took place in the Leeds Coliseum Picture Palace, in spite of great practical difficulties. If Sylvia Pankhurst's speech in Brighton had been deemed *"anti-patriotic,"* the appearance in Leeds just a few weeks later of hundreds of vociferous opponents of the war was bound to generate alarm. Hostility from the authorities compelled a last-minute change of venue from the city's Albert Hall (now the Civic Theatre) and the banning of the intended open-air demonstration.

Ken Coates quotes Dora Montefiore and Lady Constance Malleson to illustrate the hostile atmosphere. "This Leeds demonstration was so boycotted by the possessing class," Montefiore remembered in her autobiography, "that we delegates on arrival at Leeds station found that all hotels had refused to receive us. In consequence our own Leeds comrades had rapidly organised a reception committee who were on the platform of the station, and directed us to the houses of the various comrades who were offering hospitality." Malleson, who travelled with Bertrand Russell from Peterborough in a third-class compartment with "about ten others," including Ramsay MacDonald, managed to stay in a hotel — but may have regretted that before the weekend was over. A decade later, she recalled that "the hotels did their best to refuse us accommodation. The waiters slapped our food in front of us anyhow. The crowds hissed as we went through the streets to the conference. Some children threw stones. There were a lot of police about." [27] And these two were women whom one might expect to have been treated with at least some residual social deference.

In spite of such difficulties, some 1,200 people attended — 1,300 including late arrivals, according to *The Call*. Of these, 209 came from trades councils and local Labour parties and 371 from trade unions. The largest "political group" consisted of 294 members of the ILP, while the BSP had 88 people in attendance, and there were 16 representing other socialist organizations. Women's organizations contributed 54 participants, and there were a further 118 from a variety of bodies such as the Union of Democratic Control, peace societies, and co-operatives. [28]

How representative the convention was is difficult to determine. Intent on pouring every variety of cold water on the proceedings, the hostile *Justice* complained that, although the circular summoning the convention had stated that organizations should send one delegate for each five hundred members, some trades councils and local parties with much smaller memberships had sent three, four, or five delegates.[29] It seems likely that there was some substance to this complaint, given the one-off nature of the event, the organizers' desire to maximize attendance, and the enthusiasm that had been generated among the more active members of the participating organizations.

For some, however, the convention was to become in later years something that needed explaining — even explaining away. In his autobiography, Snowden devotes nearly half his chapter on the Russian Revolution to the Leeds convention, and he gives the full text of "the much criticised circular calling the Conference,"[30] plus all four resolutions passed at the convention. It is true, as he insisted, that the circular quite explicitly emphasized the need to respond to the Provisional Government's declaration concerning peace, urging emulation of "their most magnificent example." But it is also true that the circular included language that *could* be interpreted as calling for revolution when it noted: "In Russia, where the people have assumed control over their political circumstances . . . they have called on the common people of all the belligerent countries to throw over their reactionary Governments."[31]

Snowden rejected any such interpretation, however. The convention was "the most democratically constituted Labour Convention ever held in this country," he declared, and the slogan "Follow Russia" had subsequently been misrepresented "as a demand for revolution in Britain which would overthrow the monarch and the constitution and establish a Communist State." He stressed that "the Bolshevik Revolution that overthrew the Democratic Government did not occur until the November following, *five months after the date of this Convention*."[32]

At the time, the emphasis was entirely on the amazing success of the event, with *Labour Leader* headlining its report "Britain's Greatest Labour Meeting." For its part, *The Call*'s front-page report, by Fairchild, announced that "friends and foes are staggered by the success of the Leeds Convention" and went on to call for "local Workmen's and Soldiers' Councils" to be established "in every town, urban or rural district."[33]

Four resolutions were passed. The first, moved by MacDonald and seconded by Dora Montefiore, hailed the revolution in Russia. The second demanded that the British government announce its agreement "with the declared foreign policy and war aims of the Russian democracy and government" by rejecting "annexations and indemnities." Snowden moved the third, with the BSP's Fairchild seconding. This attacked current restrictions and called for a "Charter of Liberties," including freedom of speech, of the press, and of industrial organization.[34] But attention would quickly come to focus on the fourth resolution.

The "Soviet" Resolution

The most radical motion at Leeds called for the setting up of local Councils of Workers' and Soldiers' Delegates "for initiating and co-ordinating working-class activity in support of the policy set out in the foregoing resolutions"— that is, the ones "hailing" the Russian Revolution and calling for peace — "and to work strenuously for a peace made by the peoples of the various countries, and for the complete political and economic emancipation of international labour." The councils were to "resist every encroachment upon civil liberty," to give "special attention" to the position of women employed in industry, and to "support the work of trade unions." The most specific aims concerned "the pensions of wounded and disabled soldiers and the maintenance grants payable to the dependents of men serving in the army and navy and the making of adequate provision for the training of disabled soldiers and for suitable and remunerative work for the men on their return to civil life." The resolution concluded by appointing the conference convenors as a provisional committee to "assist the formation of Workmen's and Soldiers' Councils." [35]

This fourth resolution was, according to Pankhurst in the *Dreadnought*, "the only one which meant action," though she complained that it was "not too clearly drafted," possibly, she speculated, for fear of DORA — the notorious Defence of the Realm Act, which placed unprecedented restrictions on the freedom of speech and the press. She went on to say that it "foreshadows revolution, yet it concerns itself with matters of detail which are obviously part of the present system," which suggests that she already saw the soviets as the core of a new revolutionary "system." She had other criticisms. Amendments had not been allowed at the conference because there had been no time for these to be circulated to the participating bodies for decision. Otherwise, her WSF would have moved "to add to the phrase 'complete political and economic emancipation of international Labour' the words 'on the basis of a Socialist Commonwealth' in order that there be no doubt as to the intention of the Conference." Robert Williams had, Pankhurst said, emphasized this interpretation.[36]

The "soviet" resolution was moved by the ILP's W.C. Anderson, who claimed for it "special solicitation and support" on the grounds that he had gathered from press reports that it "was regarded as the ugly duckling among the resolutions."[37] His speech mocked the "dear old mid-Victorian journal, *The Morning Post*" because it saw the motion as being directed to the subversion of military authority and discipline and "clearly a violation of the law."[38] On the contrary, Anderson insisted, "they were setting up an organisation not subversive, not unconstitutional — unless the authorities cared to make it so." Not that Anderson's speech was entirely free of revolutionary rhetoric, of a sort: "If revolution be the conquest of power by a hitherto disinherited class, if revolution be that we are not going to put up with in future what they had put up with in the past, then the sooner we had revolution the better."[39]

According to *The Herald*, "the Convention was given the lead it was waiting for by Robert Williams."[40] As reported by Tom Quelch in

The Call, in seconding the motion Williams had said that "if it meant anything at all," it meant "that which was contained in the oft-used phrase from Socialist platforms 'the dictatorship of the proletariat.'" [41] And like *The Call* and *The Herald,* the *Dreadnought* had Williams urging any who had "'cold feet' about the need for revolutionary reforms and a dictatorship of the proletariat in this country to slip out before the resolution was carried." Since the concept of a dictatorship of the proletariat was to become one of the touchstones for Communists, along with the soviet system and affiliation to the Third International, it is bound to seem both surprising and significant that it was being advocated in Britain at such an early stage, five months before the Bolsheviks seized power in Russia.

Whatever may have been the case with "Socialist platforms," the phrase "the dictatorship of the proletariat" was, *as yet,* anything but "oft-used" in the British socialist press. [42] It is perhaps ironic that Williams was to become not only one of the founders of the British Communist Party but also its first member to be expelled — for his decidedly unrevolutionary activities on "Black Friday," when the National Transport Workers' Federation, of which Williams was secretary, failed to come to the aid of its "Triple Alliance" partners, the miners, who were striking against wage reductions. [43] Between Williams's speech at Leeds and his expulsion from the CPGB in 1921, talk of the "dictatorship of the proletariat" figured prominently in debates on the British Left — but, as we shall see in a later chapter, the meaning of the phrase was anything but clear or agreed upon. So what might Williams have meant in June 1917? Or what might his audience have interpreted him to mean?

Perhaps, rather strangely, it is the — very supportive — account of his speech by Snowden in *Labour Leader* that gives us the best clue. For Snowden, the "dictatorship of the proletariat" seems to have suggested the ability of workers to force the resolution of an issue, immediately that of the war, by means of strike action. Reporting on Anderson's contribution as mover of the "soviet" resolution, Snowden wrote:

Robert Williams followed with a penetrating and daring analysis of the position of the workers all over Europe in the present crisis. He appealed to delegates present to get to work, each in their own district, to make the resolutions of that afternoon, and especially the last, effective. They must be prepared as a last resort, if all else failed, to make ready as workers for the "dictatorship of the proletariat."

This was followed by a heading "The Power of the Workers," under which Snowden continued: "Running through his speech, as through the whole proceedings of the Convention, was the underlying realisation that all over Europe there was power in the hands of the workers — the weapon of withdrawn labour — which can end the war when it will. Labour will not toil interminably for a war in which it does not believe." [44]

Snowden may have placed greater emphasis than Williams had intended on the qualification about the "last resort, if all else failed." Yet it must be remembered that the explicit purpose of the proposed workers' councils was to continue to pursue the policies of peace agreed upon in the previous three resolutions and that (as *The Herald* reported at the time) Williams had said in his speech: "If the governing class of this country are convinced that you are going to give full and adequate effect to this resolution they will give effect to one, two and three in order to defeat you." [45] There were only two votes against the "soviet" motion.

But certainly Williams and others intended more than simply an end to the war, crucial though that was, as would be evident from, among other things, the concerted effort *The Herald* made to continue a much wider campaign (about which more below). After Ethel Snowden had spoken briefly in support of the motion — which might seem as ironic as Williams's fate, given her marked hostility to Bolshevism later on and the attacks on her this generated from its British sympathizers — Pankhurst "welcomed the resolution as a straight cut to the Socialist Commonwealth." She believed that "the Provisional Committee would some day be the Provisional Government like the

Russian Socialist Government." She then turned to particular concerns of the WSF — the limited representation of women and what she claimed was mistranslation from the Russian: her organization had wished to amend the masculine noun "Workmen" to "Workers." It had been agreed there would be no amendments, but "Mr Snowden put the point and received an ovation in doing so, especially from a band of working women waving red flags."[46]

Reactions to Leeds

The Leeds Convention has been presented in a variety of ways by those writing decades later. James Hinton sees it as "abortive" from the standpoint of the development of a revolutionary "rank-and-file movement" but as the "preface to the reconstruction of the Labour Party, on a non-revolutionary basis." For Ralph Miliband, it was "perhaps the most remarkable gathering of the period." Similarly, Fenner Brockway records that, to the end of his life, Fred Jowett, the veteran ILPer and MP, "used to refer to the Leeds Congress as the highest point of revolutionary fervour he had seen in this country." Laurence Thompson, in his biography of the Glasiers, describes it as "a Great Peace Convention." He quotes J. Bruce Glasier as writing of this "huge triumph," one that marked the "beginning of a popular tide against the War, and industrial repression." But of the "soviet resolution" Thompson says: "Coming as it did in the wake of the Russian upheaval and coinciding with mass mutinies in the French Army, this threat of British Soviets caused some concern to the Government. But the movement remained safely under the control of the ILP, among whom was no Lenin, and the Workmen's and Soldiers' Councils, when they met at all did nothing more alarming than pass resolutions." Nevertheless, Bill Jones is surely right to say that Leeds "marked the catalytic effect which events in Russia were having upon Labour's thinking," especially if we interpret *Labour* in the broadest sense.[47]

Snowden's biographers had, of course (like Snowden himself), to give some account of their subject's central role. Thus, Keith Laybourn comments that "the Leeds Conference was generally distanced from organized labour and it never captured the public imagination," while Colin Cross writes of the "giddy moment the fantasy could be played out of a British revolution on the Russian model." [48] MacDonald's role was also central. David Marquand notes that "the convention was held without the endorsement of the Labour Party Executive, and in defiance of the disapproval of many of its members." And L.J. Macfarlane remarks in his history of the early British Communist Party that these I L P representatives "quickly lost their heady enthusiasm for extra-parliamentary action." [49]

In his introduction to the reprint of the June 1917 report of the conference, Ken Coates concludes:

> The fate of the Convention, its lapse from the status of central importance, accorded to it by so many socialists in the years after 1917, to a mere episode among the footnotes of Labour history, is part of a whole succession of defeats which the Labour Movement encountered from 1920 onwards. But the episode occurred, and it is instructive to remember it. [50]

There was, however, a great deal more enthusiasm on the Left in the immediate aftermath of the conference. *The Herald*'s editorial "Leeds Leads: Who Follows?" was entirely devoted to the convention in relation to the war, and much of the rest of the paper was given over to a report on the events, "What Happened at Leeds." The conference would, the paper said, "give a moral impetus to the movement for a people's peace without conquest. It has hailed the Russian Revolution with frankness and has achieved its objective — the establishment of a Follow Russia Movement." [51]

As we have seen, *Labour Leader* headlined its report of the convention "Britain's Greatest Labour Meeting." The report ended: "It is certain that the Convention will mark an epoch in history as great as any, perhaps greater than any, our country has yet known." In the same issue, Snowden himself characterized "The Great Convention" as "a success beyond the most sanguine expectations":

It was not only the largest Democratic Congress held in Great Britain since the days of the Chartist agitation, but it differed from other Labour conferences in the fact that it was not a caucus-ridden gathering, manipulated by officials and "leaders," but was a spontaneous expression of the spirit and enthusiasm of the Labour and Democratic movement.

As for the fourth resolution, Snowden said, the convention had "accepted the suggestion by combining some of the local activities of the various Labour and Democratic bodies in a Workmen's and Soldiers' Council."[52] Even *The Guildsman*, often seen as remote from such concerns, apologized in its June 1917 issue for not devoting more space to "the great convention of Labour organisations."

Justice remained hostile. The conference had been dominated by pacifists, it complained. It also scornfully contested the alarmist *Daily Mail*'s assumption that five million people had been represented. As mentioned earlier, the paper pointed out that some trades councils and local parties had sent many more delegates than their membership could justify on the basis of the stipulated principle of representation. In addition, it reported on a letter sent by a trade unionist, George Penn, to his branch, in which he objected to sending a delegate, partly because of the cost but also because "the idea of the promoters of the Conference is to get as many individuals present as possible," whether they represented anyone or not. *Justice* concluded (with its customary quotation marks) that "the 'Convention'" was organized "not for home, but for foreign consumption, and for that purpose was well-planned, carefully managed, provided with Quaker money for 'peace-at-any-price' purposes and may therefore positively produce in Russia the effect intended — the further paralysis of Russian military effort on behalf of the Allies."[53]

A week later, a correspondent identified only as "T.D.H." was "more than ever convinced" that "the formation of 'Workmen's and Soldiers' Committees' in this country is not . . . seriously intended. It was put forward with the sole object of influencing the Russians to look favourably on the mandate which Ramsay MacDonald, Jowett and Fairchild received from the collection of people at Leeds."[54] The three named were the delegates the convention wished — vainly, as it turned out — to send to Russia. In the meanwhile, the SLP's monthly, *The Socialist*, seems to have ignored the convention entirely, although, as Kendall notes, Willie Gallacher, Tom Bell, and Arthur MacManus attended as SLP delegates.[55]

Trying to Make British Soviets Work

During the weeks that followed, there was some attempt to turn the "soviet resolution" into reality. In *The Call*, Tom Quelch was unrelenting in urging BSP members to follow up on the "magnificent and inspiring" meeting in Leeds. It should not be left to those elected by the convention: "The Provisional Committee can only make suggestions, the *real work must be carried out by the workers*."[56] Although eager to see the workers themselves take the lead, he also argued that "after every means to secure complete local working-class solidarity, the Socialists in the Councils should aim them in as clear and definite a Socialist direction as possible."[57]

Lansbury, in hospital for an operation, missed the Leeds meeting, but *The Herald* made a sustained effort to continue the movement begun there. As "the logical interpretation of the resolutions adopted at Leeds," it put forward, with "no dogmatic finality," its "Plan for the People's Party." It demanded "Conscription of Wealth and Equality of Income," which would include "Ownership by the State: Management by the Unions" and a "Minimum Real Income of One Pound a Day." There must be "economic independence of all men and women" and "a complete democracy," which would entail replacing the House of Lords with a "chamber based on the representation not of geographical areas, but of occupations, industrial, professional and domestic." Along with the abolition of titles and "state-granted" honours, the paper called for the "democratisation of the Army and Navy (as long as they exist)." The plan concluded with a call for "the opportunity to enjoy life" and for "the workers organised against war," which ended with a plea to "Unite in your Workers' and Soldiers' Council and use your power."[58] This was followed up by weekly "Charter Articles," each dealing in greater detail with one aspect of the demands.

By the end of June, *The Call* could report that the Provisional Committee was circulating a statement asking sympathetic trades councils "to convene local workers' councils." The statement stressed that the new bodies should not encroach on existing organizations and must encourage "broad toleration." With all the workers "gathered together under the banners of the local councils there is no limit to their potentialities if with clear purpose and courageous leading they deliberately aim at the rule of the proletariat." If "complete local solidarity" could be achieved, "then the next Parliamentary Election should witness the return to the House of Commons of an overwhelming mass of direct representatives of the working-class."[59]

Britain in 1917, as critics of the country's "Bolsheviks" were to reiterate constantly during the next few years, was not revolutionary Russia. The government and parliament might not be at the height of their popularity, but they were not discredited and hated, even among those prepared to demand an immediate end to the war, anywhere near as much as the tsarist regime. If the councils tried to bring about revolution, they would find little support and would be suppressed; if they simply attempted to be the voice of the organized working class and its socialist allies, what could they do that existing organizations could not? This point had been made by a delegate named Toole, of the Clerks' Union, at the Leeds conference itself, in what *Labour Leader* called "a quietly reasoned speech" arguing for linking up existing organizations to form a central executive "that could do the necessary work."[60]

But the attempt to cover the country with workers' and soldiers' councils *was* made. In July, in spite of obstruction from the authorities, district conferences were reported as planned in Scotland, the North East, Yorkshire, Lancashire, Cheshire and North Wales, the North and East Midlands, the South and West Midlands, East Anglia, London, the South, Bristol, and Wales. Three quarters of a million copies of "The Workers' Charter" had been mailed out, and more were available, said *The Herald*.[61]

But in *The Call,* Quelch was already warning of "dark forces" hindering the formation of local councils.[62] By the beginning of August, the paper reported that although local conferences in Norwich, Bristol, and Leicester had been "complete successes," the meetings in London, Swansea, and Newcastle had been "broken up by groups of ruffians organised by disreputable reactionary political bodies, with the tacit approval of the Government." There had been "scenes of sheer brutality and hooliganism without parallel in the public life of this country. The rulers of this country are copying the methods of the tsar. In their efforts to stifle free expression they are relying upon the Black Hundreds." The "wrecking of the Brotherhood Church" in Southgate Road, London, had been particularly shocking.[63] *The Herald* reported that £800 worth of damage had been done there.[64]

More was to follow. The following week, Quelch reported that the Glasgow meeting had been banned under DORA regulations, while in Manchester there had been trouble from "organised hooligans." On the brighter side, a Southern Counties conference had been switched from Southampton to Portsmouth and had gone ahead successfully.[65] But the problems continued. The organizers of the proposed London council had been unable to hire a large enough meeting place and had been reduced to appointing their national representative by means of "a letter ballot of the delegates." It was a similar picture in Newcastle.[66] The government was sufficiently worried that it did what it could to hamper the formation of workers' and soldiers' councils, not least by conscripting Quelch.[67]

By the following month, September, Lansbury was responding to enquiries from *Herald* readers asking what they could do to support the councils:

> We especially point out to our friends that it is not intended to get together a personal membership. What is intended is that Labour, Socialist, and other progressive organisations should unite through the Trades Councils and local Labour Parties, and by this means form local Councils. There is and never has been any question of advocating or suggesting a physical force revolution.[68]

The same month saw *The Guildsman* observing that the Secretary for Scotland had prohibited a conference of soldiers' and workers' councils and by doing so had "converted what would have been a small and semi-private meeting into a large open air demonstration and provided Mr Ramsay MacDonald with the occasion for a stirring oration on the right of free speech." The paper also gave an endorsement, of sorts, to the "soviet" enterprise, if hardly in the terms that its most earnest proponents would have favoured. The councils were no "negligible force":

> Indeed, we number them amongst the most portentous phenomena of these prophetic times. It is true that the military allusion in their title is so far at least, little more than a graceful compliment to the Russian Revolution, but on the industrial side they command the support of the whole force of militant trade unionism. Constitutional minds are prone to regard the movement as purely pacifist and of little account in the industrial struggle, but we are inclined to attribute to it a deeper significance. May it not possibly represent the first instinctive gropings of the workers towards an independent industrial constitution?[69]

The "dark forces" had not — or had not yet at least — deterred the supporters of the workers' and soldiers' councils. At the beginning of October, Albert Inkpin reported that ten districts had now elected delegates, including Sylvia Pankhurst for London and the Home Counties. There would be a meeting of the national council at which policy would be formulated "and a vigorous campaign inaugurated."[70] Reports of the election of John Maclean and David Kirkwood as the delegates for Scotland soon followed. At its first meeting, the national council agreed that it had been formed "as a propagandist body, not as a rival to, or to supplant," existing organizations. It was "striving to create public opinion" in favour of "a people's peace along the lines of the Russian declaration of no annexations, no indemnities, and the rights of people to decide their own destiny." The regional and national councils would defend rights, including those of servicemen, for whom they would demand increased pay. More broadly, the national council aimed "at the consolidation of the efforts of working class organisations to attain an ever-increasing share of wealth produced by workers by hand and brain, together with control over industry." A subcommittee was preparing a manifesto, "A Plea for a People's Peace."[71]

Meanwhile, what J.T. Murphy was later to describe as the "first truly *representative* shop stewards' national conference" had convened on 18–19 August. He noted "the influence of the great Workers' and Soldiers' Council Convention which had been held in Leeds only a few weeks previously."[72] According to *Labour Leader*, another member of the shop stewards' national committee, William Gallacher, had been one of only two speakers to express dissatisfaction with the "soviet" motion at Leeds. In contrast to the other, however — the cautious Toole — he had "mourned because the idea of the Councils was not nearly revolutionary enough and did not outline a method by which the workers could take control of the economic power of the country, the sources of distribution and supply etc."[73] Concluding an article in *The Call* at the end of 1917, Gallacher wrote:

> Unfortunately, this very promising organisation has apparently expended all its vitality in the issuing of a few political manifestoes. If it is possible, let us have it raised into new life, not to resurrect a dead House of Commons, but aided by the Workers' Committees that are now so active in every industrial centre, carry through the revolution by taking control and direction of all that goes to make up the life of the nation.[74]

Gallacher was not alone. A few weeks later, at the end of January 1918, Robert Williams, of Leeds "soviet resolution" fame, asked in *The Herald*, "Why Not a British Soviet?" What was needed, he argued, was "some vehicle of working-class thought and aspiration, authoritative and truly representative. Some of us projected this idea at Leeds." Efforts should be made to "fashion some instruments to create political power to reflect Labour's economic influence." And rather surprisingly, given what had just occurred in Russia, he wrote: "We may be satisfied with a Constituent Assembly. We should prefer an Association of Soviets: Workers' and Soldiers' Councils." Williams held views similar to Gallacher's about the agency of transformation, asking, "Have the Shop Stewards' Movement and the rank and file in general enough courage and determination to give us a Soviet for Great Britain?"[75]

But it was soon clear that such revolutionary hopes were not going to be fulfilled — at least not in the near future. By February 1918, Pankhurst was wondering what had become of all the good intentions at Leeds:

> How strange it is that the political strike, which is a weapon so greatly admired when used in other people's countries, is held to be so discreditable here. Even Mr W.C. Anderson, M.P., one of the promoters of the Leeds Convention, and an original member of the Workers' and Soldiers' Council which emerged from it (where is that body now?) is reported in a speech at the Nottingham Conference as having issued a warning to the workers that any upheaval in the country will prejudice the chances of securing a democratic peace![76]

"Securing a democratic peace" had been the major aim of the organizers of the Leeds Convention. But expectations went beyond this. Even in the ranks of the pro-war Hyndmanites, the overthrow of tsarism was seen as indicating the possibility of more widespread democratic and socialist change. If the reactionary autocracy of Nicholas II could be brought down in the midst of a desperate war, what was not possible? Certainly democracy was the aim, but, for socialists, democracy meant also that the power of capital should not control the economy. The soviets in Russia seemed to promise the latter's democratization. Could not something like soviets be replicated in Britain to achieve the same end?

Yet Britain was very different. No "marvellous revolution" had swept away the old regime. The House of Commons, although still not elected by universal suffrage, had a better claim to be representative, and was infinitely longer and better established in the public mind, than the Duma. The army, while under great strain, was not on the verge of general mutiny or collapse. The inclusion of soldiers in the proposed "Workers' and Soldiers' Councils" would remain notional, though the idea helped to spread outrage and even perhaps a degree of panic among those who regarded themselves as patriots. And, in Britain, the representation of the workers in the workplace was a tradition long established, with the institutions of the trade union movement and, much more radically, the new shop stewards' movement already engaged in trying to build structures not unlike workers' soviets. In such circumstances, what could soviets be expected to achieve that could not be accomplished through one combination or another of already existing homegrown institutions and movements? One feature of the "soviet resolution" episode worth noting is that it was the first instance of a Russian institution and its terminology being advocated for adoption in Britain on the Left.[77] It would not be the last.

Much of the hostility encountered by the delegates to Leeds can be attributed to the unpopularity, among the still conventionally patriotic, of the anti-war sentiments of the participants. But, against the background of the unprecedented industrial revolt that had swept the country in April and May, the fear of working-class power was also present — and because disillusion and war-weariness had much to do with the way relatively minor issues had triggered the strikes of 1917, the two factors were not so easy to separate from each other.[78]

The Leeds Convention does reveal the attraction, for the most militant of British Left activists, of the idea of soviet democracy months before the Bolsheviks seized power, ostensibly in support of that democracy. For most of the British Left, at the time the convention took place the Bolsheviks were yet to emerge clearly as a leading force in revolutionary Russia. The Leeds initiative did not succeed in setting up British soviets, but it did come closer to producing that result, and in the midst of a war, than would any of the subsequent advocates of soviet democracy.

The notion of "following Russia" by somehow mobilizing popular support to transform the British state was seriously entertained in at least some minds. The demands for constitutional change outlined in *The Herald's* "Charter" were extremely radical (and would still be deemed to be so in the twenty-first century), but they fell within the long tradition of campaigning for root-and-branch parliamentary reform — strong, radical democracy rather than soviet democracy. In August 1917, "Charter Article, No. 13" expanded on the "Next Steps in Political Reform." The people must be able to effectively control their representatives, and their representatives likewise able to control the executive. In addition to the demands mentioned earlier, *The Herald* advocated the "transferable vote," payment of election expenses, shorter parliamentary terms, the referendum and initiative, the right of recall, the control of all parliamentary appointments by the House of Commons itself, restrictions on MPs holding "permanent" or judicial appointments, transfer to the Commons of control over its own business, and the abolition of the government's power of dissolution.[79] There is no doubt that the mood among many British socialists was not only to assert the specific interests of the working class but also, as *The Herald's* own "Charter" demands illustrate, to somehow secure, if not the total dominance of workers *qua* workers, then at least strong industrial or occupational representation in the state, as well as in the workplace, and to connect the two.

3

THE BOLSHEVIKS AND THE BRITISH LEFT
The October Revolution and the Suppression
of the Constituent Assembly

The "Unknown" Bolsheviks Begin to Register

As bogeyman of the Right or icon of the Left, Lenin was so quickly to become a household name that it is difficult to recapture the degree of ignorance that was the norm among those on the British Left until well into 1917 — and in Russia as well, if M. Philips Price's *The Truth About the Allied Intervention in Russia* is to be believed. In July 1919, a review in the *Workers' Dreadnought* quoted a passage that began: "By the winters of 1915–16 and 1916–17 when no one in Russia but the intellectuals had heard of the Bolsheviks . . ." Siegfried Bloch's "Reminiscences of Lenin," published in the same paper some seven weeks later, confirmed that "generally speaking most working class organisations were ignorant of Lenin's existence."[1] In July 1919, looking back on the situation two years previously, no less than Theodore Rothstein, by then the chief Bolshevik representative in Britain, wrote that Russia had been seen as "a far-distant and almost unknown country."[2]

As a Russian émigré, Rothstein would have been among the few individuals on the British Left who was aware of the existence of the Bolsheviks prior to 1917. It is true that many of the crucial decisions that shaped the Bolshevik party were taken at congresses in London, that some of these had been reported at the time in *Justice,* and that some on the Left, especially in the SDF, had been actively involved in aiding Russian revolutionaries (which included gun-running) during and in the aftermath of the 1905 revolution.[3] But all this had little impact in terms of registering the existence of the Bolsheviks in the minds of even the active members of socialist organizations in Britain.

Little if anything was heard of the Bolsheviks in *The Call* — later to become *The Communist* — until quite late in 1917. There was much more about Rosa Luxemburg, whom the paper mentioned in July 1916, and Karl Liebknecht, whose arrest and trial was reported throughout that year.[4] As late as December 1916, a report of the court martial of "workmen" accused of belonging to "the Russian Social Democratic Party" made no mention of that party being long divided, in everything but name, into two completely separate organizations.[5] At the BSP annual conference in the spring of 1917 — which took place after the February Revolution — fraternal greetings came from Georgy Chicherin, the future successor of Trotsky as People's Commissar of Foreign Affairs. But this was "on behalf of the Russian Socialist Groups in London" rather than on behalf of the Bolsheviks.[6]

In March 1917, *The Herald* reported on the Russian Anti-Conscription League, in London, greeting the Social Democratic Party as the "true representatives of the revolutionary proletariat." In the same issue, in articles on the Russian Revolution by Lansbury and H.N. Brailsford, as well as in an editorial titled "Holy Russia," the Grand Duke Michael and Professor Miliukoff, reported as taking charge of foreign affairs, were the only contemporary Russians mentioned.[7] In *The Call,* it is Trotsky rather than Lenin who first appears, as the editor of *Nashe Slovo* who had been driven out of Europe by the Entente governments and greeted by a "great meeting" in New York.[8]

An exception to Lenin's "invisibility" on the British Left was the hostile *Justice,* already clearly anti-Bolshevik because of its positions on the war. In April 1917, the paper reported on Lenin's "discomfiture" in the aftermath of his speech to soviet delegates advocating a separate peace with Germany, which apparently failed to provoke enthusiasm.[9] And in its April edition *The Socialist* characterized the Russian Revolution as "middle class" and explained: "There are two social Democratic parties in Russia each with its own separate organisation and Duma faction. The 'Bolshevik' section endorses the irreconcilable Marxian position, the Meshevik [*sic*] section has revisionist leanings." Most of the rest of the British socialist press, however, showed very little awareness until later in 1917.[10] The Bolsheviks were first mentioned in the *Dreadnought* in June, as "the Maximalist Socialists," on the basis of a Reuter report of the Petrograd municipal elections, which gave them 117,760 votes out of 507,982 for socialist candidates generally, something the paper thought "augurs well for the Constituent Assembly." The same report had appeared in *Labour Leader* the previous week.[11]

Lenin now appeared for the first time in the *Dreadnought.* At the end of June 1917, an editorial noted the revolutionary potential of the soviets:

> Today the Council of Workers' and Soldiers' delegates, on which the Socialists are all-powerful, may become the Government of Russia if it wills. The Maximalist and Leninite Socialists desire this, but the more cautious elements on the Council are not yet prepared to take this step. They say that Russia cannot stand alone as a Socialist State, that she cannot dissociate herself from the commerce and diplomacy of the rest of Europe, and that a Socialist Government cannot take part in capitalist trading and diplomacy. They say that until it is possible to establish a Socialist Europe it is better to have, not a Russian Socialist Government, but a strong Socialist block in the Parliament, able to force the Liberals to do its will. They fear that if the bourgeois parties are given

no part in the Government they will join the counter-revolutionary parties. The Maximalists and Leninites, on the other hand, desire to cut adrift from the capitalist parties altogether, and to establish a Socialist system of organisation of industry in Russia, before Russian capitalism, which is as yet in its infancy, gains power and becomes more difficult than at present to overthrow. We deeply sympathise with this view.[12]

Meanwhile, "N. Lenin" appeared in the June issue of *The Socialist*, as the "famous Russian Socialist leader of the Revolutionary Section of the Council of Workmen's and Soldier's delegates — the organisation that overthrew the Czarist regime." Lenin was, if not unknown, at least unmentioned for some considerable time in the pages of *The Herald*. In the issue of 17 July, Brailsford referred to the Mensheviks, whom he described as the Social Democratic "Minimalists." The " 'Maximalist' Social-Democrats who follow Lenin" appeared in another of his articles at the end of that month:

> It may be true that this party has in its ranks undesirables. It has had money "from Stockholm" it is said. It is probable that these undesirables may have come from German sources, or possibly from Mr Ford's vast donations. All this is being investigated. When it is said, however, that Lenin himself is in German pay it is well to preserve a stiff and sceptical attitude. The evidence so far is flimsy and the Socialist Members who are not Leninites protested against its publication. Lenin is a man of great magnetism, great ability, some learning and a rigid academic mind.

Readers should be slow to believe him to be "a corrupt traitor," Brailsford cautioned. Such allegations were intended to "destroy Socialism." But while the "Maximalists" had arguments that should be considered, there was no possible excuse for their recent actions during the July Days, when they had made an abortive attempt to seize power in the name of the soviets. They were, said Brailsford, a minority of about a quarter in the Petrograd Workers' Council and came sixth in the municipal elections. "Their attempted revolution was happily a fiasco."[13]

The *Workers' Dreadnought* of the same day, 28 July 1917 — the first issue under the paper's new title — saw the soviets as "all-powerful." The majority lacked the courage "to break with the war" and were maintaining the government in power "though possessing the power to form a Socialist Administration, whilst the Leninites are alleged to be using violence or threats of violence to force the Council to become the sole Executive Council of Russia." On 11 August, Pankhurst wrote: "The continued refusal of the soldiers to fight, together with the severe and growing privations in Petrograd, appear at last, to be bringing the Council of Workers' and Soldiers' Delegates and the majority of the Socialist leaders to the position adopted at the outset by Lenin (a position we ourselves have advocated from the first) namely, that Free Russia must refuse to continue fighting in a capitalist war."

By this time, *The Call,* getting its French Revolution chronology slightly confused, was complaining that the Provisional Government had been "turned into a Directory with Kerensky as the First Consul." Moreover, capital punishment had been restored "by the very hands that abolished it in the first days of the Revolution" and Lenin, Trotsky, and other "Extremists" imprisoned.[14] Brailsford, in *The Herald,* interpreted all the conflicts in Russia as arising from resistance to the imminent ending of private property in land, while "the most popular organisation of the Socialist movement seems to be that most Russian and least academic of all the groups, the Socialist Revolutionary Party." In the same issue, Michael Farbman, the *Manchester Guardian's* Petrograd correspondent, blamed "the Anarchists and Extremists (Bolsheviks)" for opposition to the international peace conference in Stockholm.[15] Soon after this, the Kornilov revolt had *The Herald* declaring, "We stand by Kerensky."[16] It was left to the pro-war *Justice,* with its very different perspective, to sense an incipient coup. Following the Kornilov episode there would, said *Justice,* be "ministerial dictatorship under Kerensky, or military dictatorship under Kornilov, or committee dictatorship by the Soviet or the Maximalists."[17]

The Bolsheviks Take Power

By the middle of October 1917, *The Call,* like the *Dreadnought,* saw "the Soviet" as "the only body that can rally the people of Russia in defence of the revolution." It concluded that "the Soviet must take power." By now the Bolsheviks had come into much sharper focus, mainly via articles by "A Russian Socialist" who, at the end of September, identified "two rival Social-Democratic parties, one of opportunist tendencies, the *Mensheviks,* and the other of revolutionary tendencies, the *Bolsheviks.*" Three weeks later, the same contributor condemned "the Opportunist Socialists." It was no wonder that "the entire proletariat and most of the Soviets" had gone over to the Bolsheviks. "This means an open war, and the commencement of a new chapter of the Revolution." [18]

"Get Ready for the Downfall," the paper told its readers at the beginning of November, predicting revolutions in all the belligerent countries. "Mankind is on the eve of a gigantic Revolution which will be as universal as the war itself. Italy, France, Russia (a second time), Austria, Germany — all will be in it." The "International" page of the same issue reported "a remarkable shift to the 'Left' observable at present in Russia, which finds its expression in the overwhelming victories of the Bolsheviks (so-called Maximalists — that is to say followers of Lenin) in the elections to the Councils of Workers' and Soldiers' Delegates and the municipalities; and the rout of the Revolutionary Socialists and the Mensheviks (Opportunist Social-Democrats)." The writer produced figures to show that the Bolsheviks were now predominant in Petrograd, Moscow, and most of "Great Russia," while the Menshevik influence was confined to the "periphery." [19]

The following week, *Justice* reported: "The Maximalists appear to have obtained control of the Soviet at Petrograd. Trotsky is now its president and is reported to have sent a request to the Petrograd garrison not to execute any military orders but those approved by the Petrograd Committee. This will bring the Petrograd Soviet in direct antagonism to the Provisional Government." [20] A week later, *Justice's* "Bolshevik Coup d'Etat" headline contrasted with *The Call's*

"Second Russian Revolution." *The Call* regretted that "the Soviet" had "surrendered its power at the beginning of the Revolution." But now "Maximalist" opinion had rapidly spread, and the "programme of the new revolutionary Government brings the immediate objects of the Revolution back to what it was at the commencement: immediate democratic peace, the granting of land to the peasants, and the Convocation of the Constituent Assembly." [21] The last of these "immediate objects" is particularly noteworthy.

How the British Left Reacted to the October Revolution

It was taken for granted that the next major item on the Russian domestic agenda would be the long-delayed elections to the Constituent Assembly. In the meantime, what were British socialists to make of "October"? According to *The Call,* "Socialists — genuine and not make-believe Socialists" — had seized power in Russia. And, using a term that would become increasingly common, if not clearer or more precise, in the socialist press over the next few years, it added: "For the first time we have the dictatorship of the proletariat established under our eyes." As the paper explained a week later, the Bolsheviks had seized power only to thwart "the Imperialist classes," who were plotting "for the final overthrow of the Revolution and the establishment of a military dictatorship à la Napoleon." The Bolsheviks had from the first offered to share power with the other socialist parties "in accordance with their principle that the authority must belong not to any political party, but to the Soviet of Workers, Soldiers, and Peasants as a whole. But the other parties have refused point blank to have any thing to do with them." [22]

The "glorious meaning of the Commune of Paris" now had come true in Russia, the paper concluded, following "those steps which Karl Kautsky so well described . . . in his beautiful booklet 'On the Morrow of the Socialist Revolution.'" *The Call* complained, however, about the lack of enthusiasm in Britain "at the marvellous spectacle of the 'dictatorship of the proletariat' and of the initiation of measures with courage and intelligence, ushering in the long-yearned-for Socialist order of society." As E.C. Fairchild put it early in the new year: "The thing we hoped to live to see is come — the rule of the common workman."[23]

Labour Leader had been edited since 1916 by Katharine Bruce Glasier, though Philip Snowden — ILP chairman from 1917 to 1920 and an MP until defeated in the post-war election of 1918 — was "Supervising Editor." His role consisted of writing a weekly, signed "page of comments on political events," as well as "leading articles."[24] On 15 November 1917, he reported that "Extremists" had taken power in Russia. He blamed the Allies' failure to respond to pleas from "the Russian Government and the Soviet" for peace negotiations. *The Socialist* wondered in response how Snowden could find anything "tragic" in "the ascendancy of anti-militarist Socialists."[25]

In *The Herald,* a series of articles by Brailsford covered the international scene, particularly the prospects for peace. Like Snowden, he saw the "new Russian Revolution" as the more or less inevitable consequence of the failure of Allied governments genuinely to pursue peace. "In the towns of Great Russia there is no doubt that the masses to-day follow the Maximalists," he reported, though he was doubtful whether this support was reflected in the rural areas or, especially, in the non-Russian periphery of the former tsarist empire. At the same time, Brailsford argued that "on any reading of sane democracy the Maximalists have acted ill." With the election of the long-awaited Constituent Assembly now so close, it was "a piece of reckless and uncalculating folly" to seize power. He still doubted that Lenin and Trotsky were "corrupt" but believed that "some of their lieutenants might well be so." The "real crime" was following Kornilov in "perpetuating an epoch of violence."[26]

But by the following week, developments in Russia were starting to be portrayed more positively in the pages of *Labour Leader* and *The Herald.* In the *Leader,* Edward Bernard foresaw the emergence of "a coalition Socialist Government" following negotiations between other left-wing parties and "the Lenin-Trotzky group." This coalition would "undoubtedly" obtain "a majority in the Constituent Assembly."[27] Brailsford, who for the first time referred to "the Bolshevik or

'Maximalist' party," was now judging the "Western mistrust of the Bolsheviks" to be "grossly exaggerated." Like Snowden and Bernard, he saw the best hope for the future of Russia in the Constituent Assembly. No dictator could govern "this amorphous mass," he argued; a "government responsible to an elected assembly" was needed. "The only substitute which might conceivably serve the purpose would be an assembly of delegates from the elected Municipal and County Councils (Zemstvos)."[28]

In an article a week later, Brailsford was again critical of the Bolsheviks who had "vetoed Stockholm," the abortive international socialist meeting aimed at ending the war, thinking themselves "too pure" to meet the German Majority Social Democrats and seeming to be abandoning principle in seeking a separate peace with Germany. He thought that in this respect Lenin and Trotsky, "the Bolshevik dictators," had "rushed far beyond what Russian opinion — even Extremist opinion" desired. The beginnings of a divergence between Brailsford and *Herald* editor Lansbury are apparent in an editorial note making it clear that the former's "own personal views" expressed in the article were "not necessarily ours."[29] But, as was the case with Snowden and *Labour Leader*, the paper continued to voice support for the Bolsheviks' efforts at peace making. At the end of December, *The Herald* praised "Bolshevik Statesmanship" for working towards "a *general* peace."[30]

According to Snowden, writing in *Labour Leader* early in December, early results of the Constituent Assembly elections showed that the "Bolshevists" were "far more representative of the Russian people than we have been led to believe" and would be the single largest party in the assembly. Together with the "Peasants' Social Revolutionary Party," they would be able to "form a responsible and representative government."[31] At the end of that month, Brailsford suggested that the assembly election results meant that the Bolsheviks' "representation only entitles them to second place, and the Revolutionary Socialists thanks to the support of the majority of the peasants may have an absolute majority." He concluded: "The Constituent Assembly with its overwhelming Socialist majority would have placed the new order on secure ground. Until the Bolsheviks hasten its meeting, even at the cost of resigning power, it seems doubtful whether a united Russia can conclude a peace or lay her own foundation."[32]

There was hope in some quarters that something like "normality" might be resumed in Russia before too long. In a report dated 10 November, the *New Statesman*'s own eyewitness in Petrograd, Julius West, saw Lenin as already exhibiting familiar political skills. In dealing with the controversial question of the rights, or otherwise, of deserters, "Lenin smoothed the troubled waters by saying that the Government would consider the matter. How quickly Parliamentary technique can be mastered." And, West noted, "the new Cabinet had already acquired the vice of keeping the public in the dark."[33]

Within a few years of these events, all the confusions, ambiguities, and uncertainties disappeared. On 5 November 1921, shortly before the fourth anniversary of the Bolshevik revolution, *The Call*'s successor, *The Communist*, published a long article by T.A. Jackson and R.W. Postgate, "The Story of the Russian Revolution," which opened:

> On November 7th 1917 — four years ago! — the impossible happened. The organised workers of Russia, acting through the All-Russian Congress of Workers' Councils (Soviets) and led and inspired by the Communist Party (the 'Bolsheviks'), declared themselves the ruling authority of Russia.

Even for *The Call,* things had not seemed quite so simple and straightforward at the time.

The Crucial Turning Point: The Suppression of the Constituent Assembly

The first absolutely crucial issue regarding Russia was not the October Revolution but the dissolution of the Constituent Assembly in January 1918. Before this, it had still been possible to justify the earlier Bolshevik takeover from a conventional democratic point of view by stressing the representativeness of the soviets compared to the self-appointed elite of the Duma parties, who had set up the Provisional Government, now overthrown. That the much-delayed elections for the Constituent Assembly, for which the Bolsheviks themselves had been calling for so long, were going ahead suggested that no irrevocable breach with democratic legitimacy had been made. No one, certainly no one in Britain — *at this point* — seems to have advanced the notion that the assembly represented a now outmoded form of "bourgeois democracy," while the soviets embodied "working class democracy" and the "dictatorship of the proletariat" (although, as we have seen, the latter phrase had appeared in *The Call,* in connection with acquisition of power by the soviets).

Should the dissolution of the assembly be condemned as an act of tyranny or justified as the beginning of a transition to a higher form of society — and of democracy? This was the crucial turning point. If claims to a superior form of democracy embodied in the soviets were now to be sustained, the reality of soviet democracy in Russia would have to support these. If it could not, socialists would either have to convince themselves that some less than democratic form of socialism could still be supported or else dissociate themselves, or at least distance themselves, from the Bolshevik dictatorship.

In 1917, not even *The Call* — the weekly organ of the BSP, the organization that, in effect, became the Communist Party of Great Britain in 1920 — had criticized the election of a Constituent Assembly or rejected it as "bourgeois." On the contrary, in March 1917 the paper had associated the assembly with the triumph over the "Liberals and Radicals . . . who betrayed the Revolution twelve years ago." It was "one of the sweetest acts of revenge on the part of Dame History that now these very gentlemen have had to swallow the entire revolutionary programme down to articles about a Constituent Assembly and the organisation of a national militia."[34] The following week, a manifesto of the BSP praised the "Russian Social-Democratic workers" for insisting on "complete popular control" and demanding a "biennial single-Chamber Parliament."[35]

Similarly, at the end of June, Sylvia Pankhurst welcomed the high voting figures for Socialist candidates, reported by Reuter, in the Petrograd municipal elections, seeing them as anticipating the results of elections for the Constituent Assembly. Soon her paper was reporting that the elections were to be held in the autumn and that "the Socialists confidently expect a big majority." [36] Neither paper suggested that parliaments or constituent assemblies were fundamentally "bourgeois" and outmoded. At the end of September, the *Dreadnought* was able to report that those "variously called Bolsheviks, Maximalists and Leninites," now with a majority in the soviet, wished it to "become the Government of Russia *until the Elections for the Constituent Assembly have taken place*" (emphasis added). The provisional governments were again criticized: "The elections to the Constituent Assembly have been delayed again, but it seems that the mass of the people in Russia should demand the holding of these elections, in which all will have a voice." [37]

In a November *Workers' Dreadnought* editorial welcoming "The Lenin Revolution," Pankhurst quoted the view of *Daily News* correspondent Arthur Ransome that the soviets were "the broadest elected body in Russia" and reminded her readers that "since the first outbreak of revolution the Bolsheviks have consistently demanded that until the Constituent Assembly is elected the Workers' and Soldiers' Council shall take over the Government of Russia." She went on to conclude that "the power of the people may maintain the Bolshevik Government or if it should fall, the votes cast in the elections for the Constituent Assembly may re-instate it." [38]

As the results of the Constituent Assembly elections began to come in, there was great optimism in socialist ranks, not least among those who within weeks would be defending that body's forcible dissolution. Early in December, "a Student of the Revolution" claimed in *The Call* that "the Bolshevik success has been due to the fact that the masses of the town proletariat and town garrisons have revolted, at last, against the systematic surrender of the Revolution to the capitalists and landowners," who had attempted to "overthrow the Soviets and the rule of democracy in general." If the Bolsheviks could "last long enough to meet the Constituent Assembly they will have effected a real revolution — in a social as well as a political sense." By the following week, Zelda Coates thought the early results showed that "the Bolsheviks have the vast masses behind them."[39] Pankhurst agreed: "It is certain that whether the Bolsheviks have a clear majority or not, the various Socialist parties command a vast majority in the Russian Parliament."[40]

Julius West's eyewitness view in the *New Statesman* was less sanguine. The split within the Social Revolutionary party "made a common ticket an absurdity." Moreover, he wrote: "The Bolsheviks had virtually secured a monopoly for themselves (which they extended to other Socialist parties) by suppressing the 'bourgeois' papers. They had prohibited open-air meetings, though for that matter the provisional government had done the same, and 'the falling snow was doing its best in the same direction.' "[41]

We have already seen the hopes about the Constituent Assembly entertained by Snowden, in *Labour Leader,* and by Brailsford, in *The Herald,* in December 1917. Early in the new year, writing in *The Herald, Guardian* correspondent Michael Farbman blamed successive provisional governments for the "Bolshevik Ascendancy." They had continued imperialist policies and had tried to postpone elections for the Constituent Assembly until "after the achievement of peace." In addition, during the interval between the "Kornilov affair" and "Lenin's coup," they had created an "anti-democratic Cabinet" under Allied pressure, which had included the Cadets (members of the Constitutional Democratic Party) instead of the "expected purely Socialist Government" that would have saved Russia. The Mensheviks had mistakenly continued to back Kerensky, and "the Coalition Government was not pulled down, it faded away like a mirage. Its absurd unreality is the explanation of the miraculous Bolshevik success."[42]

The following week, the same paper published a message to British workers from Maxim Litvinov, the "Plenipotentiary for Great Britain of the Russian People's Government," which described how "the workmen and soldiers of Petrograd, Moscow, and other towns found themselves compelled to break finally with the middle classes and to restore full power to the Soviets." The "true proletarian revolution of November" had followed and "a mighty class war" had begun.[43] This can now easily be read as preparing the way for the acceptance of the completion of the Bolshevik seizure of power, but there was no expectation anywhere in the British socialist press, still less any demand, that the Constituent Assembly would be superseded. Even the hostile *Justice*, when it considered "rumours that the Bolshevik Administration would suppress the new Assembly and proclaim the Soviet Congress next Sunday a kind of National Convention," dismissed them because, it argued, such action would create conflict with the Social Revolutionaries, who had a majority in the assembly.[44]

The Suppression of the Assembly:
Immediate Reactions

Given his later anti-Communism and the "moderation" and constitutionality represented by the Labour Party, one might expect that — in spite of his participation a few months previously in the "Leeds Soviet Convention" — Philip Snowden would have been among the first to condemn the suppression of the Constituent Assembly. The reality was somewhat different — surprisingly so.

The first issue of *Labour Leader* following the dissolution of the assembly appeared on 24 January 1918. Snowden was cautious. "The situation in Russia still continues to be chaotic," he wrote, arguing that "the Bolsheviks hold power because they appear to be the only large party who have sufficient cohesion." He expressed his regret that "the Bolsheviks and the Social Revolutionaries cannot make some working arrangement, for there appears to be no difference in their economic ideas and programme." Internal divisions would, he felt, weaken the Bolsheviks in the peace negotiations with Germany. "With the limited knowledge we have of the actual state of affairs in Russia," he continued, "it would be foolish to dogmatise or take sides definitely in a temporary conflict. We are naturally prone to look at what is happening from our British point of view and to come to conclusions, or at least to be inclined to do so, influenced by our tradition and training in constitutional methods."

Though falling well short of a ringing endorsement of the Bolsheviks' action, this was hardly the blistering condemnation that might have been expected from such a quarter. The same issue's (unsigned) "International Notes" were even more forbearing, while still expressing reservations. Citing Ransome's *Daily News* despatches and Philips Price's "admirably sincere articles in the *Manchester Guardian*," they asserted that, the SRs having failed "to show the courage and determination to carry out their own programme," the Bolsheviks had decided that "the whole government of the country, both central and local, should be in the hands of the Workers' Soviets." The report went on:

> The Bolsheviks believe — apparently with good reason — that they alone are able to secure a democratic peace. The Bolsheviks were, therefore, faced with the alternative of dissolving the Constituent Assembly or allowing Russia to give way to Germany and to compromise with the capitalist forces. They chose the former knowing that it was a definite breach of the accepted standards of democratic government.

The writer went on to say that events were moving fast and that Lenin's actions might retrospectively be "justified by the support he will now receive." It was "unfair" to say that "he rules by force," since "the Soviets are assured of support locally, as well as centrally, and are in actual daily contact with the rank and file of the nation."[45]

While Lansbury's *Herald* did not explicitly endorse the crushing of the assembly, and Brailsford remained convinced that it ought to be reinstated, the paper did publish, on 9 February, a "Russian Workers' Appeal to Britons" from the "International Bureau of Workers', Peasants' and Soldiers' Deputies." The Constituent Assembly was not mentioned:

> The Russian working classes are not striving for a republic of the type of American trust magnates or French stock exchange sharks. They want to wield full political power and to replace the bureaucracy by the rule

of the Soviets as the local government organs. The Russian working classes will not be content with the establishment of democracy, but will use democracy as a means for accomplishing all the stages necessary to lead Russia step by step to an efficient Socialistic organisation of production.

The same issue offers other signs of an indulgent attitude to the Bolshevik takeover. Farbman wrote of the Bolsheviks "establishing the proletariat in power" and their "magnificent demonstration of democratic diplomacy at Brest Litovsk."[46] A week later, an editorial note referred to "our friend Litvinoff," soon to be congratulated for his speech — at a Central Hall meeting whose platform included Lansbury — for "the manner in which he dispelled and blew away into the clouds the capitalist lies which have been spread already about the revolution." The following week, the paper was scorning the "Anti-Bolsheviks" who "warn us of the terrible results of applied democracy."[47]

Lansbury's own equivocal views of the Bolsheviks appeared a week later under the heading "The Revolution I Want." "The Bolsheviks, in my judgement, have not failed and will not fail, whatever may happen to Trotsky, Lenin, and their comrades," he wrote. "They have lit a fire in the world which will never be put out." Lansbury detected in their internationalism "the true pure doctrine of Christianity," although he also thought they had "suffered a setback because they have convinced themselves that freedom of speech, freedom of organisation, would ruin the revolution. From the point of view of the moment they were right. I am certain, though, that the revolution of the near future which is quickly coming to this country, will base itself not on violence but on reason."[48]

The only *Herald* voice that really opposed the suppression of the assembly was, unsurprisingly, Brailsford's. But even he saw some positive features in the new Bolshevik regime and avoided any straightforward denunciation. He commended the "far-sighted policy" of Lenin and Trotsky, who had "shown themselves the greatest tacticians in Europe," although he questioned their "exact purpose."

Was it "a general peace or a general revolution?" He doubted whether the Bolsheviks' adoption of the tactics of the French revolutionaries in 1792, such as appealing for foreign revolutions (in this case particularly those in Germany) to come to their aid, could succeed: "Even the Minority leaders among the German Socialists are not Bolsheviks. Bernstein stands for evolution, and even the Marxist Kautsky has sharply criticised the whole Bolshevik theory (which seems to me more syndicalist than Socialist) and especially the suppression of the Constituent Assembly. Let us watch our steps when we hear the Pied Piper's flute." [49]

Returning to his critique of Bolshevik strategy early in March, Brailsford warned of the danger of intervention:

> If Russia had a government which obviously and visibly reposed on the confidence of the people, it might defy retaliation at home and intervention from abroad. There is only one expedient acknowledged by the mass of civilised mankind by which a government may prove that it rests on the consent of its people. It must have the majority of a regularly elected assembly. A Russian Government may be as boldly Socialist as it pleases, on one condition, that it has the votes of the Russian people behind it. If a Socialist Government in Russia had the Constituent Assembly behind it, foreign intervention would be morally impossible. No professedly "democratic" government could refuse to "recognise" it, or act, openly at least, against it. If to-morrow the intervention would begin our protests would be answered by the argument that the Lenin-Trotsky regime is anti-democratic, and the interfering Governments would profess to be acting in the interests of the Russian people. May I make a practical proposal, which it is not too soon to consider now? It is that when our International Socialist Conference meets, one of its chief acts should be to send a delegation to Russia to mediate between the various Socialist parties, with a view to the restoration of the Constituent Assembly. Sooner or later it will be our duty to defend Russia against European intervention. We should fail unless we can point to proof that Russia herself is content with her own Government. [50]

Pankhurst was far from calling for the assembly's restoration, but "What About Russia Now?" — her very long editorial in the 26 January issue of the *Dreadnought* — began by acknowledging the degree to which the action of the Bolsheviks had caused consternation:

"There is the democracy of your Socialists," "Substituting one tyranny for another," "Bolshevik autocracy," "What about Russia now?"; such are the cries that assail us.

And what have we to answer? Firstly that all Press news and comments must be received with critical caution and reserve, because they have passed through the censor's hand, and usually come from anti-Socialist sources in the first instance, and because all our great dailies are opposed to Socialism.

Now let us consider what the Bolsheviks have done. In the decree for the dissolution of the Constituent Assembly, as transmitted from Petrograd by the Bolshevik Agency, the Russian Socialist Government says:

The old bourgeois parliamentarianism has seen its day that it is unable to cope with the tasks of socialism.

It points out that the Soviets or Councils of Workers' and Soldiers', Sailors' and Peasants' delegates have been from the first the organs of the Revolution. The decree declares that the Revolution:

created the Soviets, as the only organisation of the exploited working classes in a position to direct the struggle of these classes for their complete political and economic emancipation.

It may be said with equal justice that the Soviets created the Revolution. They sprang into being at its outbreak, they carried through the deposition of the Czar in March, and every subsequent advance has been initiated by the Soviets.

According to Pankhurst, as events in Russia had unfolded they had given strong support to those, calling themselves Syndicalists, Industrial Unionists or simply Marxian Socialists who interpret the great teacher's doctrines from the industrial standpoint, who believe that Parliaments as we know them are destined to pass away into the limbo of forgotten things, their places being taken by organisations of the people built on an occupational basis. The failure of the Constituent Assembly, even though decided on an adult suffrage ballot, to return members prepared to support the policy of the Soviets is strong evidence that the industrialists have found the true path.

But why then did the Bolsheviks go ahead with the Constituent Assembly elections?

Pankhurst was clearly puzzled and concerned about this point, to the extent of offering three alternative explanations. For one thing, the Bolsheviks might have wished to demonstrate that "the capitalist parties have no following in Russia." The results had certainly been effective in that respect, she argued, since "the Cadets (or Liberals; no parliamentarian now calls himself Conservative in Russia) have secured only 14 seats in the Assembly, and but for proportional representation might have had not one single one." Or the Bolsheviks might have intended the whole episode — election and dissolution — "to divide definitely and clearly in the popular mind, the politicians who are in favour of Socialism, but do not want to have it in their time, from those who are, like themselves, striving for its immediate establishment."

Finally, Pankhurst argued, it might be "that the Bolsheviks have been disappointed in the elections, that having faith in the desire of the Russian people to secure peace and the enactment of the maximum Socialist programme, they believed that a majority of those prepared to carry out this programme would be elected." This view she thought supported by the statement in the decree that voters had been unable "to distinguish between the Revolutionary Socialists of the Right, partisans of the bourgeoisie, and the Revolutionary Socialists of the Left, partisans of Socialism."

But, whatever the motives of the Bolsheviks, the suppression of the assembly should, Pankhurst insisted, be defended on democratic grounds because the soviet system was "more closely in touch with and more directly represents its constituents than the Constituent Assembly or any existing parliament." And she urged readers to put aside their doubts:

> Therefore do not say that the news from Russia is bad because, in the stress of a great struggle to establish Socialism, the Russian Socialist Government fiercely assailed and hardly pressed by capitalism and its minions both at home and abroad, has found it wisest to break with the Constituent Assembly, and to confide the direction of policy to the democratically constituted organisations of the workers, instead of to an Assembly to which the wiles and crafts of politicians has admitted a large proportion of capitalist wolves clothed in the bright promises of a Socialist lamb.[51]

If Pankhurst showed some appreciation of the concerns that the Bolsheviks' action in suppressing the assembly had generated, the reaction of *The Call*, in its issue of 31 January, was much more confident and dismissive of criticism:

> The suppression of the Constituent Assembly has seemingly caused some perturbation among those who are no doubt sincere friends of the Russian Revolution. These friends do not yet appreciate that in Russia today we have the Dictatorship of the Proletariat, and it is this that some of those who pose as "revolutionaries" describe as appalling. Some people imagine that to make a revolution is as easy as making a new house. The elections took place before the subservience of Kerensky, and the parties supporting him, to Imperialism was discovered. When it was discovered, these parties were discredited, and the Bolsheviks took power backed by the will and bayonets of the vast majority of the people. The majority of deputies of the Constituent Assembly no longer represented those who voted for them. Its suppression was absolutely justified. The Soviets are the direct expression of the will

of the soldiers, workers and peasants. The Russian Revolution is a working-class revolution, and the workers must *rule* until it is no longer possible for the capitalists and landlords *as a class* to lift up their head. When that time comes, and classes are abolished, the Russian people will devise the most democratic form of administration best suited to the circumstances. In the meantime "All Power to the Soviets."

This seems to suggest that the "most democratic form of administration" would be something different from the soviets themselves. In the same issue of *The Call*, a BSP executive resolution — aimed at the Labour Party Conference — sent fraternal greetings to "the Russian Social-Democracy" and hailed "with profound admiration and deep joy the establishment of the Dictatorship of the Proletariat." It also offered its own interpretation of recent events in Russia: "The Council of Workers', Soldiers', and Peasants' delegates, which under the sanction of the great November Revolution, has assumed all the power of the State, has taken the first real step to bring to an end the bloodiest war in history." [52]

The tendency on the British Left to interpret Russian events in terms of the wishful thinking of the beholder is nowhere better exemplified than in the SLP's reaction, expressed in the February 1918 issue of *The Socialist*. Rather than empathizing with the Bolsheviks, it identified them as trying to follow the SLP's own impeccable approach. It excused those it still called the "Russian Maximalists" for being unable to "rigidly apply S.L.P. tactics" because of "the peculiar and limited conditions" under which they were operating. But they clearly shared the "emphatic insistence that the *Political State must be replaced by an Industrial Administration*." This explained and fully justified the dissolution of the Constituent Assembly: "It is because the Maximalists are *true* democrats that they have vested the industrial administration of Russia in the hands of industrial and agricultural committees." And in the March issue, the usual piece commemorating the Paris Commune commended the Bolsheviks for "avoiding the error of mis-educated Socialists, namely, the maintenance of the political State. The Bolsheviks rightly abolished the constituent assembly; rightly too, they established an industrial government of Soviets. This is the policy of the S.L.P. which we have propagated for years." As the article went on to point out, this

> was, indeed, no less than the "Triumph of S.L.P. Tactics in Russia." In Russia our friends have destroyed the political state — the constituent assembly — and are now organising industrial administrative Councils. Let every non-S.L.P.-er read "Principles of Industrial Unionism" (2d) (written years ago) and see whether, in the light now coming from Russia the S.L.P. is not *the* party of the workers.

The Labour Party Conferences of 1918: Litvinov Versus Kerensky

Unusually, there were two Labour Party conferences in 1918, one at the end of January and another in June. The first met in Nottingham and was addressed by Litvinov. In an editorial in *Justice*, Fred H. Gorle, was aghast at the prospect:

> This week we may have the spectacle of Maxim Litvinoff — the representative . . . of the suppressors of the first democratic assembly of Russia . . . being cheered at Nottingham by thousands of people under the impression that they are applauding the Russian Revolution, instead of the sabotage of the Russian Revolution; democracy and liberty, instead of the suppression of democracy and liberty.
>
> But what are we to say of Arthur Henderson, of George Lansbury, of Ramsay MacDonald, and of all those who have allowed the workers of this country to be so misled about the masqueraders of Socialism, Lenin and Trotsky? [53]

A separate note in the same issue asked who had invited Litvinov to the January conference. An answer of sorts was to be supplied at the June conference, to which Kerensky was invited — an invitation that was challenged at the opening of the event. Henderson, the Labour Party secretary, then made a statement defending the invitation.[54] According to the official conference report, having taken full responsibility for Kerensky's invitation, Henderson went on to describe how, shortly before the Nottingham conference in January, "a prominent representative of the left wing — he hoped they understood where the left wing was" came to his office to say that "another prominent and distinguished representative of Russia" was in London. Henderson did not agree with Litvinov's views, but he had been "sufficiently long in that Movement to realise that one of its most valuable assets was its spirit of toleration." So he had suggested that Litvinov be invited, and the Labour Party executive committee had agreed "with striking unanimity." Litvinov had come to the conference and made a speech. The delegates "did not agree," Henderson noted, "but they listened — they listened as ladies and gentlemen and as strong believers in the right of free speech.[55]

At the January conference, the reception accorded to Litvinov — whose address, "To the Workers of Great Britain," had already appeared in the 10 January 1918 issue of *Labour Leader* — was, said the *New Statesman*, "full of significance." The paper reported enthusiasm for the Russian Revolution and the overthrow of tsardom:

> But the solid mass of delegates who filled the floor was sternly silent and unresponsive when Mr Litvinoff, who had to bring his narrative down to date, explained that, in such times, it was impracticable to have respect for "forms of Democracy." The Labour Party has no sympathy with the arbitrary dismissal of the Representative Assembly; and the Bolshevik stock has gone down with a run.[56]

According to *Justice*, Litvinov had said that "democracy was 'all right in its way' but if it went against the desires of the Bolsheviks it was their determination to carry through their policy at all costs. This speech was received by our own Bolsheviks, who were present in considerable numbers in the gallery, with vociferous applause."[57]

In contrast, *Labour Leader* offered a very different, and rather surprising, version of the events, very supportive of the Bolshevik emissary. It said that Litvinov had been given standing ovation by delegates and reported him as telling the conference that in Russia "the land has been given to the peasants" and "the factories are under the supervision of their Shop Steward Committees" — a reference, the paper said, "to the developing British organisation which the conference appreciated." [58] Similarly, *The Herald,* the self-proclaimed "National Labour Weekly," reported that for the "Russian ambassador" the audience "rose to its feet and cheered again and again" and that his speech was punctuated by cheers "all through." His defence of the Bolsheviks was "listened to with rapt attention and when he declared that the land had gone to the peasants, workshops to the workers, and the army put under control of committees, who elected officers, settled questions of discipline, the hall rang with approving cheers." [59]

If the first Labour Party Conference of 1918 seems, in spite of the *New Statesman's* account, something of a triumph for Litvinov and the Bolsheviks, the second conference, in the summer, saw delegates more clearly polarized. This is evident from the *Workers' Dreadnought* report. When Kerensky appeared, "there were cheers; people stood up and waved their hands. He was Russian and that was enough for most of them. Someone cried 'Where are Lenin and Trotsky?' There were hisses and groans. 'To hell with Kerensky! — to hell with Kerensky!' Walton Newbold shouted." (Newbold was soon to emerge as one of the leaders of the "Left Wing of the I.L.P." and would later become a Communist M P.) According to the *Dreadnought* report, Henderson, as Kerensky's sponsor, was given a rough ride, and both Sylvia Pankhurst and Dora Montefiore were prominent in demanding, without success, that Litvinov should also be allowed to speak.

In his speech, the report continued, Kerensky attacked the Soviet government, which he described as a "dictatorship not of the proletariat, but *over* the proletariat who have lost all the political rights which the Revolution gave them." He declared that the Bolsheviks had "destroyed the liberty of the elections, even in the councils of workmen" and had "made an end of all institutions of self-government that have been elected by universal suffrage." When Litvinov tried to reply, "the chairman stopped him speaking and allowed Kerensky to make a calumnious attack." [60]

By this time, Lansbury was, for the moment, distancing himself from the Bolsheviks, criticizing their "haste and violence," which was "likely to promote a reaction against any form of Socialism." In the same issue of *The Herald*, Farbman noted the "warm welcome" given to Kerensky and regretted the "outburst of obstruction" directed at him during the conference.[61] Clearly, Labour Party opinion, as represented by the 1918 conferences, was divided on the legitimacy of the suppression of the Constituent Assembly.

Snowden's Early Optimism

The most surprising reactions to the dissolution of the assembly were those of *Labour Leader* and, above all, of Philip Snowden. Within a few years, the latter's attacks on the Bolsheviks would bring about a public conflict with the editor, Katharine Bruce Glasier, that would end with both leaving the paper and may have contributed to its replacement by the *New Leader* in 1922. In retrospect, it is easy to understand the support given to the Bolsheviks in the *Leader's* regular "International Notes," contributed by Emile Burns, who was later part of the "Left Wing of the I.L.P." and eventually joined the Communist Party in which he became a prominent figure. But Snowden's is a very different and still surprising case. There seem to have been two main factors in Snowden's early indulgence: his assumption, as a "practical" politician, that the Bolsheviks would eventually conform to a more familiar — and less "revolutionary" — pattern, and, crucially, the absolute priority he gave to ending the war as soon as possible.

Yet Snowden's optimism about the Bolsheviks persisted even after the end of the war. At the beginning of 1919, he was still viewing Bolshevik survival in power as proof that the party was "supported by the majority of the Russian people." Interventionists believed, he claimed, that "Democratic Socialism must be stamped out wherever it shows its head." A week later, he predicted that all the main sections of the Russian socialist movement would once more be united. The Mensheviks were said to have "adopted the Soviet programme" and the Right SRs to have declared against Allied intervention.[62] Early in

March 1919, a report in the *Leader*, reprinted from *Humanité*, declared that "all Russian Socialists, whatever their particular school, have rallied round the commissaries of the people." [63]

Writing his autobiography in the early 1930s, Snowden summed up the great significance of the January 1918 Labour Party conference: "The acute difference between the pro-War and the pacifist section which had showed itself so markedly at the previous conference had almost disappeared. Men who supported the continuation of the War were in such a hopeless minority that, at the Nottingham Conference, with the exception of the Chairman, who occupied a privileged position, they remained silent." [64] This almost certainly reflects his concerns and priorities at the time. Peace was everything; the Russian Revolution was important mainly because of the bearing it might have on this. Yet, having decided to give the Bolsheviks the benefit of the doubt, mainly on the basis of their peace-making potential, Snowden continued to do so for over a year following the extinguishing of the Constituent Assembly.

"Replacing" the Constituent Assembly: Retrospective Justifications

Given its virtual apologia for the suppression of the assembly earlier in the month, it is not surprising that *Labour Leader* should, at the end of January 1918, publish a sympathetic report of the recent Soviet Congress, which, it said, "takes the place of the Constituent Assembly." The editor's comments, introducing a "statement sent us by the International Bureau of the Council of Workmen's, Soldiers', and Peasants' deputies themselves," were headlined "The Russian Government's Defence: What the Soviets Have Done and Are Doing Today." She urged that "members of the I.L.P. cannot commit themselves to unreserved approbation of all the methods employed . . . but only future generations can justly sit in judgement upon what has been done." [65]

The only party of the British Left that unequivocally denounced the suppression of the assembly was the unfortunately named National Socialist Party, made up of the pro-war "Hyndmanites" who had left the BSP. Its first conference, held in August 1918, passed "with acclamation" the following motion by Hyndman and J. Hunter Watts, both long-time members of the "Old Guard of the S.D.F.":

> That this Conference sends to our Russian comrades of the Social-Revolutionary Party its sincere good wishes and hopes that after they have overthrown Bolshevik tyranny and beaten down monarchist intrigues they will succeed in re-establishing a thoroughly democratic Constituent Assembly.[66]

Shortly afterwards, denouncing Lenin as "a furious fanatic destitute of any moral sense, either personal or political," Hyndman called for support for the "Union of the Regeneration of Russia," a general coalition of democratic forces "headed by men who represent the Constituent Assembly crushed by Lenin."[67]

This was not a stance likely to find support elsewhere on the Left. At the end of May, reviewing Litvinov's *The Bolshevik Revolution: Its Rise and Meaning,* which the BSP was publishing as a shilling pamphlet, Eden and Cedar Paul noted wearily that it included "an apologia for that which the political 'democrats' regard as the Bolsheviks' greatest crime — the dissolution of the Constituent Assembly."[68] In June, the *Dreadnought* confessed surprise at an answer given to an *Avanti!* correspondent by Kamenev and Zahkind. When asked, "Why have you dissolved the Constituent Assembly?" they were quoted as replying:

> Because the fight with the capitalists is not finished, as long as it continues the Soviet must be the sole fighting organisation of the workers. When all have submitted the divers social strata will again be able to send their legitimate representatives freely to the legislative and administrative assembly.

This response seemed contradictory to the *Dreadnought's* firm belief that "the Soviet form of Government is a more modern and more democratic form than the old Parliament elected on a territorial basis."

According to Litvinov's *The Bolshevik Revolution,* as summarized in the same issue of the paper, the Bolsheviks had, with the exception of Lenin, initially thought that "the exercise of power by the Soviets would be but temporary, and would be voluntarily resigned to a Constituent Assembly representing all classes in which the bourgeoisie would form the Government." As Litvinov saw it, not to have suppressed the assembly "would have meant the reestablishment of the rule of those very classes which had nearly ruined the revolution." The split in the Social Revolutionary Party had not been apparent until after the assembly election, and "had the election been held a couple of months later it would have shown a large majority for the Bolshevik policy." Soviet rule, or the "dictatorship of the proletariat and peasant class," would continue "pending the re-construction of society which would do away with classes altogether and admit every citizen of Russia to the full exercise of civic rights."

This was all very well, the *Dreadnought* concluded, but

we do not know, and Mr Litvinoff does not enlighten us, as to whether the mass of the Bolsheviki now think that after the secure establishment of the Socialist Republic, the Soviet form of government will pass away and Russia revert to the older parliamentary type, in which candidates represent electoral constituents and are elected for long terms, without being responsible to, or having to report to any definite body of persons. For our own part, we believe that the Soviet Government will persist, no doubt with development and growing improvement, and is destined to become the new governmental model for the Socialist republics which will shortly follow Russia all over the civilised globe. The master mind of Lenin has no doubt foreseen this all along![69]

As the war ended and revolution broke out in Germany, the *Dreadnought* saw this prediction coming to pass. An editorial at the end of November 1918 quoted a statement from the Spartacist League: "The whole control of the country is now in the hands of the Workers' and Soldiers' Council. A Congress of Workers' and Soldiers' Councils is to be summoned as soon as possible. At present there is no talk of a National Assembly."[70] A fortnight later the *Dreadnought* reported that the Bolshevik government had sent a "wireless" from the Tsarskoe Selo station urging German workers not to let themselves be persuaded to call a Constituent Assembly. "You know where you have been landed through your Reichstag. Only a Council of Workers, Soldiers and Sailors and a Workers' Government will gain the confidence of the workers and soldiers of other countries."[71]

The issues surrounding the Constituent Assembly and its suppression continued to be rehearsed and debated in the years that followed. Justifications of the Bolsheviks' action came from more or less "detached" observers in Russia and from leading Bolsheviks themselves, as well as from enthusiastic foreign supporters. A year after the crushing of the assembly, *The Socialist* carried a piece by Klara Zetkin, translated by Eden and Cedar Paul, from the women's supplement of the *Leipziger Volkzeitung*. According to Zetkin, "the dissolution of the Constituent Assembly, far from involving a sacrifice of democracy, made democracy more effective." With "the economic and social power of the possessing classes . . . still sufficient to exercise considerable influence upon the election results," the assembly could not be regarded "as the unfalsified expression of the opinions and the will of the workers. In so far as we can speak of a popular will, that will was indubitably incorporated in the decisions of the soviets."[72]

A particularly vehement defence of the assembly's dissolution, republished in the *Dreadnought* in April 1919, came from a left-wing American publication, *The Public*. Whereas in the United States it was criminals and the insane who were disenfranchised, in soviet Russia it was the parasitic classes who were excluded from participation in the soviets. In any case, the Bolshevik claim that the Constituent Assembly was unrepresentative of "the Russian masses" seemed to be upheld by events, given that no effective protest at its suppression had materialized.[73] This argument had been advanced from time to time before. As *The Call* had insisted the previous summer: "The dissolution of the Constituent Assembly stirred no ripple on the faces of the immense sea of the Russian masses; while the threatened curtailment of the powers of the Soviets, two months preceding destroyed the Provisional Government."[74] Similarly, after John Ward, an implacable opponent of the Bolsheviks, gave a very hostile and highly coloured account of the assembly's suppression to the recent special Trades Union Congress at the end of 1919, the *Dreadnought* drew on the accounts of two Americans to refute him — *The Red Heart of Russia*, by Bessie Beatty, war correspondent of the *San Francisco Bulletin*, and Louise Bryant's *Six Red Months in Russia*. According to Bryant, the end of the assembly came about "because the people were with the Soviets."[75] By 1921, for the Communist Party at least, the whole issue could be dealt with dismissively. In the first part of *The Story of the Russian Revolution*, Jackson and Postgate (whose account of the October Revolution was quoted earlier) noted:

> Much has been made of this "suppression of a democratically elected body" as though it were a trampling on by an armed minority upon the rights of a liberty-loving majority.
>
> The Assembly was not the expression of anything beyond the superior propaganda resources during the Kerensky regime of the Aristocratic Kadets, the Middle Class Mensheviks, and the agricultural bourgeois Right Social Revolutionaries.[76]

A common feature of arguments in defence of the suppression was the claim that, irrespective of the assembly election results, the Bolsheviks *now* enjoyed overwhelming majority support. In June 1918, in response to Kerensky's address to the Labour Party conference, Litvinov claimed that there had been "only five anti-Soviet candidates" in the recent Petrograd Soviet elections, which had returned 233 "supporters of the Soviets" — Bolsheviks and Left Social Revolutionaries.[77] No explanation of what could be meant by "anti-Soviet" in this context was given.

When Admiral Koltchak, the White Russian leader, "as a sop to public protests," subsequently declared in favour of eventual elections to a new constituent assembly, rejecting the Allied suggestion that, if this proved impossible, the body elected at the end of 1917 should be reassembled, the *Dreadnought* claimed that his decision tacitly acknowledged that "a majority of the members of that Assembly are now in the Soviet Ranks!" and that "experience of life under the Soviets and the practices of Koltchak and his like has induced the majority of the Mensheviki and Social Revolutionaries to join in helping the Soviets." [78] Such optimistic claims continued to be accompanied by the assertion that soviets represented, in Lenin's words, "a higher form of democracy than the ordinary bourgeois republic with a Constituent Assembly." [79] It is to the arguments used to sustain this claim that we now turn.

4

THE MYTH ESTABLISHED
The Positive View of Soviet Democracy

"The Superiority of the Soviet"

In July 1918, Lenin's "What Are the Soviets?" appeared in *The Call.* Responding to this question, Lenin declared: "The superiority of the Soviet over any other form of representation is easily demonstrable."[1] In the years immediately following the revolution in Russia, this argument — that the soviets constituted a more genuinely democratic form of government — was crucial to advocates and defenders of Bolshevism in Britain. It was routine for such enthusiasts to contrast the failures, deceptions, and shortcomings of the British parliamentary system, and of "bourgeois democracy" in general, with the "real" democracy of the soviet system.

For example, in February 1918, a front-page piece in the BSP's *The Call,* headed "Learn to Speak Russian," mocked Britain's supposed democracy, which, it urged, amounted to "a Cabinet with absolutist powers, appointed by no one knows whom, with no check on the legislators, or, for that matter administrators, and with no control over foreign policy." There were, *The Call* insisted later that year, two forms of democracy, "with two underlying philosophies fundamentally and increasingly antagonistic to each other. The first is the Right of the Man of Property, the second of all sections of the people. The former, which is the keystone of the American and French Republican Democracies, is alien from the whole conception of socialism." [2]

Advocates of soviet democracy constantly stressed its direct and bottom-up nature. The BSP's Fred Willis, addressing a meeting in the Kingsway Hall to celebrate the first two years of the Bolshevik revolution, maintained that "when Kerensky's 'Revolution' took place it was welcomed by the Black International as a 'Democratic' bourgeois republic; but the direct rule from the bottom of the workshop and the politics introduced by the Bolsheviks inspired its fierce and undying hatred." [3]

It may be difficult now to understand how such a system of indirect election as that used in the soviet structure, with several layers of councils between the elector and the effective national rulers, could be regarded as more "direct" than the election of conventional parliamentary representatives. Indeed, there were critics, including socialist ones, who raised this question at the time. The key to understanding the position of supporters of soviet democracy is the difference — in theory, at least — between representatives and delegates. [4] Most people on the Left were familiar with the delegate system from their own socialist and trade union organizations. In principle, the delegates going forward from each level necessarily pursued the position agreed upon by their branch or whatever unit they were representing. That is, delegates were mandated to support the policy of their immediate constituency. Failure to do so could, if the constituents so decided, result in the delegate's immediate replacement.

Much emphasis was placed by soviet supporters on this "right of recall." John Reed's "The Structure of the Soviet State" — reproduced from the *New York Liberator* in the "Special Russian Number" of the *Workers' Dreadnought* at the end of 1918 — was keen to stress that "delegates are not elected for any particular term, but are subject to recall *at any time.*" This was the case, Reed went on, at all levels, from the local soviets to the commissars who formed the national government: "These Commissars can be recalled *at any time.* They are strictly responsible to the Central Executive Committee."[5] And, on the eve of the creation of the Communist Party of Great Britain in 1920, the joint provisional committee promoting its formation was quoted in *The Call* explaining that the committee could no longer defend "gradual evolution" and "peaceful transition" and must reject parliamentary democracy: *"Against this sham parliamentary democracy of capitalism the workers' representative places the method of direct representation and recall, as embodied in the Soviet idea, [with] only those performing useful service to be enfranchised."*[6]

The soviet franchise was a key issue both for opponents and supporters. For the former, the exclusion of various categories of the "bourgeoisie" from participation was, in itself, sufficient demonstration of the undemocratic nature of the regime. For supporters, almost the opposite was the case. The perceived working-class nature of the soviets — the absence of a British peasantry tended to obscure the fact that most participants in even a "perfect" Russian soviet system would be peasants — was a positive recommendation. It could be related to earlier events that had been mythologized in the socialist movement. Reviewing William Paul's *The State: Its Origin and Function* in *The Call,* Fred Shaw evoked an earlier phase in British radical history in the plea with which he ended:

> Let there be a Labour Convention — not a Labour Party or Trade Union Conference, but a gathering of the direct representatives of the rank and file, elected in the factories, workshops and mines on a plain and comprehensive ticket, to meet not in a provincial city, but in the capital, and to sit not for one day but in permanence as the direct expression of the will of the united working class. It should be an anti-Parliament, as the great Chartist conventions were.[7]

And in March 1920, in a piece that continued the long-established practice of commemorating the Paris Commune as a sort of socialist Easter, W.H. Ryde, writing under the banner "Vive la Commune," quoted Marx to the effect that it "was to have been not a parliamentary, but a working corporation, legislative and executive at the same time." He went on to claim that "an unbroken chain unites March 18th 1871 and November 5–6th 1917, the Commune and the Bolshevik Revolution."[8]

The franchise argument was, at bottom, a moral one. Capitalism was an evil system based on the exploitation of workers by capitalists who were either hard-nosed bosses accumulating riches by paying their workers poverty wages while squeezing as much work out of them as possible, or idle *rentiers* living in luxury at the expense of the workers' sweat and toil. In either mode, the capitalist made a negative rather than a positive contribution to society, and it was the mission of socialism to bring the capitalist system to an end. In 1920, in a piece titled "Bolshevism and Democracy" published in *The Call*, Anton Pannekoek, the Dutch "Left" Communist, began by stating: "The question of democracy is the most fiercely disputed question of the day." As he went on to insist: "A man, who merely lives upon his capital, who is only a parasite, a drone sponging upon the body of society, shall certainly not speak with equal voice with a worker through whose work alone society is in a position to exist at all." And, he added: "This is to some extent an ethical principle."[9]

Under socialism, said Sylvia Pankhurst, "everyone will be a worker and there will be no class save the working class to consider or represent."[10] That being so, the continued exclusion of members of the bourgeoisie from the electorate was ultimately the result of their own choice. These were people who, as Pankhurst put it, "instead of joining the general companionship of workers, employ others to work for them for private gain."[11] The self-exclusion argument was carried further by John Reed in his "Structure of the Soviet State." Reed maintained, essentially, that the excluded groups had had their chance — and had messed it up:

Until February 1918, anybody could vote for delegates to the Soviets. *If even the bourgeois had organised and demanded representation in the Soviets, it would have been given them.* For example, during the regime of the Provisional Government, there was *bourgeois* representation in the Petrograd Soviet — a delegate from the Union of Professional Men, which comprised doctors, lawyers, teachers etc.[12]

Yet an article by Bukharin, titled "The Soviets or Parliament" and published in the *Dreadnought* less than four months later, suggested that a very wide spectrum of groups were excluded from political activity: "The capitalists, the landed proprietors, middle-class intellectuals, bankers, stockbrokers, and speculators, merchants and shopkeepers, priests and monks, in short, all who form the black army of capitalism, are deprived of the right to vote and are without political power."[13]

It is perhaps not surprising that a year later, in April 1920, the SLP's *The Socialist* queried the accuracy of the translation of a passage from Zinoviev's *The Communist Movement in Russia,* which asserted that "more than nine tenths of the population have electoral rights." With some incredulity, the paper quoted the French version on which the translation was based. It had believed — it thought on good Bolshevik authority — that only "workers" were enfranchised, and yet now Zinoviev was saying that the middle classes were being given votes:

> With the development of our Soviet Constitution, the electoral right
> has been extended progressively and equally to the class formed by the
> middle strata of the population (?) (le droit electoral s'est étendu pro-
> gressivement également à la classe formée par les couches moyennes
> de la population).[14]

But could this be right? Whatever the reality, though, the claim to almost universal suffrage was now the "official" line. A few months later, *The Communist* reported that "the entire adult population of Petrograd," including students, intellectuals, and housewives, had participated in the recent Soviet elections there.[15]

In relation to the franchise issue, it has to be remembered that Britain, along with other leading "bourgeois" states, could hardly boast to be shining examples of democratic suffrage — as was pointed out by those sympathetic to the idea of soviet democracy.[16] In Britain, at the time of the Bolshevik revolution, all women and roughly a third of men were excluded from voting, and the Representation of the People Act of 1918 still left women under thirty unenfranchised. It also allowed a degree of plural voting that in effect gave an extra vote to some bourgeois sections, such as owners of business premises and university graduates. The act is rightly celebrated as a major step forward for women. But nearly all British socialists took universal suffrage for granted as an immediate aspiration and as often as not, as we have seen, espoused more radical democratic demands. British voting rights were unlikely to impress or even to be seen as offering a positive contrast with voting rights in revolutionary Russia.

Approval, or at least tolerance, of the restrictions that did exist on the soviet franchise went beyond embryonic "British Bolsheviks." A few months after the suppression of the Constituent Assembly, the ILP's *Labour Leader* announced: "The Soviet system is an experiment; it does not conflict with the principle of representative government, though at present the idle rich are excluded from political power."[17] The position taken in August 1918 in the BSP manifesto "The Allied Intervention in Russia" would thus have seemed reasonable to many more socialists than those who subsequently became committed Communists: "In placing the franchise in the hands of the workers, soldiers, and peasants, the Bolsheviks have swept away the false bases for the right to vote known to Western nations, such as property qualifications, or, in the case of women, age and marriage, and make the title to vote dependent upon the performance of social labour."[18] Even as late as 1920, the *New Statesman* — not usually regarded as an organ of the far Left — concluded, in an article to be examined in greater detail later, that soviet voting rights were "far wider than many franchises commonly regarded as democratic."[19]

Given the influence of the quite wide range of ideas — industrial unionism, syndicalism, guild socialism — that posited some form of workers' self-management and occupationally based politics, it was inevitable that, in addition to parallels with Chartist conventions and the Paris Commune, more familiar and contemporary equivalents would be found. A July 1918 editorial in *The Call* stressed the involvement of working people in the management of the Russian economy. The management of the railways was supervised "by Commissions of the railwaymen themselves organised through their unions. Similarly, the great works, the mines, the factories are managed by workers, and are gradually being socialised in the interests of the whole community." [20]

Solidarity, a monthly publication in August 1918, was edited by Jack Tanner, a prominent member of the shop stewards' movement who had served on the executive of the Industrial Syndicalist Education League in the years immediately preceding the war. Hostile to "politics," *Solidarity* could still support the soviets since "the Shop Stewards movement is more closely akin to the Russian Soviets than any other British movement." In the following issue, David Ramsay, treasurer of the Shop Stewards' and Workers' Committees, proclaimed: "We are the natural allies of Revolutionary Russia, and their success paves the way for ours." [21] Similarly, at about the same time, *The Herald* presented the Bolsheviks as having established "Workers' Control in Russia":

> While retaining throughout the proletarian character of the organisation, which results naturally from the Soviet form of Government, the Russians have established a system of control which bears a resemblance to what is advocated in this country by Guild Socialists. They have based their system on functional organisation. [22]

In "The Soviet as Practical Politics," published the following year in *The Call,* Fred Willis saw precursors and prototypes of soviets in contemporary Britain as well as in pre-revolutionary Russia:

Certainly the age-long traditions of Early Communism inherent in the Mir could have been no drawback in the establishment of the Soviet; but, from the point of view of analogy, an ordinary English Trades Council is at least as close a parallel. And the Workshop Committees building up, factory by factory, into larger bodies covering the industrial life of a whole town are closer than either. . . .

And, quite recently, during the railway strike, it is a matter of common knowledge that committees of organised workers sprang up like mushrooms in many towns in this country, solely for the purpose of taking control of the food supply if necessary. . . .

They were in fact, in all but name, Soviets, as the Soviets existed in that period (start of March 1917 Revolution).

Had the crisis developed further, he concluded, full-blown British soviets would have come into being.[23]

Later, the emphasis shifted to the essential role of soviets in a revolutionary crisis. The unidentified author of "When and Under What Conditions Soviets of Workers' Deputies Should be Formed," which appeared in the *Dreadnought* at the end of January 1921, asserted — in what seems to be an implicit criticism of the tendency of that paper to perceive embryonic soviets in almost every popular movement — that "Soviets without a revolution are impossible. Soviets without a proletarian revolution inevitably become a parody of Soviets."[24]

Protagonists of soviet democracy were also keen to stress the independent and highly responsive nature of the soviets, which was deemed to illustrate graphically the reality of truly democratic control. One example is a passage in John Reed's account of the soviet state where he refers to the situation in Petrograd at the end of 1917:

No political body more sensitive to the popular will was ever unveiled. And this was necessary, for in time of revolution the popular will changes with great rapidity. For example during the first week in December, there were parades and demonstrations in favour of the Constituent Assembly — that is to say, against the Soviet power. One of these was fired on by some irresponsible Red Guards, and several people killed. The reaction to this stupid violence was immediate. *Within twelve hours the complexion of the Petrograd Soviet changed.* More than a dozen Bolshevik delegates were withdrawn, and replaced by Mensheviki. And it was three weeks before public sentiment subsided — before the Mensheviki were one by one retired and the Bolsheviki sent back.[25]

A report from Julius West's "Petrograd Diary," published in the *New Statesman* in May 1918, presented the delegates to the peasant soviet as robustly resisting any attempt by their political leaders to direct them. "They frequently upset the plans of their political leaders by refusing to follow party lines," West wrote. "They refused to approve of Lenin, even when that master-humorist came down to their Soviet and harangued an audience consisting of men who called themselves Bolsheviks and Left Social Revolutionaries."[26]

The belief in the actual reality in Russia, and the potential reality in Britain, of genuine control by the industrial grassroots was very strong on the Left. At the meeting convened in Kingsway Hall to celebrate the second anniversary of the Bolshevik revolution, the veteran labour movement leader and pre-war syndicalist, Tom Mann, was welcomed by "uproarious cheering" when, having rejected parliaments as a route to socialism, he declared: "We must organise a thoroughly representative industrial rank and file, and use the workshop as the unit of workers' power."[27]

The Reality of Soviets — as Seen by Supporters and Sympathetic Observers

As is evident throughout this book, most British socialists had little idea of the real nature of Russian soviets, especially in the initial stages of the revolution, which were so crucial for establishing perceptions. When one thinks today about Russia in 1917, it is not difficult to understand that soviets were initially, in Charles Read's words, "rough-and-ready institutions" that were often "set up in a very ad hoc way." "Even the Petrograd Soviet," he tells us, "was initially composed of more or less anyone who showed up. Its founding executive was self-selecting." [28] How could it be otherwise at the outset? At the time, however, hope, enthusiasm, and commitment to the *idea* of soviet democracy among so many on the British Left meant that little, if any, hint of the possibility of such imperfections manifested itself. Still less would many British socialists have given a moment's credence to Robert Pipes's judgment that, "in no time, the Petrograd Soviet acquired a split personality; on top speaking on behalf of the Soviet, a body of socialist intellectuals organized as the Executive Committee; below an unruly village assembly." [29] Similarly, there was little appreciation of the complexities, the overlaps between different working-class organizations, and the confusions that Diane Koenker pointed to in her book on Moscow workers, especially in the chapter titled "The Evolution of Working-Class Institutions." [30] If any such structural or procedural untidiness was suspected, it was assumed to have been quickly sorted out.

Accordingly, along with advocacy of the superior virtues of the concept of soviet democracy, the socialist press offered quite detailed descriptions of the constitution and functioning of the Russian soviets. One example, John Reed's "The Structure of the Soviet State," reproduced in the *Workers' Dreadnought* at the end of 1918, has already been mentioned. Before this, in August, *The Call* had published an exposition of the fundamentals underlying the Soviet form of administration that had been specially written for the paper "by a well-informed Russian Socialist." The writer began by stating baldly: "There is hardly anyone in Western Europe who knows the constitution of the Soviet Government."

The article attempted to correct this deficiency, explaining that the All-Russia Congress, elected by country and town soviets, which had originally met every three months, was now convened at six-month intervals. Between meetings of the congress, the country was governed by the two-thousand-strong Central Executive Committee, and ministerial work was carried out by departments set up by the committee: "Any order of these Departments can be repudiated by the Central

Executive Committee." The "well-informed Russian Socialist" also reported that "the Russian Republic of Soviets has no President at its head." This was a statement some readers of *The Call* might have found confusing, given that, only a few weeks earlier, the paper had described Lenin as "President of the Council of People's Commissaries of the Russian Socialist Republic" and, just a few months later, would refer to him as "President of the Russian Republic." [31]

For its part, *Solidarity* was clear that in Russia "control of industry by the workers" was not merely an idea but a reality:

> Even now the Soviets are the Real Government and a knowledge of their composition may be of assistance. They consist of delegates representing 500 electors appointed on an Industrial basis, and general meetings of the workers: these form local soviets (taking the place of Municipal bodies). The local soviets elect delegates on the basis of one representative for every 25,000 electors to the All-Russian Congress of Soviets, which meets every three months. Provision is made for the expulsion of any delegate to a Soviet at any time. The Congress elects a Central Executive Committee of 3,000 members which has permanent control of the Government, and which also has the power to revoke any orders issued by the Government. The latter consists of People's Commissioners who are chairmen of the various departments of state. The Trade Union, Co-operative and other bodies have also direct representation in the Soviet. [32]

Readers of *The Socialist* were able to consider the full text of the "Constitution of the Russian Soviet Republic" in the September 1918 edition.

But how did the soviets operate in practice? Much depended, of course, on the sources of information. Like most socialist papers, the *Workers' Dreadnought* had no confidence in the reporting on Russia in the British press generally but thought that Philips Price, of the *Manchester Guardian,* and Arthur Ransome, in the *Daily News,* were "the most reliable of the capitalist press correspondents." [33] The anti-Bolshevik *Justice,* inevitably, had quite the opposite view: "Some day, no doubt, we shall understand the incomprehensible support of the Russian Bolsheviks by such organs as the 'Daily News' and the 'Manchester Guardian.'" It was, the paper declared, "not the leaders but what their 'correspondents' are allowed to publish" that was the problem.[34] And from time to time *Justice* would indulge in a jibe at what it called Arthur Ransome's "fairy tales," a snide allusion to the author's version of folk stories, *Old Peter's Russian Tales,* published in 1916.[35]

However, Ransome's seemingly measured assessments of Russian events gave his reports an aura of authenticity that impressed even some of those more skeptical than the committed supporters of Bolshevism. In its April 1921 review of Ransome's *The Crisis in Russia,* the *Workers' Dreadnought* made this point explicitly: "At times the author's criticism is strong and outspoken. It is never malignant but we can still detect traces of the old bourgeois mentality; in fact the author doesn't pretend to be a Communist. If anything, that fact adds value to his book, as he is an independent witness and investigator."[36] Many years later, in his autobiography, Ransome offered a less positive view of the "self-elected Soviet of Soldiers' and Workers' Deputies," describing how, early in 1917, "the eloquent dashed off to the factories or barracks to get themselves elected 'by acclamation.'"[37]

At the time, however, Ransome's *Six Weeks in Russia* convinced a *New Statesman* reviewer that "the official picture of Russia . . . which is periodically drawn in blood and thunder for the benefit of the British elector is a monstrous perversion." A key question was the nature of the soviet form of government:

> One may believe or disbelieve in the Soviet form, but for the foreigner and his Government the only relevant question is, Do the present Government and their institutions provide the regular representation and expression of popular opinion through elected organs of government? We are told that they do not, that Lenin and the Commisares are autocrats in exactly the same way as were the Tsars. This, however, is incompatible with Mr Ransome's description of the meetings of the

Executive Committee and of the Moscow Soviet which he attended. Of the Moscow Soviet he remarks that "practically every man sitting on the benches was obviously a workman and keenly intent on what was being said." And most significant is his description of the meeting of the Executive Committee at which the adherence of the Right S.Rs. who had been fighting against the Bolsheviks was considered, their recantation accepted, and a resolution passed giving them "the right to share equally in the work of the Soviets."[38]

Accounts of the practical workings of the soviets sometimes appeared in the British left-wing press considerably after they were written. "How a City Soviet Is Elected," for example, published in the *Dreadnought* in October 1919, was based on *Pravda* reports from April 1918. The *Dreadnought* article described elections to the Moscow soviet. It began with "Instructions for Elections and Re-Elections to the Council of Workers Deputies (Soviet)," which required workshop committees to announce elections three days in advance and to "guarantee all parties complete freedom of agitation." Results showed that, although Bolsheviks predominated, a few Mensheviks, Left and Right SRs, Anarchists, and Independents were also elected.[39] But there was no acknowledgement that, just a few weeks later, Mensheviks and SRs had been expelled from soviets as counter-revolutionaries.[40]

To illustrate the control of the electors over their delegates, the article cited the case of one factory in which a Menshevik-sympathizing Independent was initially elected. He resigned, however, when he found it impossible to abide by the Nakaz — the set of instructions or mandate — adopted by the workers' meeting, and a Bolshevik was elected in his place. All the same, the examples the paper offered of the instructions issued to delegates hardly reinforced the idealized view of workers taking the real decisions, which the elected then loyally carried out. The two Bolsheviks elected unanimously by the Ribbon-Makers' Society were, for example, simply told by resolution to "stand firm" and to carry on an "unfaltering labour policy without political compromise with the Capitalist Class and to remember that behind them stood the workers, ready to lay down their lives for the great Russian Socialist Revolution." Equally sweeping were the "instructions" given Railway District delegates, who were ordered "to support the Soviet Government with all their energies" and "to defend and strengthen the conquests of the November proletarian revolution" and were then further reminded that "in the event of the non-execution of these instructions the workers reserve the right to recall the deputies at any time and to elect others in their place."

Revelations — particularly ones coming from *Pravda* — that as early as April 1918 delegates from the grassroots level were being issued very general and highly formulaic mandates, instructing them to give the Bolshevik central government unqualified support, might, with a very modest degree of skepticism, have been expected to cast some doubt on the reality of workers' power. But the *Dreadnought*'s enthusiasm for soviet democracy survived. The same article went on to report:

> The general meeting of the Soviet takes place once or twice a week, the work in the intervals being carried out by an elected or salaried Executive Committee. The vast majority of deputies, therefore, continue their ordinary occupations among their fellow-workers for the greater part of the time. Thus they are kept constantly in touch with their comrades in the factories and shops, and can pass on their instructions to the full-time workers of the Executive Committee at the weekly or monthly general meetings. In this way the growth of the "professional politician" type is killed at the very outset. The same end is reached by making all delegates revocable and replaceable at any time.[41]

Evidently, then, the fact that the *Dreadnought*'s article relied on information already eighteen months old did not raise serious questions. When, as was so often the case, there was a time lag between events and reports in the British press, Bolshevik supporters would have assumed that, in the meanwhile, soviet democracy had been marching forward, continually establishing itself as a reality. One example, again from the *Dreadnought,* of how the Left *assumed* a positive trend in Russia — a steady advance in the direction of equality and real working-class democracy — is the final sentence of the response to the question, "Have the Communists Dissolved Soviets?" by "Our Own Correspondent":

> Yes, they have done so. In 1918 it was found necessary to dissolve the Soviets and take new elections in a number of country districts. The reason was that in these districts the poor peasants, still under the influence of their old life, elected to represent them rich peasants who were exploiting them, who had induced the poor peasants to sell their produce and after parting with their crops to work as employees in order to get food, or were selling their produce back to those who had sold it at a much higher price. The poor peasants had voted for their exploiters belonging to the Left Wing Social Revolutionary Party, which the peasants had been accustomed to believe their champion. The Soviet officials therefore found it necessary to dissolve these Soviets, to point out to the poor peasants that persons who employ others for private gain and live without working are not elligible [sic] for election, that the poor peasants should elect representatives from amongst themselves as their delegates. Only in the early elections was it necessary to take the step of dissolving such improperly elected Soviets.[42]

Believers in soviet democracy continued to insist, despite appearances to the contrary, that in Russia power lay with the working people themselves rather than the Communist Party. As an article (originally from *La Vie Ouvrière*) that appeared in *The Socialist* at the end of July 1920 declared: "In Russia, the Workers' Council, the Soviet is everything."[43]

By the end of 1921, the Communist Party of Great Britain had been established for more than a year and *The Call* had been renamed *The Communist*. Stung by criticisms emanating from, of all places, the *Catholic Herald,* the paper mounted a firm defence:

> The main charge made against the Soviet Republic is that it is governed by the Communist Party which numbers only 7,000,000 members

out of a population of 120 millions. What our critic does not seem to know is that the government of Russia is an executive committee which is composed of thousands of delegates elected from every workshop, mine, railroad, factory, farm — from every social sphere where people carry on socially necessary functions.

Lenin, Trotsky and the other Commissars are not elected by the Communist Party as our lying authority seems to infer. They are elected by the E.C. appointed by the All Russian Soviet Congress. It is true that masses have paid a great tribute to the Communist Party by electing its most brilliant members to the highest governmental posts.[44]

Among Bolshevik supporters in Britain there were few, if any, who doubted that, in J.T. Murphy's words, "the highest form of democratic organisation has been evolved" in Soviet Russia.[45]

Labour Leader *and "an Experiment Which Mankind Truly Needs"*

Enthusiasts for soviet democracy were not confined to those journals, such as *The Call, The Socialist, Solidarity,* or the *Workers' Dreadnought,* that spoke for organizations that quickly came to identify themselves closely with the Bolshevik cause. The ILP also included many equally committed "Bolsheviks," who would soon form the party's "Left Wing." But there was also a predisposition on the part of a much wider section of that party's membership to give a fair hearing to the claims of the soviets and of the Bolsheviks. We saw in the previous chapter that the reactions to the suppression of the Constituent Assembly were far less hostile than might have been anticipated even from future "anti-Communists" like Snowden.

The position of the ILP's *Labour Leader* was even commended by Pankhurst at the end of 1918. Having castigated *The Herald* (soon to become the *Daily Herald* again), which she called "the official or unofficial organ of the Labour Party," for its "most unsatisfactory attitude towards the Workers' Socialist Revolution" and for carrying articles by "anti-Socialist (for such we must term the anti-Bolshevik) writers such as Brailsford," she added: "The editorship of *The Labour*

Leader has maintained, as it should, a steady comradely attitude to the Bolsheviki, but some of the ILP leaders, both in speech and writing, and still more by silence in important crises, have failed to maintain this standard." [46]

The seizure of power in the name of the soviets was presented in *Labour Leader* almost as a disinterested academic experiment in democratic form: "If the moderate Socialist elements will recognise the system of Soviet government . . . an experiment in solving the theoretical dispute between the industrial and political State, as represented by the Constituent Assembly, might be set on foot." [47] Responding to a call soon afterwards from the Social Revolutionary Party in Russia to exclude the Bolsheviks from the Socialist International because they had "violated the most elementary principles of democracy," the ILP paper insisted, in May 1918, that these were in fact the principles of Western representative government as embodied in the Constituent Assembly. "But is the Western system really the only possible method of representative government?" the paper asked. Was not "a system of indirect elections," from workshop to local soviets and from local soviets onwards, also "a form of representative government?" [48]

The notion that what was happening in Russia was an experiment in working-class democracy persisted for a very long time. In May 1919, for example, Norman Angell, famous as the author of *The Great Illusion,* wrote that "the attempt to give democracy a new meaning by grafting onto its political forms some methods of industrial self-government, however blunderingly that attempt may be made, is an experiment which mankind truly needs." [49] Belief in the reality of Soviet democracy, together with the notion that what was taking place in Russia was "an experiment," did not head off all criticism, but it did allow widespread, general support for the soviets, which were perceived as authentic independent organs of working-class democracy.

Allowing the Bolsheviks a "Run for Their Money": The New Statesman, 1918–1921

Given the provenance of the *Statesman*, it would be easy to imagine that it would have taken a consistent, principled, anti-Bolshevik stance, defending parliamentary democracy against the claims of the soviet system to constitute a "higher form." However, the picture that emerges from its pages is not nearly as clear-cut — or as critical of the Bolsheviks and the "soviet system."

"No one who is not a lunatic will suspect us of a peculiar affection for Bolshevism," began the editor, Clifford Sharp, in December 1918, but he went on to insist that the situation in Russia had "changed completely." The Terror was now over and the "great mass of the professional and petty bourgeoisie have now gone over to the Bolsheviks." Responding to hostile criticism the following week, he declared: "We do not believe, as we have frequently said, that the Bolshevik organisation of industry will succeed; but we do hold that, assuming the Bolsheviks have now secured the assent of the mass of the Russian population, no prepossessions of ours should be allowed to prevent them having a run for their money."[50]

Early in 1919, however, relatively more antagonistic views began to appear in the *Statesman*. "An Englishman Recently Returned from Russia," who said he had been sympathetic to the revolution from its inception, now insisted that, contrary to the claims about massive support for the Bolsheviks, they would, in his estimate, secure no more than 25 percent of the votes in a fairly conducted election. As it was, he wrote, "if a Moscow or Petrograd factory dares to return a Menshevik, that factory is purged by the Bolsheviks' 'extraordinary police'— itself an exaggerated and more terrible imitation of the old Okhrana."[51]

But Clifford Sharp's judgment regarding the Bolsheviks' current popularity was not so easily shaken. The following week, his leading article stuck to "our central contention that — whatever the methods and aims of the Bolsheviks — their hold over Russia is stronger than has been generally admitted in the Allied countries." [52] All the same, this did not necessarily mean that the present situation would long continue. By July 1919 the "Bolshevik junta" had temporarily secured "the practical adhesion of the bulk of the nation for the purpose of resisting counter revolution or foreign intervention." But once the external threat was removed, the *Statesman* predicted, "the Russian workmen and peasants" would "prove as little inclined, we believe, to tolerate Bolshevism as English workmen are to tolerate a renewal of conscription." [53]

Within six months, however, this confident prediction was explicitly abandoned. In January 1920, under the heading "The Triumph of Bolshevism," the *Statesman* insisted that the situation in Russia had fundamentally changed:

> In the early part of last year we frequently expressed in these columns the view that peace with the Bolsheviks would be followed pretty quickly by their overthrow through the action of internal forces. It seems impossible now to entertain any such expectations. All recent information from public and other sources indicates that the Soviet Government has been gaining enormously both in prestige and popularity.

Bolshevism was, economically, "a crude and probably unworkable creed," and politically it was undemocratic and unpopular, but its leaders were "men whose personal idealism is above question or criticism." They might be tyrants, but they were "disinterested tyrants," not bent on personal gain. If it was an oligarchy, it was "a proletarian oligarchy" that was "democratic in essence if not in form." For Russians, it was "the most democratic Government that they have ever known." [54]

"We do not defend Bolshevism," the *Statesman* insisted at the time. But it looked too much like that to its critics, and there was a slight backtracking a week later, in an editorial note appended to a letter from Paul Hookham that challenged this conception of democracy. The editor conceded that "democratic in essence" was "too hasty a phrase. We should perhaps have said democratic 'in spirit' or 'in ultimate purpose.' "[55]

In March 1920, an unsigned article in the *Statesman*, "Parliament Versus Soviet," argued that ideas about democracy, especially among socialists, were "in flux" and that "we are certainly likely to witness, if not to take part in, a number of experiments on alternatives to the Parliamentary system." The soviet form of government had "captured the imagination not only of the 'left-wing' Socialists and Communists of all countries, but also a good many 'intellectuals.' " Not that soviets were necessarily the only possible form of working-class democracy. In the same issue, the reviewer of Lenin's *The State and Revolution* italicized the word "or" in quoting Lenin's reference to "the building up of a democratic republic after the type of the Commune *or* of Soviets (Councils) of workers and soldiers deputies — the revolutionary dictatorship of the proletariat":

> That *or* is extraordinarily significant. The Soviet system is a method of proletarian dictatorship, *an* organisation created by the proletariat to supplant the capitalist State; but it is not necessarily the only method or the only suitable form of organisation. The essential thing for Lenin is that the proletariat should create an organisation of its own, the form and structure of that organisation are matters of secondary importance.[56]

A very similar conclusion was reached just a few weeks later by "Hussein," who conducted *The Guildsman*'s book page, in the course, again, of reviewing Lenin. This time the work in question was *The Proletarian Revolution*. "Hussein" remarked on the "scant mention given in it to the Soviets" in Lenin's earlier *The State and Revolution* and then continued:

> Here, we find the Soviets in the centre of the picture, and at the same time we have the explanation of there [*sic*] not being in the centre before. Lenin regards the Soviet regime as constituting "one of the forms of proletarian democracy," but by no means the only possible form. He

does not say that, in order that there may be revolution everywhere, every country must set up Soviets; he contents himself with trying to show that the Soviet regime does satisfy the necessary conditions of proletarian democracy, without saying that no other system will satisfy them. This explains why, in his previous book, when he was arguing about proletarian democracy in general, the Soviets only entered into the argument as far as he applied his general principle directly to the Russian conditions of 1917.

Similarly, Lenin doesn't regard the exclusion of non-producers from the franchise "as the fundamental or characteristic feature of the dictatorship of the proletariat." A "necessary condition" was the "forcible suppression of the exploiters as a class" and therefore the Dictatorship of the Proletariat may take place "under different forms." [57]

The implication was clearly that one of those forms was likely to resemble the ideas of the National Guilds League. A little later, a *Statesman* review of G.D.H. Cole's *Social Theory,* headlined "Functional Democracy," quoted approvingly Cole's dictum that "true representation is always specific and functional and never general and inclusive." [58]

As the *Statesman* insisted a few weeks later, however, there was a dearth of information on the actual workings of the soviet system in Russia. "Most of the foreign advocates of the Soviet system," the paper argued, "appear to regard it as a form of organisation scarcely less characteristically industrial than Syndicalism or Industrial Unionism, and to hold that its most significant distinction from Parliamentarism is its adoption of an occupational instead of a geographical basis of representation." But this was not necessarily so. Soviet elections in Hungary in 1919 had been held on a geographical basis, and even in Russia peasant soviets necessarily followed "the main geographical lines based on the village." The "fundamental basis" of the soviets was not "occupational constituency, but the utilisation of the most natural popular groupings as the groundwork for the electoral system."

The system was clearly not without its defects. Direct representation of trade union federations, co-operative societies, "or even the local Association of a political party" meant that there was much duplicate representation and "almost infinite scope for manipulation; and there is no doubt that the Bolsheviks have consistently manipulated the system so as to secure a predominance of the 'active and class-conscious minority.'" A note added that when plural voting was prevented at the national congress of soviets in Berlin, during the German Revolution, the congress had promptly proceeded to vote itself out of existence in favour of a constituent assembly. So what, according to the article, were the significant differences between Russia and "the West"? As regards "local government," it concluded, the major difference was the Russian "service franchise, which is slightly less wide than universal suffrage but far wider than many franchises commonly regarded as democratic." At the level of "national government," however, the indirect nature of representation appeared "to destroy all democratic safeguards by sweeping away the direct contact of the elector with his representative." To this objection, the *Statesman* said, "Sovietists" responded with the claim that the "essential Soviet principle of the 'recall' . . . provides more real contact and greatly superior popular safeguards against misrepresentation."

And where did this leave matters as far as the *New Statesman* was concerned? The journal hesitated to form a judgment on the basis of what it regarded as insufficient information and too brief an experiment:

> All we can say is that, theoretically there is evidently much to be said
> for the Soviet system — in a purified form — as applied to a country
> like Russia, and that it is much too early for any detached observer to
> condemn it out of hand even as applied to more politically advanced
> communities. It is the only practical democratic alternative to Parlia-
> mentary government which has yet appeared.

The system had, the writer argued, had less impact in Britain than elsewhere in Europe, given that "the Soviet is there regarded hardly at all as a form of government, and almost entirely as an instrument of revolutionary and proletarian dictatorship." And the article concluded:

> We have therefore everything to gain by studying it, not as a strange and abhorrent monster associated with Bolshevism, but as a very vital and important experiment, which has arisen as a "mutation" rather than a "variation" in the evolution of democracy, and from which we may even be led to adopt such features as seem to offer a prospect of real improvement in the character of our own representative institutions.[59]

New Statesman optimism about the future of democracy in Russia continued. In March 1921, in "The Ferment in Russia," Michael Farbman detected a difference "in spirit and in attitude" at the Eighth Congress of Soviets as compared to its predecessors. It had introduced a series of democratic reforms, the chief of which was "the proclaimed end of the dictatorship of the People's Commissars (the Cabinet) and the taking over by the Central Executive Committee (the Parliament of Soviet Russia) of the actual control over the officers of state." He conceded that, with no political opposition or independent press and the suppression by the Communist papers "of everything that tells against them," it was only possible to gauge the spread of critical and oppositional ideas "among the masses" by following the movements of opinion within the Communist Party itself. "The real and fundamental cleavage of opinion" was between the various factions of the party and "the 'Labour Opposition' which represents the non-partisans — now the biggest party in Russia. The Communist Party remains the ruling force . . . but within it there is evolving a powerful democratic section."[60]

This seems to have been the *Statesman*'s last really optimistic prognosis about soviet democracy. Within a few months, the paper was castigating the Russian regime, under the headline "Imperialism *à la Russe*," for its invasion of Georgia. The British Labour movement, the

Statesman noted, had been "persistently friendly" to the Bolsheviks, sympathizing with them when faced with Polish aggression. But: if Soviet Russia meant "to tread the same path as Tsarist Russia, if new presbyter is but old priest writ large, then Soviet Russia will stink as much in the nostrils of the working class as it does in those of the House of Lords. For the 'petit bourgeois democrats' of this country will oppose Imperialism from whatever quarter it comes."[61]

Even so, there was still some hope, in the summer of 1921, that international efforts to relieve the famine in Russia might improve relations with the Bolsheviks. It was to be a few months more before the *Statesman* concluded, in November, that "the Communist experiment has failed."[62]

It is clear that the belief in the superiority of the soviet system, as embodying both a "higher form" of democracy and working-class power, played an enormous part in attracting the support of those elements of the British Left that would, during the years following 1917, be drawn towards a whole-hearted commitment to the Bolshevik cause. It is equally plain that a much wider spectrum of Left opinion took soviet democracy seriously enough to consider its claims sympathetically and, for some years at least, to give the benefit of the doubt to the Russian "experiment." As we have seen, at least until the middle of 1921, this was true to a degree even of the editor of, and some of the contributors to, the *New Statesman*.

We must not forget, though, that in spite of the surprisingly "open" attitude to soviet democracy during these years, the *New Statesman* was considerably underwhelmed by the various attempts to form a Communist Party, whether Pankhurst's CP (BSTI), which was "really too ridiculous," or the CPGB. Neither had "the smallest chance of founding in this country an effective Communist Party." Great as was the "sympathy with Russia" in Britain, the paper concluded, "British Communist activities do not even amount to a storm in a teacup."[63] Nonetheless, this disdainful view of the prospects of Communism in Britain co-existed with a view of "soviet democracy" in Russia that, if not totally positive, was far from dismissive.

From the start, of course, there were also implacable critics of the "soviet system" and of the Bolsheviks within the British Left. It is to some of them, and the debates that ensued within socialist organizations, that we shall now turn.

5

POLARIZED SOCIAL-DEMOCRATS
Denunciation and Debate

The National Socialist Party, Justice, *and the "Anti-Bolshevik Campaign"*

Until 1916, the successor organization to the Social-Democratic Party — the second largest of British socialist parties after the ILP, apart from the Labour Party, which was made up of affiliated union and socialist societies — had remained united despite some internal conflicts. Now, erstwhile Social-Democrats found themselves in hostile confrontation. On the one, and larger, side stood a group that would soon become the prime constituent of the British Communist Party; arrayed on the other were its most vociferous opponents on the Left.

For the first two years or so following October and November 1917, *outright* opposition to the Bolsheviks remained rare on the British Left, even among those who, like the editor of and contributors to the *New Statesman,* would scarcely be regarded as "real" socialists by those committed to the Bolshevik cause. The clearest exception was the National Socialist Party and its weekly paper, *Justice,* whose un-equivocal denunciations of the Bolsheviks have already been noted.

The "Hyndmanites," who had left the BSP over the issue of the war, are easily regarded as an irrelevant remnant, predominantly composed of the ageing "Old Guard of the S.D.F.," who, to their support of an appalling war, added an unreasonable hostility towards the Bolsheviks. The fact that they initially adopted the name National Socialist Party — with the awful associations it was later to acquire — has not exactly enhanced their image for posterity, insofar as they have one. This is understandable. As the historian of its later years, E. Archbold, put it in 1935, with considerable understatement: "The selection of a name considered from post-war points of view does not appear to be a happy one."[1] Granted, the Hyndmanites later reverted to calling themselves the Social-Democratic Federation. The fact nonetheless remains that the most stridently anti-Bolshevik section of the British Left has been largely ignored, even though its ideas and activities clearly formed part — albeit a very small part — of the overall picture of the British Left's response to the Bolshevik Revolution.

Members of the NSP saw themselves as orthodox Social-Democrats — Marxists — whose stance on the war was based on the doctrine of "national defence." Support for the Allies did not imply an uncritical view of either their conduct of the war or of capitalism. The *relatively* democratic systems of the French republic and the United Kingdom were, however, deemed worthy of support against the onslaught of "Prussian militarism." As the long-time secretary of the SDF and now the editor of *Justice,* H.W. Lee, argued in June 1918: "A peace based on the success of triumphant militarism will mean a disastrous defeat for what is free and democratic, so far as there is freedom and democracy under capitalism."[2] This was at a time when the German offensive still seemed to be in danger of sweeping all before it — when the "Prussian" triumph that Lee feared still seemed possible.

Hyndman himself had his own version of a revolutionary response to the danger of losing the war: "It is for Socialists and Labour men throughout Great Britain to recognise this [danger] and prepare for decisive action by formulating a definite policy and making an appeal, in the shape of a Referendum on a clear issue, to every man and woman on this island." This was to lead to the setting up of "a Committee of Public Safety." Two months later, as the military tide began to turn, he declared: "The people will win the war *in spite of our politicians*." [3] Some would later call the Second World War a "people's war." This was how the NSP regarded the 1914–18 conflict.

The firm belief that "Prussian militarism" was responsible for the war meant that in no way did NSP members see any equivalence between the German Social-Democrats — whom they regarded as having betrayed socialism in supporting the conflict — and their own pro-Ally position. Indeed, as the war came to an end, *Justice* cautioned against being too enthusiastic about the German revolution. In words that read a little strangely in the light of the party's anti-Bolshevism, it insisted that to win the confidence of Western socialists, that revolution "must go still further to the Left. Only when the Independent Socialists under, say, Karl Liebknecht, take over the Government can we believe that the Germans have really changed their minds." [4]

NSP members were scathing about the socialist and labour movement credentials and general integrity of some of the BSP "Bolsheviks." This was especially so in the case of Louis Shammes, who had been appointed as secretary to the "Russian Revolutionary Consulate" under John Maclean. According to J. Burden, the secretary of the Glasgow NSP, Shammes, a Russian, had been his workmate:

> He was an enthusiastic supporter of Kerensky, and when Kerensky and his followers overturned the Russian autocracy his enthusiasm was unbounded. Later he ordered one dozen Socialist Almanacks from me, published by the Twentieth Century Press, which had a portrait of Kerensky. By the time they were in my hands for sale developments had taken place in Russia, Kerensky had been thrown out of the saddle, and Lenin and Trotzky were in, so my fellow-worker Shammes refused to take up his order. . . . He was now a supporter of Lenin. [5]

But such disdain for his assistant had not prevented Hyndman sending in a letter protesting against the five-year sentence for sedition imposed on John Maclean in June 1918. He described it as "a preposterous sentence for purely political hallucination" and demanded action from Labour MPs to secure his release.[6]

Anticipation of victory in the war was replacing fear of defeat when the first annual NSP conference met in August 1918, shortly after the "Black Day of the German Army." According to *Justice*'s report on the conference, as regards the Labour Party delegates were told that "our presence there is necessary to uphold the pro-Ally point of view as far as we can against the strange mixture of Pacifism and Bolshevism that seems in a fair way to dominate the Labour Party unless the pro-Ally men and women who constitute a majority among the rank and file as among the leaders pay more attention than they are doing at the moment to what is going on." An attempt by H.W. Lee to change the party's name back to the "Social-Democratic Federation" was resoundingly rejected — apparently largely because "Social-Democratic" sounded German, in spite of Hyndman's reassurance (one that he had been giving since the 1880s) that the term had first been used in Britain in Chartist times by Bronterre O'Brien. Following this, the conference carried with acclamation Hyndman's motion supporting the Russian SRs against both "Bolshevik tyranny" and "monarchist intrigues."

Hyndman also moved the executive committee's motion on "Reconstruction," which urged all labour and socialist organizations to combine to prevent "the railways, shipping, mines and factories now controlled and managed by government" from being restored to private ownership and to ensure that they were "rapidly socialised." The remaining points of the program outlined in the motion called for "a minimum wage based on a high standard of life" to be provided "until the abolition of the wages system"; encouragement of co-operative distribution and production; a "good living wage" for redundant munitions workers and demobilized service personnel; state ownership of underdeveloped land; free transport for agricultural and industrial goods by rail or canal; the building of several million "good homes"; secular education for all from ages 5 to 19; public ownership of hospitals "with the profession of medicine to be a Department of State"; and maternity benefits. The motion concluded that these were all "mere palliatives and stepping stones towards the Co-operative Commonwealth of the world."[7]

Outright and comprehensive rejection of the Bolshevik revolution in its entirety meant that any notion that there might be a case for, or any reality to, soviet democracy was doomed from the outset. The war had yet to finish when *Justice* reproduced the NSP's poster for the coming general election. It proclaimed:

Our Candidates are out to kill

BOLSHEVISM

CAPITALISM

MILITARISM

Singled out for particular support were "Comrades J. O'Grady, Ben Tillett and Will Thorne," all said to be certain of re-election, and Dan Irving (Burnley), Jack Jones (West Ham), L.E. Quelch (Reading), and Arthur Whiting, all with memberships dating back "into the days of the old S.D.F." They would, said the paper, need to reiterate from time to time that they were "pro-Ally . . . because we believe the Allied armies have in the main been fighting a democratic fight." There was a difference between a war of defence and one of aggression.[8] Four more NSP parliamentary candidates were identified on the eve of the election, making eleven in all, two fewer than the number of Labour candidates claimed by the BSP.[9]

But at the start of the new year, *Justice* was able to claim 6 of the 60 Labour MPs returned, including O'Grady at Leeds South-East, who had been returned unopposed. "The Labour Party has not only increased its numbers," the paper concluded, "but also its influence by the defeat of Ramsay MacDonald, Philip Snowden, F.W. (Fred)

Jowett, and W.C. Anderson; and in the rout of the I.L.P. members known to be or suspected of being pacifist in the war."[10] The problem with the Labour party, according to a letter from L.E. Quelch, was that "people who have publicly avowed themselves to be Bolshevists, and have been advocating the Soviet form of government here and excusing the excesses of the Bolshevist Government in Russia, have been and still are in official positions in the Labour Party both nationally and locally."[11] In fact, Quelch's own family was polarized on the issue.[12]

The masthead of *Justice* proclaimed: "The oldest Socialist Journal in the British Isles. Established January 19 1884." All the same, the paper's credibility on the Left, already greatly weakened by its wholehearted support for the Allied cause, must have been further undermined by the vehemence of its attacks on the Bolsheviks. In March 1918, F.H. Gorle insisted that former Okhrana agents had joined the Petrograd Soviet. "Some are even on its executive," he wrote, and others on the staff of *Pravda*.[13] Later that year, Gorle was attacking "the Bolshevik Scum." He cited a Swiss source that claimed that "Lenin's proletariat dictatorship" comprised — in part, if not in whole — a variety of disreputable characters, which it named. These included "an ardent anti-semite," a former "chief official of the Tsar's secret police," another former secret policeman, a general involved in a corruption case twenty years earlier, a former agent-provocateur and fraudster, two former associates of Rasputin, various people in the pay of the Germans, and an academic from Riga who used to spy on his colleagues and students in the tsarist interest.[14] Quite independently of their truth or falsehood, such accusations were certain, in the atmosphere of the British Left at the time, to be dismissed as hysterical nonsense, on a par with the anti-Bolshevik scare stories in the "capitalist press."

This is evident from a letter from J. Connell published in response to Gorle's accusations. Something of the anger felt by the NSP's opponents on the Left is almost tangible in the letter's threatening prediction:

When the war is over we International Socialists (the only "real Social-ists") will take care to remember when the maintenance of Socialism in Russia was in the balance, Hyndman, Bax, Hunter Watts, Gorle, Lee, Woodroffe and the rest of the National Socialist tribe, sided with the capitalist governments who would, if they could, re-establish the rule of the Tsars. We will bear in mind that at the critical hour, all they had to offer to Russian Socialists was vilification, and if they attempt to take part in our gathering we will pelt them as F.H.G. would get pelted if he opened his mouth in Billingsgate.[15]

"Fraternally yours," Connell concluded, having in mind perhaps the Cain and Abel version of brotherhood.

Gorle, predictably, was unabashed and returned the following week with "The Ugly Truth About Bolshevism," giving more examples of alleged Bolshevik corruption and atrocities, including a quotation from *Indépendence Belge* that had the "former President of the Council of Workmen and Peasants" in Rostov pleading: "Shoot us in place of shooting children without trial or enquiry."[16] *Justice* quoted — while the war the NSP supported was still raging — part of a letter from Hans Vorst that had appeared in the *Berliner Tagblatt:*

The Soviet organisations such as that at Bezhetsk where the Bolshe-vists have not got a majority, are dissolved, and the Peasant Councils in which the voices of opposition make themselves heard are broken up. The entire non-Bolshevist Press is suppressed and the Law Courts have been abolished. The Extraordinary Commission has withdrawn the most important questions from the administration of justice, and passes the most terrible sentences and carries out innumerable execu-tions without court or verdict. The system of violence and arbitrary rule is worse than it ever was during the Tsarian regime.[17]

Exasperated with critics who failed to believe such claims, "because we have not taken the Bolsheviks to our bosom," Gorle quoted from *Izvestiya* on executions, suppression of SRs and Mensheviks, and dissident soviets. Wasn't this surely "enough to satisfy any sane man that Bolshevism is the antithesis of socialism and a scandal to humanity?"[18]

The year 1919 saw a series of public meetings organised by the NSP as part of its "Anti-Bolshevik Campaign." Targeted by supporters of the Bolsheviks, the small hall in which the first meeting took place was packed. Hyndman presided but "had spoken only a few words when interruptions began and they continued practically all through the meeting." A motion by Will Thorne and Dan Irving declared: "This meeting, recognising that the wage-earners constitute the majority of the nation, hereby declares that they have it in their power to establish the Co-operative Commonwealth by ordinary political and democratic action . . . a desire for the 'dictatorship of the proletariat' is an absurdity, in that there is no necessity for the majority of the nation to constitute themselves as a dictatorship." A week later, Thomas Kennedy hit at the ILP. Formerly, he claimed, it had reacted "with horror to any reference to class war, or to the use of physical force." But now "Lenin is their god and guide, disturbance of the right of public meeting their most important work." He had been told that the "Left Wing of the I.L.P." had been prominent in the "attempt to break up our Edinburgh meeting."[19]

Justice was critical of the Berne Conference of the Socialist International in February 1919, which had "dealt with Bolshevism by inference and not directly" instead of condemning it unequivocally.[20] But it would be wrong to imagine the NSP simply defended parliamentary democracy against the Bolshevik/soviet challenge. Continuing commitment to older forms of radical popular democracy is evident in the wartime call for a referendum and a committee of public safety. And, in a rather different context, the same commitment was apparent in the series of articles, titled "From Hun to Human," by "Robert Arch" (Archibald Robertson) that appeared in *Justice* in the weeks following the end of the war. The articles were in line with veteran SDFer Belfort Bax's earlier plea in *Justice* to "spare us diatribes of hate against the German people as such."[21] In the first, "Arch"/Robertson insisted that "when we said we were fighting 'the Huns' we meant (or should have meant) that we were fighting that old tribal morality, that narrow spirit of race, whatever its embodiment or whoever might uphold it." As he subsequently argued, it was vital that future wars should be avoided, and this presupposed "a great development of democracy." [22]

That "Arch"/Robertson did not simply mean the spread of electoral politics based on universal suffrage is clear from the remainder of the article. As we saw earlier, he reiterated the old SDF demand, "The People to Decide on Peace or War," which had figured prominently in the party's program since 1884 — as, for example, in 1899, when *Justice* had challenged "Mr Chamberlain and his fellow conspirators" to hold a referendum on the eve of the South African War. [23] The NSP had certainly not surrendered to an uncritical support of parliamentary government as practised at Westminster.

Nor was the "industrial democracy" or "worker democracy," which played such a great part in the appeal of the "soviet system" elsewhere on the Left, entirely ruled out. Hyndman's early post-war seven-point proposal, "The Only Way to Avert Anarchy," declared both that the initiative, referendum, and proportional representation should be the basis of legislation and for confirming "social action" and "that all monopolies, including the land and the great companies of every kind, shall forthwith be owned, and democratically controlled by the State and democratically socialised." There was no indication of quite how this process of democratic socialization might work, but Hyndman did insist that "the workers could not possibly manage the mines more carelessly, more wastefully, or more against the interests of the country than the mine owners do to-day." [24]

Though the "Old Guard" had always been very hostile to syndicalism, equating it with violent anarchism, this clearly did not preclude *some* form of "workers' democracy" as long as the rights of citizens *qua* citizens were also adequately recognized. This is evident from the positive view taken of guild socialism, where the criticism is virtually confined to the argument that, contrary to its continual proclamation of its own originality, guild socialism represented little that was new and mostly what SDFers had long been advocating. Towards the end of 1918, reviewing *The Meaning of National Guilds,* by Maurice B. Reckitt and C.E. Bechhofer, F.J. Gould told readers of *Justice*: "The two authors really cut ice. . . . They leave poor Sidney Webb and his Fabian baggage far behind." There was no "Bolshevik foolery" about the book, and "its scheme of progress is a development of an existing order." Although the authors sensibly insisted that "the Guild idea is an idea rather than a creed," Gould noted, what was missing was any acknowledgement of the long decades of campaigning against "wagedom" on the part of Hyndman and the Social-Democrats.[25] Nevertheless, there were thanks from the book's authors for the "generous" review in a long letter published a few weeks later.[26]

The lack of novelty — but general worthiness — of guild socialism was asserted, again by "Robert Arch," in reviewing Bertrand Russell's *Roads to Freedom: Socialism, Anarchism and Syndicalism* at the beginning of 1919:

> All that is good however, in Guild Socialism (the control of industry democratically from below, rather than bureaucratically from above) was advocated by Social-Democrats long before Mr Orage and Mr Cole had written a line, as Mr. Russell would see, for example, if he referred to Laurence Gronlund's "Co-operative Commonwealth" — one of the best works of the older Socialists.[27]

And a few months later, "T.D.H." reviewed *Labour in the Commonwealth,* by "Our friend G.D.H. Cole":

> Guild Socialism, as described by Mr Cole, is very much like what we Social-Democrats have always advocated. But some of the younger Fabians, who have revolted against the bureaucratic methods of Sidney Webb, still seem unable to realise that all they are saying has been said by the Social-Democrats years ago. That does not make their contributions to the solution of the industrial problem any the less valuable; only they are not quite as new and original as they appear at times to imagine themselves to be.[28]

Trying to convince guild socialists that their ideas had been anticipated was not the main difficulty for the NSP, however. Its real problem was that, no matter how often it repeated its attacks on "Russian Despots and British Dupes," as Archibald Lee described them, this failed to achieve the desired effect. It had to be accepted, Lee concluded, that "a larger number of British workers than some of us care to admit, though not so large as its leaders would have us believe, has been taught to pray for the preservation of that tyranny." [29] But not quite all of his former comrades in the BSP were accepting the claims made for soviet democracy as uncritically as Lee might have supposed.

Parliamentarism and Trade Unionism: The 1919 Debate in The Call

For members of the BSP during the summer of 1919, their weekly paper became the arena for the conflict between, on the one side, an uncritical acceptance of the reality of "soviet democracy" in Russia and a positive view of its short-term prospects in Britain and, on the other, a more skeptical view of both. The debate was triggered by Theodore Rothstein, who was born, and was to die, in Russia, but lived most of his life in Britain. He had been a member of the BSP and its predecessor, the SDF, from 1895 until 1914, when his opposition to support of the war by the then-BSP, and possibly also his work with the Foreign and War Offices as a Russian translator, led him to leave the party. Prior to leaving, he was active enough in the BSP to have served several years on its executive in the first decade of the twentieth century. He was to be a key player in the creation of the British Communist Party.[30]

At the beginning of June 1919, an article titled "Parliamentarism and Trade Unionism," by "John Bryan," the *nom de guerre* of Rothstein, appeared in *The Call*. It was followed by an announcement that this was the first of two articles and that other contributions regarding the crucial issues would be welcomed. Rothstein made the usual criticisms of "bourgeois democracy." Parliament was, he declared, "a mere veil disguising the dictatorship of the capitalist classes." The true failure of parliamentarism had been shown "in the light of the new institution, the Soviets." The division between legislative and executive functions meant that Parliament was a mere "talking shop." Not so the soviets:

> Under this system the class-sense of the workers is constantly kept alive and maintained in active operation by (1) the corporate (as distinguished from individual) voting in workshops and various Labour organisations, in which the individual is no longer a detached atom, but feels himself to be part of the working class, inaccessible to any influences or allurements; (2) by the right of instantaneous recall of inefficient or disloyal delegates; (3) by the natural and quite inevitable obligation of the delegates to report their doings on the Soviet to their electors in the same way that any delegate to a trades council or any shop steward does at present; (4) by the concentration of legislative and executive functions in one and the same body which prevents that body, the Soviet, from degenerating into an empty talking shop or of abdicating its functions — and (5) by the body sitting in permanence. Above all, under the Soviet system there is not one institution only to legislate and to execute the law leaving the people outside in the role of passive onlookers, but the Soviets, in every area . . . are the State authorities for that area.
>
> In other words, the people itself, in its actual collectivity, and not merely a chosen handful, carries on the government of the country, legislating, imposing taxes, appointing and controlling officials, electing judges and dismissing them, and so forth.

The result was that in Russia, in contrast to the delusions of parliamentarism in Britain, there was "real, and not merely nominal government by the people and through the people."[31] This was precisely the picture of soviet democracy in practice that so many on the Left found so convincing and seductive.

The following week, in the second of his articles, Rothstein turned to the trade unions. "In Russia there were no trade unions worth speaking of under the Tsarist regime," he claimed, but they sprang up in large numbers after the February Revolution of 1917. It might have been expected that, being of revolutionary origin, they would have "played a revolutionary part in the subsequent developments." But instead trade unions were "conspicuously unimportant" in later stages of the revolution, and "what little part they played was rather conservative in character." This was because trade unions were, in their very nature, organizations dedicated to improving workers' conditions "on the basis of the existing class-relationship" in their particular branch of production. Their structures and procedures were also to blame, with their machinery of committees and permanent officials, "ranged more or less in hierarchical order." Given this structure, "any impulse coming from below must necessarily lose both in strength and freshness, and take a long time before it reaches the apex of the hierarchy where the final decision is taken. It then often has to travel back to the base before it is translated into action." In addition, trade unions were "led for the most part by men who possess the highest bureaucratic capacities, and for that very reason lack any others." (Why this was not also likely to be true of the soviets, with their similar structure of "hierarchical" bodies, was a question Rothstein did not address.)

Trade unions were inadequate, Rothstein concluded. But they should not be attacked: as the potential seedbeds of shop stewards and workers' councils, they held promise. These councils would play "an important role in the task of Socialist reconstruction after the Revolution," which would come not through parliament and trade unions but "by direct action, political and economic, of the rank and file through their politico-economical organisations of the Soviet type."[32]

Rothstein's articles triggered a critical response from two of the most prominent members of the BSP, H. Alexander and E.C. Fairchild. The former was the national treasurer of the party and the latter the recent editor of *The Call* — "recent" because he had resigned at the end of May, a move clearly related to the controversy that was to follow very quickly.[33] The first to respond, however, was Alexander, who maintained that what was needed was "a considered statement wherein is proven the possibility of establishing in this country the

Soviet system *here* and *now*." Alexander's central objection to Rothstein's approach was that Britain was very different from Russia. There were 18 million people in Britain who had investments — in war savings certificates, post office savings, friendly societies, building societies, insurance companies — so revolution in Britain would "not be the result of despair." Rather, it would be "an outcome of prosperity, leisure, education and the people's instinctive feeling that they want more."

Rothstein, said Alexander, underestimated Parliament. It was "in its dotage," he said, "but that is not death." Simply because "the control of industry requires something radically different to Parliament," a Labour government "would be compelled to put into operation a scheme along the lines of decentralisation." It was possible that powers would be delegated to existing local authorities "to carry on industries co-opting for that purpose direct representatives from the workshop." It was possible that "the Russian model" would be more closely followed. But for the present it was not a practical proposition. Alexander ended with a warning: "If we want the transition period to be still-born, let us go to the people with a premature policy which the people shows no signs of accepting. That is just what the enemy wants." Meanwhile, in the correspondence column, a reader maintained that "Bryan" (that is, Rothstein) had contradicted himself by saying that Parliament was "not effective" yet insisting that he did not want to "abandon parliamentary warfare."[34]

The following week, Fairchild likewise picked up on Rothstein's apparent self-contradiction:

> At the end of an attack running into six columns in which Parliament is discussed as the "specific form of the political side of Capitalism" . . . and trade unionism rejected on the grounds that it "tends merely to consolidate the privileged position of trade unionists," John Bryan arrives at the conclusion that we must not abandon parliamentary methods nor leave our trade unions. He will run with the hare and hunt with the hounds.

Fairchild accepted the "ultimate superiority of the soviet or workers' committees," but their day would come "*after* ownership of the means of production is in the hands of the people." He contrasted the Russian scenario of 1917, in which the Duma "could not resist the growing strength of the Petrograd Soviet," with the situation in Britain: "Were the London Trades Council to propose the abolition of Parliament it would find its task rather more difficult than that of the soviet." Rothstein and his supporters were, he said, being totally unrealistic about the prospects of soviet rule in Britain. Moreover, Rothstein's "dainty idyll of a workman voting in the workshop" was naïve. "It would be hard to find a proposition having less touch with actuality," Fairchild insisted, "than the suggestion that in the workshop there is an ever present sense of common identity. Every clever foreman divides his men, and every discerning workman knows how it is done." Fairchild was therefore skeptical about the ability of the soviet system to ensure that "the people itself" would govern with "unfettered democracy" and about the assumption that "a village committee thousands of miles from the Congress of Soviets, remote and isolated, not only preserves its autonomy, but is part of a system inherently incapable of bureaucracy." He ended by questioning why "an innocuous proposition to revive the moribund shop stewards' movement and establish highly unstable workers' committees needs so elaborate a political philosophy."[35]

But Rothstein had plenty of backing in the BSP. Or so it would seem from the contents of *The Call* during the weeks that followed. One reader, Robert Lowe, contributed a long letter in his support at the beginning of July, while J.F. Hodgson, a member of the BSP executive, thought "the crux of the whole controversy between ourselves and those who agree with Fairchild" was "whether the war is to be followed quickly by world-revolution," adding: "We believe strongly that it is." Fairchild was, according to Hodgson, "a little too previous" with his characterization of the shop stewards' movement and was equally misguided in his view of Parliament:

The dispossession of the capitalist class by consent is the most childish illusion. That happy confirmation can only be reached by the dictatorship of the working-class. The instrument of that dictatorship will be developed in due course. Parliamentary "democracy" is not such an instrument. The instrument must be such as will enable power to be used where it really resides, that is, at the point of production. It must be able to be quickly responsible to the popular will and be formed on the axiom that, differently from the false "democracy" of our masters, true democracy demands that all power must originate and remain with the working masses. The Soviet Republic of Russia has developed such an instrument.[36]

Another supporter of Rothstein's view was the veteran socialist and suffrage campaigner Dora Montefiore. Others included W. McLaine, who failed to see the logic of Fairchild's position — "Fairchild appears to believe that soviets will be required after the revolution so why not prepare before?" — and Jack Carney, editor of *The Truth* in Duluth, Minnesota.[37] Meanwhile, in another contribution, A.E. Adshead — the author of the letter calling attention to what he saw as Rothstein's inconsistency — took what was becoming the position of the Communist "Left Wing," criticizing both "the equivocation of Comrade Bryan" on parliamentarism and Fairchild and Alexander. A week later, yet another correspondent, H. Steward Ryde, defended Rothstein's rejection of Workers' Socialist Federation–style anti-parliamentarism.[38]

Fairchild was allowed a rejoinder at the end of August. He began by remarking: "It is worth comment that seven comrades all with more than common skills in argument deem it necessary to enter the lists and support each other against Alexander and myself." Fairchild's critics had, he observed, a variety of opinions:

[It] would appear that John Bryan has yet to spend a deal of effort before there is intellectual unity between the conflicting pleas that Parliament is a grand propagandist platform, that a Parliamentary majority is impossible, that such a majority could hurry on the "demise and interment" of representative institutions, as W. McLaine puts it, and that Parliament cannot be of any use at all as Adshead would have us believe.

Fairchild went on to explain his own beliefs. "Parliamentary action is the readiest way, with all its difficulty and danger, when supported by the industrial power of the unions, to gain the central, national, use of political power," he wrote, "which marks off the Socialist method from preferences for violence and aimless revolt." It was the "fevered imaginations" of those such as the members of the Workers' Socialist Federation that cherished the illusion that "the workers here move rapidly towards an immediate Soviet administration."

As Fairchild's article progressed, it became evident that his doubts about the "soviet system" were not confined to its short-term prospects in Britain but extended to how the system actually operated in Russia:

> How far the People's Commissaries act under the control of the Russian workers is an interesting point in contemporary history, and if the truth were more widely known, many uncritical supporters of a Soviet for this country would have some rude shocks. Lenin knows his people and knows how far towards Communism technically backward Russia can advance at this stage. Our concern is with the people we meet face to face in daily life. They are more the means of Socialism than ourselves. If the workers are silly when voting and stupid in trade unionism, it is at least inconsequent to assume their sudden change into grand Socialist citizens when confronted with the magnificent problems of supply to meet the artistic and material demands engendered by an ordered commonwealth.

This was very dangerous ground for Fairchild, challenging not just the immediate prospects of creating soviets in Britain but casting doubt on the reality of soviet democracy in its homeland — a belief in which so many had invested their hopes. His critics, he claimed, had only "the haziest ideas when the Soviets are to be formed" in Britain. What had led to the whole debate, he maintained, was "the wordy, ambiguous, windy, 'Sovietist' resolution sprung on the B.S.P. Annual Conference at the last minute with the consent of a too complaisant and wholly invertebrate Executive Committee." And he added: "Doubtless they will all soon be assisting Alexander and I to bury it fathoms deep." In spite of this confident assertion, one cannot help wondering whether by this time Fairchild really believed this or whether he was at least beginning to suspect that the bulk of the BSP membership was now firmly behind Rothstein.

Either way, Fairchild was undeterred. Previously, he continued, he had been of the opinion that the executive, having consented to the mysterious appearance of the "Sovietist" resolution at the conference, "should at least say what they understand it to mean, since they denied my interpretation was correct. But the wily men know the dangers of definition: or was it weakness?" These charges were rejected in an editorial note at the end of the article, which asserted that "the resolution to which Fairchild takes exception was no more 'sprung on the Annual Conference at the last minute' than were three other resolutions. All three of which were drafted by Comrade Fairchild and one of which he himself moved." [39]

But Fairchild was not going to concede. In a letter published "with regret" the following week, he claimed that there was a "vital difference" between the first three resolutions and the fourth. The ones he had drafted were the outcome of prolonged discussion and were approved by the executive committee. The "Sovietist resolution" was "quite otherwise." It was "never discussed by any committee. At an Organisation Committee meeting the Secretary reported he had arranged for a resolution on the international situation to be prepared. I am of the opinion that the Party's officials exceed their duties when they make arrangements of that character and come to a committee with a *fait accompli*."

Furthermore, the "authenticity" of the resolution was questionable since it did not originate "from any member of the Party's responsible committees." "Its author is not even a member of the B.S.P.," he wrote, although, he added, he was known to the executive committee. An editorial note followed denying Fairchild's assertions, which were all in "comrade Fairchild's imagination" and "quite untrue." Walter Kendall has speculated that the "author" referred to was Rothstein himself who, though a pre-war member of the BSP, had resigned from the party in 1914.[40] This seems very likely — a racing certainty, in fact — particularly when the final sentences of Fairchild's letter are taken into account: "If the policy of the B.S.P. does not spring from its own ranks, the Party ceases to have any title to existence. It becomes a mere appendage of another."[41] Presumably, the "another" of which the BSP had become an appendage was the Russian Communist Party, of which Rothstein was, in effect, the British representative.

Rothstein was now allowed to sum up the debate. Fairchild's "uncharacteristic acerbity" was due to the fact that he and Alexander were "in a hopeless minority in the party." Rothstein maintained that recent events had made it even clearer that Parliament was "a wonderful invention of the bourgeoisie and is utterly incompatible with the requirements either of a socialist revolution or a socialist, i.e., really popular, regime." Anyone wishing to "abolish the dictatorship of the capitalist class and to establish the rule of the working class must repudiate the parliamentary form of government both as a permanent system and as a means of bringing about the socialist revolution." The revolution would, he argued, be brought nearer by "making it clear to the masses that the present is a dictatorship of the capitalist class and must be replaced by the dictatorship — or call it undivided rule — of the workers and that the specific form under which the rule of the workers can be realised is the Soviet form." A further letter from Fairchild, in the same issue, provoked a note from the editor stating that the paper was "unable to concede to him, any more than anyone else, the unrestricted right deliberately to mislead the members of the B.S.P."[42]

The defeat of Fairchild and Alexander is mainly attributable to the widespread enthusiasm for soviet democracy in the BSP as elsewhere on the Left. But there was another factor at work. "John Bryan" — that is, Rothstein — had become the representative of the Bolshevik government in Britain following the arrest and subsequent deportation of Litvinov in September 1918. If, as Kendall suggests of Rothstein's influence in the BSP, "an inner core of party members were aware that *Bryan* was speaking in Litvinov's place, with the full authority of Moscow," this could only help to secure the acceptance of his views.[43]

Certainly, by now it must have been clear to readers that Fairchild's membership in the party was unlikely to continue for much longer. He faded away quite quickly, though not abruptly, from the pages of the paper he had edited, still appearing towards the end of September on its front page with "Lloyd George: The Political Tramp."[44] He was the author of a number of pamphlets, such as *The Economics of War* and *Socialism and the League of Nations*, advertisements for which had hitherto appeared in *The Call*, along with the rest of the BSP literature. By mid-October there was still an ad for his *Ten Lectures for Students of History, 1760–1832, and Political Economy*, which included one called "Strikes and the British Constitution." But there was now nothing by him advertised in the pamphlets and books section.

The debate that had gone on over the summer of 1919 in the pages of *The Call* was continued at public meetings. The same October issue of the paper reported on a packed meeting concerning the question "Socialism Through Parliament or Soviet?" where "all the fire and grimness" had come "from the champion of established order, comrade Fairchild." The BSP Hall, Willesden Green, had also hosted a debate titled "Soviet or Parliament: Is the Dictatorship of the Proletariat Necessary in England to Realise the Social Revolution?" between Fred Willis, who had taken over the editorship of *The Call* following Fairchild's resignation, and H. Alexander.[45] Fairchild and Alexander seem to have resigned from the BSP soon afterwards, however, following its overwhelming decision in favour of affiliation to the Third International.[46]

The debate in *The Call* reminds us that the BSP's 1916 "split," which had led to the withdrawal of the Hyndmanites and the inception of the NSP, had specifically turned on the issue of the war. The division in the party had never been about the correct interpretation of Marxism with respect to democracy and dictatorship or about the attitude that should be taken toward Parliament or the trade union movement. By the summer of 1919, it was clear that two prominent BSP members, at least, were rather closer on these issues to the reviled NSP, a charge they would no doubt have indignantly rejected. But very few in the BSP were to follow the lead of Fairchild and Alexander.

6

EQUIVOCAL REFORMISTS
The Independent Labour Party, the Guild Socialists,
and the Reaction to Kautsky

ILP Critics: Giving the Bolsheviks Some Benefit of the Doubt

The BSP was by far the largest of the would-be Bolshevik organizations in Britain and, in 1920, was to form the core and provide most of the initial membership of the Communist Party of Great Britain. But both the ILP Left Wing and the guild socialist movement contributed key individuals to the new party. From the ranks of the ILP came, for example, J.T. Walton Newbold, Shapurji Saklatvala, Helen Crawfurd, and Emile Burns. The guild socialist contribution included William Mellor, Ellen Wilkinson, Palme Dutt, and Page Arnot. Some, like Wilkinson, had been active in both contexts.

Numerically, the BSP was greatly inferior to the ILP. Moreover, with Labour's new constituency organizations still in their infancy, the ILP remained the main means by which individuals participated in the Labour Party as socialists. It would be the ILP that, more than any other single party or grouping, would decide the fate of Bolshevism in Britain during the crucial few years following 1917. And at first, indeed, the prospects for a pro-Bolshevik ILP seemed far more hopeful than hindsight might suggest.

The fervently pro-Bolshevik atmosphere on the British Left in early 1918 is evident even in the first real criticism of the Bolsheviks to appear in *Labour Leader*. The prominent pacifist Dr. Alfred Salter contested their democratic legitimacy, but only after applauding them at length "for their unflinching courage, their incorruptible devotion to first principles, their uncompromising devotion to the ideal (called fanaticism by the worldly-wise), their openness and frankness." He argued, however, that "with full allowance for the dangers and isolated position in which the Bolshevik movement finds itself, we must definitely dissociate ourselves from its violence, its suppression of opposing criticism and its disregard for democracy."

"It is fashionable in certain Socialist circles," Salter went on, "to decry Constituent Assemblies and Parliaments elected by universal suffrage, to sneer at them as 'bourgeois' and to extol the method of Soviet government as 'proletarian.' But except by universal suffrage how can every single citizen make his voice heard and his influence felt?" True, "a development" of the Soviet machinery "might make it possible that every single citizen might acquire a similar power," although this would be difficult. Moreover, "with the Soviets as they are today, less than half the nation is represented. Only a very few women are organized in the Workmen's and Soldiers' Councils, and probably a bare third of the total population of Russia can at present make its protest against, or give its sanction to, the acts of the Bolshevik Government."

"Socialism apart from true democracy," Salter concluded, "is not only meaningless but valueless." Faced with the Bolshevik stance in the peace negotiations with Germany, which confronted "the might of the Central Empires with nothing but principles, the whole world stood amazed. Ideas and ideals were suddenly seen to be the most powerful of all high explosives." But the Bolsheviks had now done "much to frustrate their own appeal." They were "ruling by bayonets" and had undermined their moral authority by their acts of violence. In the long run, he predicted, this would prove a fatal weakness.[1] Salter's biographer, Fenner Brockway, writing nearly thirty years later, quoted parts of this article, which he commended as a "balanced view" of the Russian Revolution.[2]

There did appear the occasional comment hostile to the Bolsheviks, but an equivocal tone, somewhat similar to Salter's, was usually present, reflecting, in part at least, a wish to separate the "pro-peace" aspect of the Bolsheviks from the more disturbing features of their rule. As we have already seen in the case of the suppression of the Constituent Assembly and the presentation of soviet rule as an "experiment," there was a desire, even among critics, to give the Bolsheviks the benefit of the doubt wherever possible, as is exemplified by Ramsay MacDonald's statement in early July 1918 that "the Russian Government has committed acts which no Socialist can condone. But we have to remember that the Revolution is still on."[3]

It was not until August 1918 that the *Leader* carried the first letter from a reader *unequivocally* condemning the Bolsheviks' actions. Richard Robinson insisted that "the forcible dissolution of the Constituent Assembly was a crime against Democracy which should be emphatically repudiated by all Socialists." The letter was followed by a long and ambivalent editorial note that, while critical of the "Bolsheviks' appeal to force," argued that "where Bolshevism has slain its hundreds for ideal ends, capitalist imperialism has slain its millions for the basest ends known to mankind."[4] Robinson was responding to a piece by R.C. Wallhead that had appeared the previous week. Two years later, Richard Wallhead was to succeed Snowden in chairing the ILP and a few years after that was to become Labour MP for Merthyr. But in the 1918 article he was fulminating against Allied intervention against the Bolsheviks. In the course of this, he had referred to "the first great Socialist Republic" and had claimed that "the Socialist Government of Russia has behind it 85 per cent of the people." British workers were "demanding the democratic control of industry: the Russian workers have it," he declared.[5] Rather surprisingly, his statements and Robin-son's rejoinder led to no further debate in the paper.

Even after the war had ended, outright opposition to the Bol-sheviks and criticism of the soviet system — either in principle or in practice — only very slowly became more common in the pages of *Labour Leader*. The tendency to give the Bolsheviks *some* benefit of the doubt is evident in Ramsay MacDonald's anti-intervention article, "Hands off Russia," written in the summer of 1919:

> In supporting the Russian Revolution we are not necessarily taking sides either for or against Soviets or Bolshevism. We are recognising that during a revolution there must be Jacobinism, but that if that Jacobinism be evil the way to fight it is to help the country of the revolution to settle down and assimilate the revolution. Bolshevism can be tested only by the free operation of political opinion and ex-perience in Russia. If it be said that it is maintaining itself by force and repression, it is the Allies who are creating the conditions which allow it to do that.

He then drew an historical parallel with the French Revolution. If the Russian Revolution survived,

> its Soviets may disappear by being modified into some new type of democratic government, but it will start a new liberal movement of thought which will be as fruitful later on in the century as the French Revolution was in the century that is gone. Lenin will occupy in the 20th century a place akin to that held by Rousseau in the 19th century.[6]

A similar line was taken in an article in September by Joseph King, which ended: "If the Soviet idea spreads either as an adjunct or an al-ternative to Parliamentary Government, then Lenin and the Russian Revolution may well be viewed by historians of the next century as the greatest and the outstanding event of the world war."[7]

A key factor in understanding this equivocal view of Bolshevism and soviet democracy was the opposition to intervention in Russia — something that united the entire Left, including even the NSP. In May

1919, Hyndman declared: "Bitterly opposed as I am to Bolshevism in all its forms, I regret that British armies should have been sent to Russia in order to defeat the Bolsheviks." As became clear some weeks later, Hyndman's belief was that by "invading Russia and supporting Admiral Koltchak and General Denikin, we are actually strengthening, not weakening the Bolsheviks." [8]

The front page of the 17 July issue of *Labour Leader* — the one that included MacDonald's prophecies regarding the possibly benign longer-term influence of Lenin — opened with emphatic headlines:

STOP THE WAR ON RUSSIA. IT IS A WAR AGAINST DEMOCRACY! IT IS A WAR ON SOCIALISM! LONG LIVE THE RUSSIAN SOCIALIST REPUBLIC! [9]

But behind such displays of solidarity, the division of opinion concerning Bolshevism within the ILP was becoming increasingly clear in the wake of initial attempts to affiliate the party to the Third International.

Early in 1920, the growing division was reflected in *Labour Leader's* "I.L.P. Debating Column." It opened with an article critical of the Bolsheviks written by H.J. Stenning, whose translation of Kautsky's *The Dictatorship of the Proletariat* was about to appear. [10] Among the first to respond to Stenning was Mark Starr, who defended the Bolsheviks against the charge of instituting anything but a temporary dictatorship. Starr went on to make the familiar point about soviet democracy being based on industrial rather than territorial constituencies. In Russia, "workers through their Shop committees control the conditions of their lives," he claimed. He then turned to the aspect of the soviet model that is in fact indispensable for understanding what attracted so many socialists to the early soviet system. Critics of the soviets, claimed Starr, "seem invariably to miss that *delegates* and not representatives" were the means of carrying out the wishes of the voters in the soviets. "In our miners' lodges we already have an approximation to this," he argued. "When questions are discussed the delegate is mandated to vote upon particular questions instead of being elected to 'represent' his fellows for a lengthy period. This with the power of recall is certainly a step in the right direction." [11]

As the debate continued, George Benson replied to Starr, under the title "Our Soviet Impossibilists." There was "no magic in a Revolution to bring a man from the wrong side of a ballot box to the right side of a barricade," he wrote. The vote was more than part of the governmental system; it was "a symbol of personal liberty":

> Mr. Starr's most effective blow at our British Sovietists is his unconscious ridicule of the cry for delegation not representation by showing that they wish to run complex affairs of the Nation and indeed the world, as if they were the comparatively simple business of a Miners' Lodge.
>
> Because a T.U. branch can instruct its delegates how to vote upon a special point nothing will satisfy our revolutionary friends than that the immense mass of national legislation shall be discussed point by point by the whole nation, the function of M.Ps being merely to carry out the mandate of their constituents.
>
> There is a considerable amount of legislation passed nowadays. In a period of social change it would be increasingly more. Is the whole nation to sit day by day in solemn legislative conclave to decide what mandates it shall give, or is legislation to be reduced to a week's congress once a year? The former would not be good for industry, while the latter would tend to delay the Social Revolution a little.

There were other voices taking part in the debate that week. R.K. Weaver questioned whether there was any essential difference between the soviets disfranchising non-workers and the disfranchisement in Britain of "certain classes such as women under thirty," further pointing out that, in Russia, the disenfranchised could "always obtain representation by becoming workers." He also asked whether the Bolsheviks could have survived without being accepted "by the majority of the Russian nation." C. Manne believed that an "intelligent minority" must always be in control during revolutionary periods and that the length of time they stayed in power depended on "the number of people who they are able to make class-conscious."

For his part, P. McOmish Dott thought it unfair to "discuss the machinery of the Russian state while it is fighting for its very existence." In any case, he insisted, the Bolshevik leaders had publicly declared that the present form of the state was transitional, and the elections showed that they represented the majority of the Russian people. Dott concluded that if the Soviet government "adopted the Swiss method whereby no law becomes effective until voted on and approved by the whole people at the half-yearly election, even Kautsky's criticism would fall to the ground." [12]

Conflicts in the National Guilds League

If the membership of the ILP was to become vehemently divided over what attitude to take towards soviet democracy and the Bolsheviks, the same was true of the National Guilds League (NGL). *The Guildsman*, published monthly, had been launched in 1916 by the Glasgow Group of the NGL. Subtitled *A Journal of Social and Industrial Freedom* starting with its fifth issue, in April 1917, the paper became the league's "official organ" when it moved operations to London in the spring of 1919 and from the following September was edited by G.D.H. Cole and Margaret Cole. Since the beginning of that year, the former had been advocating that the organization change its name to the "Guild Socialist League." [13] This proposal produced considerable fervent debate among Cole's supporters and opponents alike. It divided NGL members broadly along the lines of those who, like the Coles, were at least initially supportive of the Bolsheviks, believing that "soviet democracy" had sufficient reality to be potentially a step in the direction favoured by the NGL, and those who saw them rather as suppressors of democracy in every form — including industrial democracy.

The name of the paper, if not of the NGL itself, *was* eventually changed. In April 1921, it appeared as *The Guild Socialist: A Journal of Workers' Control*. This abrupt change was carried out without warning to readers but with the NGL executive's approval. It was, the paper explained, the consequence of receiving a letter from the editor of a journal called *The Guildsman,* as a result of which it was learnt "that there was another, and a much older, and more respectable, monthly journal bearing the same name and devoted to the interests of certain movements within the Church of England." [14]

Back in 1919, taking the lead in opposing Bolshevism — and Cole's proposed name-change for the NGL — were C.E. Bechhofer and Maurice B. Reckitt, the authors of *The Meaning of National Guilds,* which had been so praised in *Justice.* Reckitt thought that "socialist" was "a hopelessly stale and exhausted word, which gives rise to endless misunderstanding and can be construed to mean anything from Bolshevism to Bureaucracy." Bechhofer agreed, believing that the word might "still be a rallying cry for professed Socialists; but it certainly is not for the vast mass of the people to whom our propaganda is directed." [15]

Before this, in the summer of 1918, Bechhofer had put forward an analysis of Russian developments that combined broad approval for the soviets with total rejection of Bolshevism. In his version of events, the workshop and factory committees had been set up by Russian workers as the chief means "to improve industrial life." Some success had been achieved: "The general result, as the workers improved their conditions, was that output was increased and discipline maintained." The soviets had begun well:

> Then came the Bolsheviks with their mischievous "politicising" of industry. The Workers were encouraged to elect — not as hitherto, the men best qualified to administer the work, but those who were the best exponents of certain political views. As a result, factories in which the workers were predominantly Bolshevik in their political views elected Bolshevik orators to their Committees, Mensheviks elected Mensheviks, Cadets, Cadets.
>
> Thus commenced the reign of the Demagogue in Russia — the dominion of the "worker's representative" who represented him not as a worker but as a proletarian.

The result had been the "ruin of Russian industry" by the Bolsheviks, whose industrial policy, insofar as they had one, was "clearly 'Syndicalist,'" in contrast to that of the Mensheviks, whose industrial constitution was "very near the National Guilds."[16]

The next month's issue of *The Guildsman* apologized for the absence of a pro-Bolshevik reply to Bechhofer, which had been "unavoidably held over." The same issue also reported on the NGL's third annual conference, during which Bechhofer and Reckitt — now members of the newly elected executive — were prominent in opposing a motion by Cole supporting the Bolsheviks, whom Cole described as the "only effective opposition to capitalism in Russia." In response, Bechhofer rehearsed the arguments he had deployed in his article the month before, and Reckitt urged that "Guildsmen ought not to commend a policy based on methods which repudiated democracy and depended on terrorism." He added that, in any case, a motion such as Cole's, which was "political in character," was outside the scope of the guilds movement.[17]

The carrying of a "previous question" ended the conference debate, but the underlying argument in the NGL was only just beginning. In August 1918, M.I. Postgate, soon to marry and become better known as Margaret Cole, replied to Bechhofer's anti-Bolshevik attack in an article titled "National Guilds and the Bolsheviks." Drawing on data published in *The Board of Trade Journal*, she explained that the first fundamental decree of the Bolshevik Council of People's Commissaries had been "designed to introduce the control of industry by the workpeople." She stressed the "inclusion of the technical classes and the salariat" — something that was a major preoccupation in the NGL — and the recognition by the Bolsheviks of what she called the "dual principle of Government." This, she thought, should "rid the minds of Guildsmen of the idea that the Bolsheviks are merely syndicalist proletarians."[18]

Claiming that she had misquoted him, Bechhofer remained unmoved by these arguments:

Miss Postgate must forgive me if I suggest that her obvious sympathy with the internationalist and pacifist programmes of the Bolsheviks has made her blind to the industrial side of their revolution. What holes would she have pulled in that decree if it had been issued by any other Russian political party! I submit that National Guilds were implicit in the industrial arrangements of the first revolution, but that they are neither sought by, nor realisable under, the Bolsheviks.[19]

What makes Bechhofer's position significant is that, in contrast to most enthusiasts for soviet democracy at the time, he saw the Bolsheviks not as promoters and defenders — still less originators — of grassroots workplace democracy but as its enemies and destroyers. Writing in *The Guildsman* early the following year, Reckitt was, as one would expect, equally clear about the incompatibility between the guilds movement and Bolshevism: "National Guilds cannot (in my view) be squared with Bolshevism any more than with Collectivism. The Guildsman takes his stand on industrial democracy, as opposed equally to the 'dictatorship' of the bureaucrat and to the dogmatic neo-Marxist (often a 'bourgeois') who mistakes himself and his clique for 'the proletariat.' "

In the same issue, Bechhofer insisted, in a letter opposing Cole's "Guild Socialist League" proposal, that members of the NGL "do not want to establish State Socialism *alias* State Capitalism . . . because it means the Servile State. Nor do they want its opposite, the 'Industrial Society' of the S.L.P."[20] The term "Servile State" had become quite widespread on the Left and was used in many different contexts to suggest the danger that state control and the nationalization of industry might result not in the emancipation of the workers but in their virtual enslavement. For example, in a piece on the effects of the war published in *The Herald* at the beginning of 1917, Edward Owen Greening, who was prominent in the co-operative movement, concluded that "Great Britain is becoming a Servile State; Germany already is one."[21]

The phrase went back to Hilaire Belloc's pre-war book of that title, which had generated considerable discussion in the socialist press at the time.[22] Belloc, though not himself a "Guildsman," or indeed any variety of socialist, was an occasional contributor to *The Guildsman*, which regarded him and G.K. Chesterton — together nicknamed "Chesterbelloc" — as "friendly critics." The very first issue of the journal, that of December 1916, had announced: "The Guildsman comes with a warning, a summons, and a plan — a warning against the Servile State which all unsuspected is fast being established in our midst." This was followed by a piece by Belloc titled "The Coming of Servile Labour," which appeared in February 1917. It was in this context that at the special conference at the end of 1920 — which, according to the December issue of *The Guildsman*, had been called to decide whether there was "any future for Guild Socialism" — Page Arnot charged, not without some justification, that the NGL's "right wing had abandoned the class-struggle and were moving rapidly towards Mr Chesterton and the Distributists."[23]

Bechhofer's and Reckitt's commitment to industrial democracy and their suspicion of "politicising" were paralleled in the syndicalist-influenced shop stewards' movement. The widely held view of the guild socialists as a group of middle-class theorists remote from the working class and the world of industrial work is understandable but is in need of considerable modification. Even without taking into account the ill-fated attempts to actually create working guilds — clearly a step well beyond mere theorizing, even if a failed one — such a view does not do justice either to the backgrounds of some key NGL activists or to the close interest that others, most obviously G.D.H. Cole, took in the shop stewards' movement.

The Guildsman was founded and initially edited by John Paton, in Glasgow. Following his early death, at the age of only thirty-four, his obituary, as well as noting his recent work as manager of *The Guildsman* and as organizing secretary of the NGL, gave an account of how, having been trained as an engine fitter and having "roughed it for some time in America," Paton had "worked in the drawing office and returned to the shops, soon becoming the most prominent shop steward in his native Paisley."[24]

At the beginning of 1918, *The Guildsman* declared on its front page: "The Shop Stewards are the back-bone of the trade unions!"[25] And, although there were some criticisms of Murphy's *The Workers' Committee*, the NGL annual conference of that year was "unanimous in welcoming the Shop Stewards' movement as a force of infinite possibilities for the attainment by the workers of the control of industry."[26] *The Guildsman* continued to follow Murphy's views closely enough to take issue with him later in 1918, when he changed his line and advocated "complete severance from the established organisations" in *Solidarity,* the organ of the shop stewards' movement. *The Guildsman* argued that craft unions were on their way out, in any case, and that the road forward, especially in the engineering industry, should be joint recognition of shop stewards by several unions. "Unofficial" committees were not likely to succeed "since workers will not readily forsake their Unions to follow groups of men whose only recommendation is revolutionary opinions they detest."[27]

The issue of the organization's name was debated again at the NGL's fourth annual conference in 1919. There was a clear correlation between the positions taken on this issue and attitudes towards the Bolsheviks. The proposal to change the name to the "Guild Socialist League" was moved by the London Group, which believed that "the present name is vague and misleading." There was some support for the motion, but also opposition, from, inevitably, Reckitt, who argued that it was rather "late in the day to make a fetish of the word Socialism. It is inadequate and inaccurate, has a myriad of interpretations, nearly all nasty." Opposition also came from Paton, who was afraid of being associated with "bureaucratic Fabianism." The original instigator of the suggested change, Cole, then made the defeat of the proposal more or less inevitable. Although he had intended the change of name "to exclude from the League people who were not Socialists," he said, it had now become clear that the new name would exclude "too many others." The vote was lost, with about two-thirds of those present rejecting the proposal.[28]

By the time the fifth conference was held in the summer of 1920, disagreements within the NGL had moved on from arguments over its name. The process that was to lead to the formation of the Communist Party of Great Britain occupied much of the attention of many on the Left at this time. Accordingly, the issues that caused *The Guildsman* to anticipate, in April 1920, the "biggest crisis of its career" for the NGL concerned "the Soviet system, democracy, and 'the dictatorship of the proletariat'":

> First there is a tendency represented by the present majority on the Executive. This section has manifestly scant belief in the triumph of Socialism by the constitutional accession to power of a parliamentary majority. It welcomes the Soviet as an instrument for the overthrow and supersession of capitalism; it desires to expunge the reference to "a democratic state" from the constitution of the League; and it expects Socialism to be brought about not by a converted majority, but by an energetic minority. It has clearly no objection to the principle of proletarian dictatorship, and we may add, it clearly regards Guild Socialism as a form of Socialism and the Guild more as part of the Socialist movement. . . .
>
> At the other extreme stands the group led by Mr Reckitt and the Executive minority. This group dissents from resolutions dealing with "Democracy" and "The Soviet System," and Mr Reckitt and certain others have put down a resolution of their own which is probably a direct negative of the former. In this they categorically repudiate the dictatorship of the proletariat.[29]

The next issue of *The Guildsman* demonstrated the accuracy of this analysis. Arthur J. Penty, then a member of the NGL executive,[30] believed that if the resolution concerning soviets were passed it would "entirely change the character of the League from being a body which seeks to guide the Labour movement by the quality of its thought to one that seeks to stampede it by the violence of its opinions." After a brief period of triumph, it would "dwindle into impotence," caught up in a reaction against Bolshevism. A.E. Baker questioned the way that the "supporters of the resolution on Soviets and Minority Dictatorship, proclaiming themselves the left wing of the Guild movement, assume their opponents to be relatively on the right." This raised, he said, the question of "Leftwardness." He could only suppose "that a movement far enough to the extreme left reaches the extreme right — a proposition with which Professor Einstein would agree." Reckitt declared that if the NGL was faced with the challenge "'your democracy or your life,' they had better surrender the life of the League than the most vital of its social principles."

Representing the other side of the argument, a letter from Ellen C. Wilkinson of the Manchester Group concluded by insisting:

> The question posed by the "Soviets and Democracy" resolutions on the Conference agenda can be reduced simply to this. Is the National Guilds League content to amuse itself with its box of bricks, or will it range itself with the revolutionaries throughout Europe who are working for an immediate revolution, offering the Guild theory as its contribution to the building of communist society after the transference of power has taken place?[31]

Matters came to a head at the conference, whose "most striking feature," according to *The Guildsman,* was "the appearance of two parties — a right wing and a left wing," something the paper attributed to the influence of the "Russian movement." The tone of its report on the conference was light-hearted. "The Chairman's error in putting the 'revolution' to the vote was greeted with loud applause," it commented, adding: "In the course of the discussion Cole, Mellor and Page Arnot were compared to Robespierre, Danton and Marat, and Hobson was asked whether he would be prepared to take the role of Charlotte Corday. The suggestion that there was a Judas in the League led to some competition for the part amongst the stalwarts of the extreme Left." Meanwhile, "another speaker elicited a formal (and necessary) protest by suggesting that the Left were the sort of people who did not drink and held eccentric views on marriage."

Light-heartedness could not disguise fundamental differences of opinion, but it is interesting that, even though, as *The Guildsman* reported, "the Lefts had a working majority of 67 to 55" and the "Soviets" resolution was "decided on strict party lines," which reasserted themselves at the end of the conference in the vote on "League Policy," the fourteen other motions on the agenda were carried unanimously or by large majorities. And, as was reportedly the case with other British supporters of the Bolsheviks in these years, those who presented themselves as members of the "Left" were at pains to insist on the independence of their judgement: "P.H. Cohen led a forlorn hope in the shape of an amendment proposing to rule out parliamentary action entirely. Being told that he was out-Lenining Lenin himself, he replied that he was not to be dictated to by Lenin or any other man. This display of spirit was much appreciated." [32]

The conference was followed by a stormy aftermath, centring on the "policy pamphlet" that it had instructed should be drawn up. In the meantime, Rowland Kenney, in an ironic letter to *The Guildsman* despairing of "Our Faction Fight," argued that those on "the Left" were concentrating on the wrong things from their own point of view:

> Machine gun practice and the study of street fighting, the acquisition, equipment and arming of aircraft, the manufacture of tanks and poison gas, these are the matters that should surely be occupying their time. Men consciously and deliberately working for revolution by force in England — with its absolutely dependable armed forces and its powerful anti-revolutionary groups — surely cannot hope to achieve much by agreeing on a few phrases like "dictatorship of the proletariat" and then sitting down to wait for a discontented mob to make the revolution they intend to guide into fruitful activities for establishing a more ideal state. [33]

What is clear is that the focus of the argument had shifted. The guild movement had always opposed the notion that the parliamentary system was, or could be developed into, an adequate approximation of democracy. The movement had always campaigned for "industrial democracy." In 1918 and 1919, the question had been whether soviet democracy had some degree of reality in Russia or whether, as Bechhofer argued, the Bolsheviks had decisively crushed its early flowering. In the spring of 1919, G.D.H. Cole had given a series of lectures in London, in which, according to *The Guildsman*, he referred to "the Russian Soviet Government providing so interesting an experiment in the political organisation of society." Here was the familiar experiment metaphor yet again:

> He did not actually advocate swallowing the Soviet system whole, explaining that it expressed a need rather than a theory and was, to a certain extent improvised, but suggested that the most interesting fact was the tendency to divide, to set up workshop committees, for the controlling of industry, leaving the rest to local soviets linked up federally in a Central Soviet, and a National Congress of Soviets. These two facts — the separate representation of industry and politics and the federal organisation of the State — are what commend the Soviet system to Cole's mind.[34]

By 1920, with the long, drawn-out creation of the CPGB about to come to fruition and the Left Wing of the ILP aspiring to lead their party into a Third International, which was insisting on the endorsement of "the Dictatorship of the Proletariat," the issue for NGL members was whether this doctrine could be reconciled with soviet democracy," or indeed with any kind of democracy at all, however limited — and, if so, how. The publication of Kautsky's assault on the concept and its practice by the Bolsheviks was a factor in crystallizing the issues at stake.

The "Aunt Sally of the Third International"

The ILP and *Labour Leader* were equivocal about soviet democracy and generally prone, for a surprisingly long time, to giving the Bolsheviks the benefit of the doubt. Yet it was the ILP's National Labour Press that published Karl Kautsky's *The Dictatorship of the Proletariat*, translated by H.J. Stenning, at the beginning of 1920. It was advertised in *Labour Leader* as an "incisive criticism of Class Dictatorship and a powerful defence of democratic government, by the greatest Socialist writer on the Continent."[35] Kautsky, "in the pre-war years the veritable

pope of the Second International,"[36] was a key critic of Bolshevism
— arguably *the* key critic. There was nothing equivocal about his response. Although he certainly had support among the "reformists" of
Britain, their overall reaction to his work was nowhere near as positive
as might be expected, while the response of "revolutionaries" was, as
would be anticipated, totally negative.

At the end of the January 1920, John Scurr reviewed Kautsky's
book for *Labour Leader*. He anticipated a "storm" when readers realized that "Karl Kautsky regards the revolution in Russia as being the last
middle-class revolution rather than the first Socialist." It was "middle
class or bureaucratic inasmuch as a party seizes power and exercises
it." And, like so many others, Scurr stressed that the soviet republic
was "an experiment, an experiment carried out under peculiar and
exceptional circumstances," in a country whose social and economic
conditions were vastly different from those of Western Europe. But
socialism "as a means to the emancipation of the proletariat, without
the self-government and good-will of the people is unthinkable." And
he concluded with a ringing endorsement of the book: "Everyone who
reads the LABOUR LEADER must buy this book. I congratulate the
I.L.P. on its courage in publishing it. It stimulates thought on every
page."[37]

Yet it had taken a rather long time for a book of such importance
to be translated and published in Britain. After all, it had been written well over two years earlier, in August 1918, before the end of the
war.[38] The *New Statesman* reviewer, writing in March, was much less
impressed than Scurr. Kautsky's opus had to share critical scrutiny
with three other works, one of which was Lenin's *State and Revolution*. The (anonymous) reviewer identified Kautsky as "the principal
theoretical exponent of 'orthodox' German Social Democracy" and
noted that he and Lenin shared "an intense desire to prove their respective points by citing the authority of Karl Marx." But the contest was
not an equal one, since "Lenin's book is immeasurably better argued
and has infinitely more life in it than Kautsky's somewhat pedestrian
effort":

Kautsky enters the field as a "democrat" and combats the theory of "dictatorship" from a "democratic" standpoint. He somewhat misunderstands the Bolshevik position when he assumes that its essence lies in the establishment of Socialism by a minority movement. That is not its essence and it would be a point of indifference to Lenin whether his violent revolution was made by a majority or a minority, provided that it is made by enough to secure its success. The essence of the "dictatorship" position lies in the assumption that every State is a class State and that a "democratic State" in any real sense is impossible. The character of the State depends on the character of the coercive organisations which are its instruments, and while opposing classes exist, one of these classes is bound to dominate the State. If this is true, clearly a dictatorial proletarian State is the only alternative to a dictatorial capitalist State. The argument for "democracy" which Kautsky interprets on somewhat narrow orthodox political lines is therefore not very effective against Bolshevik theory.[39]

The *New Statesman* was not the only critic of the appeal to Marxist orthodoxy. From a very different perspective, and before Kautsky's book appeared in English, an article in *The Socialist* — Klara Zetkin's "Through Dictatorship to Democracy" — was presented by its author as a response to "Comrade Kautsky." If the reformists of the *New Statesman* were equivocal, the revolutionaries of the SLP were not going to be exposed to any doubts. Zetkin was not impressed either by Kautsky's or by "Comrade Martoff's" citing of Marx's writings in support of their position. What did it matter, she wrote, if "having at first been inclined to a 'Jacobin' outlook," Marx "subsequently came rather to adopt an 'evolutionist' and 'parliamentary' view"? Historical evolution "was not arrested when the pen fell from Marx's hand."[40]

When the English translation appeared, *The Socialist* reviewer, R.M. Fox, found the book "interesting" but insisted that Kautsky's comparison between Wilhelm Weitling and the Bolsheviks broke down because "the Bolsheviks *do* believe in democracy in a socialist community." They were "simply endeavouring to make a condition of real democracy possible." Once it was admitted that the workers, as a class, had the right to carry out their will, the right to vote became irrelevant. Kautsky might cite Marx on "the Civil War in France," but Marx "believed we must ignore the other side and use our sledge-hammer majority to carry out our work irrespective of them." And, in reality, Kautsky knew very well that "in a society of classes, one class must rule and that democracy is impossible." [41]

Whatever the merits or shortcomings of Kautsky's book, British "Bolsheviks" did not have to wait long for a vehement response from Lenin himself. On the first of April, *The Call* announced: "In Press, Lenin replies to Kautsky [in] 'The Proletarian Revolution and Kautsky the Renegade.'" Three weeks later, Tom Quelch provided readers with "An Appreciation" of Lenin's reply: "This book is a fierce polemic. It is hot and strong. There is a flavour of Tertullian, a touch of Calvin, in the Communist sense, about this keen proletarian theoretician." Quelch presented Kautsky as "the intellectual head and front of all those prole-tarian forces which still fall under the spell of social patriots." Lenin's work had, he said, effectively demolished the arguments of "those who still adhere to pre-war Socialist concepts of bourgeois parliamentarism; it tells why it is necessary to shatter the capitalist State, and to replace it with the Soviet system, and to establish the worker's dictatorship." [42]

Kautsky insisted that "democracy is the essential basis for building up a Socialist system of production." [43] "A Letter from Lenin: Greet-ings to Communists Abroad," published in May 1920 in the *Workers' Dreadnought,* rejected this as cant:

> The hatred which the capitalists of Russia and of the outside world feel towards the Soviet Republic is camouflaged by high-sounding phrases about "real democracy." The fraternity of exploiters is true to its own tradition; it represents bourgeois democracy to be *the* "democracy" and it includes all the Philistines, including Messrs. Adler, Kautzky [*sic*], and the majority of the leaders of the "independent social-democratic party" of Germany, which is independent of the revolutionary prole-tariat, but dependent on petty bourgeois prejudices. [44]

Hitherto, "phrases about 'real democracy'" were more likely to refer, without the quotation marks, to the soviet variety. In the case of the *Dreadnought,* the shift of emphasis visible in Lenin's letter would not be a permanent one, but it is indicative of the direction in which much of "Bolshevik" opinion in Britain was moving.

By the end of that year, 1920, the Communist Party of Great Britain (in reality still little more than a name-change for the BSP) had been formed, and *The Call* had become *The Communist.* C.M. Roebuck, reviewing Kautsky's *Terrorism and Communism,* was predictably scathing about its author, "whom once we should have called 'Comrade,'" after Kautsky's latest attack on Bolshevism had been published — like the earlier book, by the National Labour Press:

> Kautsky's desertion of the fundamentals of Marxism, in his notorious "Dictatorship of the Proletariat"— so readily published by his British co-religionists in the N.A.C. of the Independent Labour Party — has already been exposed and branded with the infamy it deserves by Comrade Lenin in his book on the "Proletarian Revolution and Kautsky the Renegade" and Comrade Trotsky has produced, by snatches of work at 3 o'clock in the morning . . . a crushing and complete exposure of Kautsky's historical errors and political methods.[45]

Early in the new year, Trotsky's response to Kautsky was advertised in *The Communist* as "ready shortly."[46] In the meantime, a *New Statesman* review of *Terrorism and Communism* — grouped with Bertrand Russell's *Practice and Theory of Bolshevism* under the title "The Bolsheviks Contra Mundum" — had noted that "Kautsky has become a kind of Aunt Sally for Lenin and the Third International."[47]

For its part, *The Communist* was not short of "domestic" Aunt Sallys — particularly when it could link them to the international one. In August 1921, in a disparaging report on the recent congress of the "little band of Hyndmanites known as the Social Democratic Federation" (the NSP having reverted to its older name by this time), *The Communist* noted that, according to reports, Kautsky had said in a letter that he was "following with pleasure" the SDF's "campaign against Bolshevism." [48]

The most surprising aspect of the response of the British Left to Kautsky's critique of Bolshevism is, surely, the dismissive attitude of the *New Statesman* reviewer. But consideration of this response has taken us somewhat ahead of the sequence of events. By 1921, it was clear that the British Communist movement that had now emerged had as its core the old BSP, to which adhered a number of smaller fragments of the Left. A year earlier, however, it had seemed possible, even at some stages likely, that something closer to the pattern of the French "split" after the Tours congress would make the ILP the largest Left component bent on affiliation to the Third International. That this did not take place had a great deal to do with perceptions of the meaning of the phrase that became more and more dominant in left-wing discourse — "the dictatorship of the proletariat."

7

THE DICTATORSHIP OF THE PROLETARIAT

The Dictatorship of the Proletariat and Soviet Democracy

The "dictatorship of the proletariat," a phrase that had appeared somewhat sporadically in the writings of Marx and Engels, was to prove simultaneously troublesome and useful: troublesome because difficult to define, useful — for the Bolsheviks and their supporters — because of this very ambiguity. Kautsky's observation that "Marx had unfortunately omitted to specify what he conceived this dictatorship to be" seems a considerable understatement given the importance that came to be attached, by a wide spectrum of Left opinion, to the correct interpretation of Marx's legacy.[1]

In everyday discourse in the years following the Great War, as now, dictatorship was the antithesis of democracy. Dictatorship meant absolute rule by a single person; to talk of the dictatorship of a *class* would therefore have seemed a little odd — and presumably metaphorical. No doubt the early exponents of the Bolshevik version of the dictatorship of the proletariat, who contrasted it with the "dictator-ship of the bourgeoisie," did not imagine that the entire capitalist class directed day-to-day government. What they were trying to assert was that the economic, social, and cultural hegemony of the bourgeoisie distorted or negated formal political equality, making democracy, ac-tual or potential, a delusion in capitalist countries.

Clearly, the fact that Robert Williams used the phrase at the Leeds Convention of June 1917 shows that the notion of a dictatorship of the proletariat was not unknown on the British Left before the Bolshevik takeover in Russia later that year. But it was not something that had featured prominently in pre-1917 socialist discourse in Britain, at least not in most of the socialist press. On at least one of the rare occasions when the phrase did appear, the context was derogatory. In 1913, writing in *Justice,* J. Hunter Watts, a prominent member of the BSP, used it to attack syndicalism, which he saw as "a recrudescence of the theory of the Dictatorship of the Proletariat which may be traced to Robespierre, and which deluded Marx when he stated that the Paris Commune would 'serve as a lever' to overthrow capitalism."[2] Signifi-cantly, perhaps, this was the view of a Hyndmanite who would be part of the pro-war and anti-Bolshevik NSP a few years later.

When use of the phrase subsequently became widespread — oblig-atory in some Left circles — there was a great deal more agreement that this dictatorship was both desirable and necessary than there was agreement about the precise meaning of the phrase. Those attracted to the Bolshevik cause by the idea that the soviets represented a "higher" form of democracy were to have great difficulties in reconciling this vision with the idea of dictatorship — unless "dictatorship" simply referred to the replacement of bourgeois socio-economic hegemony with that of the working class. The apparent democratic superiority of the soviets was a key element in the appeal of the Bolshevik cause. If the "dictatorship" of the proletariat was understood merely as a rather extravagantly vivid way of characterizing an uncompromising and un-remitting commitment to achieving socialism by means of a system of soviets, the use of the term might be acceptable. But if it meant "real" dictatorship in any shape or form, that was obviously going to be much more difficult to reconcile with the notion of soviet democracy.

Though much more was heard of it after the Bolsheviks came to power, the phrase began to be mooted at least occasionally in the months prior to October 1917. Apart from Robert Williams at the Leeds Convention, another early advocate of the dictatorship of the proletariat was the future leader of the ILP's Left Wing and later Communist MP, J.T. Walton Newbold. In a front-page article in *The Call* in July 1917, titled simply "The Dictatorship of the Proletariat," his emphasis was on the direct role of the working class. "Through the Workers' and Soldiers' Councils or through some other medium, now or in the not far distant future," he wrote, the working class was going "to make an end not only to the capitalist system of industry, but also the capitalist system of social organisation known as the State, and of the capitalist system of ideas, education, and in fact the capitalist system of civilisation. It is going to create one of its own — that of Social-Democracy." A fortnight later, in a piece titled "Forging the Weapon," Newbold referred to "the conquest of absolute power, the Dictatorship of the Proletariat."[3]

If the "dictatorship of the proletariat" and the "soviet system" were not simply two ways of saying the same thing, then the difference was that the soviet system constituted the means, or the "medium," to use Newbold's word — one means (or medium) among others theoretically possible, but unspecified, to the desired end. As we have seen earlier, the exclusion of all but "workers" from participation in the soviet system was quite widely seen as unproblematic since socialism *meant* the abolition of classes. Therefore, everyone would quickly acquire proletarian status — unless they perversely refused to accept it — in what might be called the doctrine of voluntary exclusion. Ultimately, the proletariat would vanish, along with all other classes in a classless society.

The notion of voluntary exclusion is well illustrated in a piece by W.N. Ewer, which appeared in the *Workers' Dreadnought* in August 1918. Ewer commented on the queer notion of some Socialists that the "dictatorship of the proletariat" is a bad thing and that all classes should be on an equality in the new society. Surely the abolition of the other classes by their absorbtion [*sic*] into the workers is precisely the first object of a socialist revolution and surely while they persist in maintaining a separate existence they can scarcely be accepted as part of Socialist society. The amiable folk who want to see a capitalist and rentier class preserved and protected by a Socialist Regime have scarcely grasped the elements of the matter.[4]

Similarly, in the summer of 1919, when the Workers' Socialist Federation declared itself, briefly, to be the "Communist Party," it issued a manifesto that interpreted the dictatorship of the proletariat in precisely this way: "We recognise that the dictatorship of the proletariat, which is the restriction of political power to those who live by their work and not upon accumulated wealth, or by employing others for their private gain, is necessary for the success of the workers' revolution."[5] Earlier, in "A Soviet Republic for Britain," *The Socialist* had anticipated a system in which "each adult member of the Co-operative Commonwealth functions as a co-controller of its society and the co-worker of its industries." In more general terms, "the control of the Commonwealth is by the democratic vote of its adult members."[6]

The voluntary exclusion argument was not confined to Bolshevik sympathizers in Britain. For example, in May 1919, the *Dreadnought* published an article by Albert Lantos, described as "a Soviet Official in Budapest," that defended the soviet system. According to Lantos, capitalists had no rights. But they could easily acquire political rights by engaging in "fruitful labour," he insisted.[7] Similarly, later in the year, a small item in *The Call* reported the following statement of I.A. Martens, the Russian Soviet representative in the United States, under the heading "The Dictatorship of the Proletariat." Soviet Russia's government, Martens said, the Council of People's Commissaires, is a Government controlled by and responsible to all such members of the population of Russia as are willing to perform useful work, physical or mental. Those who, while not unable to work, deliberately refuse to exercise their productive abilities, choosing to live on the fruits of the labour of other people, are eliminated from participation in the control of my Government.[8]

The objection to "bourgeois democracy" was that the economic power of the capitalists, exercised in a myriad of social, cultural, and political settings as well as in purely economic ways, would always determine the policies pursued by governments, no matter how democratically elected. The result was the de facto "dictatorship of the bourgeoisie," a situation that was unavoidable within the framework of "bourgeois democracy." As *The Socialist* quoted Zinoviev as putting it: "Soviets signify the Dictatorship of the Proletariat: the National Assembly signifies the Dictatorship of the Bourgeoisie."[9] The "dictatorship of the proletariat," then, surely meant the transfer of economic power to the working class. In Russia, this is what soviet democracy seemed to be implementing. But given that the "dictatorship of the bourgeoisie" was compatible with an (apparently) democratic state, one featuring broad freedom of expression and political action, did this not mean that such freedoms would, or at least could, also co-exist with the "dictatorship of the proletariat?"

It was not that "harder," more uncompromising versions of the dictatorship of the proletariat were unknown — or even that they were confined to those who disapproved of them. As early as April 1918, *The Call* reported on a speech by Lenin to the All-Russian Congress of Soviets in which he claimed that "Soviet Government" had profited from the experience of the Paris Commune by constituting itself "exclusively on the authority of the workers and poorer peasants to the exclusion of capitalists and Imperialists." Lenin reportedly went on to say that "during the protracted period of transition . . . the proletariat must exercise a dictatorship" and to claim that "never in history have the questions at issue in the struggle between classes been solved in any other way than by violent methods." In fact, the paper declared, "when it was a question of suppressing the exploiters in the interests of the exploited classes, he frankly was all for violence."[10]

But most homegrown Bolsheviks preferred to put a great deal less emphasis on the use of force and to stress instead the democratic nature of the soviets. In "Dictatorship and Democracy," published in *The Call* in September 1918, "W.A.M.M." (another of Theodore Rothstein's pseudonyms)[11] spoke of the way the Paris Commune had been supported by socialists and "even sections of bourgeois radicals"— the Positivists were later mentioned. He contrasted this situation with the current state of affairs, in which

> the official Socialist parties almost everywhere are vying with the capitalists in heaping calumnies and curses on the Socialist regime in Russia, and what may be called the centre parties, the official minorities, who abstain from joining in that infamous sport, think it necessary, each time they mention the Bolsheviks, to add apologetically "of course, we do not approve of everything they do." Traitors to the one side, fainthearted neutralists on the other.

Kautsky, he continued, regarded as democratic the "couponocracy of France, the plutocracy of England — in the latter moreover, millions were at that time still excluded from the franchise," And yet, he complained, "the Soviet regime which has realised the rule of the labouring classes, which has placed the machinery of government directly in the hands of 15,000,000 industrial workers and 80,000,000 peasants, and only excluded from all participation in the government a few million intellectual saboteurs of the Revolution and capitalist reactionaries of all kinds, as a temporary measure during the period of armed conflict and pending the complete realisation of Socialism and the abolition of all classes" was, according to Kautsky, "tyrannical." "Socialism is certainly Democracy," W.A.M.M. ended, "but the way to it lies through Revolution and Revolution means fight."[12]

This "fight" was a great deal more ambiguous and abstract-sounding than Lenin's "violence." The same notion of a road to democracy via temporary dictatorship was implicit in the very title of Klara Zetkin's "Through Dictatorship to Democracy," which appeared in *The Socialist* late in 1919. Critics of the Bolsheviks seemed to forget, she asserted, that the disqualifications from the soviet franchise were "merely provisional" and would be enforced only "for the period during which the dictatorship of the proletariat and peasantry must persist." [13]

Comparisons with authoritarian behaviour by "bourgeois" governments, to the advantage of Bolshevik Russia, were often made. Dora Montefiore reminded readers of *The Call* that the declaration of war in 1914 had triggered a "capitalist revolution," in which bank depositors were compelled to accept "scraps of paper," and that the government had gone on to seize transport and other undertakings and to introduce both the ultra-restrictive Defence of the Realm Act and conscription:

> The law regulating the duration of a Parliament was arbitrarily put on one side, and all these acts of violence were carried out by a Government which had no mandate from the Parliament; so that the Government of the United Kingdom has, for the last few years, been virtually a Dictatorship and workers organised for a revolution have an object lesson of how the thing may be done.
>
> At the end of four years of peace from the clash of militarism we should with the aid of a temporary revolutionary Dictatorship of the People (such as we have been undergoing for four years at the hands of the capitalist-militarists) have evolved a working form of socialisation of the means of life: and should, with the aid of International Socialists all over the world, have replaced the competitive struggle of capitalism by the human co-operation of Socialism. [14]

As we saw earlier, Lenin tended to place much more emphasis on dictatorship in the conventional sense and on the use of violence, but those who wished to see the "dictatorship of the proletariat" as little more than a poetic way of characterizing soviet democracy could still draw comfort from at least some of his statements that appeared in the British socialist press. For example, in February 1919, the *Workers' Dreadnought* reprinted "Lenin to American Working Men," together with a picture of "Nikolai Lenin." As Lenin explained:

> The Workmen's and Peasants' Soviets are a new type of state, a new highest form of democracy, a particular form of the dictatorship of the proletariat, a mode of conducting the business of the State without the bourgeoisie and against the bourgeoisie. For the first time democracy is placed at the service of the masses, of the workers, and ceases to be democracy for the rich, as it is, in the last analysis, in all capitalist, yes in all democratic republics.[15]

Even as the Communist Party of Great Britain was beginning its life in the summer of 1920, *The Communist* carried Zinoviev's report of the "Theses" passed by the congress of the Third International in Moscow: "The Soviets are the dictatorship of the *proletariat*. The Constituent Assembly is the dictatorship of the *bourgeoisie*. To try to reconcile the dictatorship of the workers with the dictatorship of the bourgeois is impossible."[16] That December, *The Communist* also published Tom Bell's "Open Letter to the Rank and File of the I.L.P.," which urged:

> Against the parliamentary democracy, comrades, you must oppose the principle of direct representation of the working class through the Workers' Councils. This dictatorship of the proletariat is and *must* be the means for the expropriation of capital and the elimination of private property in the means of production.[17]

Little wonder that optimistic British socialists continued to conflate the "dictatorship" with "soviet democracy," a form of democracy they believed to be superior in its democratic reality to anything that was or could be available within the limitations of "bourgeois" states. Besides, the dictatorship element in the Bolshevik revolution was already becoming redundant — or so it seemed.

The Temporary Nature of the Dictatorship

In the spring of 1919, Eden and Cedar Paul wrote of "communist ergatocracy — the administration of the workers by the workers — with (as a preliminary stage) the dictatorship of the proletariat exercised through workers' committees or soviets."[18] Just how long this "preliminary stage" might be expected to last was, as always, left unestimated, although the Pauls' formulation in the same letter implied a much longer time scale than that envisaged by most other writers of the period. They could see, they concluded, "no way of avoiding these temporary dictatorships so long as great bolshevist communities and great capitalist states confront one another within the confines of one narrow planet. The Russian revolution of 1917 must become the world revolution. Not until then will there be peace on earth."[19]

But it was much more common on the Left to suggest that the dictatorship — if not yet the state itself — was already beginning to "wither away." As early as August 1918, the *Workers' Dreadnought* included the following reassuring piece of dialogue about the situation in Russia in an article titled "Socialism in the Making":

> "What is the thing which most impresses you in your daily life under Socialism?" we asked one of our friends.
>
> He smiled: "It's freedom."
>
> "But is there not a dictatorship?"
>
> He replied: "Every government is in some degree a dictatorship however mild. During war the dictatorship became everywhere more rigorous. Here too."

But such dictatorship as there was in Russia was not only mild but temporary — at least according to the friend, who assured his comrades that "when the counter-revolution has been vanquished the Revolutionary dictatorship will relax." He also noted that "in Russia the bourgeoisie, the counter-revolutionaries, have more freedom than the ordinary workers have here":

The bourgeois counter-revolutionaries constantly hold public meetings. They have complete freedom except to bear arms, and the inoffensive bourgeoisie may carry arms; it is only the counter-revolutionary who is not allowed to though he usually does!"

Not that there *were* many counter-revolutionaries, or opponents of the regime of any sort, in the friend's view:

"The moderate socialists have no programme except the substitution of the Constituent Assembly for the Soviet. But if the Constituent Assembly had not been abolished by the Bolsheviki; if the Mensheviki had then obtained power, the Mensheviki reign would have been very short, for the mass of the people are Bolshevik." [20]

Again, in February 1919, reporting on the setting up of a commission of enquiry on Russia by the Berne Conference of the Socialist International, *The Call* commented:

Neither Mr J. R. MacDonald or Mr Branting can quite make up their minds on the subject the commission is to enquire upon. Both appear to agree that the dictatorship of the proletariat, in certain circumstances, is justified and even necessary, whilst both contend that the dictatorship must not be made the permanent basis for government or administration. Long before they reached these equivocal conclusions the Bolsheviks had made a continued dictatorship unnecessary by the profoundly just rule that every able-bodied person should give some labour service to the community. When all are proletariat there can be no dictatorship. [21]

But if some managed to virtually spirit away dictatorship in this fashion, it was also in the context of the dictatorship of the proletariat that the role of the "revolutionary party" began to occupy a more prominent place in Left discourse.

The Revolutionary Party and the Dictatorship of the Proletariat

The distinction between class and party was becoming blurred. One example of the new emphasis came from Charles Roden Buxton's explanation of Lenin's view of revolution, which appeared in *Labour Leader* in May 1919.[22] For the Communist, the starting point was recognition that "*the present state of society is the dictatorship of the minority that owns property in considerable quantities, which controls our minds*, particularly through education and the Press." The initial step towards changing this situation "must be taken by a minority acting on behalf of the non-propertied. . . . It is futile to expect that you can convert a majority of the people at once to the new view of things. Universal Suffrage and Parliamentary Democracy, under the prevailing conditions, will merely register the acquiescence of the mass in the present condition of society." Therefore, Buxton argued, "an 'advanced guard' as Lenin calls it . . . must take control of the Government. This minority will in practice be found among the industrial workers."

Eventually, he continued, the propertied would "come over to the regime," a process hastened by penalizing those who did not. In the meantime, the transition would be "essentially a stage of civil war, but it need not be carried on by methods of violence." The revolutionary government must refuse its opponents any share in political power. At this stage there could be no constituent assembly chosen by universal suffrage, and the revolutionary government "must keep in its own hands the machinery by which public opinion is formed." There could be no free press, freedom of assembly, or uncontrolled education. Yet at the same time this process "must be clearly recognised as one of transition only." The "ultimate goal" was "complete democracy."[23]

In November 1919, the *Workers' Dreadnought* published extracts from the Manifesto of the Comintern, which sought to explain the role of the dictatorship of the proletariat. The proletariat was to be given "the favoured position in the community," though only as "a provisional institution," until such time as the bourgeoisie was "gradually absorbed into the working groups." In the meantime, the soviets would "draw constantly increasing numbers of workers into the State

Administration," by which process would "the entire working population gradually become part of the Government." As the manifesto also noted, "the industrial proletariat is favoured in this system because it is the most aggressive, best organised, and politically ripest class, under whose leadership the semi-proletarians and small farmers will be gradually elevated."[24]

The sociological concept of the working class was giving way, not without resistance, to a political definition of the proletariat. The conflict between these two conceptions was captured in a book review in the September 1920 issue of *The Guildsman*. "Hussein" contrasted two differing descriptions of the dictatorship of the proletariat, those of R.W. Postgate's *The Bolshevik Theory* and of Cedar and Eden Paul's *Creative Revolution*. Postgate, "a Guild Communist," was "very much 'down' on what he called 'Blanquism' and does not like to have his 'DP' confused with minority rule. Mr and Mrs Paul, on the other hand, explicitly recognise that 'DP' means dictatorship of a minority, and stress the point that the term 'proletariat' only included the class-conscious workers."

The idea that the Communist Party, as such, might legitimately stand for the proletariat appeared quite gradually. In May 1919, the *Workers' Dreadnought* carried an article by Karl Radek titled "The Dictatorship of the Proletariat." To begin with, Radek affirmed the role of the (otherwise unidentified) "class conscious" minority. Responding to those who argued that the dictatorship was only applicable to countries like Russia, where the working class was a minority, he asserted: "In no country in the world will the Revolution be the act of the majority of the population. For Capitalism is not merely physical control of production, but everywhere it controls the minds of the masses as well." Consequently, it was always a minority that carried out the revolution, though its success depended on "its affinity to the interests of the masses." Only during the "development" of the revolution "does it attract the majority and, thereby conquer."[25]

By early in 1920, W.H. Ryde was referring, in *The Call*, to "the dictatorship of the proletariat and poorer peasants under the leadership of the Russian Communists." [26] By July, L. Leslie of the Aberdeen Communist Group, who had attended the founding conference of the Communist Party (British Section of the Third International) as a "proxy delegate," was brutally clear. He was concerned particularly about the Glasgow-based Scottish Workers' Committee, which had "no spine" and included "opportunists" from sections that were still part of the Second International:

> The Soviet or Committee system must come under the dictatorship of the Communist Party, and a firm hand should be kept above the vacillating Menshevik persons and committees such as you have in Britain. The least rope given to the parties in Soviet Russia who come under Communist surveillance would be the betrayal of "All Power to the Soviets." [27]

This was unusually frank. Advocacy of Communist Party rule was generally expressed in softer terms. For example, in April and May 1922, *The Communist* published a series of five articles by T.A. Jackson, intended "for beginners" and jointly titled "What Communism Means." In the penultimate article, on revolution, Jackson exposed "the 'Democratic' Fallacy of bourgeois states." His final contribution concluded that "the Communist Party is not secret, it is not a conspiracy, it will only be violent when forced to in self-defence." The alternative to capitalism was "by way of the Dictatorship of the Toiling Masses, which in turn can be expressed and exercised only through the medium such an organised, trained, experienced, and disciplined Party." [28]

But, long before this, the growing appeal of soviet democracy had, in the eyes of some, begun to pose a problem. In July 1920, A.A. Watts, who had succeeded H. Alexander as BSP treasurer the previous year, noted in *The Call:* "The 'Soviet idea' is now recognised in words by many 'independent' Socialists and even by Right Socialists. We shall only be able to prevent these elements from distorting the Soviet idea if we have a strong Communist Party capable of defining the policy of the Soviets and leading them in its train." The preaching of wide "autonomy" would only weaken the party, he argued, and assist "the petty bourgeois, anarchical, centrifugal elements." The same article had renewed the attack on the German "Lefts" who wanted the Communist Party "to melt into the Soviets," which would then take the place of the party. This, said Watts, was "fundamentally incorrect and reactionary."[29]

It remained vital for proponents of the role of the party to stress its mass support. This is illustrated in an exchange that took place in *The Guildsman* in the last three months of 1919 between R. Palme Dutt, who was to become a leading figure in the CPGB, and Maurice Reckitt. Their arguments over the meaning of the "dictatorship of the proletariat" also illustrate the gulf that was opening up between supporters of Bolshevism and their opponents in the socialist movement. Dutt began by defining his terms: "*Dictatorship*, an extraordinary power for a specific purpose. *Proletariat,* the workers regarded as in conflict with the capitalists — therefore containing potentially all workers, including the managerial, but actually according to their alignment in the immediate struggle." All socialism, Dutt went on, implied a belief in "what is in effect the dictatorship of the proletariat; the only difference concerns form and sanction. Even parliamentary socialists agree on the employment of force . . . to oust the capitalist class." And while parliaments claimed to "hold the assent" of the majority, the soviets could more justly be said to represent its will. The role of the party was to provide sufficient leadership to avoid chaos: "The only safeguard against the horrors of a fumbled revolution is the existence of a clear, direct, and powerful revolutionary party."[30]

For Reckitt, the phrase in question, "as commonly employed," suggested "the capture of power in *the name of* the 'proletariat' by a violent section acting outside the recognised Labour movement . . . in accordance with a set of economic doctrines not understood outside a restricted circle; and refusing to share its authority not merely with the 'bourgeoisie,' but even with any other section, however numerous or important, of its own Labour movement." In response, Dutt claimed that the Bolsheviks not only had the support of the soviets "but have successively received into their midst each section of the Russian labour or Socialist movement as soon as it has shown its readiness to be labour i.e. by leave off [*sic*] co-operating with the bourgeoisie."[31]

What would come to be called the "leading role of the Communist Party" was emerging in "Bolshevik" rhetoric, but as yet it was not greatly stressed and was hedged with qualifications emphasizing the sovereignty of the soviets and the reality of massive popular support. However, defenders of certain aspects of "real" dictatorship were beginning to appear.

Defenders of Dictatorship

It was to be expected that those on the Left who had rejected Bolshevism from the outset would be implacably hostile to any notion of the dictatorship of the proletariat and dismissive of any semblance of reality that it might have. Thus, Archibald Lee, writing in *Justice*, rejected the idea that socialism or democracy of any variety existed in Russia: "There is not even that latest development in class rule, the dictatorship of the proletariat; there is merely an oligarchy of a dozen adventurers or so, originally thrust upon Russia by the German Kaiserdom to dish the Entente."[32]

Much more significant is the appearance of statements from pro-Bolshevik sources that, in substance and/or in language, defended the use of authoritarian and sometimes violent methods by the Bolsheviks. In a piece titled "Russian Bolshevism — Tyranny or Freedom?" that had originally appeared in the American newspaper *The Public* and was reproduced in the *Dreadnought* in 1919, the writer informed readers that "Lenin, when he overthrew the Kerensky government, made no claim to be the creator of a new democracy. . . . There is no other road to Socialism except the dictatorship of the proletariat and the merciless suppression of the rule of the exploiter."[33] Granted, this was still rather abstract and open to interpretation. But was J.F. Hodgson, later to become an early member of the Communist Party executive, simply resorting to metaphor when he wrote in *The Call*:

"The Socialist Revolution is no matter for kid-gloves; perhaps soon, like Napoleon's ragged army, a proletarian army will sweep through Europe and we must do our share in the fight"?[34]

Defence of dictatorial methods became more explicit in 1920, although the use of such methods was usually presented as the fault of the workers' opponents. Reviewing Lenin's *The Proletarian Revolution* in *The Call*, Tom Quelch charged the leaders of the ILP and others who held similar views with failing to realize that in the event of a "Workers' Government" gaining power in Britain, the ruling class "would resort to violence which the workers in their turn would have to counter with violence." He therefore concluded that "the fierce logic of facts compels the establishment of the dictatorship of the proletariat."[35]

In an article titled "Democratic Republic Versus Soviet Republic," which appeared in *The Socialist* early in 1920, N. Ossinsky was clear that a dictatorship was necessary in order to defeat the bourgeoisie. Therefore, "we must have an unlimited power, an iron power, otherwise called a dictatorship. (A dictatorship is one invested with the power of exacting obedience under pain of death.)" However, according to his account, the Bolsheviks were far from being all-out dictators: "The Bolsheviks do not wish to control all power. They do not wish to exterminate all the demi-bourgeois parties which have one eye on the employers and one on the workers and peasants. The Bolsheviks are pitiless only to the bourgeoise, the wealthy, because such is the will of the Russian workers."[36]

At this stage, in the summer of 1920, even the *Workers' Dreadnought* was in favour of certain limitations being placed on the press:

> The proletarian dictatorship will not misinterpret the principle of the freedom of the press into allowing newspapers and other publications to advocate the return to a state of society that was based on class exploitation. With this limit only, the discussion of ethical and economic ideals and principles of administration and social organisation will be unrestricted and the press will be entirely free.[37]

This was followed three weeks later by the publication, over the period of a fortnight, of Lenin's article "Democracy and the Proletarian Dictatorship." The first instalment included among its subheadings "Thieves to Be Shot," "Dictatorship: A Great Word," and "The Necessity of Force." According to Lenin, "the trouble with previous revolutions was this — that the revolutionary zeal of the masses, which kept them vigilant and gave them strength, mercilessly to suppress the elements of decay, did not last long." Defining the dictatorship of the proletariat as "the dictatorship of the class-conscious people," Lenin claimed that the "exploited toilers" were now discovering that "the disciplined class-conscious vanguard of the people is their most reliable leader." The problem, he said, was that the revolution in Russia was "too mild":

> The nearer we get to the complete military suppression of the bourgeoisie, the more dangerous become for us the petty-bourgeois inclinations. And these inclinations cannot be combated by propaganda and agitation only, by the organisation of emulation, by the selection of organisers, they must also be met with force.

The instalment concluded with Lenin's statement that there is "absolutely no contradiction between the Soviet (Socialist) democracy and the use of dictatorial power of individuals." What this might mean in the workplace was revealed the following week, when Lenin asserted:

> We must learn to combine the stormy democracy of the meetings, overflowing with fresh energy, breaking all restraint, the democracy of the toiling masses — with *iron discipline* during work, with *absolute submission* to the will of one person, the Soviet director, during work.[38]

It would be unduly cynical to see all those who tried to conjure away the really "dictatorial" aspects of the dictatorship of the proletariat as deliberately indulging in a smoke-and-mirrors exercise intended to deceive. Rather they were, for the most part at least, struggling to reconcile their faith in soviet democracy, which had been a crucial part of what had attracted them to the Russian Revolution in the first place, with the desire to support the actual regime that had now emerged from it. Much of the reported violence and dictatorial behaviour of the Bolsheviks could be dismissed with the comforting thought that it was the result of hostile capitalist propaganda and the Russian reality was in fact much closer to what Bolshevik supporters in Britain wanted it to be.

Statements such as those quoted above from Lenin's "Democracy and the Proletarian Dictatorship" now seem to be clear and explicit enough. Yet the British Left was generally reluctant to recognize that a dictatorship of the proletariat might mean anything more than a real, working-class democracy of the soviets, from which, at the end of the day, exclusion was purely voluntary. It was not until 1921 that the *New Statesman* reviewer of Arthur Ransome's *The Crisis in Russia* would conclude that "Mr Ransome's account of the working of the proletarian dictatorship . . . shows very plainly how the effective government in Russia has passed from the Soviets into the hands of the Communist Party, so that the dictatorship is in effect exercised by the Communist Party."[39] As we shall see, it was, surprisingly, the "British Bolsheviks" of the Socialist Labour Party who were to have the most disparaging and dismissive things to say about the whole idea of the "Dictatorship," at least as applied to Britain and comparably "developed" countries.

Meanwhile, in 1920, it had been Bertrand Russell — who, as noted earlier, was sympathetic to guild socialism and was well aware of the less "dictatorial" interpretations that many on the Left were giving to "the Dictatorship of the Proletariat" — who wrote:

> Friends of Russia here think of the dictatorship of the Proletariat as merely a new form of representative government, in which only the working men and women have votes, and the constituencies are partly occupational, not geographical. They think that "proletariat" means "proletariat," but "dictatorship" does not quite mean "dictatorship." This is the opposite of the truth. When a Russian Communist speaks of dictatorship, he means the word literally, but when he speaks of the proletariat, he means the word in a Pickwickian sense. He means the "class conscious" part of the proletariat, i.e., the Communist Party.[40]

By the time Russell wrote, the issue of the immediate future of the party had been resolved. But it had been the efforts to come to terms with the implications of the "Dictatorship of the Proletariat" that had, more than anything else, marked the struggle in the ILP over the determination of its Left Wing to seek affiliation to the new Communist International.

8

THE INDEPENDENT LABOUR PARTY AND THE THIRD INTERNATIONAL
A Crucial Test for Belief in Soviet Democracy

Which International?

A willingness to accept the claims made for the soviet system as a "higher" form of democracy, or at least a willingness to give these claims the benefit of the doubt, goes a long way towards explaining the degree of support the Bolsheviks enjoyed and the eagerness evident among the members of small groups who were already seeking to achieve "Communist Unity" to join with them in the Third International. But for the ILP, and especially for its official organ, *Labour Leader*, the affiliation issue and that of the Bolshevik revolution in general were extremely divisive. The conflict generated would help bring about the paper's demise. Arguably, it also set a pattern that was to endure within the Labour Party for decades.

Still a major component of the Labour Party at the time, the ILP's membership fluctuated between about thirty thousand and perhaps twice that number in the immediate post-war years.[1] This was a very modest figure, but it was very large in comparison to the membership of rival groups on the British Left. *Labour Leader*'s circulation rose from 51,000 in the summer of 1917 to about 62,000 by the time of the October Revolution.[2] The paper had been edited since 1916 by Katharine Bruce Glasier, who had taken over from her ailing husband, although Philip Snowden — the ILP Chairman from 1917 to 1920 and an MP until his defeat in the post-war "khaki" election of 1918 — was billed as the "Supervising Editor." A regular contributor to the paper throughout 1915 and 1916, his role now encompassed a weekly "page of comments on political events," to which his name was attached, as well as "leading articles."[3]

As already noted, the immediate response of the editors of *Labour Leader* to the Bolshevik revolution and the dissolution of the Constituent Assembly was at least of the "benefit of the doubt" type, while much more positive reactions were found in its letter columns and in the articles of some contributors such as Emile Burns. Even Snowden, as we have seen, took a surprisingly optimistic view until sometime after the end of the war. Subsequently, Allied intervention in Russia muted criticism. An editorial in May 1919 summed up a common ILP view: "We are not Bolsheviks, if by Bolshevism is meant a permanent system of Government in which any section of the community is denied its proportionate share of representation in a democratically elected assembly." All the same, the Bolsheviks had to be defended against the "vile . . . and in large measure unfounded charge of barbarism and terrorism," and intervention in Russian affairs had to be opposed in accordance with the "the right of self-determination."[4]

By summer 1919, the crucial issue had become whether to remain affiliated to the Socialist (or Second) International or to seek to join the Communist (or Third) International founded in Moscow in March. "The whole Socialist International," wrote Ramsay MacDonald, "is anti-Bolshevist. It is indeed the only real bulwark against Bolshevism." Fred Longden, president of the Aston branch of the ILP in Birmingham, denied MacDonald's claim and expressed "great dissatisfaction" that *Labour Leader* "did not contain severe criticism" of the offending article. The Bolsheviks should be defended, he insisted:

> A proletarian dictatorship in the hands of Lenin and Trotsky and their like, on behalf of the masses of 85 per cent of the people, is far more decent and far preferable to either despotism by a Tzar and Black Hundred or so-called "constitutional" rule at the behest of a few nobles and upper middle class tyrants like Lloyd George. . . . The Soviet Democracy is at least as admirable as the best in Western Europe.[5]

For MacDonald, Longden's letter revealed a "movement which is being assiduously worked in the I.L.P." In response, Longden insisted he was not "a member of any disruptive group" and continued to challenge MacDonald, describing as "monstrous" his presentation of the Socialist International as a "bulwark against Bolshevism."[6]

MacDonald's *Parliament and Revolution* was greeted with a fanfare. "No socialist writer," wrote J. Bruce Glasier, "not even Kautsky, has more thoroughly digged down to the roots of political institutions, or searched out the implications of Socialist dogmas." But he went on to comment: "Perhaps the most surprising thing in the book is his proposal for a sort of Soviet Second Chamber of Parliament. Coming from one . . . who has implacably opposed all devices calculated to lessen the responsibility of the popularly elected House of Commons, this is a piquant innovation."[7]

David Marquand, in his biography of MacDonald, describes *Parliament and Revolution* as "in many ways the most effective polemic he ever wrote."[8] The part that so surprised Glasier defended "territorial" constituencies representing "citizens" rather than "constituencies of narrow influences — whether of trades or profession." But MacDonald conceded that Parliament was "moved by class interests and class assumptions just as much as if it were elected by a stockbrokers' guild, a guild of city merchants, a guild of landowners, a guild of lawyers" and urged that reform was urgently needed to bring the country's "industrial life . . . into more direct contact with its political life." This might be accomplished through replacing the House of Lords. However its members were elected, a reformed second chamber based on citizenship would demand equality with the Commons, whereas "a nominated Second Chamber, though from the point of view of practical politics the most convenient form of such a body, is so contrary to democratic assumptions that it will not be adopted." So what was MacDonald's solution?

> Let us, then, have a Second Chamber on a Soviet franchise. . . . Guilds or unions, professions and trades, classes and sections could elect . . . their representatives, just as Scottish peers do now. It would enjoy the power of free and authoritative debate (no mean power); it could initiate legislation, and it could amend the Bills of the other Chamber; it could conduct its own enquires, and be represented on Government and Parliamentary Commissions and Committees.[9]

This was clever. Soviets — controlled by the workers and elected in the workplace — were central to the appeal of the Bolsheviks, which was nudging ILPers towards affiliation with the Third International. The attraction of guild socialism, which attempted to combine both "geographic" and "industrial" representation for citizen *and* worker, was also great at this time, especially for the younger members of the ILP such as Clifford Allen, who at this point, Marwick tells us, "hoped to bring the British Labour movement, or at least its vanguard, the I.L.P., into communion with the new Third International."[10]

MacDonald's new line therefore had much more appeal than a conventional defence of parliamentary government. And his "Open Letter," published in *Labour Leader* on 1 April 1920 and addressed "To a Young Member of the I.L.P.," deftly associated the Bolsheviks with *both* the (allegedly) "cataclysmic" socialism that had preceded the ILP *and* Fabian elitism: "At that time there was no word of 'the Dictatorship of the Proletariat,' but there was the corresponding Fabian idea that by clever manipulation you could capture the Government and thus give an innocent nation the benefits of the rule of an enlightened Junta."[11]

There was little support in the ILP for the existing Socialist

International. Early in December 1919, a *Labour Leader* editorial lambasted it. The Socialist International will "deservedly collapse, unless it can do something to justify its existence" predicted the *Leader*.[12] This theme was taken up by MacDonald himself. The Socialist International seemed "a gathering of compromised sections," unable to "give a pure sounding call to the working classes," he wrote. Yet what was the alternative? To commit to "Moscow" would mean becoming "a mere wild revolutionary minority, and throw back the movement to where it was generations ago." If the upcoming Socialist International meeting at Geneva failed, the ILP should try to "recreate a new International" composed of "national sections which, standing firm upon Socialist ground, recognise national differences and see the necessity of keeping in touch with every manifestation of the working class spirit — even the most extreme forms born of the war and its mischiefs."[13]

On New Year's Day 1920, in "A Talk with Jean Longuet," Francis Johnson, writing in the *Leader*, quoted the prominent French socialist as calling for "a meeting of what might be termed the left wing element in the Second International" with others including, crucially, "representatives from the Russian section of the Moscow International." It was not "essential or necessary," Johnson urged, "that the International should be divided into Parliamentary and Soviet sections," and G.D.H. Cole described the soviet/parliament split as "a great calamity."[14] It was in this conciliatory spirit that the ILP subsequently took part in the "Vienna Union" — the so-called Two-and-a-half International — which attempted to reconstruct a united socialist international.

Such a policy was never going to satisfy those members of the ILP who were demanding that the party affiliate to the Third International. But if support for this demand was growing in some sections, others who had previously taken a sympathetic view of the Bolsheviks were having second thoughts. By the beginning of 1920, R.C. Wallhead was far less enthusiastic than he had been in the summer of 1918. He accepted the "dictatorship of the proletariat" as a temporary expedient but believed that this was "totally different from exulting it into a philosophy or adopting it as an integral part of a programme."[15] And yet it was precisely such an embrace of the concept that was a condition of affiliation to the Third International.

Clifford Allen joined the debate. He complained about the attitude of the ILP leadership:

> We are left to pick up what we can from rather superficial controversies in the LABOUR LEADER, and when we do publish any considerable work on Socialist policy, we choose Karl Kautsky's attack on Russian ideas and leave our members to go to other organisations for almost all the original documents of Soviet Russia.
>
> Our leaders blame us for offering our platforms to speakers from other sections of the Socialist movement. But is not this partially due to the fact that the N.A.C. tends to ignore important Socialist developments and by refraining from encouraging us in careful and impartial study, forces us into the hands of sectional propagandists?[16]

Allen clearly believed that it was the failure of the ILP leadership to pursue such "impartial study" of Russian developments that had opened the way for "sectional propagandists" committed to the Bolsheviks to exercise a significant degree of influence among the ILP membership, a situation that a more intellectually vigorous approach on the part of their leaders would have avoided. Time would tell what consequences this influence would have for the ILP.

Third International Support in the ILP in Early 1920

While the issues were debated week by week in *Labour Leader*, the divisions of the ILP were holding regional conferences. The first to report, early in January, was the Scottish ILP conference. The *Leader* summed up the results succinctly. "By decisive votes" the delegates to the conference

> decided in favouring:
>   The Labour Alliance
>   The Third International
>   Prohibition of Alcoholic Liqueurs

There had never been any doubt as to how the vote would go on the proposal to affiliate to the Third International, and, when it was announced that the resolution:

> That the I.L.P. sever its connections with the Second and affiliate to the Third International

had been carried by 158 votes to 28 there followed a demonstration of enthusiasm such as had never been equalled at a Scottish I.L.P. Conference. Delegates jumped to their feet in one delirious frenzy, surprised and gratified that they were united in their desire to link up with the Moscow International.

It was a spontaneous outburst of cheering which astounded the Press agents, who asked what it was all about.

This enthusiasm notwithstanding, a motion to condemn those "members of the I.L.P. who are so blinded by thoughts of governmental power as to assist the enemies of the first Soviet Republic" was rejected, by a vote of 103 to 51. No "enemies" were named in the motion, but — inevitably — MacDonald was mentioned during the debate.[17] Snowden noted that several other divisional conferences had in fact passed similar resolutions. This, he believed, was due to ignorance among the membership, including a failure to understand that the Third International had categorically declined to negotiate with a number of parties, including the ILP, which it deemed unfit "to enter the temple of the elect."[18]

Some divisions were hesitant about Third International affiliation. One frustrated delegate — presumably a Third International supporter — thought that "those who wanted more information about Russia, in view of all that had been published, should change their song from the 'Red Flag' to 'Lead Kindly Light.'"[19] Among the most hostile to affiliation was the Yorkshire conference. William Leach, of the Bradford branch, insisted that because "the Soviet system is not governed by delegates of the people but delegates of delegates etc *ad infinitum*, the rulers at the peak of this complicated pyramid were so far removed from public control that the recall was of no value." At the Yorkshire meeting, the motion to affiliate lost by 43 votes to 10. In contrast, "a long resolution from Bradford in favour of the Committee System" to replace the cabinet government, moved as ever by Fred Jowett, was passed unanimously without discussion.[20]

Meanwhile, in mid-January, MacDonald's "Open Letter V to a Branch Secretary" — the fifth in a series that appeared in the *Leader* — had criticized the practice of inviting speakers who expounded "other doctrines" to ILP meetings, a practice that both lent itself to "hostile propaganda" and obscured the ILP's "own mission." ILP branches should promote the party's own ideas; they should not behave like a "Debating Society and a Dilettante Lecture Club."[21]

Somewhat ironically, in the light of its future failure to merge with the Communists, the Socialist Labour Party claimed a large share of the credit for radicalizing members of the ILP. Ramsay MacDonald's plea to branch secretaries to exclude outside speakers was "undoubtedly" due, *The Socialist* insisted, to "the growing number of invitations from numerous I.L.P. branches to 'Left-Wing' speakers (especially S.L.P. speakers) to address their public meetings." Such invitations inevitably led "to odious comparisons being drawn; the weakness and reactionary character of the Labour Party being exposed and revolutionary 'poison' being instilled into the veins of the I.L.P. rank and file."[22]

In spite of the doubts of some divisions and the hostility of the party leadership, there was certainly a groundswell of enthusiasm within the ILP for Third International affiliation, as the Scottish conference had exemplified. So, as it had done before the war at times of internal crisis, as the party's annual national conference approached *Labour Leader* urged branches not to mandate delegates but to leave them a free hand to consider the arguments put forward.[23] The most important question for delegates to the upcoming national conference at Easter was the relationship of the ILP "to the International Socialist Movement." "It would be in the interests of the Party, and of the International," the *Leader* suggested, "if branches would refrain from sending their delegates to the Conference definitely pledged to support certain resolutions."[24] This proposal went to the heart of the debate on the "soviet system," since its perceived democratic superiority rested not only on its "industrial" base but also on the belief that, under that system, delegates were mandated by their electors, at the equivalent of the branch level, and could be recalled and replaced, unlike the representatives — as distinct from delegates — in parliamentary systems, who enjoyed an entirely free hand between elections.

The wider implications of this were not lost on Snowden. Following the ILP's Easter conference, he commented, in "The Tied Delegate," on the conference of the Russian Communist Party. The chair, Kamenev, had, Snowden reported, "announced to the Conference that certain delegates had come pledged to vote in a particular way. He pointed out that by the tradition of the Party, the decision of the Conference would be binding on all members and that no tied voting was permissible. 'Every delegate,' he said, 'must vote according to his own conscience, and not according to the views he and others had formed before the debates.'" This, said Snowden, "runs counter to the whole idea, as we have been given to understand it, of Soviet Government." The pro-affiliation vote at the conference would have been smaller, he claimed, "if the delegates had followed the Russian plan of voting according to their own consciences, after hearing the debate, instead of following instructions given on the basis of very inadequate knowledge and information."[25]

Meanwhile, just before the conference, a letter from McOmish Dott, supporting a new international for "all genuine International Socialists," insisted that it was unclear whether the Third International demanded "a forcible revolution as a necessary means of establishing Socialism" or whether the "Dictatorship of the Proletariat" required "a minority governing even for a transitional period." For him, "Dictatorship of the Proletariat" simply meant *the holding of power by the army and police to compel the people to obey the Government.*" This state of affairs would end when "the capitalists agree merely to use their voting power and give up recourse to Koltchaks, Denikins and Entente Allies."

In the same issue, Clifford Allen, rejecting "the old Parliamentari-anism," argued that the ILP should "become identified with the new industrial thought of the trade union world." It should disaffiliate from the Socialist International and attend "the International Conference of Left Wing Socialist bodies," that is, the meeting of the Vienna Union. But it should also announce its desire to become part of the Third International. It should set out the party's own opinions on three points and ask for the Third's reaction to them. In addition, Allen wrote, the ILP should reject the "Armed Revolution of the Workers," as applied to Britain, but accept the dictatorship of the proletariat because "de-mocracy is meaningless until economic equality is established." The party should also refuse to accept the "soviet system" as a "general 'must.'" But, he added, "if they say that the fundamental idea of gov-ernment by Soviet is government through working class organisation then we agree."[26]

The 1920 ILP Conference

Early in April 1920, at the start of the ILP's Easter conference, those who supported affiliation to the Third assembled for an initial meeting. According to the report in *Labour Leader,* this "Third International gathering," chaired by C.H. Norman and addressed by Helen Craw-furd, Walton Newbold, and J.R. Wilson, drew about two hundred participants. It was agreed that they would "act together" and "hold further meetings during the Conference proceedings."

At the conference proper, the mover of the affiliation motion, Herron, launched the crucial debate. According to the *Leader*'s re-port, he insisted that if members of the party sought affiliation, "the Communists would not seek to impose upon them something that was absolutely foreign to their nature." MacDonald's "wonderful book" had shown that "Parliament could not express the will of the people; it could not function for the working class." If those in the ILP could not accept "the whole Soviet system, at least some modification of that sys-tem was the only thing for them." The "dictatorship of the proletariat" was about "declaring an economic blockade against the parasites of society." The seconder of the motion declared that "whether the Soviets were a failure or a success," their underlying principle — namely, "to govern from the bottom not from the top" — was sound. As regards the dictatorship of the proletariat, a dictatorship had in fact existed ever since the institution of private property, the only difference being that the wrong people had been the dictators.[27]

MacDonald was "enthusiastically received," despite being "constantly interrupted by a few delegates." But he was conciliatory. Listening to Herron's speech, he said, his "heart had gone up" as he saw at last a chance for agreement. But what with the Socialist International now almost on its last legs, the party was being asked to join another that was "bound to slap revolutionary conditions on every sentence it issues." They could not duck the question of bloodshed: "The manifestos that have been issued calling the Moscow Conference say you must arm the proletariat and disarm the bourgeoisie." This brought applause from the supporters of Third International affiliation.

George Benson opposed Herron's motion, insisting that "the Third International favoured not merely the defence but the capture of the State by armed force." There were cries of "No!" from part of the audience. John Barry, from Merthyr, denied that the Third International imposed "inflexible" conditions: "The question of force only arose as a weapon of defence." Clifford Allen, making, as Fenner Brockway later wrote, "his first mark as a national figure in the I.L.P.,"[28] supported the motion to postpone the affiliation decision until the ILP had made further enquiries. Those who were of two minds could rally behind his reminder that "the majorities in the branches were narrow, a thing that extremists on both sides were apt to forget."

Three votes were taken. Delegates voted 529 to 144 to disaffiliate from the Second International, but the motion to affiliate to the Third garnered only 206 votes. A motion for further consultation and the holding of a special conference in the future was carried by 472 votes. The conference closed on a less dramatic note, with Jowett's motion for the "abolition of the Cabinet system" carried by a large majority.[29]

Snowden's *Labour Leader* editorial following the decision presented the outcome as historic: "Not since the I.L.P. came into existence has it been called upon to deal with a more critical situation than at this week's Annual Conference," he announced. Affiliation to the Third International would have meant the ILP abandoning "its anti-militarist and civic principles." But, he said, he was left "with a feeling of relief rather than satisfaction." Those who still supported the move to affiliate were, he said, misleading themselves: "The kind of Socialist International they approved would bear little or no resemblance to the Moscow International with which they desired the I.L.P. to affiliate."[30] The actual Third International would not, in other words, live up to their romanticized expectations.

Reports from Russia

Until this time, *Labour Leader*, like other socialist papers, had had to rely on journalists such as Arthur Ransome (of the *Daily News*) and Philips Price (of the *Manchester Guardian*) for firsthand accounts of Bolshevik Russia written from a British perspective. But, as visits became easier, this began to change. Reports broadly sympathetic to the Bolsheviks started to appear, such as those of Professor William Goode and H.G. Wells.[31]

In the spring of 1920, Snowden criticized George Lansbury's *Daily Herald* dispatches, which were based on a relatively brief visit to Moscow and were soon to form the basis of Lansbury's *What I Saw in Russia*. In the preface to his book, Lansbury would write: "I see the Socialists of Russia as a band of men and women striving to build the New Jerusalem."[32] This was not a view Snowden now shared, whatever his early optimism about the Bolshevik takeover. "The Third International stands for everything [to] which Mr Lansbury declares himself to be opposed," Snowden argued. It aimed at "what it calls the Dictatorship of the Proletariat, which is a euphemism for the establishment, as in Russia, of an autocracy as tyrannical as that of the Tsar." Affiliation to the Third International, he concluded, was tantamount to "being committed to a silly and futile attempt at armed revolution;

it means violence as the method of Socialism; it means autocracy and not democracy; it means dishonest and disingenuous propaganda; in short it means the complete reversal of everything the I.L.P. has preached and practised up to the present." [33]

For the ILP, of much more serious consequence than Snowden's views was the joint Labour Party/TUC delegation to Russia in May and June of 1920. This expedition had its origins in the "Hands off Russia" campaign against Allied military intervention. [34] Attached to the delegation was an unofficial ILP duo, Clifford Allen and Richard Wallhead, whose mission was to clarify the terms on which the ILP might affiliate to the Third International. [35] Bertrand Russell also travelled with the party. One of the interim reports to *Labour Leader*, sent while the delegation was en route to Russia in May, claimed that "the Norwegian Party" had been allowed to affiliate, on the basis of "equal treatment of peasants and workers" and — crucially from the ILP perspective — the rejection of the "arming" of the proletariat. An editorial in the same issue seemed to confirm this report, encouraging the belief that affiliation terms were negotiable. [36]

In mid-June, an article titled "What We Saw in Russia," written by Ben Turner, who chaired the delegation, received front-page treatment in *Labour Leader*. They had seen what they wanted, he reported; there had been no "organized camouflage." They had had free access to Mensheviks. There was no "anarchy," and trade unions took part in "the actual government of Russia as well as in the government of their respective industries." But, he noted, the Bolsheviks did not deny that they had "used repressive measures": "They say that, so long as a great part of the world is plotting against them, they must have exceptional powers to arrest the counter-revolutionaries, monarchists, and officers of the old White Guard who act as agents and spies for the enemies of Russia." The Extraordinary Commission (the Cheka) was "above ordinary law, but its members assured us that they always give the prisoners a trial and provide the indictment within 24 hours. The members of the delegation were given every opportunity to see the British prisoners and the Concentration Camp." [37]

The fact-finding visit may have clarified the issues at stake, but it certainly did not produce a lasting consensus about the situation in Russia — although the members of the delegation did agree on the crucial and immediate issue, as was reflected in their official report, which condemned Allied intervention as "criminal folly."[38] But, writing in *Labour Leader* in early July, Brockway reported that the delegation had returned with "very differing views about the Soviet regime":

> A.A. Purcell and Robert Williams can find no words of praise too unbounded, Mrs Snowden . . . finds it difficult to criticise sufficiently strongly. Reading the various accounts, one gets nevertheless an intelligent picture of the whole. It is not so much the facts which are disputed as the interpretation of the facts.

He went on to note that "Bolshevism . . . is shown to involve great restrictions on personal liberty — suppression of freedom of speech, Press, and association, and industrial conscription with an almost military discipline. Apparently, too, even in the Soviet system there is little rank and file control."[39]

In the meanwhile, Lansbury presided over a "welcome home" for the Labour delegation, held at the Albert Hall and attended by all the members of the group except Tom Shaw, Clifford Allen (who was still in Russia, quite seriously ill), and, significantly, Ethel Snowden.[40] As the *Leader* informed its readers, "Arthur Purcell and Robert Williams declared out and out for Bolshevism" whereas Haden Guest's "plucky speech" criticized "the method of violence," while Margaret Bondfield noted the "pragmatism" of the Bolsheviks in reintroducing "one-man management."[41]

Williams had already offered his very positive assessment in "Impressions of Soviet Russia," a series of articles in the *Daily Herald* that had, he noted, originally been commissioned by the *Daily Mail*, which now refused to publish them without major changes. Calling Soviet Russia "an entirely new civilisation," he admitted that "I went frankly and avowedly as a supporter of the Proletarian Dictatorship. My impressions will, therefore, be coloured by my essentially working-class outlook."[42] At the Albert Hall meeting, the *Daily Herald* reported, Williams had displayed the "Soviet Military Medal" presented to him in Russia "for work on the industrial field in England to promote direct action." The paper also reported that Haden Guest had been heckled when he was critical of the fact that "the Russian people had called in force as their ally" and expressed the wish that "all the forces of Socialism" could be "combined for constructive purposes."[43]

In late July, the *Leader* reported on the questions that the ILP's Clifford Allen and Richard Wallhead had put to the Third International. But in mid-August, after his return from Russia, Allen announced that he could not recommend "unconditional affiliation to the Third International until it agrees that the policy of violence as a means of attaining power shall be an open question for the decision of each national party."[44] Allen's earlier enthusiasm for affiliation to the Communist International had been based on certain assumptions about its nature and, especially, about its openness to negotiation regarding the terms of membership, which his subsequent experiences in Russia had shown to be without foundation.

The threat of British intervention against the Bolsheviks in the Polish war complicated responses, to a degree. The members of the "Labour Delegation who have just returned from Russia" appealed to every trade union branch, trades council, local Labour Party, and socialist branch for "direct action" to prevent such interference in Russian affairs. The members who did so included not only Arthur Purcell and Robert Williams but also Harold Skinner (another of the TUC's representatives), Ben Turner, and Richard Wallhead. Yet Wallhead, at least, had come to have serious reservations about events in Russia.[45] As noted earlier, Wallhead, now chairman of the ILP, no longer had anything like the positive attitude towards Bolshevik Russia that he had expressed two years earlier. The reality of rank-and-file democracy was now in doubt. In September 1920, he wrote:

A short time ago, for anyone to question the immediate practicality of Workmen's Committees controlling industry, was to run the risk of having one's personal integrity impugned and drawing on one's head the charge of treachery to Socialism. If one dared to suggest that this particular experiment in Russia might fail, the effect was to arouse antagonism of the most violent character.

Yet the Bolsheviks themselves were now saying that such committees were impractical and were introducing "one-man management." [46] For Wallhead and other ILPers who had initially been attracted by the promise of soviet democracy in Russia, that country now seemed to be heading in the opposite direction. Roughly two months earlier, the *Daily Herald* had quoted Lenin as describing freedom as "a bourgeois notion" and had reported that "the trade unions are about to be transformed into State departments." But the paper made no further comment. [47]

Meanwhile, at the beginning of July, Emile Burns complained in *Labour Leader* about how the *Times* and the *Morning Post* were "making great use of interviews given them in Stockholm by Dr Guest and Mrs Snowden." [48] This complaint was followed by further protests "against the hostile interviews on Soviet Russia being accorded to the Capitalist Press by Mrs Snowden." There were demands that the NAC take action. [49]

Lansbury's *Daily Herald* also targeted Ethel Snowden, reporting that she had "given to the Capitalist Press an interview strongly critical of the Soviet regime in Russia. The Capitalist Press is delighted naturally." According to the *Herald*, Snowden had said of the Russian Bolsheviks: "They believe in what they call the dictatorship of the proletariat, but they have not even got that. They have only got the dictatorship of the Communist Party. It does not stop there. The Communist Party is dictated to by a handful of people inside the party." But this, said the *Herald*, was not easy to reconcile with her further statement that "the Soviet Government is quite stable and supported by the whole population, in spite of the fact that probably the majority do not like it." [50] In September, under the heading "Lenin to Mrs. Snowden," the paper would quote from an attack by Lenin on critics of the Bolsheviks. It was natural, Lenin commented, for "bourgeois democrats," who were "quite like our Mensheviks," to oppose the Bolsheviks, and it was likewise "natural that revolutionary workers execute Mensheviks." [51]

Ethel Snowden's book, *Through Bolshevik Russia,* further angered her critics. Reviewing it in the *Daily Herald,* George Young regretted that "her Anglo-Saxon attitude while providing Bolshie busters with valuable quotations" had "detracted from the value of her 'impressions de voyage.'" The book, he said, abounded with "sweeping and superficial indictments." [52] Of the ILP reaction, Keith Laybourn says, in his biography of Philip Snowden, that it was "the party's treatment of his wife," which Snowden took as a "personal insult," that drove him from "the mainstream of I.L.P. politics." [53] His point is well taken, although, as we shall see in the concluding chapter, Snowden's conflict with the editor of *Labour Leader* was surely another, related, factor.

The Left Wing of the ILP and the 1921 Conference

Although *Labour Leader* reported on the initial meeting of Third International supporters at the party's 1920 conference, it was only at the very end of that year that references to the "Left Wing of the I.L.P." began to appear regularly in the paper. In a letter reproduced in the SLP's *The Socialist* in May, however, the BSP secretary, Albert Inkpin, referred to "the unofficial Left Wing Committee that has been established in the ILP" as taking part in one of the meetings on Communist unity. [54]

Soon after the 1920 conference rejected the motion for immediate affiliation with the Third, a letter appeared in *Labour Leader* whose author, A.T. Rogers, argued that it was now the "bounden duty" of every Third International supporter to "immediately withdraw from the I.L.P." This alarmed leading figures of the party's "Left Wing," who expressed the hope that no one would take this advice. They were, they insisted, "seeking to unify the movement, not disrupt it." [55]

Although it was plainly very active throughout the remainder of 1920, little more was heard in *Labour Leader* of the campaign of the Left Wing until the end of the year. In the meantime, supporters of Third International affiliation published a fortnightly paper, *The Internationalist*, and a pamphlet titled *Moscow's Reply to the I.L.P.*, which had been sent to Walton Newbold by the Comintern executive. The crucial 1921 conference, at which the final decision on affiliation would be taken, was now in sight. At the beginning of December 1920, Philip Snowden noted that the Comintern had "instructed" all the Communist groups in Britain to unite, including "the Left Wing of the I.L.P.," while in the correspondence column H. Parker subsequently attacked "the attempt to establish and build up within the I.L.P. an undemocratic and questionable group, namely 'The Provisional National Committee of the Left Wing of the I.L.P.'"[56]

Others still emphasized unity. Jim Simmons, chair of the Midland divisional council, praised the "Left Wingers" in his division "who had refused to take part in any 'wrecking movement' inside the party." He was to plead the following month for tolerance of "loyal Left Wingers, like Fred Longden . . . who have refused to take part in the wrecking tactics of the last twelve months."[57] The policy proposals of the "Provisional National Committee" had by this time already appeared in *The Socialist*. In the opinion of the committee, the "Object" should begin: "The I.L.P. is a Communist organisation whose aim is to destroy the capitalist system." The dictatorship of the proletariat was to be declared a "necessary condition for Social Revolution."[58]

Meanwhile, Ramsay MacDonald was contesting the Woolwich parliamentary by-election, and Brockway's eve-of-poll report in *Labour Leader* confidently predicted that he would win by a large majority.[59] But, with the CPGB attacking him and recommending abstention, MacDonald was defeated. Angry letters followed in the paper a week later. The Reverend William J. Piggott blamed the Communists, who he said "torpedoed their Comrade's work," but supporters of the "Left Wing" were held at least partly responsible. H. Parker wrote: "The Labour Party candidate at Woolwich was an I.L.P. member and the

National Labour Party is entitled to the satisfaction of knowing that in future our nominee cannot be fought 'relentlessly, ruthlessly and in the open' by members (?) of the I.L.P. who have sought to purloin our title and malign our name."

Summarizing the content of these letters, the *Leader*'s editor, Katharine Bruce Glasier, concluded by commenting on the opinion of yet another critic of the "Left Wing":

> Mr R Sedgwick writes with our full sympathy, that he thinks it will be agreed that the time has now arrived when Mr Walton Newbold and his like must conduct their "relentless and ruthless fight out in the open" of Mr MacDonald and our other I.L.P. leaders, outside the ranks of the I.L.P. . . . . It can hardly be doubted that these men are out to smash our Party. . . . Therefore let the Party give them clear notice to quit.[60]

Under severe pressure from all sides, Glasier refused to publish "defamatory libels on individuals unsupported by evidence." These included both a letter attacking Walton Newbold and one from him, written, she said, "under the kindly title 'MacDonald Must Go.'"[61]

This was by no means the first time that Glasier and Newbold had clashed. Back in June 1918, under the heading "More Suppressions," *The Socialist* had published an exchange between Newbold and the *Labour Leader* editor. The former began by explaining that he had wanted to respond to the criticisms of the Bolsheviks made by Dr. Alfred Salter (detailed in chapter 6) but that he had waited to see what MacDonald would have to say about the issue "before putting the point of view of the Bolshevik I.L.Per"— that is, of himself and fellow members of the "Left Wing." In fact, Newbold's June letter had concentrated on *Labour Leader*'s failure to make enough of the publication by the Bolsheviks of the "secret treaties" between the Allies and tsarist regime, to which *The Socialist* had devoted most of its April issue. "We care not one fig for 'Democracy'!" Newbold had proclaimed. "We have no wish to greet the political democrats of the Constituent Assembly. We are concerned only about Social and Industrial Democracy." He had gone on to defend the "Dictatorship of the Proletariat," though "no one pretends he likes the prospect of a dictatorship." In her brief reply, Glasier merely explained that "the tone and temper left no alternative but to return the article."[62]

Once again, in 1921, the ILP's annual conference at Easter was dominated by the affiliation issue. But by now it was clearly a lost cause. Reporting on the Scottish ILP conference back in January, P.J. Dollan, a dominant figure in the Glasgow ILP, noted in *Labour Leader* that there had been "some surprise" at the rejection by the Scottish ILP, by a vote of 93 to 57, of a motion for joining the Third International, in the light the very different vote at the Scottish conference the previous year.[63] Far less surprised, by his own account, was the veteran Scottish socialist John Maclean. Writing in an edition of *The Socialist* published the same day in January, he commented: "In response to the timely and cunning appeals of Ramsay MacDonald, the Scottish I.L.P. branches have turned from the Third and will drift back to the capitalist-controlled Second International. The I.L.P. wirepullers have consequently won the day."[64]

This proved to be the case, though how much "wirepulling" was now required is highly debatable. According to *Labour Leader*'s report on the Easter conference, in his chairman's address Richard Wallhead attacked the "criminal record" of the British government in relation to Russia and referred to "the great Socialist experiment" there. But on the issue of dictatorship he was clear:

> In the end Socialism can only be effectively established upon the freedom and frank acceptance of the new order by the mass of the people. Permanent dictatorship and repression is its very negation and could only result in a hideous travesty.

Turning to the issue of the ILP's "Left Wing," he continued: "There cannot be permitted allegiance to an outside body whose mandates are to be carried out against the expressed will of the Party. . . . They should leave and join with an organisation to which they can honestly give their allegiance." A request from the British Communist Party that its president, Arthur MacManus, be invited to address the conference on the issue of the Third International was rejected.

In the light of Walton Newbold's ILP candidacy at Motherwell, John Beckett attempted to refer back for further consideration by the NAC the section of its report dealing with prospective parliamentary candidates. "It was absurd of the Party to put up candidates who were active members of another and hostile association," he argued. Beckett withdrew his objection after Newbold's wife — Newbold himself was not a delegate at the 1921 conference — insisted that her husband was "never a member of the Communist organisation." But she also explained that "he had received sanction to stand from Moscow so long as he stood on the maximum program." She had, she said, returned from Moscow with a message to the Left Wing that "their duty was to remain in the I.L.P."

Even-handedly, Beckett also tried to block the nomination of Ethel Snowden to represent the ILP on the Labour Party executive. Although Beckett's motion was defeated on a card vote by a margin of 235 to 191, this led to acrimonious debate. According to the *Leader*'s report on the conference, Beckett "drew special attention to the article that appeared in the *London Magazine*. It was accompanied by pictures which had never been outdone for bestiality by the capitalist press in their propaganda against the Germans (Hear, hear). The Bolsheviks were shown dragging women half-naked from their homes." But Mrs. Snowden had her defenders. As R.L. Outhwaite declared: "During the war Mrs Snowden played a braver part than any man or woman in the country in her championship of the liberty of the I.L.P.ers who withstood conscription (Hear, hear). When she found that Trotsky shot C.O.s she was naturally revolted."

George Benson, moving the motion to reject the Third International's 21 conditions for membership, argued that their acceptance would hand over the ILP, "bound hand and foot, to a foreign organisation." This provoked loud dissent, general exception being taken to the word "foreign." Referring to Comintern's requirement that the ILP change its leadership, Benson asked, "Was the I.L.P. a political party or a Christmas party? Was it an organisation or a pantomime?"

In contrast, the "Moscow amendment," moved by J.R. Wilson, sought acceptance of the 21 conditions. Wilson argued that the "Communist Party was using the power of the dictatorship on behalf of the mass of the Russian working class." Seconding his motion, Helen Crawfurd insisted that dictatorship was "a temporary institution." But the majority of delegates were more convinced by John Paton's argument that "in the Communist International as at present constituted there was no place at all for freedom of discussion." *Labour Leader*'s report commented that "Paton's analysis of the 21 points was remorseless, and uttered with high spirit."[65] In his autobiography, Paton, a future secretary of the ILP, gave his own account of his speech at the ILP conference. Convinced that the 21 conditions were "generally unknown" to the delegates, he had learned them by heart and found it easy "with such material to make a devastating attack" on the proposed affiliation. The climax of his speech, he thought, came when he listed the ILP leaders whom the Comintern insisted should be "flung out to the Party." At the mention of MacDonald, someone in the public gallery shouted derisively "Twister!" Paton retorted that he'd "sooner go to hell with Ramsay MacDonald than to paradise with some of the leaders of our own Left wing." As he spoke, he recalled, "the delegates rose to their feet and my voice was lost in a roar of cheering which continued for several minutes."[66]

Following a contribution from Shapurji Saklatvala, MacDonald picked up on Mrs. Newbold's admission that the Left Wing "had been officially instructed from Moscow to remain inside the I.L.P. to disrupt it." Charles Baker then offered yet another view of the meaning of the dictatorship of the proletariat, arguing that it referred simply to nationalization, inasmuch as that would involve "the imposition of the will of the masses upon a dissentient few." In the end, the Moscow amendment was overwhelmingly rejected, by a vote of 97 to 521, at which point the Left Wing contingent walked out. *Labour Leader* summed up the result:

The Conference ended with many empty places owing to the secession of the Communist minority. There are many whom we shall miss, but we believe it will be better for them and for us that the two sections pursue their separate courses. The secession will probably not number more than a thousand.[67]

This contrasted, as would be expected, with the view presented in *The Communist*. The organ of the CPGB saw the ILP as having "voted for nothingness" and claimed that 20 percent of its members — five thousand or more — had deserted in favour of the Communist Party.[68] There is no doubt that the *Leader's* assessment was the more accurate. As Walter Kendall points out, if every member of the ILP branches that voted in favour of affiliation to the Third International had joined the CP, the total number of defectors would still have been "only about 4,850." He estimates that the actual number of CP recruits was about five hundred or, "at the absolute maximum, one thousand."[69]

Not long after the conference, in a piece titled "Communist Efforts to Disturb I.L.P. Branches," the Reverend Gordon Lang attacked what he viewed as subversive activities in Scotland on the part of the ILP's Left Wing. He recalled branch officials selling *The Communist* rather than the *Leader* and other ILP literature, as well as the heckling and bullying of chairs and speakers at meetings. The "wild men" should be careful, he cautioned: "They had better remember . . . that they cannot all sit at the desk signing the death warrants of sentimental I.L.Pers and the like. The plain truth is that they do not believe in their own vaguely defined 'dictatorship of the proletariat.' What is desired by them is a dictatorship of the Party."[70]

In his biography of MacDonald, David Marquand sums up the significance of the ILP's decision on the issue of Third International affiliation at this time:

In Britain, only a few tiny and unrepresentative Marxist sects, with no significant following in the working class and no hope of building a mass party, had so far made overtures to Moscow. The I.L.P. was a very different proposition. In comparison with the Italians or the German

Independents it was a small party. But its membership was booming, its morale was high and it enjoyed influence out of all proportion to its size. If the I.L.P. decided to affiliate to the Third International, there was a distinct possibility that a strong Communist party, able to speak in native accents and appeal to native traditions, might come into existence on British soil. In the turbulent climate of 1919 and 1920, such a party might have made considerable headway.[71]

That this did not occur in 1921 is probably more attributable to the combined effect of growing disillusionment with the Bolsheviks, the fading of belief in the reality of democracy in Russia, as is exemplified in Wallhead's conference address, and, above all, the intransigence of the Third International itself than to the efforts of outright opponents of affiliation. To most ILPers, the 21 conditions were outrageous. But MacDonald's apparent espousal of something vaguely approaching guild socialism, together with the final judgment of erstwhile supporters of affiliation such as Clifford Allen, must also have contributed to the outcome. The debate in the ILP had centred, more than anything else, on the much-contested notion of the dictatorship of the proletariat. It had become increasingly difficult to maintain the view that this was simply a "poetic" way of describing working-class dominance through a genuinely democratic soviet system or that the ideal of soviet democracy, if not yet fully achieved in Russia, was a real possibility there in the foreseeable future.

Attitudes towards communism remained diverse within the ILP. A corollary of the fact that there were relatively few defections to the CPGB was the continued presence in the ILP of members who had voted for Third International affiliation even at the 1921 conference. The spectrum of views established by this time foreshadowed Labour Party opinion for most of the rest of the century. These views ranged from various degrees of sympathy with communism to outspoken condemnation, with, in the middle, the view summarized by P.J. Dollan in his report on the 1921 Scottish ILP conference. Referring to the Third International affiliation motion, he noted that "the delegates were asked to give unqualified obedience and support to Moscow as dictator of policy in Britain, and the delegates rejected the proposal." And he concluded succinctly that "the delegates did not repudiate Bolshevism for Russia, but they were not prepared to accept it for Britain." [72]

Yet, as F.S. Northedge and Audrey Wells point out, neither the Labour Party's constitutionalism nor its gradualism could entirely offset the "almost instinctive feeling that simply because the new Russia was socialist, or called itself socialist, it *must* be right in the basic things whatever its critics might say." [73] Such a feeling was experienced by a wide range of Labour Party members and supporters, and certainly it would be characteristic of a great many members of the ILP until at least the late 1930s.

9

"AN INFANTILE DISORDER"
Communist Unity and the Brief Life of the Communist
Party (British Section of the Third International)

The Khaki Election of 1918

By the time the ILP had finally rejected affiliation to the Third International, two versions of a British Communist Party were in existence — and about to be amalgamated. But it had been a long, hard battle to achieve this union. If doubts over the legitimacy of the dictatorship of the proletariat and its compatibility with *any* variety of democracy were at the root of the Left Wing's failure to capture the ILP, it was soviet democracy itself and its apparent incompatibility with participation in "bourgeois parliamentarism" that was the sticking point for Sylvia Pankhurst and her group.

The British socialist movement had long been characterized almost equally by schisms and by unity campaigns. The Socialist League split from the SDF in the 1880s, and both the SLP and the Socialist

Party of Great Britain left the SDF in the "impossibilist" split early in the twentieth century. Blatchford's *Clarion* had campaigned for an ILP-SDF merger in the 1890s and first decade of the 1900s, and the BSP was born at the 1911 "Unity Conference," still leaving all but a minority of dissident branches continuing with the ILP.[1] The outcome of the campaign for Communist unity, in terms of the composition of the Communist Party of Great Britain that ultimately emerged, had some resemblance to this earlier episode.

To begin with, "the various British Revolutionary groups groped towards unity under their own initiative, and independent of any outside interventions," as Kendall puts it, without, achieving any discernible progress.[2] But with the founding of the Third International in March 1919, this changed. Now the pressure came from the Comintern, with all the prestige of an apparently successful revolution and resources that were huge by the standards of the small-to-tiny British groups accustomed to operating on the proverbial shoestring. Even so, the desired unity took a very long time to come to pass, and then only imperfectly, with some of the earliest and most fervent supporters of the Bolsheviks still outside the ranks of the "official" party.

The divisive issue for the WSF first emerged clearly during the post-war "khaki" general election of December 1918. The *Workers' Dreadnought* was critical of members of the SLP who had chosen to run for Parliament — MacManus (a candidate in the West Yorkshire district of Halifax), J.T. Murphy (running in Gorton, Manchester), and William Paul (running in the Ince, Wigan district):

> MacManus and the S.L.P. stand for a Workers' Industrial Socialist Republic. So does THE DREADNOUGHT and the W.S.F. But whilst we wish MacManus success in his parliamentary fight since he has entered on it, we think he somewhat sacrifices his consistency in seeking a seat in Parliament, and we know that, if he is elected, he will find Parliament a waste of time.[3]

As W.F. Watson put it in the following week's edition:

Men who should be concentrating on the Shop Stewards' movement are either Parliamentary candidates or actively working for candidates.

I am more than ever convinced that the revolutionary industrialists will sooner or later have to repudiate the Parliamentary machine entirely and build up, through the Workers' Committees, a National Administrative Council outside of any Capitalist structure, and supersede the functions of the Parliamentary machine.[4]

The article the week before had been headlined "The S.L.P. Candidates: The British Bolsheviks and the Parliamentary Election." For Pankhurst and company, the SLP were the only real Bolsheviks in Britain — apart from themselves. The issues of participation in parliamentary elections and of affiliation to the Labour Party were to bedevil attempts to create a united Communist movement.

Waiting for the Soviets:
The "True Believers" of the Workers' Socialist Federation

Nowhere was the notion of soviet democracy greeted with more enthusiasm and more sustained belief than in the pages of the *Dreadnought*. Just over a week before the armistice, Pankhurst wrote:

> We have heard another voice, the voice of the future, now comes with great inexorable steps, bringing the elements which shall form the social structure of the 20th century. The old husks of the 19th century do not charm us. We are waiting for the Soviets, as they are called in Russia, the councils of delegates appointed by the workers in every kind of industry, by the workers on the land, and workers in the home. Through the medium of these workers' councils the machinery of the coming of the Socialist Commonwealth will be evolved, here, as in Russia.[5]

Nor, in the pages of the *Workers' Dreadnought,* was this degree of optimism entirely confined to Pankhurst and members of the WSF. Fred Silvester, secretary of Birmingham branch of the SLP, had never dreamed that the "Industrial Republic" would be realized in his lifetime: He had not anticipated that "the golden dream of a Morris Utopia would immediately follow the nightmare of Czardom but it is good to know that the Bolsheviks are, under the most adverse circumstances, putting into practice the kind of Socialism I want in this country — the administration of affairs by the workers democratically organised where they work."[6]

With such total belief in the inevitability of soviet democracy conquering the world, signs of its inexorable spread were quickly identified. By the end of March 1919, the *Dreadnought* was announcing that the Hungarian Revolution has "declared for the Soviet form of government and has at once allied itself with Soviet Russia." Soon the soviets had reached Bavaria: "The Independent Socialist Party of Germany has now definitely declared for the Soviets and the dictatorship of the proletariat," Pankhurst wrote in April. There could be no doubt that "Austria will shortly establish the Soviets," and all this confirmed "the belief that the British revolution is coming and that the Soviets will shortly be established here."[7]

In July and August, it was Italy's turn. According to the *Dreadnought*'s "special correspondent," Hiram K. Moderwell, Italy's seventy-four *camera del lavoro* had been called "the Soviet of the future." They were "wholly of and for the proletariat." But while "the Milan chamber is much like the Russian Soviet," there were elements of "true soviet organisation" missing. Its executive was elected not by the general council "but by the cumbersome method of universal ballot." He went on to point out that general council delegates are "elected for a fixed period and are not in practice recalled as they would be whenever they cease to represent the change of temper within the membership." These defects, which meant that the *cameria* fell somewhat short of the *Dreadnougtht*'s ideal of soviet democracy, were, however, expected to disappear before long.[8]

Meanwhile, the vital task was to bring soviet democracy to Britain. And, undeterred by what had followed the Leeds Convention in 1917, this was to be the task of the WSF. In March 1920, Pankhurst appealed to working women to create "Soviets of the Streets." They should "hold their own street meetings and set up their own soviets."[9]

Then, in its issue of 19 June, the *Dreadnought* published "A Constitution for British Soviets," which went into considerable detail about the structure, if not other vital details, of the proposed soviet system.

Every urban district was to be divided into household soviets of about 250 women — members of families who were mothers and housekeepers — who would meet weekly to deal with issues such as housing repairs and decoration, food and clothing, water supply and sanitation, and "co-operative housekeeping." One correspondent, E.T. Harris, protested: "Surely comrade you would not adopt a form of organisation that restricts household management to women." [10] These household soviets were to elect delegates to district household soviets, meeting fortnightly, and these would be represented both on "the District Soviet which deals with general political questions & public matters" and the regional, and, via the regional, the national household soviets, each of which would have delegates on the general soviet body at the appropriate level.

As far as industry was concerned, the constitution envisaged workshop committees and factory committees of delegates elected by all workers, with "foremen and managers . . . appointed by vote of the workers in the factory, and on the advice of the District, Town, Regional, or National Council for the industry." How possible conflicts between workers' preferences and the advice of these councils might be resolved was not explained. The workers in each industry would prepare schemes to be ratified by the National Council of Soviets. National, regional, and district economic councils composed of delegates from the various industries and from the general soviets would be formed "to co-ordinate the various industrial functions and overlook questions of distribution and supply."

There would also be "Public Health Soviets" — composed of equal numbers of medical workers' delegates and delegates of the "general local soviet" — and "Educational Soviets," whose structure began with "teachers' and pupils' soviets" at each school, with children under sixteen represented by their parents. These types of soviet would be continued at the district, regional, and national levels. The constitution also envisaged that "the army, so long as it remains, will have its Soviets organised according to military grouping. As the present forces are disbanded and the Red Army takes their place, Red Army Soviets will be formed." There were also to be sailors' and seamen's soviets, and agricultural soviets. In the letter quoted above, E.T. Harris also protested that there was no need for a different kind of soviet in rural areas because in Britain there was no "a small-holding feudal peasantry"; rather, the country had a "class-conscious and dispossessed agricultural working-class."

The timing of the appearance of this long exposition, written by Pankhurst herself, is significant. The next issue of the *Dreadnought* added "Organ of the Communist Party" to its masthead. The WSF had, with the adherence of some even smaller groups, proclaimed itself the Communist Party (British Section of the Third International). The "Constitution" was its vision of communism.[11]

"Left" and "Right" Communists

The rather grand "subtitle" of the new party is very significant. For Pankhurst and her comrades, the urgent desire to identify themselves as part of the international revolutionary movement outweighed the commitment to Communist unity in Britain, desirable as the latter remained — in theory at least. It was not the first time the WSF had declared itself "the Communist Party." A year previously, the *Workers' Dreadnought*, describing itself as "published by the Communist Party," reported that the WSF annual conference had

> received a recommendation from the Third International in Moscow that a Communist Party be inaugurated in this country. A resolution that the name of the organisation be changed in order to make it clear that it takes its stand with Russian Communism was already on the Agenda. The Conference decided to adopt the name *Communist Party*, and instructed the newly appointed Executive Committee to approach other organisations of like tendency with a view to the formation of a United Communist Party.

This proved extremely short lived. A week later, the reversion to "Workers' Socialist Federation" was announced with a note explaining that the executive committee accepted that the use of the name "Communist Party" should "be delayed during the progress of these negotiations."[12] The Comintern's "recommendation" had been misinterpreted, it seemed.

Pankhurst was fully involved not only in the WSF, in the People's Russia Information Bureau (which she and others had set up in September 1918 with some funding from the Bolsheviks via Rothstein),[13] and in the "Hands off Russia" campaign but was also a very active participant in the emerging international Communist movement. She attended the 1919 conference of the Italian Socialist Party in Bologna, which declared for the Third International, and witnessed Bordiga's attempt to commit it to an anti-parliamentary stance. She also made dangerous and illegal crossings first into Switzerland and then Germany, where she travelled with Klara Zetkin to Frankfurt for a clandestine Comintern meeting, and then went on to Amsterdam, where the short-lived Comintern Sub-Bureau was being formed.[14]

The Amsterdam bureau was, like Pankhurst, firmly anti-parliamentarian. The leading figures of the Dutch movement, Herman Gorter (1864–1927) and Anton Pannekoek (1873–1960), were both people of major intellectual substance outside as well as inside the socialist movement. Gorter was well-known as a poet, while Pannekoek's standing as one of the founders of astrophysics can be judged from the fact that to this day the Astronomical Institute of the University of Amsterdam still bears his name. Both were also serious Marxist theoreticans. They were to feature prominently in future issues of the *Dreadnought*. Little wonder, then, that Pankhurst entered 1920 — such a crucial year for the British Communist movement — confident that she and the WSF, rather than the "Right Wing Communists" of the BSP, represented the "real" international Communist movement.

In the meantime, at home the problem was that, whereas the SLP, the South Wales Socialist Society, the Communist League, and several other small groups might be deemed fellow Bolsheviks, the BSP's claim to such a status seemed dubious. Reporting on the BSP's 1919 Easter conference, the *Dreadnought* thought it had "not quite made up its mind yet to throw in its lot with the Socialist Revolution."[15] The immediate reason for doubting the wholeheartedness of the BSP's commitment was the failure of its annual conference to disaffiliate instantly from the Second International and declare for the Third. But there were other reasons to be wary. As we saw earlier, the events of the summer that followed were to show that E.C. Fairchild and H. Alexander had little support in the party for their opposition to the "soviet" policy it was adopting. But they had both been prominent in its leadership.

A year and a half after the fact, Pankhurst gave an account of relations with the BSP in the summer of 1918:

> Members of the W.S.F. hearing that almost the whole of the B.S P. Executive would be affected by the raising of the conscription age, approached the B.S P. in the spirit of comradeship, with a tentative offer of fusion which was very cordially received. The W.S F., however, drew back from the negotiations, because in the course of them, E.C. Fairchild stated that he did not think the organisation should decide between Parliament and bourgeois democracy, and the Soviets and the proletarian dictatorship, as the goal towards which our propaganda should be aiming.[16]

The "Leading English Communist"

Clearly confident that he would support her own anti-parliamentary views — otherwise what was the suppression of the Constituent Assembly in favour of the soviet system all about? — Pankhurst wrote to Lenin in July 1919, giving her impressions of the various organizations of the revolutionary Left in Britain, especially in relation to their attitudes towards parliamentary participation, and inviting his response. Her letter, published anonymously as from "an English comrade; a well-known Communist," and Lenin's reply appeared in the fifth issue of *Communist International,* the Comintern executive's official organ.[17]

Quite unexpectedly, for Pankhurst, Lenin failed to support her. In January 1920, the correspondence was brought to wider left-wing attention in Britain by *The Socialist,* which strongly objected to Pankhurst's claim that the SLP "had dropped its 'anti-parliamentary position.'" The party had *always* recognized "the necessity of parliamentary and electoral action." [18]

A week later, Tom Quelch, writing in the BSP's paper, *The Call,* was able to claim the Bolshevik leader's support for his own party's position in an article titled "Parliamentarism: Lenin and the B.S.P." Lenin had described parliamentary elections as *"one of the means* to prepare the proletariat for revolution." This, he explained, was why the BSP supported participation, not because of "any of the thousand and one reasons which some simple-minded or muddle-headed anti-Parliamentarians" had put forward. Quelch then turned to the "letter from a leading English Communist." He quoted Lenin's advocacy of parliamentary participation and his belief that the refusal to participate was "a mistake," although it was "better to accept this mistake than to postpone the formation of a strong Communist Labour Party in England," which should include "all the elements and groups . . . who sympathise with Bolshevism and are sincere advocates of a Soviet Republic." While plainly delighted with Lenin's endorsement of the BSP's stance, Quelch was extremely irked by the letter that had triggered the whole business:

> Perhaps it would not be too strong — as we feel that the intention was deliberately to mis-lead our comrade Lenin — to stigmatise the statement that the B.S.P is "too much occupied with electoral success, and after the election their representatives, elected by the workmen, usually forget the workmen and their interests" as *a lie,* because of the simple and apparent fact that ever since the B.S.P. expelled the social-patriots, four years ago, long before the Russian Revolution, it has had *no* representatives in Parliament.

Quelch ended with the claim that "to all intents and purposes the B.S.P. *is* the Communist Party — though there are many outside its ranks who should be inside." [19]

A fortnight later, *The Call* came closer to identifying the culprit. Only *The Call* and *The Socialist* — and, by implication, *not* the *Dreadnought* — had published Lenin's response: "We might have advised the 'Leading English Communist' beforehand that he (or should we say she?) would get small change out of Lenin's answer; but his (or her) continued silence is none the less remarkable." In April, Fred Willis announced in *The Call* that the "leading English Communist [is] now revealed as Miss Sylvia Pankhurst." There had still been no reference in the *Dreadnought* to Lenin's reply, he noted: "Presumably suppression was the better part of valour." [20]

Pankhurst had not been without support, however. In the February issue of *Solidarity*, Eden and Cedar Paul contested the accuracy of the present version of Pankhurst's letter, which, they insisted, had been translated three times before it reached *The Call*. It had first been published in Britain by the *Newcastle Daily*, whose version was based on a translation into Swedish that appeared in *Folkets Dagblad Politiken*, "the organ of the Swedish Bolsheviks," that was itself based on the Russian translation published in *Communist International*. And the Pauls were, of course, fully supportive of Pankhurst's antiparliamentary position. [21]

The February 1920 issue of *Solidarity* also contained support for the anti-parliamentary position from Jack Tanner, the paper's editor. The question needed to be settled before the Communist Party was formed. "We say that no good can be got from Parliamentarism," he wrote. "The energy, time and money expended in it is absolutely wasted." Aspiring "to function in what is acknowledged to be an effete and rotten institution, and which has to be abolished before real changes can be brought about, seems to us to show a lack of revolutionary principles." The fight in Britain would "take place in the industrial field."

The WSF position was similarly boosted, that same month, by a letter from William Gallacher on behalf of the Scottish Workers' Council, a group he described as "definitely anti-Parliamentarian." Moreover, in Scotland the "rank and file" of the ILP was becoming "more and more disgusted with the thought of Parliament, and the Soviets or Workers' Councils are being supported by almost every branch." The BSP "doesn't count at all here. I say this as one who has been a member since its inception."[22]

From Pankhurst's point of view, Lenin's failure to support the position of those she believed were the *real* British Bolsheviks was a blow — but not a decisive one. He seemed to be saying that the issue was less important than getting all the would-be Communist groups into a single party. In any case, Lenin was not the Pope! He and Zinoviev, who chaired the Third International, might support the BSP's view, as Tom Quelch had claimed, but was this the view of the movement as a whole? At first it seemed not.

Early in March, *The Call* reported that at the Third International conference in Amsterdam it had been decided that the basis for Communist unity in Britain

> should be disconnection from any body affiliated to the Second International, or from any "social patriotic" organisation. The B.S.P. delegates explained fully the general position of the working class movement in this country and the loose structure and composition of the Labour Party, but failed to induce the delegates to alter the general terms of the resolution.[23]

It was against this background, with Pankhurst and the WSF believing that they were in tune with the advance guard of the international revolutionary movement, that the efforts to create a British Communist Party continued. The SLP, which supported parliamentary participation but was quite unwilling to contemplate Labour Party affiliation, had already dropped out of the negotiations by this time, leaving a fragment of its former leadership, the Communist Unity Group, still participating in the process.[24]

On 8 May the *Dreadnought* published a communication from the Amsterdam Sub-Bureau: "We strongly appeal to our English friends to unite on the basis of 'no affiliation to the Labour Party.' "[25] This was the policy that Pankhurst had already persuaded the "Unity Conference" of 24 April (at which the SLP was not represented) to adopt. To have followed the advice from Amsterdam would still leave open the more fundamental question of participation or abstention in parliamentary elections. But the Sub-Bureau's intervention must have seemed like a strong nudge in the desired direction. What the editor and readers of the *Dreadnought* did not know was that the Comintern had revoked the mandate of the Amsterdam group six days earlier on the grounds that it had consistently opposed the views of the Comintern central executive in Moscow.[26]

The Call announced this dramatic change on 20 May, but two days later the *Dreadnought* was still taking comfort in its own interpretation of the Third International executive's statement on parliamentary political action:

> We are glad to notice that the Executive of the Third International has declared that the "most vital part" of the workers' struggle for Communism "must be outside Parliament." We believe that in this country the struggle outside Parliament would entirely supersede the struggle inside, and that British Communists will discard Parliamentary action in the near future.[27]

By June, *The Call* was reporting progress towards the formation of a united Communist Party. "Hail! The Communist Party," A.A. Watts proclaimed, and pleaded for everyone to put the cause of unity before "minor matters." But parliamentary participation and Labour Party affiliation were anything but minor issues for the WSF. Nor was it prepared to go along with the decision that at the upcoming Unity Conference, provisionally scheduled for 1 August, all participating organizations would be pledged in advance to accept its resolutions and merge their assets. WSF participation must be "conditional upon a referendum of their membership now being taken." But the other participants — at this point essentially just the BSP and the ex-SLP Communist Unity Group (CUG) — were determined to continue without waiting for the outcome of the WSF referendum. This, as Kendall says, "proved a turning point."[28]

A week later, *The Call* was complaining about Pankhurst's tactics after *The Socialist* published a letter from her urging the SLP to participate in the "rank and file convention" but insisting that if the results were "not satisfactory," they would not be bound by outcome." The response from the SLP executive had been "what was to be expected. It is rigid and doctrinaire, but quite honest. The Calvinists of the Socialist movement will have nothing to do with the proposed convention. They do not favour Miss Pankhurst's brilliant tactic of running away from the unity proceedings in the event of not being able to stampede them."[29]

By this time, however, Pankhurst's tactics had moved on. Believing that the convention was likely to commit the embryonic Communist Party to the "Right Wing" policies it feared, the WSF had called a "preliminary conference" to decide whether to participate in the BSP-CUG event. To this preliminary gathering were summoned "representatives from the various Communist Groups which have lately sprung into being, and from the Social Soviets and Workers' Committees, which accept the Dictatorship of the Proletariat, the Third International and the Soviet System, and which are definitely non-parliamentary and opposed to affiliation to the Labour Party."[30] They met on Saturday, 19 June, in London and declared themselves to be the "Communist Party (British Section of the Third International)."

"A Wrecking Policy" and the Failure of the "Appeal to Caesar"

The decision was explained in the *Dreadnought* the following week. Delegates from the Aberdeen, Croydon, and Hull Communist groups, the Stepney Communist League, the Gorton Socialist Society, the Abstentionist Labour Party, and the Manchester Soviet had met together with those representing the WSF.[31] The SLP's withdrawal from the BSP-centred unity negotiations, along with the non-attendance of the fourth original participant in the process, the South Wales Socialist Society,[32] had, they concluded, left "the right wing in a preponderant position," which it was now using to insist that participants to the August convention "should be bound *beforehand*" to accept its decisions, which were likely to include parliamentary participation and Labour Party affiliation. Therefore, the *Dreadnought* told its readers, "We Revolutionary Communist delegates" decided not to take part in the convention and had instead launched the CP (BSTI).[33] Mark Shipway estimates the initial membership at about six hundred.[34]

The new party's position was made clear. A report on its provisional program by Edgar T. Whitehead, the party's secretary (formerly secretary-treasurer of the Abstentionist Labour Party),[35] explained: "In our opinion it is a matter of first principle absolutely to repudiate the bourgeois instrument of class oppression, Parliament, and to get on with the work of forming the network of Soviets, which will be the corresponding proletarian instrument of political power, not only for maintaining that power, but for seizing that power." The "proletarian ideal of economic democracy" required that the franchise be confined to workers (those fulfilling a "function of social utility"), that voters be "grouped industrially, according to industry, trade, profession or other function of social utility which they fulfil," and that delegates be subject to "recall and control by the persons electing them." None of these conditions were met by the rules governing elections to Parliament.[36]

The BSP response was angrily dismissive. *The Call* published extracts from the "Theses of the Executive Committee of the Communist International" declaring that anti-parliamentarism, "in the sense of an absolute and categorical refusal to take part in elections or parliamentary revolutionary work," was "a naïve, childish doctrine." This was, the paper said, "a sufficient answer to the attempts of Sylvia Pankhurst and her grandiose 'Communist Party, British Section of the Third International' to sabotage the efforts now being made to establish a genuine Communist Party."[37]

It fell to A.A. Watts — whose name was always followed by "LCC" in *The Call,* to remind readers of his role as a member of the London County Council — to continue the attack on the front page of the paper two weeks later. He regretted that "one person and one party (?) thought themselves of so much importance as to set themselves above the great principle of unity":

I refer to Miss Sylvia Pankhurst and her W.S.F. I cannot condemn too strongly her action — *her* action — in trying to jump the claim and set up a little chandler shop Communist Party of her own. This is emphatically

A Wrecking Policy

I say unhesitatingly to those few whom she inveigled into attendance at "her" conference, "comrades, you are being led into a morass."

Miss Pankhurst appealed to comrade Lenin for his views, hoping to get something from him to support her anarchist views and action; Lenin's views appear on this page. The appeal to Caesar has recoiled upon her.

As regards Lenin's views, Watts was referring to a "wireless message," printed in an oblong box in the middle of the page, that contained the following message "from Lenin to the Provisional Committee of the Communist Party":

> I consider the policy of comrade Sylvia Pankhurst and the Workers' Socialist Federation to be wrong. I personally am in favour of participation and of adhesion to the Labour Party on condition of free and independent Communist activity.

Lenin's view, according to *The Call,* was that the BSP and SLP were "the main potential formers of the CP." The paper also claimed that he hoped that "the I.W.W. and Shop Stewards' Committees" would be "brought into close touch" prior to "complete union."[38]

"Left-Wing" Communism: *Wary Shop Stewards Remain Aloof*

Lenin's authority was again brought to bear the following week when *The Call* published extracts from his extended pamphlet *"Left-Wing" Communism: An Infantile Disorder,* newly, and as yet only partially, translated. Of the ten chapters that had so far been completed, the only ones targeting "infantilism" in specific countries were the fifth, on Germany, and the ninth, on Britain. The latter was based on a report of a speech by Lloyd George, from the *Manchester Guardian,* and otherwise on an article by Pankhurst and the letter from William Gallacher nentioned above, both of which had appeared in a single issue of the *Workers' Dreadnought*, that of 21 February 1920.[39]

Lenin's lead was being followed even before the party was formed. The Second Comintern Congress, which members of "anti-parliamentary" British groups, including Pankhurst, attended, took place between 19 July and 7 August in Petrograd. In a September report on the congress, W. McLaine told how he and Quelch had represented the BSP at the meeting. But "as it drew nearer August 1 we felt so confident that we were truly representative of what the new Communist Party would become that we let it be known that we represented the Party." On its behalf they argued in favour of parliamentary action and they

> also laid down that correct revolutionary tactics for Britain at the present time included application to the Labour Party. All the Shop Stewards and ultra-left delegates from Britain opposed us, but the Congress as a whole agreed with us. Lenin declared that when he wrote his recent booklet he was not sure about the Labour Party question, but had since spoken to many English — and Scotch — comrades and was now convinced that the Communist Party should certainly affiliate.[40]

This may have been the first time that the term *ultra-Left*, which was to become a standard part of Communist Party vocabulary, was used in a British socialist organ, and it is noticeable that the shop stewards — though equally guilty of deviating from "correct revolutionary tactics" — are subtly distinguished from the greater sinners.

Solidarity was certainly skeptical about the claims of the CPGB. As a monthly publication, it commented on the formation of both Communist parties in the same issue. Presenting the shop stewards' and workers' council movements from the perspective of "a looker on" taking an interest in "the progress of the various political parties in red hot pursuit of unity," it expressed surprise at the "lack of originality" in the criticisms of the formation of the CP (BSTI) and its "strictly anti-parliamentary programme," criticisms in which "Lenin is quoted ad lib and the rest is mere abuse." It singled out both Watts's "Wrecking Policy" attack in *The Call* and the "facetious paragraph which culminates in an attempted analysis of Sylvia Pankhurst" in the same week's issue of *The Socialist,* objecting that the latter had referred to her "fundamental instability and erratic character." It was not attempting to defend the CP (BSTI), *Solidarity* declared, but "we would ask for a little more intelligent argument and the use of better weapons than that of abuse." Turning to the more recent formation of the CPGB, *Solidarity* rejected, in line with its syndicalist hostility to "politics," the notion "that the work of the British Communist Party is to be done inside the workshops, factories, mines etc. because as a political party it is outside the realm of industrial activity in the workshops and factories." And, it reported, while Hodgson had supported affiliation to the Labour Party, "lest they should fall victim to [the] 'Infantile Sickness' of the Left Socialists," William Paul had opposed such affiliation, arguing that "while Lenin advocated affiliation it was not understood by Communists that Lenin had the authority of a pope and should not be subjected to criticism like any other Communist." [41] The prospect of the shop stewards' movement throwing in its lot with the CPGB still seemed, at this stage, quite remote.

Gorter Rejects Lenin's Criticism

In September 1920, the *Workers' Dreadnought* published Herman Gorter's "Open Letter to Comrade Lenin" — his response to *"Left-Wing" Communism: An Infantile Disorder.* Gorter began, somewhat sycophantically, by stressing how much he had learned from Lenin. He insisted, however, that Lenin's views on the situation in Western Europe were based on false premises. There were virtually no peasants in Western Europe, but the issue of the reliability of leaders was very much a current preoccupation everywhere: "We still seek leaders *who do not want to dominate the masses* and who will not betray them," he wrote. In the current conditions, Lenin's stress on iron discipline and "the strictest centralisation" was playing into the hands of *"the opportunist elements in the Third International,"* who used his arguments to insulate themselves from criticism.[42] This was very much what the CP (BSTI) wanted to hear. The anti-parliamentary and anti–Labour Party beliefs of a substantial proportion of the earliest and most committed British supporters of soviet democracy seemed, in the late summer and autumn of 1920, to have helped produce a stalemate as far as Communist unity was concerned.

Apart from more or less syndicalist shop stewards and Pankhurst's rival Communist Party, the new CPGB had failed to keep on board the "Calvinists" of the SLP, who, unlike the CP (BSTI), were prepared to accept participation in parliamentary elections but drew a definite line at seeking affiliation to the Labour Party. Even when, a little later, under considerable pressure from the Comintern, unity negotiations were renewed, as well-informed an observer as the *New Statesman* remained skeptical of any reconciliation between these apparently irreconcilable groupings:

> There are now three separate Communist Parties — the Communist Party of Great Britain, the (largely Scottish) Communist Labour Party, and Miss Pankhurst's Communist Party (British Section of the Third International). In addition the old-established Socialist Labour Party sees itself as a Communist body, and the English and Scottish organisations of Workers' Committees and the Left Wing group of the I.L.P. have also been invited to take part in the Communist Unity negotiations. All these bodies between them have only quite a small number of members, but it is very doubtful whether they will be able, even under strict orders from Moscow, to combine into a single effective organisation.[43]

But events were speedily to demonstrate that this seriously underestimated the strength of the "strict orders from Moscow," which produced a "Communist unity" that amounted to a surrender to the CPGB and its positions on the part of many — but, as we shall also see, by no means all — of those who saw themselves as "Left" Communists.

The Short but Eventful Life of the CP (BSTI)

On New Year's Day 1921, on the eve of its disappearance as a separate entity, the secretary of the CP (BSTI), Edgar Whitehead, writing in the *Dreadnought,* expressed his sadness that after six months of the party's life its membership still stood at about six hundred — a tenth of what its founders had hoped for. But its tiny size did not inhibit the party's optimism about the imminent revolutionary prospects for Britain nor lessen its conviction that it and not the "Right Wing" Communists, with their "revolutionary parliamentarism," were on the right track for bringing these possibilities to fruition.

In the weeks following the formation of the CPGB, anyone relying on the *Workers' Dreadnought* to estimate the likelihood of the CP (BSTI) achieving "Communist unity" with that organization would have been as skeptical as the *New Statesman.* As one *Dreadnought* contributor, John Nicholson, put it: "With us the question of Political Action does not arise. It is a delusion."[44]

The summer and early autumn of 1920 was a period during which the expectations of the would-be revolutionary Left for an all-out assault on capitalism seemed, for a short while, about to be realized. With Britain apparently preparing to side actively with Poland in its war with Russia, virtually the entire Labour movement was united in setting up councils of action at national and local levels and in threatening a general strike if Lloyd George, under pressure to intervene from Churchill and the French government, went ahead with this plan.[45]

Whitehead was keen to establish a distinctly different approach to the councils of action, one that clearly originated from the party's commitment to soviet democracy. Members of the CPGB (the "Maiden Lane Communists," he called them) were demanding representation of their party on the national body and presumably also on local councils of action. But, Whitehead argued:

> Such a course can only confuse class-conscious industrialists and bring discredit on Communism by the advocacy of false principles of [the] delegation of power. For consider. The "action" contemplated

is industrial action, and the people who are going to act are industrial workers. And what right or mandate has the Communist Party to decide on such action? And if they do not know, I am sure the Workshop Movement of this country will very quickly give them the information.

Not that the CP (BSTI) intended or advocated leaving the councils of action to their own devices. On the contrary, members were urged to get elected to them as delegates from "industrial bodies, able to take part from an unfettered Communist standpoint." Their prime mission should be to "SOVIETISE THE COUNCILS OF ACTION." To accomplish this they needed to persuade the local councils to admit only delegates "from such bodies as are to be called upon to act: Trade Union branches, Shop Committees, and organised industrialists." Councils should "knock out all political representation," and delegates at all levels should be subject to "instant recall." With a national council of action organized along these lines, it would, he said, be possible not only "to stop the war on Russia, but to destroy the Capitalist System and substitute economic equality and Communism just as soon as the workers wanted to do so." [46]

The CPGB's interpretation of soviet democracy was putting increasing stress on the "leading role" of the party, exercised by directly establishing as many of its members as possible in positions of power and influence. The "Left Communists" of the CP (BSTI) still aspired to such a leading role, but it had to be one exercised in accordance with the principles of soviet or working-class democracy as they understood them. This meant refusing all possible shortcuts, such as getting the party represented directly on the councils of action. Rather, it would seek the support and endorsement of workers at the base — shop-floor or branch — level. Left Communists would act as delegates only for workers in "industrial" organizations, and they would accept delegation only once the workers had agreed to the "unfettered Communist standpoint." [47] This was, to put it mildly, setting the bar very high. As a very long-term strategy, it might have been a viable and non-manipulative approach to the problem of converting the working class to the party's position and advancing its cause. But the CP (BSTI) was an unlikely convert to the inevitability of gradualism. It was impatient for revolution tomorrow — if not sooner.

The Communist published "The Conditions for Admission to the Third International," which stressed that Communist parties were to be organized "on the principle of democratic centralisation" with Communist "nuclei" in unions and other working-class organizations "completely subordinate to the general control of the Party."[48] It was going to be difficult to reconcile such demands with the strategy to which the CP (BSTI) was committing itself with regard to the councils of action. Yet its very name demonstrated that the party was committed to being part of the International; indeed, it insisted that it was already one of its sections.

The way the party was being pulled, and was pulling itself, in opposite directions became clear a fortnight later, when, in the same issue of the *Dreadnought* that contained Gorter's defence of the Left Communist position, Pankhurst's editorial "A Call from the Third International" appeared. The Comintern executive wanted to hold a conference, within four months, to form a single British Communist Party on the basis of Zinoviev's theses that the Comintern congress had endorsed. Pankhurst regretted that the text of the theses might not be "in the hands of our members, in order that delegates might have been fully instructed" in time for the forthcoming CP (BSTI) conference. But, in words that inevitably suggest religious conversion, she insisted that "our Party has been received into the Third International." The International could only be "an International of action" if its decisions were binding on its component parts. She recognized the problems that this created for her party: "The fact that in some respects the tactical policy of the theses (though not its essential object and theory) differs from what has been our own, lends great responsibility to our Party's discussion of the theses."[49]

While still clearly at odds with the "Right-Wing" Communists, Pankhurst had been persuaded during the international congress in Moscow that its demand for the unification of Communist parties and groups in Britain must be accepted.[50] The National Inaugural Conference of the CP (BSTI) took place in Manchester on 18 and 19 September. The delegates agreed to participate in the unity conference that the Comintern executive had proposed but also to call "another conference of our own in December," to which the Scottish Communist Labour Party and all other groups "with principles which correspond with our own" would be invited. The affiliation conditions of the Third International were read and adopted "with the reservation that the passages referring to discipline to be applied to Parliamentary representatives does not apply to our Party, which does not take parliamentary action."[51]

Just a few weeks before, Whitehead had issued branch circular No. 5: "Work Through Industrial and Non-Party Mass Organisations of Our Class." The circular instructed members to accept delegation from union bodies only when this did not "necessitate denial of their Communist principles," to refuse otherwise to act as delegates, and to "seek to capture the local Trades and Labour Councils" not by means of direct affiliation but "through their industrial organisations." Once "captured," these bodies should be transformed "into purely TRADES COUNCILS" by the exclusion of "all political parties such as I.L.P. branches and local Labour Parties." Furthermore, "all members of the Party exercising power and influence on the industrial field should refrain from outdoor propaganda and confine themselves to the industrial field."[52]

At the CP (BSTI) conference Pankhurst had moved "that the Communist Party must make itself able to control the industrial policy of the workers in order that it may direct them in mass industrial action leading to revolution and the overthrow of the capitalist system. After the overthrow of capitalism the Communist Party must maintain its control in order that the industries may be administered on Communist principles." Delegates must have been surprised, or even alarmed, at this, but they dutifully passed the motion and agreed to withdraw — "provisionally" — circular No. 5, in which Whitehead had taken his stand.[53]

But it is clear that Pankhurst had not really been converted from her anti-parliamentary views. She did not believe that parliamentary participation would be "so rigidly enforced as to hinder us in revolutionary action," and there was, she insisted, "a growing tendency in the Third International to reverse the policy with which we disagree." She predicted that, what with the growing weight of "Communist abstentionists" in many countries, the next congress of the International would reverse, or at least "greatly modify," the policy on parliamentary participation. It was already so "hedged around with conditions that it seems like a poor shrivelled chrysalis from which the butterfly has flown away, a chrysalis that is just left as a memorial to a past epoch, in order not to seem disrespectful of the honoured Socialist dead, who believed in it in the days that are gone." [54]

It was soon after this that the *Dreadnought* reported the arrest for sedition of its editor by "Scotland Yard sleuths." [55] The prosecution, carried out under the draconian Defence of the Realm Act, arose as a result of an article titled "Discontent on the Lower Deck," which had appeared in the paper on 16 October. Convicted of attempting to cause disaffection in the armed services, Pankhurst, who had fallen foul of DORA before and who had served a number of prison sentences in her suffragette days, found herself sentenced to six months.

Meanwhile, the CP (BSTI) was preparing for its own special conference in Cardiff in December as well as for the Comintern "unity" conference with the CPGB and others the following month. The task of the first of these was to accept — or reject — what Whitehead, in his "National Secretary's Notes," referred to as "the remaining conditions of affiliation to the Moscow International." Embarrassingly, Whitehead himself had received no copy of the theses that the Cardiff conference was supposed to accept, and no pamphlet version was going to be available in time to be put into the hands of branches or even their delegates. But he undertook "to extract as far as possible, the contentious points and major matters for decision" and to publish them in the paper starting the following week "so that delegates, as far as possible, can be mandated by Branches how to vote on the main points." As for the January conference, Whitehead supported the policy of the Communist Labour Party to accept the theses, which would be followed by an effort to "get them altered by a special demand from the United British Party *after* the merging." Whitehead concluded that "our Scottish friends" were urging that, without the help of the CP (BSTI), they would have to "carry on the devil of a struggle to keep the British Revolutionary Movement sound and clear." [56]

A week later, Whitehead's "National Secretary's Notes" highlighted the "stupendous task" facing the CP (BSTI) conference in Cardiff. The theses presented to the Communist International Congress amounted to "a thick book of one hundred and twenty pages." The theses, statutes, and conditions that had been adopted were laid out in a similar volume of eighty-one pages. The previous conference of the CP (BSTI) had resolved in favour of sixteen of the conditions — but this covered fewer than five of the pages, leaving seventy-six to be somehow dealt with at Cardiff. And how were branches to mandate their delegates when they were unable to obtain copies of the document?

To extract the most contentious parts, as he had previously undertaken to do, was very difficult, he insisted, "because the whole thing hangs together in such a way that it would be unfair to the Communist International to extract one small portion away from its context." It was clear that the real task of the party's conference was to decide whether to "remain affiliated to the Communist International" or to "remain untrammelled by Moscow discipline." The first would entail accepting all the conditions and "theses" and passing "a statute which condemns anti-parliamentarism as a naïve and childish doctrine that cannot bear criticism." Would members accept this? He was now skeptical about the possibility of carrying out "our anti-parliamentary propaganda so as to alter the theses at the next world congress" in the merged party. As he pointed out, the last of the Third International's 21 conditions, regarding the expulsion of dissident elements, would seem to mean that "if any Comrade speaks against the thesis on 'Revolutionary Parliamentarism' he risks immediate expulsion." [57]

The Cardiff conference was poorly attended, but delegates voted by 15 to 3 to accept the theses. The "decisive factor" in the vote had, it seemed, been the plea of "Comrade Leslie" — whom Kendall describes as having "returned from a difficult and adventurous trip to Soviet Russia"[58]— who "pictured the amazement" of the hard-pressed Russian workers at the sight of conference delegates "academically splitting hairs over dialectical discussions of Parliamentarism." This speech, said Whitehead, "put the finishing touch on any waverers present, and every vote, with the exception of those definitely mandated ones, with strict instructions to vote against acceptance, went for a united party."[59] Nevertheless, there were, unsurprisingly, clear signs of discontent in the branches. At Christmas, Fred Alder of the Manchester division reported that the four local groups were "absolutely solid" in their insistence on retaining the right to oppose the Comintern theses "to the *last ditch* and the *last man,*" while Norah Smyth's Bow branch wanted a referendum on whether members were in favour of participating in the unity conference at all.[60]

By the new year, Whitehead was having to deny the contention of the Gorton branch that the CP (BSTI) executive was proposing that "we should eat our programme in the interests of Communist Unity," while the Sheffield and Altrincham branches joined the call for a referendum and from Manchester came the criticism that the executive had already reneged on a commitment to hold one.[61] The Manchester branches withdrew in protest a week later, though the executive insisted that "our Party is better conducted from the point of view of rank and file control, soviet principles regarding party government, Communist principles as regards election and payment of party officers, than any other party."[62]

With the acting editorship of the *Dreadnought* alternating between Jack O'Sullivan and Norah Smyth, the following week saw an editorial from the still incarcerated editor. Pankhurst's argument, along the lines of the view Whitehead had earlier attributed to the CLP, seemed oblivious to the secretary's concerns about the extreme unlikelihood of any sort of "party within the party" being tolerated, even temporarily.

Were she free to attend the conference, she would, she said, support the creation of a united party, but she would do so on the basis that "the Left Wing elements keep together and form a strong, compact, block within the Party. Lenin advised this when I discussed the question with him in Moscow, and I think the advice is sound. The Left block should have its own convenors, and its own special sittings, prior to Party conferences, to decide its policy." With or without Lenin's alleged advice, this was clearly not at all the sort of unity that was going to be tolerated by the Third International, any more than would Pankhurst's further demands that the "Left elements" should be free to campaign for their policies "in the Party and in the Third International as a whole" and that the party's executive, elected by its conference, should be "subject to recall by a special Party Conference called on the initiative of one-third of the branches." Whether or not a "merger" was achieved, concluded Pankhurst, the *Dreadnought* would become "an independent organ giving independent support to the Communist Party from a Left Wing standpoint."[63]

The SLP had for years been warning other socialist groups of the importance of establishing ownership and control of their own press, as it had done in the case of *The Socialist* and the Socialist Labour Press. When the wartime split in the BSP occurred, it was evident that this party did not fall into the same category, and it had lost control of *Justice*. Now the same sort of thing seemed to be happening with the *Dreadnought*. The day after Pankhurst's editorial appeared, a meeting of the CP (BSTI) executive declared that the paper was no longer the official organ of the party. The *Dreadnought* seemed unshaken by this decision: "This formal change in no way affects the policy or the financial position of the paper, because the Party has never made itself responsible for any part of the burden of maintaining it."

A statement in the same issue, signed "A.T.," defended Pankhurst's position. To be independent had not been her choice. She had made repeated requests to form a *Dreadnought* finance committee. The editor should not, as proposed, be appointed by the executive but by the party as a whole, "subject to recall by a special conference . . .

on requisition of 1/3 of the branches." The idea of letting "little sub-committees of the members of the Party who live in London, the most reactionary centre of the movement put a brake on the policy of officials elected by the national movement" was to be resisted.[64] On 22 January, the *Dreadnought*'s masthead was changed from "Organ of the Communist Party" to "For International Communism."

In the meantime, while the Staines branch declared itself willing to accept the whole of the theses and statutes without a referendum, others took a very different view. There were complaints that insufficient copies of these documents had been sent to branches, while the Sheffield branch favoured participating in the unity conference only if it was "not binding." Portsmouth protested against the executive committee's decision to send ballot papers only to branches in which half the membership had requested a referendum and insisted that ballots should have been sent for each member rather than one per branch: "Surely, if we believe in the principles of Soviet rule, we should apply it to our own Party."[65]

Whitehead's well-founded doubts about whether "the Left" would be allowed to pursue its own agenda in the united party had deterred neither Pankhurst nor the most determined opponents of parliamentarism in the branches. They were supported in the supposition that they would be able to carry on advocating "Left-Wing Communism" within the united party by an article by William Leslie entitled, rather grandly, "An Appeal to Communist Comrades of Great Britain and Ireland." He acknowledged that the "Theses and Statutes" had been put together by the hastily convened second congress of the new International. There was "nothing to hinder *us*," he wrote, from the plan "to unite into one Party where we can mould a real National Programme to amend these Theses and Statutes at the coming Third Congress of the Third International."[66]

At last, the unity conference took place on 29 and 30 January in Leeds, and the short life of the CP (BSTI) came to an end. A leader in the edition of the *Dreadnought* following the conference, presumably written by Jack O'Sullivan, saw the policies of the paper justified by the events and took it for granted that "the new Party" was going to be very different from "the ex-CP of Great Britain." The new party "should be resonant to the demands and the views of the rank and file, and it should avoid the pitfall of organisations where leaders only have a voice, to the detriment of full expression of opinion by even the humblest member."[67]

The "Left Communists" who had created the CP (BSTI) saw themselves as the true revolutionaries. The BSP and its successor, the CPGB, had always been highly suspect. Both remained tainted with "Hyndmanism," according to the *Dreadnought* editorial quoted just above. For the "Lefts," the dictatorship of the proletariat simply described a soviet system from which those unwilling to accept the socialist principle that all should contribute to the general good of society were excluded. Soviet democracy was so superior to the representative, parliamentary, democracy of bourgeois society that to engage at all in conventional electoral politics was both pointless and confusingly inconsistent.

The belief that the new democracy had to be more genuine, more truly egalitarian, and that, in its organization and its procedures, a Communist Party should prefigure the soviet democracy of the future by applying the norms of that democracy to itself is evident from the concerns, expressed in letters and reports from branches as well as in editorials and articles in the *Dreadnought*, about all aspects of the unity process. All this was accompanied by the equally strong desire to demonstrate maximum solidarity with the world revolution and to play a proper part in the Third International that was the agent of that revolution. The requirement that the anti-parliamentary stance be abandoned put these aspirations in conflict with each other. Pankhurst's notion of the International was not one of a rigid organization ruled by the principle of "democratic centralism." Rather, it was one in which power was not concentrated exclusively in Moscow and where radical factions could fight for their corner. The unity conference at the end of January 1921 saw the end of the CP (BSTI), but it was not the end of "Left Communism" in Britain or of the *Workers' Dreadnought* as its advocate. But before we return to that strand of the story of soviet democracy in Britain, it will be helpful to explore the attitudes of the other main left-wing organization to which the plea for Communist unity was directed — the Socialist Labour Party.

10

The Socialist Labour Party

Some Limits of SLP Sectarianism

Pankhurst and the *Dreadnought* were soon to return to their position as left-wing opponents of the "orthodox" Communists, advocating soviet democracy as vehemently as ever, while the CP (BSTI) as such was absorbed — with little trace — into the CPGB. By contrast, the Socialist Labour Party was to remain outside and hostile to the CP. True, some of its most prominent members formed the Communist Unity Group (CUG) in 1920 and subsequently enjoyed high-profile roles in the CPGB. True, also, there continued to be plenty of defections to the CP, both of members and entire branches. But, even though the issue of "unity" with the Communists remained a controversial issue within the SLP, as an organization, however much dwindled from its (not exactly massive) former size, it remained obdurate.

The SLP's refusal to take part in the initial formation of the CPGB in the summer of 1920 or in the Leeds Unity Conference in January of 1921, or to merge itself with the Communist Party subsequently, was less clearly related to the notion of soviet democracy than is the case with the hesitations of the CP (BSTI) and Pankhurst's subsequent position in the *Workers' Dreadnought*. But there was a relationship nevertheless. In his account of the SLP, *The Origins of British Bolshevism*, Raymond Challinor cites the 1920 SLP conference report, which gave the party's membership as 1,258, "almost a third of whom had joined in 1919." And contrary to what he calls the "myth" that "the SLP was largely confined to skilled engineers on the Clyde," he concludes that "probably by 1920 four-fifths of the SLP's membership lay South of the Border."[1] The SLP and its paper were based in Glasgow, but it is certainly true that branches from all parts of the UK featured in conference proceedings and branch reports published in *The Socialist*. While the January 1915 edition of *The Socialist* lists only one Scottish branch (Glasgow) and twelve English ones (Birmingham, Bristol, Croydon, Derby, Dewsbury, Leeds, Newcastle, Nottingham, Oxford, Sheffield, Southampton, and Wallsend-on-Tyne), the branch directory at the end of 1919 listed far more Scottish — and English — branches, totalling forty-four in all.[2] Some, at least, seem to have been active. The issue of 6 May 1920, for example, included branch reports from Oxford, Mid-Rhondda, Dewsbury, Belfast, Birmingham, Birkenhead, Coventry, Sheffield, Fleetwood, Edinburgh, and Paisley. As Challinor says, the SLP was by no means confined to Scotland.

In an earlier chapter we saw how the SLP had been very quick to identify itself as the "Bolshevik" party of Britain. Challinor cites several instances where this identification was made both by the SLP itself and on at least one occasion by no less than Lenin himself. And as late as 10 March 1921, after having rejected two opportunities to merge with the CPGB, the SLP was still insisting, in *The Socialist,* that "we belong to the Third International, and we are Bolsheviks." In Challinor's account, the problem was Lenin's failure to understand the British socialist and labour movements and his consequent insistence on Labour Party affiliation.[3] Seen in this light, it was a case of the SLP trying to be, if not more Catholic than the Pope, more genuinely Bolshevik than the Russian Bolsheviks' preferred collaborators in Britain. But on closer examination the position seems to have been, as is so often the case, rather more complicated. Before examining the party's version of soviet democracy and the — surprisingly "un-Bolshevik" — view it had of the "Dictatorship of the Proletariat," it is worth taking a look at the extent to which the sectarianism and dogmatism often alleged at the time, and widely taken for granted subsequently, was actually reflected in the party's principal organ, *The Socialist*.

There is no shortage of instances that may illustrate the self-congratulatory isolationism and sectarianism for which the SLP was noted. But this characterization is misleading if presented as the whole picture. At the time, what was striking about the SLP was its differences from other socialist organizations in Britain; today one is likely as frequently to notice the similarities. It is difficult to escape from a sort of template of total left-wing sectarianism derived from later times when one considers the SLP, but the attempt needs to be made if its nature is to be understood.

The SLP published a wide range of works by Marx, Engels, Bebel, and Kautsky, as well as those of "our late Comrade Daniel De Leon," whose portrait was advertised for sale in *The Socialist* following his death in 1914.[4] De Leon remained central to the SLP's distinctive approach to Marxism. One might expect *The Socialist* to be constantly invoking the authority of Karl Marx, but in fact he is mentioned quite sparingly, except in articles that specifically discuss Marxist theory. Though *The Socialist* was always ready to point out the "incorrect" positions taken by other socialist groups, and De Leonist coinings such as "fakir" found their way into the language of its publications (and indeed became more frequent again in the paper's latter days), some sense of membership in a common movement was always present. For example, early in 1921, when Helen Crawford, a prominent member of the ILP "Left Wing" and later of the CPGB, complained about *The Socialist*'s erroneous report that she was going to stand against John Maclean in the Gorbals election, the editor printed an apology in which he referred to her as "our comrade."[5] And the SLP shared many points of reference with the rest of the British socialist movement.

Like other socialist organs in Britain, *The Socialist* would mark the March anniversary of the Paris Commune with a special supplement and, in an issue that must have gone to press before the March 1917 news from Russia could be noted, by the reprinting of an 1890 article by William Morris that might just as well have appeared in the pages of one of its rivals almost anywhere on the British Left.[6] Material from other non-SLP sources appeared frequently in the paper. The December 1915 edition, for example, featured both extracts from Brailsford's *War of Steel and Gold* and Tolstoy's anti-militarist writings. In 1917, J. Walton Newbold, of the ILP, appeared as a contributor on several occasions (in the November issue, for example).

Many other works that were far from supportive of SLP orthodoxy were praised from time to time. In the space of little over a month in the summer of 1920, James Clunie, reviewing *Economic Democracy,* by Major C.H. Douglas, the apostle of Social Credit, thought it "in many ways a good book," while Tawney's *Acquisitive Society,* published by the Fabian Society, was declared "epoch-making." Similarly, R.W. Postgate's *The Bolshevik Theory* was described, again by Clunie, as "a valuable contribution to the literature on the Russian Revolution," though he added, making a claim that might well be treated with a degree of skepticism: "Note. We would like to impress upon Mr. Postgate that the S.L.P. did NOT expel all its active members in 1920. Active S.L.Pers are never expelled."[7] Much later, at the end of 1922, when *The Socialist* had again been reduced to monthly publication, a December review of Postgate's *Out of the Past: Some Revolutionary Sketches* praised his treatment of Blanqui as being "as fascinating as a good short story." Later still, in the issue of March 1923, John Henderson cited Brailsford's *The Russian Workers' Republic* in support of his argument on "Moscow and the S.L.P."

Nevertheless, suspicion of "intellectuals" manifested itself from time to time. "We of the working class have nothing to thank Messieurs les Intellectuals for," wrote one regular contributor, Jay Hen, in 1920. "They have ever attempted to deflect us into the Serbonian Bogs of Reformism."[8] And in November 1921, Henderson — who at various times held the positions of national secretary of the SLP and editor of *The Socialist,* as well as secretary of the Industrial Unionist Groups in the Amalgamated Engineering Union — dismissed guild socialism as an attempt to create "a 'safety valve' for those 'social superiors' of the workers, namely the intellectual middle-class whose theory of 'rent of ability' has now led them to forsake the propagation of State Capitalism, and to consider how to compromise with the ever-growing advocacy of Industrial Administration by the workers for the workers." This statement appeared in a review of G.D.H. Cole's *Workers' Control* pamphlets. The following week, in a contribution titled "A Critical Examination of Guild Socialism," Henderson concluded that the movement would result in a state of affairs where "instead of keeping up Capitalist masters, the workers, by the surplus wealth they produce, will keep up an intellectual despotism." [9]

But not all contemporary "intellectual" currents were dismissed in such a wholesale way. In 1921, D.J. Williams, reviewing the Plebs League's cheap edition of the Pauls' *Creative Revolution,* applauded the attempt to "apply the new Freudian psychology to the practice of mass action. Psycho-analysis does for psychology what the materialist conception of the study of history did for the study of history." [10] The Pauls — if not Sigmund Freud — had been close to the SLP with their insistence on "ergatocracy." But *The Socialist* often had positive things to say about ideas from sources far more distant, even remote, from the party.

In 1918, *The Socialist* carried a largely favourable review of J.A. Hobson's *Democracy After the War.* Hobson's presentation of the problems with the parliamentary system were, the reviewer said, "brilliantly worked out." However, not being a "Marxist Socialist," Hobson came to grief when it came to solutions. [11] Even the proportional representation advocate J. Humphreys's *Electoral Reform* was not ignored, its reviewer noting that "in political democracy proportional representation is certainly the ideal method of voting and is undoubtedly the most democratic," albeit adding that in view of the imminence of the infinitely more democratic "industrial republic" there was no point in tinkering with the current electoral system. [12] A brief notice of Walter Citrine's

The Labour Chairman, published by the Labour Publishing Company, concluded: "May it help to aid the efficiency of the movement."[13]

Literary figures such as Jack London and, more surprisingly, George Eliot were occasionally recommended to readers.[14] Such authors could be attacked, too, when they had the temerity to venture into what the SLP regarded as its own territory. In 1920, Jay Hen mocked "Mr 'Hilarious' Belloc, the Intellectual Harlot," while the following year, another regular contributor to *The Socialist,* Tom Anderson, urged, much more gently, "Think it over, my dear Belloc," and concluded: "I admire your 'Hills and Sea' but in politics and religion you are out of it entirely."[15] Yet the phrase "servile state," which originated from the book of that name by the non-socialist Hilaire Belloc, was just as likely to appear in the pages of *The Socialist* as in other left-wing publications and was used in an editorial as late as September 1921.[16]

Nor was the SLP as isolated from other parts of the Left — at least when real threats loomed — as its "Calvinistic" reputation might suggest. When one of its Birmingham members, William Holliday, was convicted under the Defence of the Real Act (DORA) in 1916 as a result of his anti-war speeches in the Bull Ring, *The Socialist* set up an appeal fund. Donations included contributions from ILP and BSP branches, the Bristol Socialist Sunday School, and the Glasgow Clarion Scouts.[17] This was not a one-way street. However much distaste the SLP had for other socialist organizations, it always rallied to their support when they in turn were threatened by suppression. Admittedly, this could be done very back-handedly, as it was in the issue of January 1918: "As consistent opponents of certain melancholy and nebulous theories scraped together and called Guild Socialism we wish to record our protest against the attempt to suppress their meetings in London. The S.L.P. believes in free speech for everybody, because only thereby can we consistently claim the liberty of free discussion ourselves." Not, we may note, an attitude to free speech that would normally be characterized as "Bolshevik."

The formation of the CPGB was followed by what the SLP perceived as a vicious and unprincipled attack on its own organization by the new party.[18] When, in February 1921, it was reported that CP branches were not allowed to sell the SLP paper, *The Socialist* referred to a report in the *Workers' Dreadnought* "that a sinister resolution was put forward at the Leeds Unity Conference, to the effect 'that nothing but official literature should be handled and sold by the members of the Communist Party.'" In contrast, it claimed, "in the central shop of the S.L.P. and any one of our branches, one may purchase 'The Worker,' 'Workers' Dreadnought,' 'Communist,' 'Plebs' and last but by no means least the 'Socialist' along with other revolutionary literature." There were limits, however: "Only we must protect the workers against reformist stuff." [19] But there was no suggestion that such "protection" should extend beyond *failing to sell* ILP and other "reformist" publications. As Challinor says of the Communist ban, this was "a new departure in British politics." [20] Again, it marks another way in which the SLP seems more "old-style British Left" than "new Bolshevik." Two years later, admittedly in a context where the paper was struggling to survive, *The Socialist* carried advertisements for the *Workers' Dreadnought, Plebs,* and *The Worker.* Even though such ideas did not entirely correspond to the position of the SLP, the ad for the *Dreadnought* proclaimed: "For Pure Communism. No Parliamentarism. One Industrial Union of Workshop Committees." [21]

"Jokes and funny stories may serve some purpose but do not serve the purpose of the Revolution," a "Management Announcement" concerning the future of the paper solemnly declared in August 1921, thus reinforcing the image of the SLP as an organization composed exclusively of dour, humourless dogmatists. Yet just over a month later there appeared on the same page of *The Socialist* "A Story About a Story" and "Dan Dusty's Jemmy." [22] The attempt, in 1922, to attract the younger generation by means of a "Children's Corner" in the paper, with stories such as "Papuans, Ploughs and Proletarians" and "The Squire, the Robin and the Boy" by "Uncle Tom," does not have to be read as a sign of un-Calvinistic levity; taken in conjunction with the SLP's Sunday schools, it could be seen as quite the reverse. [23] But even in 1923 there still seem to have been members whose levity was suspect in the minds of the more austere.

The founder of the Young Marxian Schools for Proletarian Education, Tom Mitchell, had been at various times national secretary of the SLP and editor of *The Socialist* and was now managing secretary of the Socialist Labour Press. In a July 1923 piece devoted to congratulating the Glasgow SLP in particular and the party in general on eluding the wiles of "the 'unity at any price' fellows," he detected "yet another element of extraneous matter" in the party: "I refer to the social element, that section of the working class, who, willy nilly find themselves within the revolutionary movement, a class of people who mistake Socialism for Social and who endeavour to make a Socialist club a purely social club."

Nor, in spite of its self-perceived role as the exclusive repository of revolutionary truth, was the SLP immune from the suspicion of the very notion of "leaders" or "leadership" that was so common elsewhere on the pre-Leninist Left in Britain. W.R. Stoker's opening address, as he chaired the 1915 SLP conference, had concluded: "So long as the workers put their trust in leaders — as the term is understood today — so long will they be led astray." Granted, the qualification in the middle of his remark might be seen as an "escape clause," but, all the same, Stoker continued: "The workers by the power of their organisations must emancipate themselves, they alone can do it." And on the centenary of Marx's birth in 1918 an editorial titled "Hero Worship" proclaimed: "The S.L.P. is not a band of hero-worshipers. We do not believe in 'Leaders.'"[24]

This attitude was not something that faded as the Bolshevik stress on "correct" leadership and the "vanguard party" came more to the fore elsewhere. At the beginning of 1922, for example, in its 5 January issue, *The Socialist* included an "Industrial News" supplement that featured adamant opposition to paying trade union officials higher wages than the members they were supposed to represent. The working class needed to guard against the setting up of a labour bureaucracy. The piece concluded that the creation of such a social group constituted "a real danger to the working class — the placing between itself and the capitalist class of an ORGANISED body of PROFESSIONAL LEADERS or 'negotiators.'" This could easily have come from the pen of one of the supporters of the *Clarion* trade union scheme, which had briefly been realized in the form of the National and International General Federation of Trade and Labour Unions a quarter of a century previously. And the aspiration (quoted earlier) of the scheme's promoter, P.J. King, who, in 1898, wished to see the end of "a few well-paid and well-groomed officials" thwarting the wishes of the members that elected and paid them, would have chimed happily enough with the attitude of *The Socialist* in the 1920s.[25]

As regards the conduct of its own affairs, the SLP was always insistent on the reality of its internal democracy. At the time of the CUG breakaway and the expulsion of Bell, MacManus, and Paul, branches were urged to strengthen the hand of the executive by resolutions of support and were exhorted — with the use of the boldface type that *The Socialist* favoured for emphasis — "Remember that **you**, the rank and file, can turn out **your** officials at any time should **you** desire." Just before this, when the issue of unity seemed likely to cause problems at the party's 1921 conference, *The Socialist* declined to attempt to influence the outcome, insisting that "the S.L.P. is a rank and file organisation almost to the point of detail," while its editorial declared: "In the name of the principles of Communism we support whole-heartedly the agitation for free speech and a free press."[26] The decisions of the 1921 conference were confirmed by a referendum of members, as seems to have been the normal practice.[27]

The SLP was insistent on the openness and transparency of its activities. When a branch officer's home was raided in search of "Bolshie Gold," *The Socialist,* having remarked that "the secretary wishes to heavens that he had gold of any kind," asserted that "everything in the S.L.P. is above board and can bear the light of day. The S.L.P. is no hole-and-corner band of conspirators but an organisation of Class Conscious Working Men and Women." All information about the party was readily available from the National Secretary at 50 Renfrew Street, Glasgow. "When applying," the paper added, "state whether [it's] Mr, Mrs, Lieutenant, Sergeant or just plain 'Bobby' trying to 'get on.'"[28]

There is much, then, that tends to modify the image of the SLP as the sectarian body of the British Left par excellence. At the same time, it would be just as misleading to conclude that the S L P was — contrary to its usual image — consistently devoted to internal democracy, free speech, and transparency. Challinor mentions, as a noteworthy S L P activist, Sean McLoughlin, who had previously participated in the Easter Rising and subsequently joined the Socialist party of Ireland before coming to Britain, but he fails to note McLoughlin's eventual fate in the S L P.[29] McLoughlin contributed at least one article to *The Socialist* ("Bourgeois Dictatorship," 1 July 1920) and made tours giving talks to branches. On 8 September 1921, the Leeds branch enthusiastically reported in *The Socialist* that McLoughlin was staying with them for a full week and giving six lectures. And yet the very next week, on 15 September, the following notice appeared: "To whom it May Concern. Sean McLoughlin is not now a member of the Socialist Labour Party, having been expelled by the N.E.C. on September 10th 1921." No further explanation was forthcoming — at least not in the pages of *The Socialist*.

The expulsion may have been amply justified, but the absence of any explanation in the party's weekly paper seems to cohabit uncomfortably with the S L P's declared commitments to openness and democracy. As we shall see a little later, the expulsion of an even more prominent member of the party at the end of 1922 was dealt with in an identical fashion.

Parliament and the Labour Party

While the sticking point regarding unity for the C P (B S T I) before 1921 had been participation in parliamentary politics, for the S L P it was affiliation to the Labour Party. In the run-up to the 1918 election, William Paul, a future defector to the C P via the C U G, stressed that the S L P was "not a parliamentary party." According to him, the S L P believed in contesting parliamentary elections "only as a means of sweeping away all the antiquated institutions that stand in the way of the industrial union controlling the means of production."[30]

The S L P stressed that its position in no way resembled that of the "reformist" organizations. In contrast to the I L P and the B S P, the S L P was "*not* a parliamentary organisation," *The Socialist* insisted at the end of January 1919, and it would not, therefore, "swallow its revolutionary principles by being affiliated to the Labour Party." A week later, Margaret Watt, who seems to have been one of the few female SLP members at this time and was certainly one of the few women to contribute to the paper, claimed that the SLP was the first British socialist party to "direct the attention of the working-class to the impossibility of achieving the social revolution through Parliament." Its candidates participated in elections "for the deliberate purpose of *revolutionary agitation* and with the intention of seeking to *destroy* the Parliamentary institution."[31]

The SLP always declared itself heartily in favour of "unity"— but not if it entailed Labour Party affiliation. "The time has come," *The Socialist* proclaimed on May Day 1919, "for those who are not obsessed with the constitutionalism of bourgeois Parliamentarism to withdraw from the Labour Party once and for all." Labour Party affiliation would put the SLP in a "false position," it reiterated the following year.[32] And, on 1 September 1921, *The Socialist* announced that "the Labour Party reflects the interests of the auctioneers of the Working Class, whose economic domain is the Trade Union Movement."

Throughout the BSP-led unity negotiations and subsequently, its total opposition to Labour Party affiliation kept the SLP from making any agreement to merge its forces. At a meeting on 13 March 1920, Thomas Mitchell, the SLP's national secretary, stressed again that the party "could never agree to sink the identity of the Revolutionary movement in any compromise with Social-Patriots such as the Labour Party." The SLP would agree to unity only if the BSP dropped the idea of Labour affiliation altogether.[33] The prospects were to be no better from the SLP's standpoint after the CPGB was formed. In the issue of 3 March 1921, a *Socialist* editorial titled "The Futility of Parliament" deplored Labour as having "no class war basis":

> Yet the vain, self-important Communists talk about helping the Labour Party into power in order to prove its uselessness, and then the masses will swing over to them! To them indeed. To whom, may we ask? To men, who have not the courage of their own convictions?

The Communist Unity Group and the "Unity Gag": The SLP Declines to Unite

In the early part of 1920, with the protracted negotiations that eventually led to the formation of the Communist Party still not seeming to offer many signs of progress, Tom Bell, Arthur MacManus, and William Paul, who had earlier acted as SLP negotiators for unity, formed their own faction: the Communist Unity Group (CUG). The CUG then proceeded to hold a conference in Nottingham at the same time that the SLP conference was taking place in Carlisle. *The Socialist* responded with a predictable mixture of anger and dismissiveness. A third of those attending the breakaway conference, said its "Headquarter Notes," had no connection with the SLP at all and were in fact "guests of those who wish to disrupt the S.L.P. and make it a Party of compromise." In the same issue, which stressed the party's willingness to negotiate with others to achieve what it called "Revolutionary Unity," the rather oddly titled "Random Reflections on the Carlisle Conference," by Jay Hen, reported:

> The "late Unity Committee" might have been discredited by its self-imposed absence from the Conference. In this connection the Rochdale delegate in reporting that he was deputising for a member of his branch who was attending a "conference" at Nottingham presumably called by the "Unity Committee" created a painful sensation.[34]

Bell, MacManus, and Paul were duly expelled from the SLP. *The Socialist* published messages of support from branches but also reported ones that resolved to "take no action" or, in the case of the Birkenhead branch, to offer "support for the unofficial manifesto" of the CUG. Mitchell, explaining the SLP's rejection of an invitation to take part in another "Communist Unity" meeting at which the CUG was represented, referred to the expulsions and expressed surprise that, at the projected meeting, "the three persons mentioned had equal voting rights with a National Organisation such as the B.S.P."[35] Like Sylvia Pankhurst and her comrades, the SLP was heartened by the fleeting appearance of Third International support for their position. The editor of *The Socialist* put in bold the statement of the ill-fated Amsterdam Sub-Bureau urging "English comrades" to unite on the basis of opposing Labour Party affiliation.[36]

At the beginning of July 1920, under the heading "The Unity Gag: What a Game!" *The Socialist* published a disdainful assessment of the attempts to achieve Communist unity. Signed "T.E.," it began: "After eighteen months [of] useless palavering, after a mountain of labour a mouse has come forth." Pankhurst had started a Communist Party "with the help of a few Anarchist and Anti-Parliamentary elements." But "knowing her fundamental instability and erratic character," the SLP had turned a deaf ear. Pankhurst had "jumped the claim," leaving the BSP and CUG "in a devil of a fix." After a lengthy account of the unity negotiations, and after prophesying that the BSP would "pack the rank and file Convention on August 1st to carry the affiliation to the Labour Party clause," the article concluded that this protracted search for unity might result in the creation of three separate Communist parties. There might be Pankhurst's anti-parliamentary Communist Party, the South Wales Communist Unity Council might form a "Parliamentary Communist Party," and the BSP and CUG might together create a "Labour Party Communist Party." If, as seemed likely, the Left Wing of the ILP joined the latter, this would "only weaken still further the proposed new party."[37]

But, as would soon become evident, there was much more that kept the SLP from uniting with the Communists than simply the question of Labour Party affiliation, crucial though that was.

The Third International and the 21 Conditions

As members of the SLP saw it, the British Communists were responsible for misleading Lenin about Britain. The result was the attempt to impose the inappropriate "21 conditions" of the Third International and all that went with them. At the time of the Leeds Unity Conference early in 1921, *The Socialist* published a letter explaining the non-attendance of "our comrades" of the British Section, International Socialist Labour Party — another small Left grouping founded, according to the letter's signatory, its national secretary

Louis Gordon, in 1912. "We had neither a voice nor a vote in the framing of the 21 points" Gordon complained, and the "tactics of the Thesis were inapplicable to the conditions obtainable in this country." In Britain, "a measure of freedom," which allowed the open advocacy of socialism, prevented "the possibility of police spies and agents provocateurs doing the work of the capitalist class."[38] It was soon evident that this was also the position of the SLP.

As we saw earlier, the party regarded itself as part of the Third International and, in the summer of 1921, duly sent James Clunie as its representative to the Third Congress of that body. He went with the intention of presenting the case of the SLP on Labour Party affiliation and other issues, only to find that the credential committee rejected him "because we had failed to obey the instruction to join up with the Communist Party." But there were "certain tactics stipulated in the thesis and statutes of that Congress" that the SLP "did not approve" and consequently "it was impossible for us to agree with the 21 conditions entirely." Clunie was not even allowed to attend as a "fraternal delegate" but only as a guest.[39] His lengthy report was published in instalments over a period of over two months and then as a six-penny pamphlet, *The Third Communist International: Its Aims and Methods.*[40]

Clunie's report pinpointed the policy positions and practices unacceptable to the SLP. The Communist Party's industrial policy entailed "the formation of Communist nuclei within the trade unions," whose function was to propagate Communist principles. These were "simply political weapons for the achievement of political power" subordinated to the Communist Party.[41] This subordination of "the industrial factor" to "the political faction" was quite the reverse of the SLP position. Logically, it "excluded the cardinal point of industrial unionism which holds to the prime need for control within the workshops." Concluding his report, Clunie summarized his party's position: it aimed at working-class unity and economic control, revolutionary political action to "foment and register this," working-class education, and independence from reformism. And he included a passage that came about as near as anything that ever appeared in *The Socialist* to criticism of the

Bolshevik regime itself. The Bolsheviks' "New Economic Policy" was seen simply as the beginning of a return to capitalism:

> In Russia there is no Communism and the people are not Communists and for many reasons the political dictatorship, necessary as it may have been up to now, has been undermined because of the poverised condition of economic resources and means of production. With the growth of Capitalism in Russia, the proletariat will be drawn more and more to study revolutionary progress from the industrial side. These things point to the absurdity of the Third International imposing its psychological outlook upon the rest of the countries whose conditions dictate otherwise.

The fault did not lie with Lenin, however, who had been ill advised and misled by British Communists.[42] In contrast to the pages of the later *Workers' Dreadnought,* where disillusion and criticism gradually but increasingly manifested themselves in the early 1920s, Lenin's reputation in *The Socialist* remained unsullied right up until his death, which was reported on the front page of the very last issue of the paper, that of February 1924. Indeed, it seemed that, belatedly, Lenin had become aware of what the SLP had been saying all along.

In March 1923, Henderson cited Lenin's speech, "Five Years of the Russian Revolution," delivered at the Fourth Congress of the Communist International, in support of the Socialist Labour position. The "21 points," Lenin was quoted as saying (with *The Socialist*'s usual boldface for emphasis) were "**Russian through and through**. Should some exceptional foreigner master the meaning of our resolution he would **find himself incapable of carrying it out**." Two months earlier, the paper had castigated a once prominent SLP member who had passed through the party on his way from the syndicalism of his *Workers' Committee* pamphlet to the Communist Party: "Mr J.T. Murphy, like many other ex S.L.Pers, got 'drunk' with revolutionary romanticism after having waded through many fine but altogether unnecessary Russian pamphlets on theses and statutes which are now reckoned by Lenin as being useless and unfitting for the people of the western part of the world."[43]

The SLP and the Soviets: A Changing Emphasis

The SLP shared the positive view of the Russian soviets that was so widespread on the British Left, as we have already seen in the party's response to the suppression of the Constituent Assembly. "Government by the Soviets," said *The Socialist* on 13 March 1919, "representing directly in committee, the industrial and social affairs of the common people and reaching the remotest hamlet is a challenge to the class rule of capitalism." And as the paper's editorial on the Easter conference in 1919 put it:

> To the bourgeoisie the unpardonable crime of Revolutionary Socialism in action has been the levity with which the Parliamentary machinery has been treated. In Russia and Hungary, in particular, the National Assemblies have been swept aside to make way for the more proletarian machinery of Soviets or committees, which places complete power in the hands of the masses.[44]

Shortly afterwards, in a piece titled "Let Us Be Communists" that appeared in the 22 May issue, Fred Sylvester explained: "As the Soviets were from the first democratic organisations of soldiers, workers and peasants . . . they are now the unit of the Russian Socialist Republic — the complete expression of the revolutionary movement." And later in the year, in the course of reviewing Ramsay MacDonald's *Parliament and Revolution,* "E.S." presented the usual idealized view of the democratic superiority of the soviet over the parliamentary system:

> A monthly meeting of a Workers' Committee which receives a report of its delegate's activity, considers his recommendations, and instructs his further activity, is more likely to be an institution productive of intelligent membership than an electorate dragooned, cajoled or exhorted once in four, three or one years.[45]

So far, so familiar. But, even during its most "soviet" phase, the SLP was less keen than other enthusiasts for soviet democracy to use the Russian nomenclature. The August 1920 version of the "Platform of the Socialist Labour Party" sketched the "the Communist form of organisation," regarded as "essential for Socialist Communism," as being "dual in character — i.e. industrial and residential." The basic unit would be the "Workshop or Yard Committee," which would send delegates to and be "co-ordinated by the formation of Works or Plant Committees." These would then be represented on the (more familiarly named) Workers' Council, which would also have delegates from the "Residential or Ward Committee, the unit of organisation at the point of residence." The "residential" electorate would consist "only of those who render service to the community." At regional and national levels there would be "Regional or National Administrative Committees." This describes a structure very like other models of ideal soviet democracy but, significantly, with more "British"-sounding titles.[46]

That there might be a good deal more to this than mere choice of vocabulary became clear in 1921, when there was a self-conscious reassertion of the party's De Leonist origins. That March, a very long letter from David Sherriff, secretary of the Glasgow branch, urged a return to "Industrial Unionism as laid down by the Workers' International Industrial Union and spoken to by Daniel De Leon in July 1905." According to Sherriff, during the war "the Anarchist tendency composed of that element known as the 'prominent members'" had gained ground within the SLP. The April 1918 conference had "buried" the 1905 platform, "despite the fact that the conditions of production **here** are no more like those of Russia than night is like day." Sherriff's letter ended with the uncompromising claim that "Daniel De Leon, of the Socialist Labour Party, was the **real** founder of the Third International, **not** Moscow."[47] And, early in 1922, noting the "decision of the Bolshevik Government to revert to a Capitalistic form of industry," the ever-astringent Jay Hen poured scorn on the "parroting of Russian phraseology, and attempts to popularise the Soviet form of government in a country which has long passed the stage when this political form was either possible or desirable."[48]

The Revival of De Leonism:
The "Industrial Republic" and the WIIU

If *The Socialist* avoided overuse of "Russian phraseology," it is noticeable that, from 1921 onwards, there was a resurgence in the paper of the De Leonist equivalent. In several of the issues in the early weeks of 1922 alone, we find expressions such as "taking and holding," "Labour Fakirs" (and the variant used to characterize Communists and their sympathisers: "Marxian Labour Fakirs"), "boring from within," and "pure and simple trades unions." References to De Leon also became more frequent again, usually in contexts intended to underscore his impeccable Marxist credentials, his appreciation by Lenin, and his continued relevance: "Lenin, a really great man, a man at whose feet one would have pleasure in learning, paid a lasting tribute to the work of De Leon as being the greatest contribution to Socialist thought since Marx." [49]

The SLP was, contended the "Platform of the Socialist Labour Party" at the beginning of 1923, "the only political party in this country that blazes the trail to the Workers' Industrial Republic." There was now, significantly, no mention of "residential" organization:

> In place of the Capitalist system the Socialist Labour Party aims to substitute a system of social ownership of the means of production, industrially administered, by the workers, who assume control and direction as well as operation of their industrial affairs.
>
> We, therefore, call upon the wage-workers to organise themselves into a revolutionary party under the banner of the S.L.P., and to organise themselves likewise upon the industrial field into a Socialist Industrial Union, as now exemplified by the Workers' International Industrial Union, in keeping with their political aims, and we call upon all other intelligent citizens to place themselves squarely upon the ground of working class interest and join us in this mighty and noble work.[50]

The Workers' International Industrial Union (WIIU), which is not mentioned in Challinor's *Origins of British Bolshevism* (though its predecessor is), had emerged from the Advocates of Industrial Unionism, a body open to non-SLPers that went back to the early pre-war days of the party.[51] Industrial unionism was the De Leonist version of, or alternative to, soviets — without peasants, soldiers, or, most significantly, direct representatives of political parties. The WIIU revival had much to do with attempting to counter the Red International of Labour Unions (RILU), organized by the Communists internationally, and the Workers' Committee Movement, which, Challinor says, "had degenerated into a CP-dominated rump" by this time.[52] The WIIU began to be brought to the fore again towards the end of 1921, with reports and articles about it appearing in *The Socialist*.[53]

Early in January 1922, as the Sheffield SLP announced the formation of a WIIU group — one sign of the revival — its relationship with the party was becoming the subject of controversy. Throughout January and February, the issue was debated in the paper under the title "The Problem of Policy," the chief protagonists being John Henderson, who had made a hostile "critique" of the RILU in December, and his adversary, Willie Allan.[54] An issue of *The Industrial News* — the organ of the impressively titled Shipbuilding and Engineering Trade Group of the Workers' International Industrial Union and said to be regularly available in no less than sixteen named locations throughout Britain — was published as a supplement to the 5 January edition of *The Socialist*. The following week, Allan complained that, even though Henderson and others acted and spoke as though it were, "the W.I.I.U. is *not* the S.L.P." An editorial note to Allan's letter invited further contributions from readers on "the question of an industrial and political policy," a process that the paper hoped would continue until the Easter conference in order to enable the Party to "openly thrash out the problems of party policy."[55]

Allan favoured participation in the National Workers' Committee (NWC) movement. He presented the choice between the NWC and the WIIU as one of viability: "The N.W.C. policy is practicable. The W.I.I.U. is impossible, both from the point of view of Dubb, who is afraid of losing his funeral benefits, and of the Socialist who does not see the need for a duplication of organisation."[56] Judging from the correspondence in the paper, Allan was not alone in taking this view. But the SLP as a whole was with Henderson. It was, however, much more than a question of which form of organization was the more practical — or perhaps we should say the less impracticable.

For Henderson there were three "cardinal points." The first was "class struggle," with its aim of overthrowing "the political state." Second was the successful establishment of the Socialist Industrial Republic, which, he said, implies "Industrial Administration, and which accordingly implies Industry as the Governmental constituency." Third, there was "the One-ness of the Proletariat" and the organizing of workers on the political as well as on the economic field:

> Taking that position prevents anyone — logically — from working in harmony with, say, the Workers' Committee Movement which aims at "The overthrow of Capitalism, and the setting up of a workers' dictatorship under which a system of workers' control and management of industry shall be developed."
>
> It should be recognised that Socialist Industrial Unionism is not a "post-revolutionary" machine, but a necessary requisite to the accomplishing of the Social Revolution here, in Great Britain where the proletariat, in contradistinction to Russia, is the greatest portion of the population.[57]

How "Bolshevik" was an SLP that, committed to something very like soviet democracy, albeit in the form of "Industrial Unionism" and the "Industrial Republic," rejected the dictatorship of the proletariat? As Henderson had written a few weeks earlier: "Unity at the top can only proceed from unity at the bottom. In this country the proletariat constitutes a majority of the population. When they assume power it is the rule of the majority. Dictatorship of the Proletariat is a nonsensical term in relation to conditions here."[58]

The Dictatorship of the Proletariat and "Civilised" Conflict

The key words in Henderson's statement are the final five: "in relation to conditions here." This was not a rejection of the dictatorship of the proletariat and the Bolsheviks role *in Russia*: "Whatever we may say regarding the Communists in this country, the Russian Communists are earnestly and modestly striving to see World Communism established," declared *The Socialist* on 22 September 1921. A few months later, an editorial note affirmed: "We have always insisted and shall continue to emphasise the fact that our duty as revolutionaries is to study the struggle in Russia in the perspective of Russian circumstances and to stand by her in her struggle against World Capitalism." The blame for the concessions and retreats forced on the Bolsheviks was laid, by William Leslie in 1922, at the door of "the disorganised Proletariat of the advanced countries who were unable to seize economic and political power during the last four years."[59]

It was the absence of "a European or World Proletarian Revolution" that had determined events in Russia. In the view of *The Socialist*, the results were predictable:

> We Marxians know that the Dictatorship of the Proletariat — the wielding of the Political State as a Proletarian State followed (as night does day) in Russia in conformity with the political and economic requirements of that country — it could not have been otherwise. The industrial proletariat was the advance-guard, the revolutionary class, but it was a feeble minority and lacked the material basis for the realisation.[60]

In Britain, the main culprit for the country's failure to come to the aid of the Russian Revolution was, of course, the Communist Party. "Where are the mighty to-day?" Tom Mitchell asked rhetorically in the issue of September 1923: "The mighty who betrayed our Russian Comrades in the first years of the Bolshevik revolution. The mighty who carried such glowing, but false reports about the strength of the revolutionary movement in this country in general and the mighty strength of the C.P.G.B. in particular."

The previous year, during the "Problem of Policy" controversy, Henderson, touching on the issue of the dictatorship of the proletariat, had complained that too many on the Left had their "feet in Great Britain, but their heads in Russia."[61] A few weeks earlier, in a long piece titled "The Foundations of Revolutionary Activity," Jay Hen dismissed "talk of controlling the State, through the 'Dictatorship of the Proletariat,'" which was "being indulged in by people calling themselves 'Marxists.'" Apparently, he complained, "the ability to memorise a number of rather ponderous phrases is considered a sufficient qualification, in some quarters, to justify self-investment with this title." In Britain, the proletariat was "by far the greatest numerical section of the population, and, assuming a real revolutionary situation reached, with the workers organised industrially, and actually in possession of the workshops and factories, dictatorship is resolved into the familiar 'majority rule' on an occupational, instead of a geographical basis."

Hen objected to the use made of quotations from Marx concerning both the dictatorship of the proletariat and the withering away of the state by "colorature Bolsheviks," who spent so much time memorizing the words of Marx, Lenin and other "notable thinkers" that they had "none to spare for an intelligent use of the theoretical matter of either Marx or anyone else." He went on:

> The plain fact of the matter is that no such extended period of unstable social equilibrium (with society poised on the knife edge of class strife) is possible in a country where capital has advanced to the high composition it has with us, and where, as a necessary corollary, the State has perfected its functions of oppression — both psychological and physical to the utmost.
>
> We shall have to kill the State, break it up, and scatter it to the four winds. What is needed is the extension of the functions of society, organised industrially, to every field of social activity, politics included.[62]

For the SLP, the advocates of the dictatorship of the proletariat as applied to Britain and similar economically developed "western" countries were simply, and often wilfully, misinterpreting Marx and Marxism.

David Sherriff had been typically disparaging about the CP in the summer of 1921, after press reports of violence in Sheffield, where there had been baton charges against a demonstration by the unemployed "who are popularly associated with the Communist Party." He presented this as a "stupendous attempt in Sheffield to establish the Dictatorship of the Proletariat! Rant and Riot, window smashing and nonsensical words." The time had come for the SLP to wage vigorous war against **"this treason to the Proletariat."** The incident revealed how capable the CP was of leading the proletariat — "to damnation and massacre." It was up to the SLP to show the workers how to organize themselves as an industrial union capable of taking economic power and carrying on production "for the whole of society." The party had, furthermore, to show that

> Peace and Order is implied in such actions and that the Political Party at the Polls must register approximately the strength of the revolutionary Movement; that discipline is essential to the result of the Polls; if the majority decide in favour of wage-slavery then the power is in the hands of those who have most to gain from such a system; they enforce its conditions upon the whole of society; the Party of the Workers must carry on and try again — time is always with it. If it triumph at the Polls, i.e. gains the majority, it has the power the POWER IMPLIED IN THE INDUSTRIAL UNION of the workers to destroy the "robber burg" of Capitalism; to declare wage-slavery no more.

The phrase "civilised methods" was acquiring a deeper meaning for the SLP, concluded Sherriff. It implied carrying out the necessary education and developing the strategy and tactics capable of conquering

> not only the petty, old-fashioned barbarism of fisticuffs, hay-forks, and pocket pistols; the barbarism that is lingering in the minds of our pitiable burlesque bolsheviki, but, moreover, that will know how to make powerless and ineffectual the revised and improved barbarism of the modern Field of Mars. Education and organisation, not rant and riot, is the necessity of the hour.[63]

For Sherriff, the SLP's policy of encouraging workers to participate "in all forms of activity" in existing unions while also presenting craft-unionism as "pro-capitalist" was contradictory. Trade unionism was a diversion, he insisted in a letter to the paper in July 1921. He wanted to see the "working-class marching in a direct line to their emancipation," and to accomplish this "social peace must be their war cry." Only industrial unionism as represented by the WIIU would succeed:

> The W.I.I.U. places itself on the principle of a **peaceful solution** of the organisation of the workers around the tools of production to take and hold these means by and for Society. **Its method is to keep the ruling Class to the Civilized, i.e. the Peaceful method of settling disputes; to test the strength of the Industrial Organisation of the Workers and take and hold by the easy method of counting votes.**[64]

For the following two weeks, *The Socialist* gave front-page prominence to articles by Sherriff titled "To Prevent Strikes" and "Trade Unionism and 'Peaceful Submission.' " It was futile to expect anything but defeat from a "Trade Union strike" when market conditions were against the workers. They should "keep focussed" on socialism rather than frittering away energy "by fighting incidentals." Organized as a class in one union, they should "take and hold all the means of production, distribution and exchange and to administer these things for the whole Society." Politically, "as a means of endeavouring to accomplish by **peaceful methods** the abolition of wage-slavery," they should "**endeavour to solve by means of the vote, by disciplined submission to majority rule, the burning question of the time.**"[65]

Building "Socialist Industrial Unionism" might be difficult, but it was the correct way forward, as opposed to the "Civil War stunt" advocated by the Communists. "We live in a Political society, in Civilised Society," *The Socialist* insisted. And, in bold uppercase letters, it laid down its position unequivocally:

CIVILISATION IMPLIES ORDER
NO DICTATORSHIP OF THE PROLETARIAT CAN
SOLVE THE SOCIAL PROBLEM

The latter was, it declared, "a historical and social impossibility in these days." The capitalist system continued, and the capitalist class ruled "by the consent of the vast majority which is the Proletariat."[66]

Only when this majority awoke to its real position and organized itself as an industrial union could this situation be changed.

In February 1922, with the shop stewards' movement, its membership much dwindled, now merging with the CP, *The Socialist* devoted two whole pages to a response to an article in *The Worker*, the shop stewards' movement's northern organ. Written by J.R. Campbell, who now chaired the organization,[67] the piece summarized his position as advocating the necessity of "a working class dictatorship" resulting from "a physical force struggle." The SLP's "belief in the possibility of a peaceful Revolution" was, according to Campbell, "a monstrous and dangerous delusion." This, said *The Socialist,* was "the negation of revolutionary principles and a menace to the working class." Who, it asked, would "wield the dictatorship" in the absence of "a proletariat which is not sufficiently conscious to adopt civilised methods of establishing its power?" What "guarantee of protection" would there be for "an industrial proletariat, which is too weak to protect itself?"

As "ordinary proletarians," the SLP believed in an "open platform and frank discussion":

> If we cannot discuss our ideas in the light of day, before the masses, which must vindicate the realisation of our views, then we have no right to hold such ideas. . . . The establishment of Socialism is not possible with hush-hush-here-comes-the-policeman-hide-the-plans methods. No, no, we have had enough of that kind of stuff recently.
>
> We would like to impress on Campbell that Marx nowhere, to our knowledge, gives any reason to believe that he believed in dictatorship, physical force, and political revolution, in Great Britain, as those ideas find expression in his article, or as presently expressed by certain persons who insult the memory of Marx by calling themselves Marxists.[68]

The SLP was determined to maintain that it, not the CPGB and its acolytes, were the true Marxists. Writing in October 1922, P. Marsden compared the original *Communist Manifesto* with its 1872 preface. Conditions "in highly developed capitalist countries (England, the

U.S.A. and Germany for example)" were very different than they were in 1847. He quoted Engels's "Landmarks of Scientific Socialism" to the effect that armies were now entirely dependent on "economic conditions." To Marsden this meant that, should the ruling class attempt to use force to resist the coming revolution, "if the proletariat is organised to prevent regular supplies and unhindered transport, the capitalist armed force would become a rabble." An 1894 *Neue Zeit* article by Engels (helpfully translated in *Plebs,* from January to April 1921) had demonstrated "the absurdity of the workers attempting to organise an armed force to put through a revolution, or, once organised, the impossibility of doing anything with it." Marsden continued:

> Now, since political dictatorship (of one class over another) is the rule of a minority over the majority, the proletarian dictatorship can exist only when the proletariat is in a minority. If the proletariat is a majority, its rule is majority rule and majority rule is not dictatorship; it is one of the principles of democracy.

So, while the dictatorship of the proletariat might be "correct in a country like Roumania or Russia," it was "out of date" in countries such as Britain, Germany, and the United States. "In civilised society (capitalist variety especially) the methods of settling quarrels by an appeal to force (violence) is out of date. Today we recognise the peaceful method; by public speeches, by free press, by balloting, by the gaining of majorities." How could SLP propaganda reach workers if "we advocate violence which would get us crushed"?[69]

It was soon after this, in the issue of November 1922, that a brief notice, headed "To Whom It May Concern", and signed by Henderson as national secretary, appeared in *The Socialist,* announcing that Sherriff had been expelled from the SLP by its National Executive Committee. As with the earlier expulsion of Sean McLoughlin, no explanation was given. Whether there was a connection between Sherriff's expulsion and any of the uncompromising views he had expressed during the previous year is not clear. But it seems unlikely that *The Socialist* would publish without critical comment material that the

SLP leadership objected to or that they would wait for over a year to take action. In any case, Sherriff was hardly alone in his conclusion. The emphasis might sometimes differ, but the conclusions were the same: "The Dictatorship of the Proletariat" was totally inappropriate and unnecessary in the British context.

The Nature of the Revolution and the Role of the Revolutionary Party

It must be evident by now that the position of the SLP on the nature of the anticipated British revolution and the role of the revolutionary party in it had little in common with what would be normally understood by "Bolshevik" and that, with the defection of the CUG and subsequent transfers of members to the CPGB, this became increasingly clear. In an editorial in the March 1918 issue, *The Socialist* had concluded:

> When the political expression of revolutionary socialism captures the state it will proceed at once to use such power to *enforce the will of the revolutionary proletariat*. It will call upon the *industrially organised workers* to take over and control the industries of the country. It will use the power over the State, which includes the armed forces of the nation, to see that no capitalist counter-revolutionary movement stands in the way of the industrial unions electing their local and national administrative councils.

With its stress on the political, as distinct from the industrial, and the anteriority assumed for the capture of the state by political revolutionaries, this may possibly have been a departure from the strictest interpretation of De Leonism. But, according to a piece written in April 1919 by the future chairman of the CPGB, Arthur MacManus, the role of SLP was still to ensure that the coming revolution was a "Social *and not* a Political" one.[70] At this stage the party seemed to put the stress on differentiating itself from "the hare-brained schemes of wild-eyed and lopsided Anarchists," which it did by emphasizing that "the political and industrial organisations of the working-class" were "not antagonistic and separate, but complementary phases of the movement for Socialism."[71]

The SLP's job was to convince workers of the "necessity for Social Revolution and for converting our Party into a Ways and Means Committee to accomplish that historic task," argued a *Socialist* editorial that focused on the party's Easter conference in April 1920. Rather difficult to reconcile with its later statements concerning peaceful revolution and "civilised" methods was the paper's call later that year, when British intervention in the Russo-Polish war seemed likely: "Let the capitalists declare their war if they dare; the workers, with rifles in their hands, will create a greater civil war at home and render their proclamation futile." [72] But such bravado was very uncharacteristic of *The Socialist*.

If there was to be a revolution, it would have to be the work of the workers themselves. The SLP's role was to show the way. It would accomplish this by preserving the correct, De Leonist, version of Marxism, by propagating the classics of the faith, and by educating the working class and encouraging it to organize itself into one big industrial union willing and able to challenge capitalism at the point of production. At the same time, the growing revolutionary consciousness that made this challenge possible would be registered by workers voting for, and eventually electing, revolutionary socialist candidates. But the real protagonists of the revolution had to be the workers themselves: "The organised workers must make the Revolution while the individual, and even parties, can only function more or less as units of the mass." [73]

As we have seen, in 1921 the focus increasingly shifted to re-emphasizing the De Leonist approach and promoting industrial unionism. In June, one correspondent, rejecting the line of the "so-called Communists," saw the need for "a strong nucleus" to prepare for the "last struggle." Its role would be to point out "that science not leaders, can determine the end of wage slavery." [74] *The Socialist* insisted on the need for education "on Marxist lines." Hence the classes in industrial history and economics offered in 1921 by W. Lusty, secretary of the Coventry branch, as well as the SLP "Sunday schools" and other similar initiatives. [75] Above all, a "Socialist Industrial Union" was vital. "Political power to the working class is essential to the accomplishment of Socialist Revolution," the paper argued a week later, "but political power is only effective inasmuch as it is a reflex of the economic power of the class that wields it." It was the task of the SLP to promote this, while the CPGB, that "great monstrosity," was "heading through Labour Party affiliation for the Servile State."[76]

There was no way that the revolution could be carried out without overwhelming working-class support. *The Socialist* insisted in November 1921 that what it called — rather oddly for a paper based in Scotland — "Capitalist England" could only "be changed when the **wage-workers** desire it, not before." At the beginning of 1922, an article titled "The Problem of Industrial Organisation" concluded that the SLP must "show the workers a social constructive policy, which will lead them to work for their own emancipation."[77]

The SLP certainly saw itself as a vanguard, but it was an ideological rather than a politically directive vanguard. Those who left to join the Communists may have had a more ambiguous notion that blurred such a distinction. But those who remained faithful to their De Leonism rejected any idea that a revolutionary minority could carry out a revolution in a country like Britain. The SLP's task was to prepare the way, not to direct the revolutionary process. As *The Socialist* put it in June 1922: "Our work is to Agitate, Educate and Organise for Socialism — nothing else."[78]

11

PANKHURST'S *DREADNOUGHT*
AND THE (ORIGINAL) FOURTH INTERNATIONAL
"Left Communism" and Soviet Democracy

The Dreadnought *Before Pankhurst's Expulsion*

As we have seen, even before the "merger" of the CP (BSTI) with the CPGB at the Unity Conference of January 1921, Sylvia Pankhurst's *Workers' Dreadnought* had ceased to be "The Organ of the Communist Party" and now presented itself as a paper giving "independent support" to the united party "from a Left-Wing standpoint." This was not a position that was going to be tolerated for very long by those in charge of the party or by their Comintern mentors.

Pankhurst was serving what was to be her final jail sentence during the period of the January Unity Conference and was not released from Holloway prison until the end of May. The decision of the executive committee to expel her from the party was made on 10 September.

Until then, the *Dreadnought* had made some effort to give what a later generation of Communist dissidents would call "critical support" to the party, while continuing to promote "Left-Wing" Communism. The fact that, following Pankhurst's release, no dramatic change can be discerned in the way the issues were presented suggests that — however small in numbers — "Left-Wing" Communism was at least more than a one-woman band. It soon became clear that Pankhurst, like the SLP, viewed the freedom to debate and criticize as a necessary pre-condition of soviet democracy.

There was also a renewed emphasis on women during this period, with, for example, a leading article by Dora Montefiore ("Why We Celebrate a Communist Women's Day") and a piece by Alexandra Kollontai ("International Solidarity and the Proletarian Woman of To-day") appearing in the *Dreadnought* in April.[1] This continued after Pankhurst's break with the CPGB with, for example, a new edition of "Kolontay's Splendid Pamphlet *Communism and the Family*," advertised in the paper early in 1922. Kollontai's *The Workers' Opposition in Russia* and Rosa Luxemburg's *Russian Revolution,* together with her letters, were featured a year later.[2]

Much of what appeared in the *Dreadnought* during the period before Pankhurst's expulsion reflected Communist orthodoxy, with reports and articles by Lenin, front-page prominence given to the "Red Trade Union International Conference," and a piece titled "Prison Life in Russia," which contrasted that enlightened regime with "the prisons of 'Democracy.'"[3] There was little here, or in the paper's report on the party's conference in April, to disquiet the Communist Party leadership. The main function of the April conference had been to ratify the party's constitution and rules. Its most dramatic event was the expulsion — for what was deemed his treacherous behaviour on "Black Friday" as secretary of the National Transport Workers' Federation — of Robert Williams, the stirring advocate of the "dictatorship of the proletariat" at the Leeds Soviet Convention in 1917.[4]

But the *Dreadnought* also published material that was bound to cause leadership eyebrows to be raised. There was little to annoy in the spring 1921 serialization of Sylvia Pankhurst's *Soviet Russia as I Saw It in 1920,* in which the 21 conditions of the Communist International were hailed as "disciplinary measures aiming to give power to the old forces of Socialism." (Indeed, later in the year, the paper's reviewer was to complain that "Miss Pankhurst throws no light on the 'Cheka.' ")[5] But the same could not be said for the serialization, spread over three months, of an extended version of Herman Gorter's response to Lenin's *"Left-Wing" Communism: An Infantile Disorder.*[6]

In July, the Bow branch of the CPGB protested when the *Dreadnought* published a letter criticizing the policies pursued by Communists elected on the Labour Party ticket as members of the Poplar Poor Law Guardians, the local authority that administered aid to the poor. No "information likely to cause injury to the Party or to prejudice the Communist reputation of any other member" should be published without the consent of the branch, the Bow branch insisted. In response, Pankhurst said that it was the duty of Communists to criticize the Labour Party. What was it to do "when members of the Communist Party go into the Labour Party and become an indistinguishable part of it, displaying all its weaknesses and faults?" If the branch had the right "to control the public activities of its members," why then had "the Party left its representatives to do as they please, and only passed a vote of censure on those who, at long last, have called attention to the fact that these representatives are not moving in the path of Communist tactics"? The Bow branch could not safeguard the Communist Party's reputation by "a policy of 'Hush! Hush!' " Pankhurst ended by claiming that she shared the CP's aim to affiliate with Labour "in order to draw it into the path of Communism." But this could only be accomplished "by constant vigilant criticism and discussion."[7]

Soon after, Pankhurst questioned Communist tactics in running a candidate in the Caerphilly by-election. In the same issue, her editorial criticized some of Zinoviev's "pronouncements" to the Comintern, in particular his contention that the "tactics of creating Communist nuclei within the Trade Unions" had been successful in (among other countries) Britain. She would like to hear from such groups. "It would do our heart good," she wrote, "if they really are advanced enough to be called *Communist*, and really powerful enough to achieve results. Let us hear from you, O Communist nuclei." It was also "not quite accurate" to say that the shop stewards' movement had joined the party — only "certain members" had done this so far. Furthermore, she declared, Zinoviev was wrong about the Labour Party. At the second Comintern congress, Lenin had used "Comrade Rothstein's" argument in support of Labour Party affiliation. Rothstein had argued that Labour "was really not a political party at all but a loose federation of Trade Unions, within which one could carry on any sort of propaganda one chose." But subsequent events had demonstrated that Rothstein's argument was false. And already the Labour Party had twice refused to accept the CP's bid for affiliation. If all this was not enough raise hackles, Pankhurst concluded by reiterating her claim that, in Moscow, Lenin had advised her that her group should join a united party and work within the Comintern on behalf of their own anti-parliamentary policy:

> "If the decisions about the Labour Party and Parliamentarism are wrong," he said, "they can be altered by a subsequent Congress. Form a Left Block within a United Communist Party."
>
> On this advice we have continued to act in good faith.[8]

What must have been the final straw followed a fortnight later. The *Dreadnought* headline proclaimed: "A New International. Left Wing Communism's Anti-Parliamentarians Consolidate." The impetus for the new international, Pankhurst said, came from Germany and Holland, with Pannekoek and Gorter as "leading theorists." There would be an international newspaper, published in several languages. An anti-parliamentary party was being formed in Holland to join the existing German KAPD (Kommunistische Arbeiter-Partei Deutschlands, the Communist Workers' Party of Germany), and *Dreadnought* readers should "watch these developments with attention." She concluded by restating the familiar anti-parliamentarian case: "The change of system will not come until the old forms of government are discredited and the workers break away from them." [9]

The following week's *Dreadnought* introduced Alexandra Kollontai's *The Workers' Opposition* under the headline "The Workers' Opposition in Sovrusssia." Although she was, the paper explained, a member of the central committee of the Russian party, her "brochure" on "Working-Class Organisations" had been refused publication. It had then been "printed illegally" and retrospectively approved, but, at the same time, its distribution among Communist Party delegates had been forbidden in Russia. Kollontai complained that the unions had "become depopulated," with only "little groups that did not take part in the race for a career in the Soviet bureaucracy" still "intimately bound up . . . with the workers." [10]

Meanwhile, applications for five-shilling shares in a new "Dreadnought Publishing Co." had already been sought, and the editorial preceding the "New International" piece had dealt with the *Dreadnought*'s financial difficulties. Whatever "Moscow gold" the paper had previously received had clearly been discontinued by this time.

Pankhurst's Expulsion, "Freedom of Discussion," and the Dreadnought Reprieved

A week after her expulsion from the CPGB, in the 17 September issue of the *Dreadnought*, Pankhurst gave her own account of the decision. The party was, she said, "passing through a sort of political measles called discipline, which makes it fear the free expression and circulation of opinion within the Party." Ever since its formation, it had "fretted itself" about the "independent Communist voice" of the *Dreadnought*, and, apparently, the January conference had "even debated whether members might be permitted" to read the paper. Informed that the question of the *Dreadnought*'s future was "in abeyance," some party organizers interpreted this news as a prohibition on its circulation. The "struggle for existence as an unsubsidised paper was intensified," she noted, "in the face of the *Communist*, heavily subsidised, largely advertised and sold at 4d a quire cheaper to newsagents and branches."

Soon after her release from prison, Pankhurst explained, she had met with a subcommittee of the CPGB's executive, which proposed that "as a disciplined member of the Party" she should hand over the paper unconditionally: "The disciplinarians set forth their terms to one who had for eight years maintained a pioneer paper with a constant struggle and in the face of much persecution." She had refused but had promised "to consider carefully and in a comradely spirit" any alternative proposition the party might make. The original demand was repeated, however, with the executive committee insisting that she "should surrender the *Dreadnought* to it within the space of two weeks." She had not replied, she said, and at the end of the two-week period had "received a summons to meet the Executive," which she did on 10 September:

> "We are not here to consider the good the *Dreadnought* might do, but the harm it might do," said Comrade MacManus, his red silk handkerchief showing so smartly from his pocket.
>
> "What the Committee wants is the death of the *Dreadnought*," said another comrade.
>
> Discipline was the watch word of the meeting.

Pankhurst went on to stress the necessity of an independent organ "giving expression to Left Wing ideas." She cited recent developments, especially the decision of Third International to exclude the KAPD, which she described as "the industrialist, anti-Trade Union, anti-Parliamentary and highly revolutionary Communist Labour Party of Germany, which played so important a part in the Ruhr Valley rising." The Kollontai article of the previous week had demonstrated "the growing cleavage between Right and Left in the Russian Communist Party" and "the tendency to slip to the Right" in Russia. But such questions were not discussed in *The Communist,* "a Party organ under the control of the Right Wing of the British Communist Party, and of the Executive in Moscow, which is at present dominated by the Right Wing policy."

At the 10 September meeting, Pankhurst reported in her account, after the executive had confirmed once more its unwillingness to "tolerate the existence of any Communist organ independent of itself," she had announced that the *Dreadnought's* financial problems meant that the next issue of the paper would be its last. Rounding off the debate, MacManus then concluded that there was no alternative but expulsion.[11] The CPGB position was quite explicit, and in its 17 September issue *The Communist* gave front-page prominence to the expulsion of Pankhurst for refusing to "hand the paper over to the control of the party." A few weeks later, in an article in *The Communist* titled "Party Organisation," Tom Bell would emphasize that *"no paper may be recognised as a Communist organ if it does not submit to the direction of the party."*[12]

Pankhurst really does seem to have believed that the issue in which this long account of her expulsion appeared — that of 17 September 1921 — would be the end of the *Workers' Dreadnought*. Quite apart from her unrepentant comments about her expulsion, it looked as though the paper would die with stings in its tail. The editorial, headed "Farewell," regretted "the growth of opportunism in the Third International," and a letter, from A.J. and F.E. Symes, congratulated Pankhurst on her expulsion and announced their own resignation from the CPGB, regretting the "end of our little fighting B.S.T.I." and the sacrifice by the merged party of its principles. Another letter protested emphatically against the expulsion and attacked the CP executive: "It has made the 'Power of recall' a mere phrase, well buried in the constitution. It has interpreted the Dictatorship of the Proletariat as the Dictatorship of the gentlemen who happen to be in power, or rather in office. It has gagged the voice of the rank and file." The issue also featured an article titled "Transition to and from Communism," signed "A. Ironie," that attacked the recent retreat towards market economics and the reinstatement of private property in Russia and contrasted "free Communism" with "Communist Partyism." Finally, in a boxed inset, Pankhurst protested against the way the *Daily Herald* had dealt with her letter concerning her expulsion. The paper had submitted the letter to MacManus for his "cuts and criticisms," while not reciprocating by according her "the similar courtesy" of seeing the CPGB's statement before publication (something that MacManus had refused). She also insisted on the truth of her statement that no member of the Communist Party would be allowed to publish anything without the sanction of the executive.

Had the 17 September issue really been the last *Dreadnought*, that battleship would have certainly gone down with all guns blazing. In fact, the paper managed to struggle on — and indeed appeared the following week. Much of this edition was given over to Pankhurst's exposition "Our Point of View," in which she explored the differences of the Communist Left Wing with the CPGB, which were a matter "partly of principle, partly of practical utility." The Communist Party's representatives on local bodies did not "operate the Parliamentary policy in the destructive sense laid down by the Third International," she complained. In other words, they failed to use their election to local bodies simply as a means to discredit these institutions but insead tried to play a positive role as conventional local councillors. Pankhurst also repeated her claim that Lenin had "urged" her to join a united Communist Party and "form a Left block within it." Her hope had been that this would allow the Left Wing to achieve "final ascendancy in the united Party, failing that they could, should some crisis render it advisable, break out later on."

The CPGB and the Third International were bent on the "excommunication" of the Left Wing. But new tendencies were developing. On 11 September, in Berlin, the KAPD had held an international conference of Communists opposed to the Third International, and in a recent speech Lenin had announced that the Workers' Opposition was leaving the Russian Communist Party. It seems clear that Pankhurst assumed that the "Right" would soon be discredited in Russia and throughout the international Communist movement. She seems genuinely to have believed that Lenin was sympathetic to the formation of a "Left block" and at least to have hoped that he was already siding with the Workers' Opposition.[13]

William Gallacher — whom Lenin had recently criticized, along with Pankhurst, for being in the grip of an "infantile disorder" because of his "Left-Wing" views — now alleged that she had deliberately provoked her own expulsion "because someone was willing to finance The Workers' Dreadnought." The retraction and apology that Pankhurst demanded was not forthcoming.[14]

Perceptions of Russian Reality: The Beginning of the Change

Pankhurst's *Soviet Russia as I Saw It in 1920*, serialized in the *Dreadnought* over the course of many weeks in 1921 while its author was in prison, presented a rosy view of Soviet Russia in general and soviet democracy in particular. Though still "incomplete," the Russian soviet constitution already contained "a system of democratic checks and balances quite foreign to the Parliamentary and Cabinet system of capitalist states." In a subsequent instalment, the change to one-person management in industry was accepted uncritically with a positive gloss: "The steady tendency is for the election of management to give way to selection, based on practical experience, technical competence and organising capacity."[15]

In the *Dreadnought* edition published on 10 September, the day of Pankhurst's expulsion, an article by Dennis E. Batt, recently returned from Russia, answered the question posed in its title — "Does Moscow Soviet Represent the Workers?" — with a definite affirmative. Batt reported that he had witnessed a normal election campaign in which "Mensheviks, Left and Right Socialist-Revolutionaries, [and] Anarchists" participated, although together they managed to secure only 2 percent of the delegates. Following the election, Batt reported, the "support of the non-partisan vote was pledged to the Communist Party by the non-party spokesman at the opening session." There was no comment on the oddity of this or its apparent lack of consideration for the views of the supposedly sovereign electors.

Until now, *Dreadnought* dissent had focused on the policies and actions of the *British* Party and, to a lesser extent, on the International's misguided policies regarding parliamentary participation and Labour Party affiliation. Only the very recent Kollontai article, published on 3 September, suggested any real disquiet about the state of affairs in

Russia itself. But this was swiftly to change. Whoever's identity lay beyond "A. Ironie" in the (temporarily final) issue of the *Dreadnought*, he or she was clear about that nature of Bolshevik rule:

> We were told that however much we might object to government of any sort, on principle, government in the form of the dictatorship of the proletariat was necessary to bring about the transition from Capitalism to free Communism, and that such a dictatorship would be shorn of the objectionable qualities of other forms of government. Some of us never assented to this, and the trend of things seems to show we were right when we maintained that the dictatorship of the proletariat could only amount to a dictatorship *over* the proletariat of an official class, which would partake of the common nature of all officialism, even if some or all of those officials should be drawn from or voted for by the proletariat itself. We maintained that bureaucracy never proved the transition to anything save increased bureaucracy, or towards the revolt of the proletariat which should discover that those aspirations towards Free Communism which some have never relinquished, others have newly awakened to, are yet far from realisation.[16]

The positive view of Russia under the Bolsheviks, exemplified by Pankhurst's account of her visit the previous year, was by this time giving way to one that was much more critical. The Comintern — with which her earlier organization, the CP (BSTI), had been so anxious to identify that it included the claim to be a "section" of the Third International in its name — was no longer the guide and inspiration it had been. Now Pankhurst and the *Dreadnought* were investing their hopes in a new Communist International.

The Original Fourth International and the Communist Workers' Party

As we have seen, the advent of a "Left-Wing" Communist international had been broached even before Pankhurst's expulsion in September 1921. Early in October, an editorial appeared in the *Dreadnought* under the heading "The New Communist Workers' International." The Third International had "through force of circumstance developed along lines which have caused it to become the defender of Soviet Russia rather than the champion of World Revolution." The actions of affiliated parties were controlled by a "Moscow Executive wholly dominated by Russian Policy," and a new Fourth International had become inevitable. "The Workers' Dreadnought was the first British paper to welcome the Third International; it now has the honour to be the first to welcome the Fourth International." Like-minded individuals and groups were invited to send in their names for enrolment in a new Communist Workers' Party soon to be formed.[17] There was, of course, a big difference between Pankhurst's tiny group and the German KAPD. In August 1920, the month that the CPGB was formed, the KAPD had about forty thousand members — although, as Marcel van der Linden tells us, following an all too familiar left-wing pattern "from then on, the Party was decimated by a series of splits and splinter groups."[18]

The manifesto of the new international was spread over two issues of the *Dreadnought* as extracts from it reached the paper. It was now clear the Bolsheviks had possessed no ability to skip a bourgeois revolution: even the Bolsheviks could not "evade the law of history," the paper commented. While the contest in the industrial towns had been between capitalism and socialism, in the countryside it had been between feudalism and capitalism, with the peasants demanding private property rights. Once victory over the feudal aristocracy was achieved, the divergence of interests led to conflict and eventually to the New Economic Policy. The state and the "economic machine" had gradually been "strongly penetrated by bureaucracy." The reaction to this was the Workers' Opposition, which represented "more than the mere desire to choose for itself the management of the branches of industry." As the conflicts escalated, there had been demonstrations in Moscow and the "insurrection of Kronstadt." Meanwhile, there was famine and, as the paper stated emphatically: "*The call for succour by the Soviet Government to the whole world has illumined the situation like a searchlight.*" The Soviet government was surrendering "its country, its revolution, its proletariat, to the International bourgeoisie."[19]

In the *Dreadnought*'s view, the Communist Workers' International would have to "be created from down below."[20] The objects and methods of the Communist Workers' Party were set out in the issue of 11 February 1922. The party aimed "to overthrow Capitalism, the wages system, and the machinery of the Capitalist State, and to establish a world-wide Federation of Communist Republics administered by occupational Soviets." The statement of methods was largely negative: the new party would take no part in elections and would expose "the futility of Communist participation therein." It would refuse affiliation to "reformist" organizations such as the Labour Party and seek to "emancipate" workers from the "merely palliative" trade unions. More positively, they would seek to "spread the knowledge of Communist principles" and to set up workers' councils "in all branches of production, distribution and administration, in order that the workers may seize and maintain control."

The activities of the Communist Workers' Party now appeared regularly in the *Dreadnought*. Membership cards could be obtained for a shilling.[21] Meetings, usually featuring Pankhurst as the main speaker, were advertised. Early venues included the Minerva Café, at 144 High Holborn, and the St. Leonards Academy in Leytonstone, as well as a meeting in Tatton organized by the Portsmouth Communist Workers' Party, a breakaway from the CPGB.[22] The latter was "a crowded meeting," held on 26 March in Tatton's Trades Hall, that included a musical program by the Proletarian Socialist Sunday School featuring "The International" sung in Esperanto, as well as an address by Sylvia Pankhurst. In a manner very reminiscent of the early days of *The Clarion* in the 1890s, members were urged to respond to requests for propaganda and propagandists from rural districts by becoming "Communist Pilgrims" and organizing village meetings on the weekends, at which the "simple and beautiful gospel" of communism could be proclaimed.[23]

Much hope was invested in the Workers' Opposition in Russia, which, the *Dreadnought* reported at the beginning of June, had now "allied itself with the Communist Workers' Party (Fourth

International).” This it had done by sending a manifesto to the KAPD, signed “Group of Revolutionary Left Communists (C.W.P.) of Russia,” which greeted “the unanimous determination to set up the Fourth International as being the central body that will unify the genuine Proletarian forces of the revolution.”[24] A further statement by this group appeared in the *Dreadnought* a fortnight later under the headline “The Workers’ Opposition Joins Fourth International”:

> In all theoretical matters and practical problems, the C.W.P. of Russia
> will be influenced by the *Communist Workers’ Party of Germany, and it
> pays regard also to Communist Workers’ Parties in Holland, Bulgaria,
> and Czecho-Slovakia, which have united with it,* as well as to all other
> Left Wing Communist parties and groups which adhere to it.

An advertisement for Kollontai’s *The Workers’ Opposition,* in the same issue, said that the book “describes and explains the Communist Proletarian Movement which has grown up in Russia to oppose the Soviet Government’s ‘New Economic Policy’ of reversion to capitalism.”[25] By mid-July, the *Dreadnought* was appealing for financial help for the Workers’ Opposition. The organization had collected “several million roubles” to print the publications it was prevented from producing in Russia, only to find that, owing to the exchange rate, its funds would “scarcely pay postage” in Germany. Because of the favourable rate of exchange for sterling, however, even small contributions would help.

There must have been some confusion in the offices of the *Dreadnought*, for another page of the issue carried a report from the Russian Communist Workers’ Party, which, the paper insisted, was “not to be confused with the unprincipled and backboneless leaders of the so-called Workers’ Opposition.” This was followed by a report on the Fifth Special Congress of the KAPD, which had been attended by delegates from ten industrial districts as well as an observer from the Dutch KAP and another from the “Left-Wing Communists of Russia.”[26] The financial appeal seems to have had some effect, because a letter from the “Revolutionary Left Wing Communist Group (C.W.P.)” thanking readers for their assistance appeared later in the year.[27] All this is very difficult to disentangle. But clearly there was a group — variously named in the *Dreadnought* — that the paper had initially assumed was the same as the Workers' Opposition associated with Kollontai.

Most of the Communist Workers' activities advertised in the *Dreadnought* were London based and featured a small group of speakers that included Pankhurst, Norah Smyth, and A. Kingman. The addresses of the secretaries of the Willesden, Portsmouth, and Sheffield branches were published on 30 September 1922, in the same issue that contained the agenda for the Second Congress of the Fourth International, to be held in Berlin on 1 October. The Communist Workers' organization was, the paper subsequently said, "essentially a rank-and-file movement. It has no place for leaders as commonly understood." [28]

In October 1923, the *Dreadnought* reported on the formation of a "Communist Workers' Group" in Austria, and, a few weeks later, on the protest of the Russian Communist Workers' organization at the expulsion from the Communist Party of five "old Worker Comrades," whose names it listed. In the same issue, the paper also published the organization's manifesto, "typewritten copies of which at the beginning of the year were circulated all over Russia." [29] More of the manifesto — now described as coming from the "Workers' Group of the Communist Party of Russia (Bolsheviki)" — was published early in 1924. According to the *Dreadnought*, the struggle in Russia against the "liquidation of the conquests of the October Revolution" needed united working-class support from outside the country. The Workers' Group had been unable to publish the manifesto in Russia, the paper reported, and those suspected of sympathizing with its views would be "excluded from the party and trade unions simply upon suspicion, arrested and spirited away." [30]

In May 1924, the aims of the "Communist Workers' Movement" were again said to be "to spread knowledge of Communism amongst the people" and to build an "All-Workers' Industrial Revolutionary Union of employed and unemployed workers" on a workshop basis "covering all workers regardless of sex, craft or grade who pledge themselves to work for the overthrow of Capitalism and the establishment of Communist administration by the workers' councils." The minimum cost of membership in the "Communist Workers' Movement" was a mere tuppence a week, which illustrates the huge gap between ambitions and resources.[31]

Around this time, the *Dreadnought* reported, the *Daily Mail* had noted that in Hyde Park "Communism was represented by a little woman wearing a bright green coat and a red tie, who was speaking on behalf of the Workers' Communist Movement." This, said the *Dreadnought,* was "Comrade Norah Smyth" — and she could use some help.[32]

The Role of the Soviets in the Coming Revolution

The "Left Communists" may have been miniscule in number even by the standards of the British Left, and the *Dreadnought*'s struggle to survive would end in failure. But it does illustrate the persistence of uncompromising notions of "Left Communism" well into the 1920s. Towards the end of 1921, and into the following year, Pankhurst published a series of pieces called "Communism and Its Tactics," which offered a more comprehensive exposition of her view of the nature and role of soviet democracy. In her view, the soviet structure was something that arose "naturally when the workers are thrown upon their own resources." It might eventually be superseded by "something higher," but for some time to come it would be "the organisational structure of Communism." During the revolutionary crisis, the "guiding and co-ordinating machinery" would take the form of soviets, which, after the revolution, would run industries and services.[33]

Pankhurst totally rejected Zinoviev's "Thesis," one of those adopted by the Second Congress of the Third International, that "no attempt should be made to form Soviets prior to the outbreak of revolutionary crisis":

> The idea expressed and insisted upon in that Thesis of Zinoviev was
> that the Soviet must be a great mass movement, coming together in the
> electrical excitement of the crisis; the correctness of its structure; its

actual Sovietness to coin an adjective, being considered of secondary importance. A progressive growth, gradually branching out till the hour of crisis; a strong and well-tried organisation is not contemplated by the Thesis.

In Russia the revolution had been "an affair of spontaneous outbursts with no adequate organisation behind it." Russian trade unions had been feeble and had, in any case, been crushed at the outbreak of war. The revolutionary parties had been incapable of making a revolution:

> The disability arising from the disorganised state of the workers was not felt in its true weightiness until after the Soviet Government had been established. Then it was realised that, though the Soviets were supposed to have taken power, the Soviet structure had yet to be created and made to function. The structure is still incomplete: it has hardly functioned at all. Administration has been largely by Government departments, working often without the active, ready co-operation, sometimes even with the hostility of groups of *workers* who aught to have been taking a responsible share in administration.[34]

It would, she said, be "monstrous folly" to replicate Russian unpreparedness elsewhere. "Workshop soviets" should instead be set up whenever possible because they were "a good fighting weapon and a preparation for the Soviets after and during the revolution." Unlike the unions, which were "governed from a central office," the soviets were self-governing organizations. With soviets there was "no official class." As Pankhurst explained:

> As the breakdown of Capitalism draws nearer, the conflict of opinion as to what shall replace it grows keener. Is it to be State Capitalism pure and simple; or is it to be some dual control of society by a Parliament of professional politicians and of officials of the Trade Unions, and perhaps also Cooperative Societies? Are the Trade Unions and Co-operative Societies to be the controlling force? Are all these to make way for the Workers' Committees?
>
> The issue is vital, for on the decision depends whether the new

society is to be a combination of the Post Office type of administration and trusts, or some modification of that, or a free Communism. The question is whether the basis of social organisation is to be government and control of persons, or the administration of services, to be freely used by all.

The questions, said Pankhurst, for anti-parliamentary Communists such as Guy Aldred — those who argued that "soviets of the workshop must not be organised until after" the revolution or that "they may only be started during the revolution" — were "What force is to make revolution?" and "When is the revolution to begin? Who can be sure of recognising its beginning, who can predict its duration?" [35]

Pankhurst's view of the CPGB seemed confirmed when, at the end of July 1923, the *Dreadnought* reported:

> Mr Walton Newbold, speaking on behalf of the Third International in the House of Commons, said that when the Capitalists are expropriated, production will be organised either by the general councils of Trade Unions or by the workshop committees. To Mr Newbold the difference seems to be immaterial. It is, however, of vital importance. It is nothing less than the question whether industry is to be controlled by an outside authoritarian body composed of professional officials, or whether it is to be organised by the equal co-operation of the workers in the industry.[36]

The soviets would be the instrument of the dictatorship of the proletariat — "a much misused phrase," for "when Communism is in being there will be no proletariat, as we understand the term today, and no dictatorship." Insofar as it was "genuine and defensible," the phrase meant "the suppression by Workers' Soviets of capitalism and the attempt to re-establish it. This should be a temporary state of war," if an inevitable one. But when any serious attempt to re-establish capitalism had reached its end, "then away with the dictatorship; away with all compulsion. Compulsion of any kind is repugnant to the Communist ideal." [37]

According to Pankhurst, the "special fitness" of the soviet system was its construction along the lines of production and distribution. Soviets would replace not only the institutions of national and local government but also "the capitalists, managerial staffs and employees of today with all their ramifications." As she noted: "The Soviets may also conduct the fight for the actual overthrow of capitalism, though in Russia the power was actually seized by the Bolshevik Party and then handed to the Soviets." Pankhurst then outlined the familiar "generally accepted theoretical structure of the Soviet community." In Russia, however, this had "only been very partially applied." Soviets had not been "regular in structure." Moreover, the "new economic policy" of a reversion to capitalism "strikes at the root of the Soviet idea and destroys the functional status of the Soviets." Even before this, the Russian soviets had been "irregular from the theoretical standpoint":

> The Soviets, instead of being formed purely of workers in the various industries and activities of the community, were composed also of delegates of political parties, political groups formed by foreigners in Russia, Trades Councils, Trade Unions and co-operative societies.

Consequently, "the essential administrative character of the Soviets was thereby sacrificed. Constituted thus they must inevitably discuss political antagonisms rather than the production and distribution of social utilities and amenities."[38]

The workshop council was, for Pankhurst, "the germ of the Soviet." During the war, "when the Shop Stewards' movement flourished," even employers had seen the merits of such councils and of the election of workers' stewards. This was demonstrated by the "general spread of Whitleyism" — joint consultative boards of employers and workers in each industry, recommended by a wartime committee chaired by J.H. Whitley. As Pankhurst noted:

> The trend of the times supports the view that the Soviet Government made a serious blunder when it decided (and put its decision into practice) that "workers' control of industry" is only a slogan useful for

securing the overthrow of the capitalist, and must be discarded once the workers have turned out the capitalist, in favour of management by an individual or committee appointed by some centralised authority.

She finished the series by recapitulating her view in three propositions. First, soviets or workers' councils would "form the administrative machinery for supplying the needs of the people in Communist society, after having made the Revolution by seizing control of industries and services." Second, the revolution in Russia had been possible only because the government had broken down, capitalism was weak there, and the country was in a chaotic state. In Britain, the machinery of soviets must be prepared in advance. Finally, trade unions were useless for this purpose: what was required was industrially and nationally co-ordinated workers' councils.[39]

Admiration for the murdered Rosa Luxemburg, whose *Russian Revolution*, and later her letters, were serialised in the *Dreadnought*, did not deter Pankhurst from adding dissenting footnotes at the point where Luxemburg criticized Lenin and Trotsky for not introducing another Constituent Assembly at a later stage. "In our view, the soviets, not the Constituent Assembly, form the essential administrative machinery of the Revolution," declared one footnote. In another, Pankhurst asserted: "The substitution of the Soviets for a Parliament would have meant not a setting aside, but a development of democracy had they functioned adequately."

As Pankhurst emphasized, the road to the soviets in Britain was to be *"One Big Revolutionary Union organised on a workshop basis."*[40] The denial of workers' rights in Russia was "the clearest possible evidence of the fact that until the workers are organised industrially on Soviet lines and able to hold their own and control industry, a successful Soviet Communist revolution cannot be carried through nor can Communism exist without that necessary condition."[41]

Pankhurst was optimistic that sooner or later a crisis would precipitate the formation of soviets in Britain. On 23 September 1922, the *Dreadnought* called for a general strike to prevent the war against

Turkey that Lloyd George seemed intent on beginning. An advertisement appeared for an "Open conference for the General Strike against the war," to be addressed by a number of Communist Workers' Movement speakers, including Smyth and Pankhurst herself. By May 1924, the *Dreadnought's* statement of "What We Stand For" included — in bold: **"A centralised Government cannot give freedom to the individual: it stultifies initiative and progress. In the struggle to abolish capitalism the workshop councils are essential."** [42]

The Nature of Soviet Democracy

In 1921, as Pankhurst and the *Dreadnought* grew ever more libertarian in tone, some aspects of the notion of democracy the paper espoused became clearer. The demand for "freedom of discussion" within the Communist movement that preceded and accompanied Pankhurst's expulsion, the contemptuous rejection of the notion that the party should determine what members were allowed to publish, the idea that "compulsion" was alien to "genuine Communism," and the criticism of Russian soviets for extending representation to political parties and interest groups instead of being based solely on the workers on the shopfloor: all form part of this emerging picture.

The rejection of "leadership" was another aspect. At the beginning of 1922, the Congress movement in India was criticized for appointing a single individual, Gandhi, "as its sole executive authority," although there was optimism that the "absence of democratic tendency" would be short-lived in this case. In much the same way, British trade unions were condemned for, in some cases, making eligibility for office dependent on long periods of prior membership, for electing executives for periods of up to eight years, and for having "no general congress of branch representatives." [43] An unsigned review of G.D.H. Cole's *Guild Socialism Restated* (1920) noted how his ideas had changed since *The Self-Government of Industry*, published in 1917. Having previously borrowed from Fabians and syndicalists, he was now following the popular course and borrowing from Soviet Russia. He had endeavoured to "Soviet-Governmentalise" his structure, with "Communes" at all levels formed from delegates of the "smaller" bodies:

> In his earlier book, Mr Cole made the general ballot of members in given districts, or in given trades, the main method of electing his Guilds. But now he chooses the Russian method, saying he approves of indirect election, if checked by recall. He even boldly cuts the roots of popular election away by dictating that if a delegate be appointed by a committee to represent it as a delegate, he would cease to be subject to recall by the original electors. Only the committee which has sent him can now recall him.[44]

For Pankhurst, soviet democracy was to be a system that excluded politics as normally understood. It presupposed the achievement of social harmony and a virtually conflict-free society. Soviet democracy would have to grapple only with the predominantly technical questions of production and distribution. As we shall see in the next chapter, she and other Left Communists were by no means alone in this assumption.

Pankhurst's anti-political views were made very clear in March 1922, in a *Dreadnought* article in which she considered the possibilities of reform within the parliamentary system — and rejected them. The monarchy and the Lords, or any second chamber, might be eliminated, the prime minister might be chosen by a majority in Parliament or directly by the electorate, as might the cabinet, and the "doings of Parliament might be checked by Referendum," but Parliament would still remain "a non-Communist institution." However, "under Communism we shall have no such machinery of legislation and coercion," Pankhurst declared. "The business of the Soviets will be to organise the production and supply of the common services; they can have no other lasting function."[45]

Pankhurst summed up her view of soviet democracy in a *Dreadnought* editorial in November 1922, at the time of the general election. The "Capitalist machinery of Parliament and the local government bodies of the Capitalist State" did not administer production, distribution and transport. Rather, Parliament, "with much talk and little effect, merely passes laws to palliate the inevitable ends which arise from the private ownership and management of the means of production, distribution and transport." She continued:

> Members of Parliament receive no instructions from their constituents, nor do they report to them except by holding some public meetings in the constituencies, at which vague speeches are made. Members of Parliament have really little to report. They merely sit in Parliament, listen to speeches and vote according to the instructions of the Party Whip.

The soviets, by contrast, would administer production, distribution and transport. "Every one of us will take part in the Soviets; we shall all belong to the Soviet where we work" [46]

There was even greater emphasis on local autonomy in a series of articles that appeared early in 1923 under the title "Communism and Its Tactics." In the workshop, a state of affairs reminiscent of Morris's *News from Nowhere* would pertain: "Dictation from the so-called 'higher councils' will neither be needed, nor could it be accepted. There will be no conflict of class interest: all will be working towards a common end." Therefore, under communism, "the arguments which will arise in the Soviets will be as to the efficacy of this or that technical process, as to whether this or that proposed innovation will increase or improve production — an end desired by all." [47]

This scenario contrasted with other "utopias" on offer — including that of the Webbs. Reviewing the *Constitution for the Socialist Commonwealth of Great Britain* at the end of April 1923, Pankhurst concluded:

> The entire failure of the Webbs' Utopia seems to us fundamentally anti-socialist. They visualise an assembly of warring interests and competing claims, and no doubt under the constitution they propose they would get such an assembly.
>
> The Utopia of the Webbs is that of the policeman and the inspector. It is a Utopia of class distinctions and economic differences. It will not do. [48]

In a more immediate way, the nature of democracy was at issue in the Poplar Board of Guardians incident in 1923, following which Councillor C. Key, the prospective mayor of Poplar, challenged his opponents among the unemployed to a debate — chaired by Pankhurst. The *Dreadnought* report concentrated on Key's defence, before offering an emphatic rebuttal:

> He said that the Guardians were tired of being menaced by the unemployed, and that no party or body of elected representatives would stand being ordered to do things under menace. They must come to a decision according to their own judgement.
>
> *This contention of Mr Key is not new. It is as old as Parliamentarism. Elected persons habitually say to their constituents, "We will not do what you ask, but what we think right." If the elected persons were really the representatives of the unemployed, instructed by them, and subject to recall, they would be compelled either to do what the unemployed desired or to forfeit their positions. The present so-called representative system does not represent at all: for apparently representing many diverse interests elected persons actually represent no one, and in practice usually do as their party dictates, not as their constituents wish. Indeed, their constituents have diverse wishes and diverse interests.*[49]

Moreover, the "elected persons in the Parliamentary governing system" had only "an indirect power which cannot be constantly exercised," Pankhurst insisted on 1 December 1923, in a piece titled "Soviets or Parliaments?" *"If Parliament were to take over the industries the House of Commons could neither administer them, nor represent them,"* she declared. This stood in contrast to a soviet system "built on industrial lines" and based on *"the rank and file in the workshops."*

Contemplating the new Labour government early in 1924, Pankhurst predicted that "nationalised industry, managed as the Post Office is managed, would be managed with radical inefficiency at the top and would offer to the worker no freedom, no share of intelligent co-operation." Jowett-style proposals to replace the cabinet by committees would produce a system that would be "only a shade less evil than the Ministerial system." Both ministers and committees were detached from what they were supposed to be managing. "It is the workers in the department or industry itself who should, and will in a true democracy, undertake all management. Management in the form of an autocratic outside body, imposed from above, will no longer exist when democracy is actually achieved."[50]

Yet Pankhurst was prepared to concede that something short of a total commitment to "free Communism" might constitute at least a very small step in the right direction:

> The London Central Branch of the I.L.P. is advocating a four or rather five chamber Parliament. The proposal is adapted from the proposals of Mr and Mrs Sidney Webb in their book entitled "A Commonwealth for Great Britain." We cannot subscribe to the I.L.P. proposal. It is out of keeping with the free communist society we desire. Nevertheless we welcome the fact that even in the I.L.P. people begin to realise that King, Privy Council, Lords and Commons together represent a machinery which is incompatible with the Socialist ideal.[51]

The Degeneration of the Russian Revolution: "Right-Wing" Communists Abandon Soviet Democracy

Like the SLP and *The Socialist,* the *Dreadnought* was quick to detect signs of degeneration in Russia. Unlike the former, however, it saw this not simply as an inevitable consequence of the "backwardness" of Russia, compounded by the failure of the working class of the West to come to its aid. Rather, there had been a series of avoidable wrongs committed by the Bolsheviks.

At the beginning of 1922, Pankhurst noted signs of this deterioration. One was the arrest in Russia of the Rumanian KAPD member, Henry Kagan, who was "suspected of having entered relations with Left Social Revolutionaries and with the Workers' Opposition." This was probably the consequence of "a decree lately given out by the Soviet Government, in accordance with which all who oppose the new economic policy are to be treated as enemies of the state." White

Guards and other counter-revolutionaries, who had "fought, weapon in hand, against Soviet Russia," the *Dreadnought* claimed, were being amnestied in order "to make room in the prisons for our comrades of the Workers' Opposition and the Left Social Revolutionaries."[52]

About a month later, the paper reported that "Anarchist-Communists," as well as SRs and the Workers' Opposition, were being suppressed by the Bolsheviks. The same issue contained a letter protesting the arrest by the Cheka of the All-Russian Section of the Anarchist Universalists, as well as an appeal by Alexander Berkman, Emma Goldman, and Alexander Shapiro on behalf of anarchists imprisoned in Russia.[53]

By March 1922, the *Dreadnought* was arguing that whereas the Russian Soviet government was a "target for capitalist abuse, Communists had refrained from criticism." But now, what with the reversion to capitalism in the form of the New Economic Policy and "the chorus of praise swelled by bourgeois politicians," it was time to consider the views of those Russian workers in whose opinion "the proletarian revolution is being betrayed." An article by a "Russian comrade," translated from the anarchist *Le Libertaire*, followed. From the outset, in 1918, "the roles of the Communist Party and of the proletariat in the revolution were rigidly defined; on the one side the material, the herd, the proletariat; on the other, the Communist Party, which organises, administers and directs all. 'The Communist State' in its essence is the dictatorship of the Central Committee."[54]

A second article, from the same source, attacked the Terror: "All shapes and forms of human liberty were torn up by the roots; freedom of speech, of association, of assembly, and of free labour were proclaimed to be middle class ideas and prejudices." The Cheka had become a "hideous sore for the whole country." The Bolsheviks had taken over the revolutionary movement, and, "under cover of the Dictatorship of the Proletariat," they had turned on "all who understood the social revolution as the self-organisation of the labouring masses," beginning, as of 12 April 1918, with the violent suppression of anarchist clubs and press and becoming systematic thereafter. The advertisement for Pankhurst's *Soviet Russia as I Saw It in 1920,* in the same issue, now carried the warning "Written before the Policy of Reversion to Capitalism was Instituted."[55]

In *The Workers' Opposition,* serialized in the *Dreadnought* in the spring of 1922, Kollontai argued that the revolution had benefited the peasants and the middle classes, who had "cleverly adapted" and taken over all responsible positions in Soviet government, while the working class was told to "suffer and wait" as their conditions became "more unbearable." Pankhurst complained that in a debate between speakers from the ILP and the CPGB, Ernest E. Hunter and Palme Dutt, both had assumed that "state socialism" existed in Russia, "entirely ignoring the fact that the land of Russia is privately worked by the peasants, that vast tracts of it are being offered for private capitalist exploitation, and that the industries are fast passing away from the State into private hands."[56] Further evidence of the Bolshevik's descent "from depth to depth" was to be found, said the *Dreadnought,* in a *Daily Herald* report that there would be no workers' participation or compulsory trade union membership for the employees of foreign "concessionaries." The *Dreadnought* hoped that the fact that "the Soviet Government expressly permits the capitalist to employ non-unionist labour will open the eyes of the proletariat of the Western world."[57]

"Oh! For another workers' uprising to cleanse this augean stable that is being created in what was once Red Russia!" wrote Pankhurst in August 1922. Lenin was "hauling down the flag of Communism and abandoning the cause of the emancipation of the workers." He preferred "to retain office under Capitalism than to stand by Communism and fall with it if need be."[58] And on 7 April 1923, responding to reports of the execution of a Roman Catholic priest in Russia, Pankhurst commented: "It is the very worst sort of propaganda for Communism which, though some people are apt to forget the fact, is based upon human fraternity." A little over a year later, as the *Dreadnought* neared its end, Herman Gorter concluded in "The International and the World Revolution" that "Russia and the Third International are the greatest enemies of the world revolution."[59]

Parallel degeneration was evident nearer to home. When *The Communist* argued that the question of "whether the workers are to rule through a Soviet Dictatorship or through a Parliament" would become "a vital and immediate issue" only once the Labour Party was in power, Pankhurst concluded that the Communist Party had "abandoned the establishment of the Soviets as an essential part of its policy" and that "to the officials of the CPGB the Soviets mean dictatorship. They have no conception of a free Communist life in which Soviet workers in the industries will administer the production and distribution of the social product."[60] The CPGB was "now more reactionary than the old B.S.P of pre Russian Revolution days."[61]

The Irish Communists were no better. Instead of demanding the replacement of the *Daìl Eirean* and the existing local government bodies with soviets, their proposals on the ownership and management of industry were constructed "on truly Fabian lines."[62] When the *Workers' Weekly* (which had replaced *The Communist*) insisted that the CPGB was striving to establish "a Workers' State," Pankhurst dismissed this as "State Capitalism":

> They are great statists, great disciplinarians, great dictators, these latter-day Right-Wing Muscovites. It should be noticed that unfortunate humanity is expected to bow to the rod of the super-disciplinarians for at least a generation after the Workers' State has come into being.[63]

In September 1923, the *Dreadnought* once again attempted to clarify its own understanding of communism: "When we use the terms 'Communist' and 'Communism,' we are far from meaning the blood and thunder, physical force, follow-your-leader- discipline nonsense which passes for Communism in many quarters."[64] But while the Bolshevik revolution degenerated, and at home the shop stewards' and workers' council movements seemed virtually dead, there had been encouraging signs elsewhere.

The Spread of Soviets and the Dictatorship of the Proletariat

The *Dreadnought* kept discovering soviets in embryo in many locations — some of which seem anything but likely. In February 1922, the temporary seizure of some mills and creameries near Mallow and of stations in the city by Cork railworkers was headlined "The Soviets in Cork." A month or so later, it was Austrian workers' councils that were seen as forerunners of the soviets, and in May the takeover and running of some butter factories earned an editorial headlined "Another Irish Soviet" [65]

Hopes for a "soviet" Ireland were not, however, encouraged by the publication of the draft constitution of the Irish Free State, which contained, said Pankhurst, "some features which have not yet found their way to this country." These included proportional representation and some provision for the use of the referendum and initiative but also "checks on the working of democratic government, notably the Senate." She concluded:

> From the democratic standpoint the draft constitution therefore leaves
> much to be desired: whilst to those who are Sovietists, like ourselves,
> it is wholly unsatisfactory. Of course that was inevitable. On with the
> Soviet movement.

The lack of permanent progress towards soviets in Ireland was frustrating. For

> soviets have again and again risen in that green island across the sea.
> The Irish workers have given evidence that they can act. What they lack
> is a general comprehension that the soviets should be regarded not as a
> weapon for forcing concessions from the employer, but as a permanent
> successor to the employer, so that the employing system may go out of
> existence altogether. [66]

By 1924, there were few "soviets" to report, although the *Dreadnought* detected signs of a desire for soviets in the 1924 National Union of Teachers conference when, in a debate on a motion urging co-operation with the Board of Education, some speakers called for "teachers' control to put a check on the bureaucratic control." Similarly, two weeks later, the paper was encouraged when the Railway Clerks' Association conference discussed workers' control of industry:

> Its executive opposed the principle and procured a vote in favour of joint control of industry by the workers therein and by the community. The idea of workers' control is moving onward and securing wider and wider circles of adherents. When it is fully understood, we shall see spring up the workshop councils which eventually will take over industry.[67]

While soviets were advocated enthusiastically and unconditionally and every instance of self-initiated working-class activity was seen as potentially leading to their establishment, Pankhurst was having second thoughts about the dictatorship of the proletariat. In July 1923, the *Dreadnought* published the manifesto of the Unemployed Workers' Organisation, which, it hastened to point out, was not connected "with another organisation known as the National Unemployed Workers' Movement." According to the manifesto, the organization was opposed to affiliation with a "counter-revolutionary party as the Labour Party or such a reformist party as the Communist Party of Great Britain" and likewise with the TUC or RILU. The manifesto, signed by J. Mummery (chairman) and G.E. Soderberg (secretary) continued:

> We firmly believe in the application of a rigid dictatorship of the proletariat when the collapse of Capitalism comes, but until that time we strongly object to the dictatorship of a caucus of self-seeking politicians who make the "united front" an excuse for their own self-aggrandisement.

The *Dreadnought* declared its general support for the Unemployed Workers' Organisation. But it had reservations:

> One phrase has crept into the manifesto . . . which requires discussion. It is a phrase of which all Communists have made use, both of late and also in the days of Marx, Engels and Bachunin [*sic*]. We refer to the term "the dictatorship of the proletariat." This in its original use

meant the rigid suppression of the middle and upper classes in so far as they may endeavour to resist the coming of socialism and to combat the popular will.

Latterly, under the inspiration of Russian bureaucrats, the term ... has been used to justify the dictatorship of a party clique of officials over their own party members and over the people at large. So far as the dictatorship has been carried that the parties submitting to it have become utterly sterile as instruments of education and action. In Russia the dictatorship has robbed the revolution of all it fought for; it has banished Communism and workers' control.

Liberty is an essential part of the Communist revolution. We must not sacrifice it to the ambitions of would-be dictators.[68]

Early in February of the following year, in the course of commenting, supportively, on the manifesto of the Russian Communist Workers' Group, which touched again on the question of the "dictatorship of the industrial proletariat," Pankhurst wrote:

In spite of the time-honoured character, we must affirm that, in our view, the use of the term "dictatorship" is responsible for much confusion and misunderstanding.

No reasonable person believes that what was required in Russia was that the relatively small number of industrial workers in Russia should act as the dictators — in the sense that the Czar and Napoleon were dictators — over the peasant masses of Russia.

But a week later the *Dreadnought* carried two series of articles by Herman Gorter that were distinctly "anti-peasant." According to Gorter, peasant soviets had been a mistake since "it was certain that the peasants would fight for private property and against Communism. A proletarian revolution, in Germany or England, will never give the peasants political rights till they have shown that they are really communists."[69]

Gorter was equally hostile to trade unions. Only workshop councils could supply "the essential bedrock" for communism. "By making peace with trade unionism the Russian Bolsheviks and the Third International showed that they were themselves still capitalist, and neither wished or dared to smash up European capitalism." But, he went on, "the real proletarian revolution, which is preparing in England, North America and Germany, cannot be made by a stupid mass led by a few wise leaders, only by the self-conscious, self-acting mass."[70]

Though Pankhurst seems never to refer to herself as an anarchist, the libertarian emphasis in the later *Dreadnought* was strong. Contemplating the nature of "free Communism" in October 1923, she wrote: "There shall be no State, Government or Parliament." Rather, the economy would be organized on a "voluntary autonomous workshop basis." By April 1924, Pankhurst was reassessing the ideas of Proudhon in a review article based on the recent republication of some of his work by the anarchist Freedom Press. "We differ emphatically from his desire to retain private ownership and petty trading," she noted, but his "denunciation of the tyranny of majority rule and of the centralised bureaucracy advocated by the State Socialists is unanswerable."[71] In an article in which she declared that "neither legal nor religious forms can make the mating of men and women either right or wrong," Pankhurst advocated "free Communism," with "no State, Government or Parliament" and the economy organized on a "voluntary autonomous workshop basis."[72]

Like the SLP's *The Socialist,* Pankhurst and the *Workers' Dreadnought* thus maintained a "Left Communist" commitment to its own version of a pure form of soviet democracy. But how did ideas of soviet democracy fare in the Communist Party of Great Britain?

12

THE EARLY BRITISH COMMUNIST PARTY
Soviet Democracy Deferred and Redefined

The First Step to Socialism: A Labour Government

I n the early days of the Bolshevik revolution, the British
Socialist Party was as contemptuous of bourgeois parliamentary democracy and as committed to the soviet variety
as the "ultra-Left" elements of the SLP and Pankhurst's Communist
Workers. H. Alexander and E.C. Fairchild had found — to their apparent
surprise — little support for their reservations about soviet democracy
during the debate with Theodore Rothstein in *The Call* during the
summer of 1919. A year later, the BSP was to form the initial core of the
Communist Party of Great Britain. Other elements that joined the new
party — from the SLP, the CP (BSTI), and the "Left Wing" of the ILP
— had been at least equally enthusiastic proponents of the soviet system.
The same was broadly true of recruits from among the guild socialists.

Yet it soon became evident that adhesion to the "official"

Communist line meant, for Britain at least, the deferment to a more distant time of the promotion, and ultimately of the reality, of soviet democracy. Moreover, with regard to perceptions of Russian soviet democracy, a process of change was set in motion that led towards the development of a version of the ideal of soviet democracy that reconciled it, to the satisfaction of its adherents, with the actual Communist dictatorship in Russia. This accompanied and was in fact integral to the emergence of the vanguard party theory and the centralization, or "Bolshevizing," of the British Communist Party itself, along with a radical downgrading of any notion of internal democracy. The conversion of some of the most prominent former advocates of soviet democracy "from below" aided the acceptance of the new interpretation.

Deferment concerned the prospects for soviet democracy in Britain. Even before the formation of the CPGB in the summer of 1920, while Left Communists and the radical shop stewards of *Solidarity* insisted on attempting the immediate creation of workplace-based workers' committees, *The Call* (soon to become *The Communist*) saw the need for an intermediate step in the coming social revolution. By May 1920, the BSP's paper was already emphasizing the need for a radical vanguard, as well as supporting Labour Party affiliation for the future Communist Party. "The Social Revolution must be ushered in by a class-conscious minority," it argued, "which if not passively supported by the masses, then at least must not have the masses actively or passively opposed to them." The majority in Britain would support Labour, and therefore a Labour government was "the necessary preliminary to the Communist Revolution." This step was needed to shake the working class out of its delusions. As a result of Labour's election, workers would learn "the sham of Representative Government and the inevitability of the Dictatorship of the Proletariat." Communists should therefore abstain from activity that "might harm the prospects of the Labour Party."[1] Later, the continued refusal of Labour to accept the affiliation of the CPGB failed to modify this position.

Not that there was any shortage of criticism of the Labour Party, particularly as regards its views concerning Russia. In 1922, *The*

Communist was scathing about Labour's condemnation of the trial and execution of twelve leaders of the Social Revolutionary Party.[2] Nor were all CP members happy with the policy of Labour Party affiliation. The Musselburgh branch registered its disapproval. Nevertheless, it expressed its determination to carry out the party executive's instructions to withdraw candidates standing against Labour — a manifestation, said *The Communist,* "of our desire to form a working-class united front against capitalism."[3]

Any moves to implement soviet democracy were to be postponed until after a Labour government had been elected and shown wanting, with a consequent shift of allegiance to the Communists and the precipitation of a "revolutionary situation." In the meantime, the CPGB would continue to pursue Labour Party affiliation. The logic of this was to make the election of a Labour government the initial step on the road to socialism and to postpone any immediate prospect of soviet democracy in Britain.

Redefinition Begins: Democracy . . . or Ergatocracy?

Advocates of the "soviet system" had usually been content to contrast "bourgeois democracy" with "proletarian democracy." The latter, otherwise known as "soviet democracy," was presented as infinitely more authentic. But was not "democracy" — the rule of an indeterminate "people" — an irredeemably bourgeois concept? Did not the rule of the workers mean a new departure, a transition to something superior to democracy? For some, this was clearly so.

Morgan Philips Price, the pro-Bolshevik *Manchester Guardian* correspondent, was an articulate advocate of the superiority of the soviets. In a series of articles in the *Workers' Dreadnought,* he counterposed — in one of his sub-headings — "Soviet System Versus Democracy." A "democratic state," he argued, recognized "no economic divisions in the electorate," and everyone was regarded as part of what was "vaguely called 'the people.'" But soviets provided "the economic apparatus" that was able "to represent the workers' special interests and . . . reconcile them with the interests of the community."[4]

Eden and Cedar Paul took the process of dropping the term *democracy* as applied to the soviets one step further. For them, the correct way to describe the working-class rule exemplified by the soviets was their own coining: *ergatocracy* — the rule of the workers. They outlined their position in May 1919, in a letter to the *Workers' Dreadnought* that sought to explain why they were resigning from both the ILP and the BSP. The "purely political type of social organisation" had, they argued, outlived its usefulness; the future lay with the new type of industrial organization, the workers' committees and the shop stewards' movement. There was in the socialist movement, they maintained, "a hopeless divergence between those who expect to realise socialism through political democracy and those who expect to realise it through Communist ergatocracy — the administration of the workers by the workers — with (as a preliminary stage) the dictatorship of the proletariat exercised through workers' committees or soviets."[5] This argument was developed in their book, *Creative Revolution: A Study of Communist Ergatocracy* (1920). Unsurprisingly, the neologism was not one destined to enter general discourse.[6] Meanwhile, the Comintern was busy redefining the revolutionary role of the soviets.

The Role of the Soviets: Zinoviev's "Theses"

As we have seen, in the earliest years of Bolshevik rule the superiority of the soviet system over so-called bourgeois forms of democracy was as much part of the stock in trade of *The Call* as of other left-wing publications that identified with the idea of soviet democracy. But now the emphasis in accounts of this "higher form of democracy" was shifting from what had earlier been seen as a spontaneous creation by the workers towards something that suggested foresight and planning on Lenin's part. Early in 1920, *The Call* reviewed Lenin's pamphlet "Towards Soviets," which, it said, had given the very earliest formulation to the soviet idea, in 1917, and had correctly anticipated "not only the trend of events, but also the objections forthcoming from Socialist opponents of 'dictatorship and Soviet rule.'" Time had proved him right; soviets were "higher in type than a parliamentary republic from the point of view of workers' control."[7]

Later that year, with the new British party now formed, Zinoviev's "Theses" — adopted by the Third International and, as we have seen, the target of much criticism from the Left Wing — laid down three conditions necessary for the organization of soviets: a "great revolutionary impulse," an acute political and economic crisis, and a serious decision "in the minds of considerable masses of workers, and first to all in the ranks of the Communist Party" to begin the final struggle for power. In the absence of these conditions, the idea of soviet democracy should be promulgated but no action to form soviets taken. Soviets without a revolution were impossible — they would become a "parody of Soviets."[8] This was a crucial difference in point of view. For the Third International and therefore for the CPGB, soviets, prior to the revolution, were essentially a mechanism for seizing power. Until revolution appeared imminent, they might be advocated in a general way, but they were actually to be set up only at the beginning of a definite revolutionary crisis, the advent of which would be determined by the Communist Party itself. In contrast, those whom the Communists now termed the "ultra-Left" saw the promotion of embryonic soviet democracy, which seemed to prefigure the communist society of the future, as an immediate and essential task in preparing the way for revolution.

How could the new society based on working-class self-organization possibly function without the workers being well prepared for this form of democracy? How could promoting this new form of democracy possibly co-exist with participation in the discredited and irredeemably bourgeois versions of democracy? Hence, as we have seen, the rejection by Pankhurst and other "anti-parliamentarians" of any involvement in the politics of parliamentary and local government elections. And though the SLP dissented from this view to the extent of perceiving a necessity for involvement in "bourgeois" electoral politics, it, too, gave priority to trying to build a working-class participatory organization, in the form of the Workers' International Industrial Union.

The Communist — a "transmogrified" *Call*, as Willie Thompson puts it in *The Good Old Cause* — began publication immediately following the formation of the CPGB. Billing itself "An Organ of the Third (Communist) International" published by the Communist Party's executive committee, it ran as a weekly from 5 August 1920 until 3 February 1923, when it was replaced by the *Workers' Weekly*, which Thompson characterizes as "the recognisable ancestor not only of the subsequent *Daily Worker* but also of the latter-day journals of the British far left, like *Militant* and *Socialist Worker*."[9] Throughout its existence, there were hardly any invocations of soviet democracy in *The Communist* — far fewer, especially, than in the *Dreadnought* during the same period. For the CPGB, emphasis was shifting decisively to the need for a "dictatorship of the proletariat" and to the necessity for the Communist Party itself to assume the role of leader in bringing this about.

The Dictatorship of the Proletariat: From Class to Party

As we saw in our discussion of the dictatorship of the proletariat (chapter 7), the emphasis had initially been on class rather than party and also on the brevity of the period of dictatorship that was perceived as inevitable and necessary. The role of the working class in the coming revolution would be a direct one, and the transition to socialism, indeed to communism, would be short. In an article titled "The Dictatorship of the Proletariat," which appeared in *The Call* in the summer of 1917, months before the Bolsheviks came to power, the future Communist MP J.T. Walton Newbold emphasized the perceived impatience of the proletariat with reformist half-measures. The working class would not be satisfied with "that social-co-partnery known as Guild Socialism; with the democratisation of the State; the consumer's safeguard for protection against himself, the producer," but would instead bring "the capitalist system of civilisation" to an end, "now or in the not far distant future."[10]

The following year, with the end of the war at last in sight, *The Call* published Dora Montefiore's article "How Socialism Will Be

Realised." As we saw in chapter 7, Montefiore foresaw the triumph of socialism by "the end of four years of peace," following "a temporary revolutionary Dictatorship of the People," which she equated with the contemporary wartime state direction and restrictions in Britain.[11] In much the same spirit, soon after the formation of the CPGB, the party's first manifesto ended with the injunction to "CONCENTRATE UPON WORKERS' CONTROL" and the statement that "The Workers ALONE CAN FREE the working class."[12]

But party was soon elbowing class aside — or, rather, party was soon to be declared more or less interchangeable with class. Reports from the Comintern Second Congress were featured in the early issues of *The Communist,* with more of Zinoviev's strictures on the soviets given prominence. "The Soviet system not only did not exclude the idea of a proletarian party, but, on the contrary, presupposed it," he insisted. He dismissed the claim by "people like Kautsky" that what existed in Russia was a dictatorship of the party rather than of the proletariat. One followed from the other, he argued, "since the Party is merely the organisation of the most advanced elements of the working class."[13]

The focus of *The Communist* came to centre on the obstacles the Bolsheviks had faced: civil war, intervention, and the machinations of counter-revolutionaries. Harsh, authoritarian Bolshevik measures were unavoidable. These measures were retrospectively alluded to, explained but not portrayed in detail, in T.A. Jackson and R.W. Postgate's "The Story of the Russian Revolution," which began serialization in *The Communist* in November 1921. The responsibility for repression was placed firmly with the perfidious behaviour of opponents of the Bolsheviks who had attacked the revolutionary regime with total ruthlessness:

The Extra-Ordinary Commission and the Soviet authorities replied by producing a mass terror against the enemies of the Revolution. Upon the details of this we have no need to dwell. The whole country was in a chaos of conflicting pressures, and the enemies of the Republic had shown themselves utterly without scruple in their determination to compass its downfall. The Soviet Republic had no choice but to cast away scruples likewise, and deal with the wild beastlike attacks in the only possible way.[14]

The assumption among British Bolshevik supporters had been that the period of the dictatorship of the proletariat would be very brief, but now the end to this phase seemed to be retreating rapidly into the distance — and the role of the proletariat itself along with it. The decisive shift of emphasis from class to party was clearly completed when, early in 1923, the *Workers' Weekly*, which had just replaced *The Communist*, reported on a meeting of the "Communist Party Council." The report included the text of a resolution, moved by Tom Bell, which decreed that "only the workers' government, consisting of Communists, can be the embodiment of the dictatorship of the proletariat."[15] This shift from class to party was accompanied by, and complementary to, the "Bolshevization" of the CPGB.

"Bolshevization" and Democratic Centralism

Calls for tight party discipline had been made even before the British Communist Party came formally into being. In spite of Pankhurst's notions about rival "Left" and "Right" Communist parties or "Left blocks" within the party, there could, of course, be only one, monolithic, party. Robert Williams, secretary of the National Transport Workers' Federation and soon to be the BSP's "national" delegate at the founding conference of the CPGB, was to be expelled, even before Sylvia Pankhurst, following the Triple Alliance's failure to support the miners on Black Friday. But on the eve of the formation of the new party, he was very much in favour of party discipline. He believed, he told *Daily Herald* readers in the fourth of his "Impressions of Soviet Russia" articles, "more and more in discipline and organisation. Dictatorship first of all to break down the capitalist system, and then strict military and industrial discipline in order to establish the Socialist or Communist state." And a week later, in *The Call*, W.H. Ryde made a plea for "voluntary, rigid discipline," concluding that "we should be Communists first and trade unionists, co-operators, and the like after."[16]

As always, the example of Russia was inspirational. Dora Montefiore had been elected, together with five others (all men), to form the provisional committee of the party. She praised George Young's recent *Observer* article about a visit to Russia, quoting his view that "devotion and discipline are organised into a 'Red Army,' or more accurately perhaps into a Religious order — the Communist Party. . . . They are the First Hundred Thousand — a missionary and militant Lenin as Loyola." Montefiore commented: "Nothing finer could be told of these men and women." In the same issue, *The Communist* reported that the Third International had summoned "all elements standing for the mass struggle for proletarian dictatorship" to unite "under the guidance of a centralised party of the revolutionary proletariat."[17]

A fortnight later came Zinoviev's version of how Communist MPs — once there were any — should operate. He insisted that "the parliamentary group must be wholly in the hands of the Central Committee of the Communist Party." Somewhat ironically, in the same issue *The Communist* reported that the CPGB had received a letter from Arthur Henderson, the Labour Party secretary. Henderson had written to confirm that the CPGB's application to affiliate to the Labour Party had been turned down — something that made the likelihood that there would be, in the foreseeable future, enough Communist MPs to form a parliamentary group more remote than ever.[18]

Very soon the CPGB as a whole became the target of "Communist Discipline." In an article so titled, Albert H. Hawkins wrote in October 1920 that it was "necessary to examine our Party machinery and outlook in order that anything which contravenes the spirit of the Russian Revolution may be speedily remedied." The Russian party was synonymous with discipline, whereas "we have confused democracy as an ideal of government with democracy as a matter of political tactics. This needs alteration." He continued:

The Communists have declared their adhesion to the policy of the "dictatorship of the proletariat," realising that pure and unqualified democracy is not practicable during a revolutionary period or a time of transition. This abandonment of democracy for the time being must be carried into the party organisation in order that our forces may be used to the greatest possible advantage.[19]

The conference of the CPGB at Easter 1921 was not without some signs of internal debate — even dissent. *The Communist* reported a "splendid debate" about the powers of the executive committee. Some delegates (those from Central South Wales and Tooting were mentioned) wanted "some check" by "locality against the centre." *The Communist* interpreted this as a throwback to earlier attitudes triggered by memories of betrayals on the part of trade union leadership. Such anachronistic responses were swept aside, it assured readers, when William Mellor made the case for "centralised power," declaring that "a revolutionary organisation must have a central driving force able to issue orders and to enforce them." But the soviets were not completely forgotten. The conference urged "the adoption of the Soviet or Workers' Council system so successfully applied in Russia."[20]

By the autumn of 1921, there were already indications of the direction the party was heading, including the introduction of the key notion of "democratic centralism." This first appeared in the pages of *The Communist* on 17 September 1921, in the same issue as a front-page report on Pankhurst's expulsion from the party. In an article titled "Party Organisation," Tom Bell declared, under the sub-heading "Democratic Centralism":

Formal democracy, which is the curse of most institutions outside the Communist Party, represents a splitting of the organisation into *active functionaries and passive masses.* Proletarian democracy rejects formalism for the living association of common endeavour i.e. an active living organisation of struggle working up through a centralised leadership. This centralisation does not merely exist on paper; it is derived from the development and maintenance of living associations and mutual relations within the Party. Between the directing organs and the members. In other words, formal democracy produces bureaucracy and promotes anarchism. Proletarian democracy or democratic centralism is an efficient instrument which the membership feels is fundamental for the successful carrying out common activity and struggle. It represents live contact from the lowest unit of the organisation or individual membership right up to the central leadership and *vice versa* from the centre to the several units.

Another article stressed the binding nature, for every Communist, of the "instructions and resolutions of the International" and the powers of the central committee: "The representatives of the Central Committee or comrades authorised by it are to be admitted to all meetings, *with a deciding voice.*"[21]

The key stage in the "Bolshevization" of the CPGB began in 1922. Kevin Morgan has called attention to the crucial role of the Comintern control commission's emissary, Jakob Friis.[22] With encouragement and pressure from this quarter, the party conference took place that spring. It determined, *The Communist* declared, that the party would go forward united, "welded into an homogenous body." The conference ratified "the Theses on the International Situation, Revolutionary Tactics, and Tactics of the Russian Communist Party" and set up a commission, in the words of Gallacher, "to go into the whole question of party workings with a view to applying the new methods of organisation with the least amount of disturbance of the Party as it now exists." There was some disagreement about the scope of the enquiry, an issue that, on Gallacher's advice, was referred back to the executive. There were also differing views on the commission's composition. It was decided by 87 to 38 to select it from outside the executive.[23] The result was announced a little later: Harry Inkpin (Albert's brother) and Harry Pollitt, with Palme Dutt chairing. The commission was set the task of making detailed recommendations to the executive and to the annual conference "for the application of the theses." It would have access to all information, but no executive powers, and would "issue short reports on its work from time to time."[24]

A second conference followed in the autumn of 1922. In a report titled "A Strong Central Lead," *The Communist* commented: "We have grown out of the old childishness of insurrectionary posing and of democratic sentimentalising. The essential task of the Conference is the setting up of a strong and efficient central leadership." The conference had adopted, "without dissent or opposition," the commission's proposals. "For the first time in the history of the working-class movement in this country, a single centralized organisation of the revolutionary forces has been established," the paper concluded, with evident satisfaction.[25] Early the next year, an article titled "Rebuilding the Communist Party" recorded "considerable progress in the re-building of the Communist Party on the lines of the Theses of the Communist International."[26]

Desertions from the Left

The process of Bolshevization certainly accelerated during 1922, and its outcome came to be more consciously sought. But long before that the tide in that direction was marked by some notable desertions from the cause of true soviet democracy as perceived by "Left-Wing" Communists. These must have had a considerable impact, given the prominence of those involved. As early as 1920, the startling change in the thinking of J.T. Murphy that we noted in the introduction, from a purist "bottom-up" to a determinedly "top-down" approach, was already well underway.

Murphy had started 1920 as member of the SLP. Reviewing Robert Michels's *Political Parties* (translated by Cedar and Eden Paul) for *The Socialist* at the beginning of the year, he asked: "Who has not witnessed the new organisation come into being, observed the small groups, enthusiastically, democratically, carrying on their business, growing in numbers and losing their democracy in spite of their profession?" But he had rejected Michels's idea of the inevitability of oligarchy; it was too much of a "sweeping statement":

Even in Soviet Russia wherein the highest form of democratic organisation has been evolved, the conflict with capitalism modifies it and compels a degree of subordination which would be unnecessary had the class struggle ceased. Yet the whole answer to Michels' conclusions are [*sic*] there.[27]

Initially, at least, Murphy had also rejected the line taken by the Communist Unity Group. In a letter from Hamburg dated 10 April 1920, which *The Socialist* editor called "illuminating in the extreme," Murphy still saw the BSP as a body lacking revolutionary credentials and warned of the "grave danger of the Communist International being infected with compromise."[28] In "The S.L.P. and Unity — An Open Letter to the Party" (and a very long one), he identified the SLP, approvingly, as "the Extreme Left." The SLP, he declared, had more in common with the anti-parliamentary Workers' Socialist Federation and South Wales Socialist Society than with the BSP, which only "under protest" had withdrawn from the Labour Party. "Better a Communist Party without the B.S.P. than a party including the B.S.P. trailing with it the spirit of compromise to hamper the party in revolutionary practice." But at the same time this open letter signalled a break with Murphy's past. It concluded:

> A Revolutionary Party needs strong leadership, strong centralisation, and rigid discipline.

> P.S. This letter may be quoted against some of my previous utterances, well, so much for those utterances.[29]

That was in May 1920. By November, Murphy's transition was nearly complete. Writing in the *Dreadnought*, still the organ of the CP (BSTI), Murphy began by quoting Zinoviev and other Bolshevik leaders, with whose views on the need for "iron discipline" and "democratic centralism" he agreed. The problem for British Communists was that, perhaps more so than anywhere else in the world, "capitalistic notions of democracy have so saturated the social and political life of a people." As a result, the "pleas for referendums and local autonomy" were common in all parties, and "rank and file control by way of the ballot-box" had become for many the exclusive test of such control.

But now, "under the impulse of the Communist International and the growing intensity of the class war," the fight against such notions had opened in earnest. Such things as "referendums and local autonomy" could be promoted "so long as the revolutionary movement was confined to propaganda," but the entire conception of the movement was changing. This shift was occurring because of the growing realization that the movement was

> a revolutionary and insurrectionary struggle involving the penetration of numerous organisations, the harnessing of forces leading to open conflict, the mobilisation and direction of the masses first in this direction and then in that, according to the exigencies of the situation developed by the waging of war against the capitalist class, each step fraught with grave consequences, and toleration of looseness in organisation and lack of decisiveness and quick responsive action, becomes a veritable menace to the working class. We are the revolutionary army waging a many-fronted war, and an army that is not organised in such a manner that it can act in unison and work to a definite plan of campaign is destined to failure.[30]

There were still faint echoes of Murphy's syndicalist years in another *Dreadnought* article, published the following week, in which he called for "a shaping of the Party with a deeper regard for industry than hitherto." Otherwise, little remained that was reminiscent of his earlier stance. The party's executive was to exercise unfettered power between national congresses, with "no antiquated limitations of the referendum etc.," he wrote. "The General Staff of an army cannot take a ballot vote of the army before each battle to see if the rank and file are willing to fight." The executive should not be elected by a ballot of the membership; most members would know nothing about the majority of names on the list. Subcommittees of the executive should exercise the full powers of the parent body between meetings of the latter. Control by the membership would be exercised by "opportunities for recall," which were "a far more effective method of keeping the organisation at its highest pitch than the old methods of referendum etc." It had to be remembered, Murphy said, that the party was not required to think out basic principles and policy. These were all to be found in the theses of the Second Congress of the Communist International. The party's task was simply their application.[31]

A second sad defection, from the standpoint of Left Communists, and particularly in the eyes of Sylvia Pankhurst, was that of another former leading light of the shop stewards' movement, Willie Gallacher. As in the case of Murphy, the crucial moment in his conversion to the orthodox Bolshevik line had been his attendance — which included meetings with Lenin — at the Second Comintern Congress in the summer of 1920.

The *Dreadnought* ended 1921 — literally on New Year's Eve — with a long attack on Gallacher. In Moscow the previous year, he had been confronted with Lenin's *"Left-Wing" Communism: An Infantile Disorder,* which quoted him disapprovingly. "Undaunted," he had stuck to his anti-parliamentary views and had joined Pankhurst in speaking at the Third International conference on behalf of the Left — opposing Labour Party affiliation and parliamentary action. At the same time, "honestly impressed with Lenin's appeal for Communist unity," he had returned determined to secure it. Participation in the united party, however, seemed "completely to have changed William Gallacher; a revolution has taken place in his mind." Pankhurst quoted from "Are We Realists?" an article by Gallacher and J.R. Campbell that had appeared in the previous week's *Communist:*

> The class content of the Labour Party is proletarian. . . . To unconditionally repudiate affiliation to the Labour Party because of its defects leads to the most pitifully barren sectarianism. It brings one close to the position of the bewildered theoreticians of the "Three and a Half International," whose immaculate Communist Parties and theoretically beautiful, but politically impotent industrial unions are no more a menace to Capitalism than the Primrose League.

On this, Pankhurst commented:

> By the "Three and a Half International" the writers, of course, mean
> the Fourth. W. Gallacher and J.R. Campbell have indeed receded from
> their attitude of 1920 as some pages of *The Worker* will testify.
>
> We prefer the Gallacher of 1920, who said he did not like the Par-
> liamentary–Labour Party–Trade Union policy of Moscow, but would
> bow to it for the sake of unity as long as it remained the majority policy,
> and in the meantime would strive to change it for the "Left Wing" policy
> he now decries. Lenin advised us to form a Left Block with Gallacher
> in 1920. Where is Gallacher now?
>
> (Oh, Comrade Lenin with your tortuous Eastern tactics, you are
> corrupting these simple Westerners, who do not understand you, and
> whose metal is softer than yours!)[32]

Soviet Democracy Deferred

If such erstwhile ardent advocates of full-blooded soviet democracy
were now preaching the necessity for obedience to the Third International and its leadership, this must have had a considerable influence
on those on the Left, and not simply members of the CPGB, who had
hitherto been enthused by the vision of a society in which the workers — real, literal workers — democratically took all decisions from
the shop floor upwards. According to Zinoviev's theses, the soviets
were no longer to be seen as spontaneously created bodies exercising
grassroots democracy but rather as a mechanism for bringing about
the dictatorship of the proletariat, or Communist rule. They would
be called into being when, and only when, the party determined that
a revolutionary crisis was imminent.

In Russia, the ultra-optimistic prognosis of revolutionary advance
was no longer tenable. The task of the Bolsheviks was to ensure that
their rule survived in circumstances where, despite the end of the civil
war, it was threatened, both internally and externally, from all sides.
The first duty of British Communists was to do whatever they could
to support their Russian comrades, besieged in a hostile world — a

duty that now took precedence over the promotion of the idea of soviet democracy. Indeed, "proletarian democracy" could now be equated with "democratic centralism." Within the British Communist Party, democracy was to be abandoned "for the time being." Given that the path to socialist revolution had already been well marked out in Russia, what scope was there for debate on policy?

Compared to the earlier post-1917 years, there was at this point little focus on the advocacy of soviet democracy and much more on the dictatorship of the proletariat, now clearly synonymous with the imposed rule of the "vanguard" Communist Party. It is difficult to resist the conclusion that, as far as "orthodox" Communism was concerned, the full implementation of soviet rule even in Russia itself — as those enthused in 1917 and 1918 by the prospect of this "higher" form of democracy would have understood it — had now been effectively postponed until some time in a hazy future, after the "dictatorship" had completely crushed all capitalist resistance.

In the case of Britain, it would be postponed until after disillusion with a future Labour government had rallied a working-class majority to the Communist cause. In July 1922, after the Labour Party had again refused to allow the CPGB to affiliate, *The Communist* still insisted on the necessity of a Labour government and "the determination of the Communist Party whether affiliated or not *to assist them to gain that position*."[33]

Soviet Democracy Depoliticized

Yet orthodox Communism did not *entirely* abandon soviet democracy, nor did it simply relegate it to a distant future. Rather, a way was found of reconciling a conception of soviet democracy with de facto dictatorship, whose "withering away" had now been deferred to a more distant day. Crucial to this was a well-established feature of the socialist movement, arguably its Achilles' heel (or one of them): its distaste for, even rejection of, politics. Pankhurst's anti-political stance has already been noted, in the previous chapter — though she was definitely not to share in the reconciliation with dictatorship. A similar rejection of politics is present in the SLP's idea of the replacement of the political state with the "Industrial Republic," following the revolutionary takeover. Conventional "bourgeois" politics, with no real purchase on the actual distribution of power, seemed to be characterized by empty rhetoric, unscrupulous manipulation, and self-seeking egotism — all ineffectual hot air and deliberate deception. Moreover, political parties reflected socio-economic classes. But in the classless society that socialists were striving for, would not the divisions represented by these parties have disappeared?

There would have been few people active in the British socialist movement in the 1920s who had not at least a passing acquaintance with William Morris's *News from Nowhere*. In the shortest chapter of that "utopian romance," old Hammond, who guides the time-travelling Morris in the post-revolutionary future, famously dismisses politics completely: "We are very well off as to politics — because we have none." Advocates of vanguard parties might have also found some apparent endorsement in another of Hammond's statements. Asked whether "differences" are settled by the "will of the majority," Hammond confirms that this is the case but adds: "The majority must have their way; *unless the minority were to take up arms and show by force that they were the effective or real majority*" (emphasis added). He goes on to say that this is unlikely to happen since "the apparent majority *is* the real majority."[34] But that, of course, was in Morris's ideal "communist" society of the future. How would it have been read by "British Bolsheviks" in the 1920s? Kevin Morgan has noted how frequently the memory of Morris and his notions of fellowship and the transformation of work were later invoked by visitors to the Soviet Union who were well disposed to what they encountered — or believed they encountered — there.[35]

Part of the attraction of soviet democracy had always been that the debased distractions of "bourgeois democracy" would give way to the *real*, down-to-earth, practical concerns of workers. Based on this disdain for the degradations of "politics," a version of soviet democracy was evolved that saw it as flourishing — and only able to flourish — beneath a protective carapace provided by the Communist Party's authoritarian rule, which warded off both the dastardly attacks of the worldwide capitalist conspiracy and the equally vicious machinations of the enemy within.

This version of soviet democracy can already be detected in the articles by Philips Price in the *Dreadnought* in 1919, quoted earlier in the chapter. The "two great social institutions" of revolutionary Russia were, according to the *Manchester Guardian* correspondent, "the political soviet and the economic soviet." The former's duty was "to protect the Republic from internal and external counter-revolution," while the latter was to "to build up under the protection of the former the new social order once the danger of foreign intervention is removed." It was then possible that "the political soviet will reduce its functions, and that the power in the land will pass to huge economic syndicates working under the Central Council of Public Economy." [36] This was a novel interpretation of the soviet structure. Earlier accounts of soviet democracy had not distinguished separate "political" and "economic" soviets.

This emerging version is even more clearly visible in the constitution adopted by the Workers' Committee movement early in 1921. The previous year there had been no mention of the dictatorship of the proletariat in Murphy's report (in *Solidarity*) prior to the movement's national conference, though soviet democracy had figured prominently: "We fail to see how workers can control industry without the Workers' Committees or Councils." The conference report the following month noted the declaration of solidarity with the "Russian Soviet Government" and the decision to affiliate to the Third International but also the movement's commitment to "the Soviet form of organisation for the purpose of independently taking control of the industrial and social machinery." [37]

Then, in 1921, a new element entered the formulation of the movement's "Objective," which was now declared to be the overthrow of capitalism and "the setting up of a Workers' Dictatorship *under the protection of which* a system of workers' control and management shall be developed" (emphasis added).[38] This followed a national shop stewards' conference the previous month that, as Ralph Darlington puts it, "ratified this alliance with the CPGB by accepting a constitution which subordinated it to the political control of the party."[39]

Yet the reality of soviet democracy in Russia was still insisted upon. In 1922, *The Communist* serialized Trotsky's "Between White and Red." In the chapter titled "About Democracy and the Soviets," he rejected claims — attributed to the Mensheviks — about the "decay" of the soviets:

> As mass representative institutions the Soviets could not, of course, maintain that high tension which characterised them during the first period of internal struggle or at moments of acute danger from outside. It would take the dullest professor of constitutional law or the most brazen renegade of Socialism, to deny the fact that the Russian toiling masses right now, even amidst so-called "decay" of the soviet system, participate in directing all aspects of social life in a manner which is a hundred times more active, more direct, continuous and decisive than is the case in any parliamentary republic.[40]

Trotsky's phrase "all aspects of social life" is worth noting. It already suggests a kind of "soviet democracy" from which "politics" was implicitly excluded.

It is this notion of a "depoliticized" version of soviet democracy, able to operate — and indeed in Russia actually flourishing — beneath the dictatorship that protected it, that explains some otherwise baffling positions taken by Communists, and by other sympathizers with the USSR, in subsequent years. How else could one still assert the reality of soviet democracy against the undeniable — and frequently undenied — evidence of dictatorship?

The myth of soviet democracy in this strange form persisted until long after the advent of Stalin. As late as 1937, Gollancz would publish Pat Sloan's *Soviet Democracy*, which, as its title suggests, treated the myth as a contemporary reality. Sloan began his book with the claim that "well-known people of different political views make statements which suggest that, in the Soviet Union of today, there exists a system of government which possesses all the essential features of democracy." Chief among such "well-known" people were Beatrice and Sidney Webb, from whose *Soviet Communism* Sloan quoted to the effect that, unlike all previous societies, the USSR did not "consist of a Government and people confronting each other" but was rather "a Government instrumented by all the adult inhabitants." [41] Sloan complained of the inclination "to treat democracy and dictatorship as two mutually exclusive terms, when in fact they may often represent two aspects of the same system of government." The Soviet state had always had features of both. "But," he insisted, "the democracy was enjoyed by the vast majority of the population, and the dictatorship was over a small minority. [42]

Lenin had realized that "the party, as the organised leadership of the mass of the people, must not be disbanded after the seizure of power, but, on the contrary, must be strengthened, in order to ensure that the real democracy achieved should not be overthrown by the armed forces of the property-owners." [43] Protected by the dictatorship of the party, Sloan saw an essentially apolitical "real democracy" flourishing both in social institutions such as schools, trade unions and co-operatives and in the soviets themselves. As we have seen, from the early 1920s the CPGB was well on the way to this view.

Democracy is, of course, a highly complex issue, and yet, in the aftermath of the Russian Revolution, the proponents of all varieties of soviet democracy presented the choice as being simply between bourgeois and working-class democracy. One of the clearest expositions of the latter is, again, in Sloan's *Soviet Democracy*:

> The structure of democratic working-class organisations is almost always on the same general lines. Members join branches which elect local committees. On territories which cover a number of branches, either delegate committees, or conferences which elect a co-ordinating committee, are the supreme authority. And nationally, the supreme authority is usually a congress, with a committee elected at the congress

taking its place as the supreme authority between congresses. This form of working-class organisation is universal because it is the most satisfactory form for working-class purposes. By means of delegate congresses the supreme authority widely represents the rank and file of the members, who give their delegates instructions. By means of a small executive committee elected at the congress the number of permanent officers is reduced to a minimum, so that most of the delegates can return to their regular jobs in their localities. Such a system will be more or less satisfactory according as the delegates really represent those who elect them. The Soviets from their very origin, made all members of the Soviet subject to recall if they ceased to give their electors satisfaction. In this way the Soviets were more democratic than many democratic organisations of the working people in other countries even at the present time.

Later in the book, explaining the absence of opposition parties in the USSR, Sloan stated that "a 'party system' became out of place in the Soviet State, just as a 'party system' is quite out of place in a working-class organisation in any capitalist country." [44] Curiously, what seems to have been largely unexamined and unquestioned, both by supporters and by opponents of soviet democracy, is precisely the role — if any — of political parties in "working-class democracy." Soviet election results were, from the very beginning, routinely reported by all the socialist papers in terms of votes cast for, and delegates elected from, political parties. For example, reporting on the Petrograd Soviet elections in July 1918, *The Call* summarized the results as the election of "221 Bolsheviks, 12 Left Social Revolutionaries and only five anti-Soviet candidates." [45] (How someone elected to a soviet could be "anti-Soviet" was not explained.)

But if claims for the superiority of working-class democracy — epitomized by the soviets — over the bourgeois variety rested on the idea that instructions were given to delegates by their electors at the lowest level of the pyramid of branches and councils, how could the operation of such a system be represented in terms of the gains registered by different political parties? Were not political parties — or at least parties standing for election — a feature of bourgeois, parliamentary-style, *representative* democracy? Were they not totally out of place in proletarian, soviet, delegate democracy? In a properly operating system of delegate democracy there *might* be a role for parties to put forward proposals at the base level. Beyond that, however, if claims to genuine grassroots democracy were to be realized, then it was the duty of those elected, whatever their personal predilections or political affiliations, to faithfully represent the decisions arrived at by the majority of their electors — or, if they felt unable to support the policies so decided, to seek replacement as delegates.

Anyone who had first-hand experience with delegate democracy, in trade unions or other such organizations, would surely have been aware of how difficult it is to operate such a system in practice. Even when delegates made a real effort to respect the mandates they were given, such structures tended towards what could be called an "activists' democracy." In an essentially voluntary organization such as a trade union, however, the tendency for relatively more militant members to push the organization too far in a direction not favoured by less active members was restrained in a variety of ways. There was usually some provision for special conferences, requisitioned by a certain minimum number of members, or for controversial issues to be put to a referendum vote. And it was usually possible for those totally at variance with the organization simply to leave it, or even to start a rival group. But an all-encompassing state structure based on soviet delegates was a very different proposition — especially with the monopoly of real power being exercised by a "vanguard party."

Such considerations seem to not to have occurred to supporters of soviet democracy, although it is difficult to resist the suspicion that the fact that complex delegate systems tended to privilege those who had the commitment and stamina to become activists was one of the unacknowledged attractions of soviet democracy. But "council communists" such as Pankhurst and her comrades, with their sometimes naïve faith in "bottom-up" structures, could at least see that *any* kind of democracy was incompatible with the dictatorship of the Communist Party leadership and the suppression of dissent.

In contrast, for orthodox Communists, once the dictatorship of the proletariat had come to be understood in terms of party rather than class, the only available interpretation of soviet democracy was the depoliticized one, in which democracy operated beneath the protective wing of party rule. Seen in this light, the Communist Party was not a political party at all in the normal sense but was simply the authentic voice of the working class, charged with the task of safeguarding soviet democracy from internal and external subversion. This position had begun to crystallize in Britain by the early 1920s, but it was to become even clearer in the 1930s. In his 1937 apologia for Stalin's regime, Pat Sloan saw nothing contradictory in his statement, quoted earlier, that there was no place for a "party system" in the working-class movement and his endorsement of the Communist Party's dictatorship in Russia. When the Communist Party succeeded in Britain, it "would have established itself not as a parliamentary party of the old type, but as the organised leadership of the people."[46]

But by then committed Communists were not the only ones to buy into the idea of soviet democracy without politics. The popularity, during the late 1930s and the 1940s in the wider Labour movement and beyond, of the Webbs' *Soviet Communism* demonstrates this.[47] Morgan pinpoints the "aversion to politics and woolly mindedness about the state" that underlay the Webbs' "multiform conception of democracy." He concludes that the Webbs did not regard the Soviet Communist Party as a political party at all but instead saw it as a "companionship," an "order," a "united confraternity" merely "termed the Communist Party,"[48] rather like George Young's comparison of the party to a "Religious order" that had so enthused Dora Montefiore around the time of the CPGB's foundation. C.B. Macpherson's belief, in the 1960s, that the Soviet Union was democratic in "the broader sense" seems to be a late and partial echo of this notion.

So, odd though it may seem in the early twenty-first century, it was possible to combine, in this fashion, a rejection of politics, the belief that a socialist society would be naturally harmonious (an "epoch of rest" in Morris's words), the assumption that the working class had a uniformly common interest, and the faith that the Communist Party represented this interest with what Morgan aptly calls "the old socialist dream of unmediated self-government."[49] The result was a novel vision of "actually existing" soviet democracy.

13

Kronstadt and the "Collapse" of Communism

Writing in *Labour Leader* in March 1921, Bertrand Russell observed that a "Third Revolution" was in prospect in Russia. He based this view on reports by *Observer* and *Manchester Guardian* correspondent Michael Farbman, who noted "the determination of the masses, demonstrated by numerous meetings of rank and file Communists and non-partisans, to take a real share in the affairs of the State, and real power to the soviets, and to stamp out all the privileges and inequalities introduced by the Communist bureaucracy." Russell concluded: "Whether the watchword will be 'Constituent Assembly' so popular among Russian émigrées [*sic*], or the more Russian 'All Power to the Soviets' the near future will show." [1]

Russell was a little late. The "Third Revolution" had already come — and failed. The previous week, in the same paper's "International Notes," Emile Burns had reported that "anti-Bolshevik forces outside

Russia" had succeeded in "stirring up a revolt against Soviet Russia." The revolt was centred on Kronstadt, where a tsarist officer, General Koslovsky, was said by Moscow to be "directing the movement, which has been inspired by Mensheviks, Social Revolutionaries and the French Bourgeoisie." The same week, *The Communist* presented the "Revolution" at Kronstadt as "the French war-plot against Russia."[2]

In fact, the experience of Kronstadt from 1917 onwards is probably the best evidence available for anyone wishing to argue that soviet democracy was far from mythical, as the title of this book suggests. Kronstadt was a naval base with a revolutionary tradition stretching back to 1905; its sailors had been regarded as "a loyal stronghold of the Soviet regime and its Communist party."[3] It enjoyed, says Israel Getzler, "virtual autonomy" and relatively privileged treatment at the hands of the Soviet regime. Until June 1918, its governing soviet remained essentially a broad socialist coalition. "Red Kronstadt" was a stronghold not of supporters of the Constituent Assembly but of those who fully accepted the superiority of soviet democracy. According to Getzler, "Kronstadt's democracy was self-consciously egalitarian, but its body politic was confined to the mass of producers and 'toilers,' and excluded members of the propertied classes."[4] That its revolt in March 1921 (which was triggered by reports of serious unrest in Petrograd) was the Third Revolution that Russell was anticipating is evident from the rebellion's slogan, "All Power to the Soviets and Not to Parties." The revolt was ruthlessly suppressed and followed by "hundreds of executions."[5] Later it would become an icon for anarchist and far-Left critics of the Bolsheviks, and one might anticipate that it would have been a rallying point for the British "ultra-Left" at the time. But that was not so. Hostility from the pro-Bolshevik Emile Burns in *Labour Leader* was predictable, though it is a little strange that he was left unchallenged in the ILP paper. But what of those critics of orthodox Communism on the Left?

Even the SLP's paper was hostile to the Kronstadters, with *The Socialist* concluding that "the whole matter is to all appearances one of wire-pulling in the interests of reaction and against the proposed establishment of trade relations between this country and Russia."[6] *Solidarity,* which was to disappear that May, made no mention of the Kronstadt revolt in its "International Notes." It may also be indicative of the response to Kronstadt at the time — even on the libertarian Left — that "Kronstadt" does not appear in the index of Shipway's *Anti-Parliamentary Communism.*

Later, at the beginning of June, *The Socialist* re-published an article by Karl Radek titled "The International Lesson of Kronstadt." The uprising, he said, had elicited a "great shout of joy from counter-revolutionaries." Radek mocked "the leaders of the rebellion, who having proudly declared that they were ready to lay down their lives under the walls of Kronstadt, preferred to retire to Finland." The Kronstadt sailors were "imbued with a peculiar sense of their own importance" and "surrounded by a halo of their revolutionary past." Nevertheless, Radek conceded that the current situation fell short of the ideal of soviet democracy: "The Soviets . . . should exercise power. They should represent the masses as a whole, and not the Communist Party alone — We must create a **real Soviet power**." It was necessary to rid the Communist Party of "careerists and place seekers."

Moreover, not all the rebels had been reactionaries: "A section of the workers of Kronstadt were attracted to the movement by syndicalist tendencies." The article was concluded the following week, with Radek urging that "the defeat of the Communist Party of Russia will destroy the only power which enables Soviet Russia to be a great world factor for revolution, and without the Communist Party, Soviet Russia will fall victim to counter-revolution."[7] But apart from Radek's piece, *The Socialist* had nothing to say about Kronstadt — aside from a brief mention of the "Opening of Cronstadt Harbour" in its "International Notes" section early in July.[8]

The *Workers' Dreadnought* was also slow to comment on Kronstadt. In April 1921, in an article headlined "End of Martial Law in Petrograd," the paper took note of the "ending of the Kronstadt adventure." According to its report, only the "conspirators" who had not made good their escape featured in the trial of the mutineers. Everything had been "forgiven and forgotten for their misled supporters." [9] We should perhaps recall that the *Dreadnought's* editor — or "Prisoner 9587," as the same issue referred to her — was in jail and her organization had just merged itself in the "united" CPGB. As we saw in chapter 11, the paper made reference in October 1921 to "the insurrection of Kronstadt," and the *Dreadnought's* view of Kronstadt the following year would be very different from its initial reaction.

At the end of 1922, the *Dreadnought* reviewed *The Kronstadt Rebellion,* by the anarchist Alexander Berkman. Initially an enthusiastic supporter of the October Revolution, Berkman had acted as interpreter for George Lansbury during his visit the previous year and was in Petrograd at the time of the Kronstadt events. [10] As a result of those events, Berkman decided to leave Russia. His book, said the *Dreadnought,* demonstrated that Kronstadt had not been

> a White Guard insurrection, but an uprising of sailors, workers and peasants against Bolshevik bureaucracy, against the suppression of left propaganda and freedom generally and against the privileges and economic inequalities which have developed under the Bolshevik regime.

The twelve resolutions passed by the general meeting of the crews of the Baltic fleet, which formed the basis of the Kronstadt demands, were given in full. [11]

But not all assessments of the significance of Kronstadt in the later *Dreadnought* were sympathetic. Early in 1924, in the course of a series of articles attributing the decline of the Russian Revolution largely to the peasants, that leading international proponent of Left Communism, Herman Gorter, gave a very hostile interpretation of the Kronstadt events. He saw it as the moment at which a peasantry inevitably and profoundly hostile to communism brought about the system's downfall. The term "war communism," to designate the economic system functioning during the Russian civil war, had only been used retrospectively, he insisted: it was not used at the time the system was operating. [12] Then came Kronstadt:

In February 1921, *the rising in the fortress of Kronstadt, on the battleships and in Petersburg* broke out. Then — as if by a breath — Communism collapsed. Its foundations disappeared in an instant. It may be argued that the rising was very insignificant considering the huge size of the country. Moreover, the peasants were not, and are not, organised as a class; but the small act of a small group of peasants was sufficient — it is said that the warships were mostly manned by peasant sailors.[13]

Whatever its view of the Kronstadt events, in the *Dreadnought*'s eyes everything was heading inexorably downhill in Russia. The demise of the revolution was a regular theme in its final period, as we have already seen. In June 1923, a report headed "Russia Today" took up the entire front page. "A comrade returned from Russia speaks sadly of the situation there," the *Dreadnought* told readers. With the New Economic Policy, capitalism was growing "like a snowball." Little by way of propaganda for communism was in evidence, and what there was of it was mainly directed against the church. "The comrade knew little of the Workers' Opposition," the paper reported. "Its work can only be done underground, for all opposition is repressed." In terms of everyday material conditions, Moscow appeared to be better off than before, although people in Warsaw had seemed better dressed. The comrade also noted that "at the Opera in Moscow one sees people even more richly clad than in London, but children selling programmes are in rags." There were, moreover, "swarms of prostitutes and beggars." Wages were often inadequate, while "bureaucratic delays and truculence" appeared to be growing.[14]

Lenin had been such an inspiration for Pankhurst in earlier years, but, reporting his serious illness in March 1923, she now saw him as "a courageous and able tactician in the struggle to overthrow Capitalism," rather than an originator in the building of Communist ideology and practice. He lacked "the constructive conception of Communism and the practical ability to take definite measures thereto," she concluded after Lenin's death early the following year. "With the actual overthrow of capitalism, his social ideals became stationary, then receded as his physical powers waned, and as the Soviet Government became stabilised in power." [15]

But, in spite of this, Pankhurst still had *some* respect for Lenin. He was "one who fought wholeheartedly for principle, who burnt his bridges, who was not afraid to go forth alone, toiling without praise or encouragement till others should be converted to his views. Of such are the makers of history." [16]

The Decline of Left-Wing Alternatives in Britain

In 1969, Walter Kendall's *The Revolutionary Movement in Britain* caused controversy, centring as it did on the revelation of the importance of "Moscow gold" in setting up the CPGB — a revelation that has now become commonplace. As John McIlroy and Alan Campbell put it in their survey of interpretations of the Comintern-CPGB relationship: "Kendall's conclusions on the important role Moscow gold played in the party's formation have stood the test of time." As they pointed out, the opening of the Russian archives had revealed, for example, that between 1920 and 1922 less than 3 percent of the CPGB's income came from its members' subscriptions. [17] In an earlier article, McIlroy supplies a useful chart showing the annual allocations made by the Comintern to the CPGB from the time the party was founded through to 1929. And, as an article by Walter Kendall in the same issue of *Revolutionary History* demonstrates, it is certainly clear how much Russian funding contributed to the recruitment of intellectuals — students, teachers, writers, artists — during the period of the Popular Front in the following decade. [18] There has been some debate about exactly how vital this financial support was, notably in relation to the work of Andrew Thorpe and, more recently, of Kevin Morgan. [19] But there is no longer any real dispute about the huge significance of "Moscow gold."

Of course, it has to be stressed that, for many on the Left at the time, there was nothing wrong with accepting such financial assistance, which was regarded as timely help from comrades abroad rather than as cash, with implicit strings attached, from a foreign government.

For example, when, in the issue of 10 September 1920, the *Daily Herald* asked its readers, "Shall We Take £75,000 of Russian Money?" it described the offer as "a magnificent demonstration of real working-class solidarity." Many readers wrote in to urge acceptance, though the directors of the paper finally decided to refuse the offer a few days later. And as far as members of the CPGB are concerned, L.J. Macfarlane is surely right to say that "the ordinary party member did not see the relationship in terms of outside control and 'Moscow gold.' He saw himself as a member of a great working-class international movement guided by outstanding Marxist revolutionaries who were making Russia into a land of socialism."[20]

But the focus on "Moscow gold" has tended to obscure the other aspect of Kendall's central thesis that, largely as a result of this Comintern support, the Communist Party "absorbed . . . practically the whole pre-existing revolutionary movement." A Left that had once been "ultra democratic, opposed to leadership on principle, opposed to the professionalisation of the Labour movement almost as an article of faith" was replaced by one that was far more regimented and centrally directed by Comintern. The result, as he saw it, was the tragic decline of a variety of ideological alternatives: "the end of the SDF-BSP tradition, the demise of the SLP, the end of the shop steward movement and the burial of its ideas, the decline and disappearance of the movement for Guild Socialism, Syndicalism and workers' control."[21] McIlroy and Campbell are of course right to say that there is no need to "accept Kendall's conclusions as to the potential of the pre-CPGB revolutionary tradition" in order to give assent to his view of the decisive role played by the Comintern and the funding it supplied in the establishment and survival of the CPGB.[22] But Kendall's more positive evaluations of the pre-Leninist Left in Britain, which were subsequently sidelined, should not be ignored.

"Moscow gold," or the lack of its availability to other Left organizations once the CPGB was securely established, certainly played a role in this narrowing of alternatives, but the crucial issue here is as much the disappearance of these alternatives as its cause. All these pre-Bolshevik tendencies, and indeed the "Left Communism" of Pankhurst and her comrades, had in common a commitment to *some* form of robust and "strong" democracy, be it some version of "soviet democracy" or radical alternatives to both it and the status quo. The ideas may have been naïvely unrealistic, as well as seriously flawed, but the commitment and aspirations were real, even if they were not always fully reflected in practice.

Yet, as the defections to orthodox Communism of the Murphys, Gallachers, former guild socialists, and so many others on the Left shows, these alternative socialist "traditions" could be terribly fragile in the face of what decades later would be called "actually existing socialism." The organizations embodying these alternative versions of socialism were for the most part very small. The ability to keep the group's official organ afloat was absolutely crucial. Without it, that group and its distinctive ideas would almost certainly disappear from view as far as the wider Left was concerned. Within a few years of the establishment of the CPGB, the most prominent papers of organizations that stood to the left of the Labour Party and were independent of the Communist Party had all folded. And, as these papers vanished, alternative interpretations of soviet democracy or similar "industrially based" versions of the socialist commonwealth, as well as the earlier SDF version of radical democracy, were marginalized.

The Demise of Solidarity and The Guild Socialist

"Sudden Death" announced the final editorial in *Solidarity,* the paper of the shop stewards' movement, on 13 May 1921. It explained that the movement's National Administrative Council, now firmly under Communist Party control, had decided to "concentrate all their resource[s]" on the Scottish-based paper *The Worker.* Just how suddenly the death of *Solidarity* came about is illustrated by the fact that that week's instalment of the serialization of William Mellor's *Direct Action* ended with "(to be continued)." The acquisition of the rights to serialize the book had been proudly announced only the previous week. The editors hoped that a new publication, "The LIBERATOR," which would be "unhampered by any official or unofficial connection with any party or organisation," would take the place of *Solidarity*. The editorial concluded with an appeal for "HARD CASH." Clearly nothing like enough of this was forthcoming.[23]

We have already seen how divisions over "soviet democracy" and the Bolsheviks wracked the guild socialist movement. Much later, G.D.H. Cole was to claim starkly that "it was the Communists who broke up the National Guilds League."[24] This claim was not without substance, though it might be more accurate to say that it was the defection to the CPGB of so many of the most prominent and energetic Guildsmen — and Guildswomen — that sealed the fate of the NGL. As Kevin Morgan points out, most of the "leading personalities" recalled by Maurice Reckitt in 1941 in *As It Happened* had taken this path. There had been

> the Coles themselves, Ivor Brown, William Mellor, Raymond Postgate, Monica Ewer, Norman Ewer, A.L. Bacharach, R. Page Arnot, Walter Holmes, Hugo Rathbone and Rose Cohen. All but the Coles and Brown joined the infant CPGB, five of them never to resign, and within the party they at first provided the core of a not dissimilar grouping known as the "nucleus."[25]

Some others were already pulling in different directions — A.R. Orage toward Social Credit, while Reckitt became a Distributist.[26] The collapse of the Building Guild in January 1923 was undoubtedly the "shattering blow" that W.H. Greenleaf calls it, but Kendall is surely right in arguing that the divisive influence of the CPGB played "a decisive role" in the movement's demise. The final annual meeting of the NGL, in May 1923, was poorly attended, and those present empowered the executive to wind the organization up without a further conference.[27]

But, well before this, advocates of the guild approach were able to draw some comfort from the influence that guild socialism was beginning to have in the Labour Party and, especially, the ILP. Cole had noted in 1920 that the Labour Party conference agenda contained many motions on the control of industry. "Only one of these, from

Norwood Labour Party, definitely mentions the name Guild Socialism; but they are all virtually Guild resolutions," he commented.[28] Yet two years later, when the ILP adopted what was widely seen as a form of guild socialism, Cole's welcome was less than hearty. The new constitution, he thought, incorporated "as much Guild Socialism as can be put in without mortally offending the old stagers." And he concluded: "Some commentators are suggesting that the I.L.P. has been converted to Guild Socialism. Perhaps; but I do not hear of any bonfires being ignited by the N.G.L."[29]

By that time, *The Guild Socialist* had just over a year to run. The final issue appeared in August 1923. As with *Solidarity* over two years earlier, a replacement, to be called *New Standards: A Journal of Workers' Control*, was promised for October. This paper did in fact appear. It ran for a year, until an announcement appeared in October 1924: "This is the final issue."[30]

The End of The Socialist *and the Sinking of the* Workers' Dreadnought

The SLP's *The Socialist* had gone from monthly to weekly publication at the beginning of 1919, and its size increased from six to eight pages in April 1919. But such success was not to last. Though it claimed in August of 1921 to be "the largest Socialist paper in the country," the same issue announced the need for "a slight curtailment," for "purely technical reasons." By December, the paper was urging readers to buy two copies of each issue to assist its "Circulation Push."[31] Efforts continued into 1922, with pleas for help from the "Manager, S.L.P. Press." Soon it was claimed that "sales are increasing continuously week by week," but by June readers were being asked to collect "bundle orders" from railway stations to cut postage costs.[32] That August, the Glasgow branch was given a prize for selling more copies of *The Socialist* than any other branch, but two months later heavy losses were reported, and it was announced that the paper was returning to monthly publication.[33]

The Socialist managed to survive through 1922 and 1923. Its last issue, in February 1924, devoted its front page to the death of Lenin, and rather appropriately reprinted an editorial by De Leon, from the *Daily People* of 15 April 1900, that ended: "The Political Government must go. The Industrial Government must come." But there was no hint that the paper might be closing down.

The other main organ of "independent Communism," and the final one to succumb, was the *Workers' Dreadnought*. Like *The Socialist*, it did so after a long and desperate struggle to survive. In October 1922, the price of the *Dreadnought* was halved to one penny and a rise of circulation was claimed. But by the following March more regular donations were deemed "vital to the continuation of the paper." [34] A "£500 Fund," intended to keep the paper going, had reportedly risen to £470 8s 9½d by 17 March 1923 and to £501 8s 9½d by 7 April. But it had taken fifteen months to raise this amount. Now a "£1,000 Fund" aimed to achieve its target by the end of the *Dreadnought's* tenth year, on 24 March 1924.

Other fundraising efforts in 1923 included a "Social and Dance" at the Circle Gaulois in Shaftesbury Avenue, at which a "SELECTED WEST END JAZZ BAND" was promised. [35] The weekend of 5 and 6 May featured a "Grand Carnival," with "Jazz Band, Streamers, Hats, Balloons," at the same venue, as well as a "Social" with jazz band and speakers in Whitechapel. [36] August saw a *Dreadnought* holiday reunion at Pankhurst's home, the Red Cottage, in Woodford, and by December the paper was offering: "Head reading by an expert phrenologist. Proceeds to 'Workers' Dreadnought.'" [37] In spite of the problems of keeping the paper afloat, Pankhurst launched a monthly literary and artistic journal called *Germinal*. A "Germinal Circle," meeting monthly, was formed, which claimed credit for the London exhibition of works by the Hungarian artist Emerich Gondor. [38]

Notable features of the later years of the *Dreadnought* are the increased approval given to libertarian and/or anarchist enthusiasts for soviet democracy and the early attention given to the rise of fascism. To create a "vision of Communism" in the minds of the average person, no better books could be found, said the paper, than Kropotkin's *Conquest of Bread* and Morris's *News from Nowhere*. [39]

Nothing if not an internationalist, Sylvia Pankhurst was especially aware of developments in Italy, no doubt in part because her partner, Silvio Corio, was an Italian political exile.[40] Pankhurst was particularly alarmed at the sympathetic reporting of fascism in the mainstream British press, including the *Manchester Guardian,* where a leading article "largely condoned the acts of the Fascisti in Italy, and seriously discussed the advisability of such a force."[41] Even more shocking was the socialist *Daily Herald,* which she accused of "unexampled treachery to the cause of the workers" in "attempting to whitewash the White Terror of the Fascisti" and soon after castigated for "joining in the general Press conspiracy to make this evil Mussolini appear a brave, and withal rather a splendid fellow, in spite of his faults."[42] Pankhurst was active in campaigning against every variety of fascism, warning of Hitler's "storm troopers armed with hand-grenades in Bavaria" and "a society on Fascist lines called 'The Integral Race'" in Spain.[43] She spoke frequently at anti-fascist meetings and attacked attempts to form a "British Fascisti Movement."[44]

By the end of 1923, advertisements had appeared that read: "Red Cottage, Woodford Wells. For Outings and Week-ends. Parties Catered For."[45] The back page of the 24 March 1924 issue featured a large woodcut showing teas being enjoyed outside the Red Cottage, which was repeated the following week (5 April), with the announcement: "Teas provided Saturdays and Sundays from April 18 (Good Friday)." Meanwhile, as of the beginning of 1924 — at which point the £1,000 Fund had amassed only £169 12s 6½d — there was a noticeable deterioration in the quality of the paper's layout, and by early February the paper was appealing for volunteers to do "Clerical and Organisational work."[46] By May, the *Dreadnought* was claiming to be "the only weekly which maintains the idea of Pure Communism as a constructive vision."[47]

The final issue of the *Dreadnought* appeared on 16 June 1924. As with *The Socialist,* there was no warning given of its demise. Given her early awareness of threat posed by fascism, it is hardly surprising that the next paper Pankhurst launched, in 1936, was a broad anti-fascist weekly: *The New Times and Ethiopia News.* Although its primary focus fell on opposing Mussolini's invasion and subjugation of Ethiopia, it highlighted every anti-fascist and anti-Nazi cause of the time.[48]

Justice *and the Ending of the* SDF-BSP *Tradition*

To those younger socialists radicalized by the war and by the Russian Revolution, with its promise of soviet democracy, the party that had chosen to resume its old title, the Social-Democratic Federation, must have seemed an irrelevant anachronism. Hyndman had alienated the majority of BSP members by his pro-war stance, and the vehemently anti-Bolshevik line he subsequently pursued only deepened this alienation. His variety of radical democracy, with its emphasis on citizens as much as on workers (if not more so), had little appeal to those enthused by the democratic potential of the soviets or by the notion of the dictatorship of the proletariat. Hyndman had died, at the age of seventy-nine, in November 1921. Many of the SDF's remaining members — or at least those who contributed regularly to *Justice* — were, like him, part of the "Old Guard of the S.D.F."

Yet *Justice* survived longer than most left-wing alternatives to orthodox Bolshevism. It began 1925 with its masthead still proclaiming the paper to be "The Oldest Social-Democratic Journal in Great Britain." Its New Year's resolution was to "keep 'Justice' and the S.D.F living." But it was not to be. Three weeks later, H.W. Lee announced that, after forty-one years, the paper had to cease publication. It would be incorporated into the monthly *Social-Democrat*. In its final edition, *Justice* took a last swipe at the Bolsheviks, applauding Gandhi for administering "a wise and well-merited rebuke to those Bolsheviks who are seeking to use him for their hopeless Indian projects." Gandhi — rightly, the paper said — did not believe in "short, violent cuts to success."[49]

This was not quite the end of the SDF, however. The weekly paper was gone, but the party survived in an attenuated form for the remainder of the interwar period. The final chapter (written by E. Archbold) of *Social-Democracy in Britain* (1935) is entitled "Conclusion: The S.D.F. Vindicated." In it, Archbold argued that "the Labour Party has virtually become a Social-Democratic Party itself."[50] It must have seemed very ironic to those who could recall the pre-war social-ist movement that the SDF was now contrasted with the ILP, which had gone "out of the ranks of the Labour Party, and into the politi-cal wilderness."[51] Only one comment in Archbold's account seems to recognize the distinctively radical notions of democracy and socialism that had always characterized the Social-Democrats: "The tendency of the Labour Party to apply the public corporation idea as a means of securing the transition to public ownership has not been received without some trepidation amongst the S.D.F. membership." Public corporations were not what the Social-Democrats had in mind when, at the previous year's conference, they passed a resolution calling for "the public ownership and democratic control of the instruments of production and distribution."[52]

The Beginning of the End of Labour Leader: Snowden Versus Mrs. Glasier

If the end of *Justice, The Guild Socialist, Solidarity, The Social-ist,* and the *Workers' Dreadnought* marked the effective end of the organizations whose outlook they embodied and for which they were the main point of contact with the wider socialist world, the case of *Labour Leader* was different. The *paper* came to an end, but the ILP itself was to remain through all the twists and turns of the interwar period — and, in a much diminished form, beyond. But the fate of the *Leader* well illustrates the divisive effect that Bolshevism's claim to be promoting soviet democracy could have, even in a case where neither of the main participants were likely ever to become "British Bolsheviks."

We have seen how — surprisingly — Philip Snowden's *initial* attitude to the Bolshevik seizure of power and to the claims of soviet de-mocracy was equivocal and fell far short of the outright condemnation that might have been anticipated. This had much to do with his hope, during the final year of the First World War, that the Bolsheviks would be instrumental in bringing about a swift and "democratic" peace. The relative optimism of Snowden and of other prominent ILPers continued into the early post-war months. Even Ramsay MacDonald still had a sympathetic take on what was happening in Russia. In the summer of 1919, he was critical of the Allies' interventionary activities rather than of the Bolsheviks. As we saw earlier, while invoking the "Jacobinism" he believed inevitable in revolutions, he blamed the Allies' hostility for prolonging it and equated Lenin with Rousseau as an inspiration for the future.[53]

We have seen how enthusiasm for the idea that the ILP should join the Third International initially went far beyond the ranks of those who were later to leave and join the CPGB. It included Clifford Allen, who was on his way to becoming the ILP's leading figure in the early 1920s. With the "Left-Wing of the I.L.P" campaign well underway, however, attitudes were soon to harden. By the spring of 1920, Snowden was criticizing Lansbury's approving views of the Bolsheviks, and his antipathy became deeper and more bitter after Ethel Snowden's visit to Russia as part of the Labour Party-TUC delegation and the treatment she was subjected to on her return, when she came out as unequivocally hostile to the Bolsheviks.

Snowden still blamed the interventionists, but he now pulled no punches in the way he described the Bolsheviks. At the end of 1920, he insisted that

> Winston Churchill has done more than any living man to strengthen the Bolshevik Government. If it had not been for his policy the Russian people would themselves long ago have dealt with the gang of despots who usurped power by force and maintain it by tyranny aided by the help of British and French Bolsheviks like Churchill and Poincaire [sic]. The best way to kill Bolshevism is to give the Russian people goods. Even if some of the men in power remain their methods will not survive the opening up of intercourse with the rest of the world.

This was followed on the page he was still contributing to *Labour Leader* by "An Appeal to British Labour" from "a number of well-known Russian Socialists living in England." It was right to denounce the blockade and demand recognition of the Soviet government, but the Labour Party was silent about "the suppression of liberty and every form of democracy by that Government." Snowden urged that social-ists should "make it a condition of moral support that the Bolsheviks should show at least as much consideration for Russian Socialists as for American capitalist concessionaires." This was too much for Katharine Bruce Glasier, the paper's editor, who appended a long editorial note: "The Editor feels compelled to disassociate herself once and for all from Mr Snowden's bitter denunciations of the Bolshevik leaders." She had, she said, no sympathy with their "crude materialism" or their "absurd attempts to interfere with the free self-government of the Socialist movements in other countries," but she believed them to be "sincere" and "ready to die for the cause." [54]

The reason for Glasier's negative reaction to Snowden's anti-Bolshevik comments is clear from her letter to him, quoted by Laurence Thompson. Her concern was to avoid publishing "anything that could be used by the Government to help them make war on Soviet Russia or weaken International Labour's Resistance to that War." [55] Undeterred, Snowden returned to the attack the following week, applauding the Labour Party's refusal to allow the CPGB to affiliate:

Any other decision would have been an act of suicide. A great deal of harm has been done already to the Labour and Socialist movement in this country by its uncritical support of Bolshevism and by its support and toleration of Communist speakers. The Communists stand for the dictatorship of a minority, which has seized power by force.[56]

But while that week's *Leader* included a letter from Walter Ayles, a member of the executive of the NAC, in support of Snowden, Glasier reported that she had received "a number of warm-hearted letters thanking her for her editorial protest." A week later, she claimed to have received "a veritable summer shower of kindly letters and resolutions" supporting her position "and usually asserting it represents the general feeling of the I.L.P. membership." She had decided to print only one, from Clement J. Bundock, a member of the NAC — but not of its executive, which had criticized her.

Bundock defended Glasier's rights as editor and maintained that "the editorial footnote more accurately expressed the attitude of the majority of members of the I.L.P." He was concerned lest "these unsparing comments upon the Bolsheviks were to be regarded by our comrades on the Continent as the opinion of the I.L.P." He admired Snowden's work but believed that "we cannot endorse such phrases as 'gang of despots' and the general tone of the paragraphs in question."[57]

Meanwhile, the ILP executive deeply regretted "the Editor's comments at the foot of Mr. Snowden's Notes." It noted that "Mr Snowden was appointed by the N.A.C. as the writer responsible for the Editorials and the Notes on Current Affairs and any such criticism affecting policy should have been made first to the N.A.C." The editor's reply was "implied in her last week's note, which was only the culmination of a series of differences between herself and Mr Philip Snowden on the special matter at issue." The NAC met only once a quarter, and only at that point could it make the party's position clear. "The harm done to the movement by an unquestioned statement in the 'Labour Leader' is immediate," she declared.[58]

A special meeting of the NAC on 16 and 17 December 1920 tried to calm things by confirming the editor's full discretion and responsibility for the paper's contents, while accepting that Snowden should be responsible only to the NAC for his signed articles.[59] But he had had enough. On 6 January 1921, he announced: "With the writing of this paragraph my contributions to *Labour Leader* cease." His was not the only exit. The following week, readers learned that the editor had asked for "a release from her duties" as of Easter, "which will enable her to come out once again, with, she hopes a veritable host of other willing propagandists, to the market places and village greens."[60]

In her last weeks as editor, Glasier found herself refusing to print more letters, including one from C.H. Norman, in which he chided the "Vienna Union" for accepting Martov as the Russian representative on its executive committee, describing him as "an ex-ally of Koltchak, and Denikin." A fortnight later came an announcement that "Mrs Bruce Glasier has had a rather serious nervous breakdown and has been ordered complete rest by her medical adviser." Tom Johnson, the editor of *Forward,* would take over for the time being. Then, early in July, it was announced that, starting in August, Bertram R. Carter would become the editor of the paper.[61]

The former editor, whose husband, a leading member of the ILP for decades, had died the previous summer, seems to have recovered quite quickly from her illness. By mid-June, she was reported addressing large meetings in Middlesborough.[62] She was appointed as a "special propagandist" and spent much of following eighteen years on the road for the ILP and the Labour Party. She died in 1950, at the age of eight-three.[63] It is difficult not to feel some sympathy for an editor besieged from all sides.

The conflict was a defining moment for Snowden as well. He refused to accept renomination as ILP treasurer and, although he remained a member until 1927, played little or no part in the party's affairs after early 1921. As with the related issue of the treatment of Ethel, he seems to have taken the "unseemly wrangle" with Glasier very personally.[64] In his autobiography, Snowden refers to her as the "Acting-Editor" — but never by name. The chapter following his account of the "wrangle" celebrates the lives and contributions to the socialist cause of W.C. Anderson and J. Bruce Glasier. But whereas he devotes two paragraphs to William Anderson's wife, Mary Macarthur, there is no hint that Bruce Glasier was married to a woman so prominent in the ILP.

The End of Labour Leader

The impetus behind the replacement of *Labour Leader* with the *New Leader* in 1922 came from the new treasurer, Clifford Allen, later described by Fenner Brockway as "in effect the directing head of the Party."[65] According to Arthur Marwick, the NAC voted to transfer publication from Manchester to London, with three dissenters, "probably R.C. Wallhead, Ben Riley, and Fred Jowett, who represented the core of the old-stagers' resistance to Allen's innovations."[66] In David Marquand's words, Allen "forced through a radical transformation of the worthy but unreadable *Labour Leader,* which was rechristened the *New Leader* and put under the editorship of the well-known socialist journalist, H.N. Brailsford." [67] Readability is subjective. By no means all ILPers found the old paper "unreadable" or the new one worth reading. As Marwick says: "Unhappily . . . the Party membership did not take too kindly to the new paper.[68]

As a competitor of *The Nation*, the *New Statesman*, and *The Spectator*, Brailsford"s enterprise was a success. Its circulation rose to 47,000. Brockway, who took over as editor after Brailsford's resignation in October 1926 (after the "Allen régime" had given way to that of Maxton's a year earlier), agreed that "Brailsford produced a paper of great literary merit, loved by school teachers for its Nature Notes, adored by artists for its woodcuts, and revered by intellectuals for its theoretical features." [69] Robert Dowse notes in *Left in the Centre* that "particularly justified" among the complaints from members were those against "intellectualism" — and, more specifically, the "'arty' intellectualism that plagued the I.L.P." [70]

For those who see the episode as a shift from a plebeian to a comfortable bourgeois ambiance, the fact that Brailsford began with an annual salary of £1,000, in contrast to Katharine Bruce Glasier's £2 17s (rising to £3 5s) a week, was probably conclusive. "I.L.P. salaries were high under the Allen regime," notes Brockway.[71] Pankhurst was predictably scornful: "We wonder how he is able to put aside the thought that of the thousands of copies of the paper which might be freely distributed each week for the difference between the £2 or £3 a week on which he could live if he chose, and the £20 a week he actually draws." [72] There were many in the ILP who would have sympathized with Pankhurst's view. Indeed, the editor's salary was criticized by a Sheffield delegate at the 1923 annual conference as being contrary to the traditions of the ILP and extravagant at a time of mass unemployment.[73]

Dowse points out the gravity of the ILP's finances in general and those of the *Labour Leader* in particular. Its annual losses were estimated at £1,200, and its circulation had fallen to below 20,000.[74] This was a crucial factor in the paper's transformation, but there seems little doubt that Allen's project was greatly aided by the almost simultaneous resignations of Snowden and Glasier the previous year. The prolonged battle over Third International affiliation not only made the wider debate on the nature of Bolshevik Russia critically important but also increased its bitterness. One casualty was *Labour Leader* itself. But the "literary" *New Leader* would not last very long. In retrospect, it is difficult not to see this episode as, in part, a sort of attempted cooling-off period in the disputes over the correct response to the Bolshevik revolution and its "soviet democracy" that had riven the ILP during the previous several years.

Attitudes Towards Leadership and the Cult of Lenin

As we have seen, Kendall argued that, in view of the Comintern's "elevation of leadership to a cardinal principle," the advent of a British Communist Party largely funded from Moscow ultimately spelled the virtual end of a revolutionary Left "opposed to leadership on principle" and "opposed to the professionalisation of the Labour movement." [75] In his study of J.T. Murphy, Ralph Darlington notes the severely anti-leadership attitudes of the embryonic shop stewards' movement and the decision, taken at the founding conference of the national organization, that "the national committee should have purely *administrative* powers" leading to the election of "a National Administrative Council." [76] What his account might obscure is the fact that such things were not some new phenomenon peculiar to the wartime shop stewards' movement. In fact, they had antecedents in several parts of the modern socialist movement in Britain, from the time of its inception in the 1880s.

The "National Administrative Council" was precisely the name adopted for the ILP's national body at its founding conference back in 1893. The suspicion of leadership in general — and also opposition to the beginnings of a "cult of personality" surrounding Keir Hardie — was reflected in the 1896 decision to dispense with the title "president" in favour of "chairman," which did not prevent motions appearing for some years afterwards at the annual conference seeking the abolition of the office under *any* name. Opposition to leadership verged on the obsessive in Blatchford's *Clarion*. It constituted much of the driving force behind the *Clarion* federation, or, to give it its proper title, the National and International General Federation of Trade and Labour Unions, in the late 1890s.[77]

Anti-leadership and anti–hero-worship attitudes long predated this, and they could apply to the dead as well as the living. In the 1880s, the SDF paper *Justice* frequently railed against "Fabianistic caesarism,"[78] while the elaborate graveside ritual planned by the "Communistic Working Men's Club" to mark the first anniversary of Marx's death was seen as offensive. "Any renewal of the old pagan and Catholic forms of canonisation of individuals is contrary to the principles of socialism as we understand it," thundered *Justice*, adding that no one would have protested more vehemently against such an unwelcome development than Marx himself.[79] And on several subsequent occasions, Hyndman, in particular, inveighed against any tendency to "deify" Marx or to "regard his teachings as authoritative." No doubt this was motivated in part by Hyndman's desire not to be overshadowed himself by Marx — or by anyone else. Nonetheless, his protests reflect a very pronounced, indeed dominant, attitude in the SDF generally. At the same time, the fact that Hyndman criticized fellow Social-Democrats John E. Ellam and J.B. Askew for their "deification" of Marx indicates that there were tendencies in the opposite direction.[80]

Hyndman, full of his own importance and sure of the correctness of his views on all subjects, is frequently seen as dominating the SDF and BSP, until the revolt against his pro-Ally position during the Great War. Yet he always objected to being referred to as the party's "leader." Indeed, on more than one occasion he was subject to party censure — something he accepted with bad grace, but accepted nonetheless.[81]

Ernest Belfort Bax is often regarded (despite his notorious anti-feminism) as the one serious Marxist theoretician in the SDF. John Charles Cowley describes him as "uncompromising in his adherence to revolutionary socialism," adding that "it was a Babouvist conception of revolution; the seizure of power by an elite — the working class — vanguard." [82] But we also need to remember that Bax was so exercised by the dangers of control by a single individual that his essay "Democracy and the Word of Command" advocated that committees of three be substituted for ships' captains and other analogous holders of authority. [83]

It is certainly true that what was only just beginning to be referred to regularly as the "Left" of the pre-1914 British socialist movement was characterized by a suspicion of all forms of leadership and a desire to offset them with democratic checks. From this perspective, it was the Fabians on the "Right" of the movement, and, to a lesser extent, the "leaders" of the ILP and especially MacDonald, whose major defect seemed, to those situated to their left, to be a willingness to approve — even to celebrate — the leadership of elites both political and bureaucratic. It was again Bax who depicted Fabianism as "the special movement of the Government official just as militarism is the special movement of the soldier and clericalism of the priest." [84] But just how far anti-leadership attitudes had penetrated into the Labour mainstream is shown by the fact that it was not until after the Great War that the Labour Party officially adopted the office of "Leader."

This is the context in which the cult that grew up around the Bolsheviks, and Lenin in particular, needs to be understood. It was by no means confined to "Right-Wing" Communists, or to those who would become such in the eyes of Pankhurst and other self-designated "Lefts." Indeed, one of the earliest and most extraordinary statements about the Bolshevik seizure of power was made by Pankhurst herself in a *Workers' Dreadnought* editorial at the end of November 1917. Having praised the Bolsheviks for exceeding their promises as regards securing the land for the peasants and the factories for the workers and going ahead with preparations for the Constituent Assembly, she asked for appreciation of "the difficulties of those who are thus courageously attempting to put into practice the teachings of Christ." [85]

Perhaps the religious language is not so surprising in the light of the way that Lenin was awarded a species of secular sainthood. Other Bolshevik leaders, notably Zinoviev, Kamenev, and Bukharin, were singled out for personal appreciation, and Trotsky's picture, captioned "Chief of the Victorious Red Army," appeared on the front page of the 6 November 1919 issue of *The Call*. But this was just a bit of mild hero worship compared to the adoration lavished on Lenin. Earlier that year, the *Workers' Dreadnought* described Lenin as "the recognised leader of the proletarian world." [86] A few months later, reviewing "Mr Ransome's Great Book" (*Six Weeks in Russia in 1919*) in *The Call,* Fred Willis highlighted the author's stress on Lenin's cheerful temperament and sense of humour and quoted approvingly Ransome's statement that "he is without personal ambition." Writing in *The Call* in November 1919, Robert Dell noted that "everybody who has met Lenin agrees that he is perhaps the greatest man of our time." He could be regarded as "the Robespierre of the Russian Revolution," except that "Lenin has not Robespierre's rigid dogmatism and narrow fanaticism." In the same issue, the paper spoke of "the wonderful foresight of the great revolutionary leader." [87] And by September 1920 the *Daily Herald* was describing Lenin as "a great man — a man whose power is drawn from selflessness, who has never let his interests count against his ideas." [88]

A quantity of verse — of a type one might think many readers would find embarrassing — appeared in some of the left-wing papers. One example, from the 9 March 1918 edition of Pankhurst's *Dreadnought,* will suffice. "To Lenin," by "Ronald Campbell Macfie, M.A., M.B.C.M., LL. D.," began:

> 'Tis thine in places dark and desolate
> To fashion Beauty to illume the night
> Of Falsehood and of Fear with Reason's light:
> 'Tis thine from wrack of empires to create
> A commonwealth of Love, a Federal State,
> Not founded on deceit or gold or might
> But built by Truth and Justice in despite
> Of all the Powers of Moloch and of Hate.

But even this was mild stuff compared with "Lenin — A Birthday Sketch," which *The Call* published in April 1920. Although Lenin was seen in hostile quarters as a fanatic, it explained, "this fanatic has always been, and still is, the most tolerant of men — except, indeed towards the enemies of the working class and those who themselves are tolerant of them." The writer of the tribute continued: "Happy the country and the age which has produced such a man." And Theodore Rothstein, writing as "W.A.A.M.," concluded by apostrophizing the man himself: "Vladimire Illyitch, the proletariat of all countries greets you on your fiftieth birthday and cries out. Long live the proletarian revolution and its great leader."[89]

The devotion of the "great leader" was vividly illustrated a couple of months later, again in *The Call,* by Otto Grimlund's "Personal Recollections of Lenin," reprinted from the American socialist publication *The Truth*: "Long after the lights have been extinguished and only the clicking of the watch breaks the silence of the night, the light in Lenin's workroom up in the castle of the Kremlin is still burning."[90] And there was more along the same lines at the end of the year from Maxim Gorky, who declared: "The fundamental aim of Lenin's whole life is the happiness of mankind." Not that that was enough:

> His private life is such that in an age of strong religious faith Lenin would have been regarded as a saint. . . . A severe realist, a politician of intellectual ability, Lenin is gradually becoming a legendary character. And that is well.[91]

This sort of thing was perhaps predictable in the pages of *The Call* and *The Communist,* and perhaps also in the *Daily Herald,* where Robert Williams's characterization of Lenin as "simple, genial and entirely without affectation" seems restrained in comparison with some of the other encomiums. But some came from more unexpected quarters. "It is well known that Lenin himself," said the *New Statesman,* "lives on the rations of a sedentary worker, which are substantially less than those of a manual worker."[92] Perhaps this was not so surprising. In his study of the early decades of the *Statesman,* Adrian Smith commented on the "sycophancy" of Clifford Sharp, the editor, toward Lenin and other leading Bolsheviks.[93]

But not all of the *Statesman* pronouncements on Lenin at this time were sycophantic. In June 1920, the journal detected "a certain Napoleonic outlook" shared by Lenin and Churchill:

> Both are professed democrats who at bottom have not the least respect for democracy: and both without a trace of personal brutality, act always on the assumption that human life is of very small account beside the realisation of their own aims and ideals. Both . . . are intellectual fishwives who believe in the real efficacy of reiterated abuse and are themselves past-masters of resourceful vituperation: and both in certain directions, are as invincibly ignorant as they are always clever and industrious.

Lenin had been given the chance to show "what a second-rate intellect combined with self-confidence and indomitable courage and persistence can achieve," but his letter to the British proletariat seemed to have produced "a most salutary revulsion of feeling in all sorts of quarters." Anti-Bolsheviks, the *Statesman* concluded, would be wise to confiscate Mr Churchill's sword — and it would be wiser still for pro-Bolsheviks to confiscate Lenin's pen.[94]

New Statesman writers might waver between enthusiasm and skepticism as far as the Bolshevik leader was concerned, but "Affable Hawk," who contributed the paper's "Books in General" feature, remarked on his cult status in March 1921:

> Early every day during the past month I have passed a church outside which stands the announcement in red letters
>
> "LENIN? or THE LORD?"
>
> It invites us to attend six Lenten sermons. My first feeling was "Lenin and the Lord" this is really fame! My second was that perhaps even Lenin was being given rather undue prominence.[95]

There was, in short, an unmistakable shift from previous anti-leadership attitudes to cultlike celebrations of Lenin and, for the infant Communist Party, a stress on the role of the vanguard party and the adoption of "democratic centralism," which had the effect of elevating the position of the party's leaders. But if that much is clear, the question of professionalization is trickier. Men, and less often women, had taken paid roles — very low paid, usually — in British socialist organizations long before the arrival of the CPGB in 1920. And, of course, paid officials were commonplace in the trade unions. In fact, finding such work was often an economic necessity for those whose political and/or industrial militancy had resulted in dismissal and blacklisting by employers. During the war and post-war years, arrest, prosecution, and imprisonment were all too common consequences of any kind of radical socialist activity.

Working for the new Communist Party was no gateway to fame and fortune — especially not the latter. But the degree of professionalization did increase with the "Bolshevization" of the party. The policy of democratic centralism led in this direction, and so, especially, did the attempt, in the words of *The Communist,* to create a "centralized organisation of the revolutionary forces." [96] One could say that "Moscow gold" put Communist Party employees — as long as they took care to toe the notoriously swiftly changing party line — in something like the position of someone with a rich uncle. He might not think much of you, but, in the last analysis, he could be relied on to come to your rescue when total disaster threatened. [97]

But even before the Bolshevization of the British Communist Party was well underway, *some* had detected what they saw as signs of an incipient creation of an alternative officialdom. This was particularly true of some of the CPGB's critics in the SLP. At the time of the January 1921 Unity Conference in Leeds, an SLPer from Leicester, who signed himself "F.L.R.," described, with more good humour than was often found in *The Socialist,* how he had gone to the Victoria Hotel — probably, he said, the largest hotel in Leeds — in hopes of being able to report the proceedings. "A London comrade — one of the 'solidarity' lot, and of Sylvia's party tried to get me in," he wrote, "but no go." So he hung about outside the conference. A group of delegates came out, all seemingly BSP members wearing BSP badges. "Most of them looked like minor Trade Union officials," but he did see "one genuine member of the working class" who had been "sent off to find a duplicator":

> I felt sorry for him, just a humble cog in this magnificent machine, this inversion of the Soviet principle, when, instead of the power springing from the organised workers in the field, mine, factory and workshop upwards to the central administrative body, a triumphant band of omnipotents stand on the apex and give out their instructions.

"F.L.R." also queried the cost of the venue — where did the money come from? In the experience of the Leicester SLP, pub landlords — never mind hoteliers — would not let left-wing organizations book rooms because of the clash with their "class interests."[98] And when, in December 1921, *The Communist* published an apologetic editorial saying that, until further notice, no payments would be made to those who contributed articles, *The Socialist* was quick to publish a letter of comment. The correspondent, J. Brown, pointed out that *The Communist*'s announcement showed that previously the paper *had* been paying for articles and claimed that "in the majority of cases, articles are from those who were in the way of receiving emoluments for other positions and work (odd jobs!) in the C.P."[99]

Conclusions

To say that soviet democracy was a myth is not to deny the broadly democratic character of the soviets in their earliest days; it is rather to point up the importance and resonance of the *idea* of soviet democracy, which had a crucial role in the initial attraction of the Russian Revolution, both before and after the Bolsheviks seized power. This idea was an integral part of the vision of a new society of equals.

We need constantly to remind ourselves of what might be called the "bliss was it in that dawn" factor. For so many on the Left, everything about the circumstances of the revolution seemed so unexpected and so without precedent. The socialism that they had hoped — more than expected — to see the beginnings of in their lifetimes now appeared to be within immediate reach. Quite suddenly everything seemed possible.

Belief in the soviets as a "higher" form of democracy was congruent with a pre-existing widespread disposition on the Left to regard the workplace as a more "real" basis for democracy than any geographical constituency. Earlier left-wing commitment to critiques of parliamentary representation and to forms of radical democracy also predisposed British socialists who were already eagerly seeking "real democracy" in some form to view the soviets in this light. A striking example is Sylvia Pankhurst, who began 1917 advocating the referendum, initiative, and recall and within a few months was an active participant at the "Leeds Soviet Convention" and a tireless advocate thereafter of soviet democracy. Long-established opposition to the very idea of "leadership," as well as suspicion of actual leaders, also contributed to the belief that soviet democracy put the workers at the base of its organizational pyramid in real, literal, control — or at least to the aspiration that it should do so.

Enthusiasm for soviets on the British Left preceded a commitment to, and in nearly all cases any real knowledge of, Bolshevism, as the meeting at Leeds in June 1917 demonstrates. At this stage, hopes for the future of the revolution in Russia were vested in the coming elections for the Constituent Assembly — which the soviets had long been demanding. As regards beliefs about democracy, the forcible dissolution of the assembly early in 1918 was a more crucial turning point for embryonic "British Bolsheviks" than the seizure of power the previous October.

For most people on the Left, including those who would quickly come to reject the actions of the Bolsheviks, the Duma and the various editions of the provisional government had less democratic legitimacy than the soviets. But the crushing of the assembly began to force people — who were often in some uncertainty about how to interpret this development, as is most evident in the case of Pankhurst — to take a definite stand. The claim that the soviets represented a higher, working-class, truly operative form of democracy, one that made the "bourgeois" democracy of the Constituent Assembly redundant, was now voiced — essentially for the first time — by the Bolsheviks and their supporters.

For quite a considerable period, and certainly until sometime after the end of the war, there was a willingness to take such claims seriously on the part of a very broad segment of left-wing opinion that even included, to some degree, such future vehement anti-Communists as Philip Snowden and Ramsay MacDonald. A great deal of attention was given in the various socialist weekly papers both to theoretical appraisals of the alleged democratic superiority of soviets and to descriptions of how they were thought to be operating in revolutionary Russia. The attractions of soviet democracy went well beyond the ranks of those who would eventually join the Communist Party or support one of its "left-wing" rivals such as the SLP, Pankhurst's organizations, or the libertarian groups committed to "anti-parliamentary communism" traced by Mark Shipway. The view that soviet democracy, as interpreted by the Bolsheviks, was inappropriate for Britain and other "Western" countries but might well suit conditions in Russia was also widespread on the Left generally, including the ILP and, with a De Leonist twist, the SLP.

One exception was *Justice*, which, in addition to its pro-Ally position on the war, rejected the whole Bolshevik enterprise as being totally undemocratic and tyrannical. But *Justice* spoke essentially for the "Old Guard of the S.D.F.," who were being carried away by time, rather than having much influence with younger generations. In 1914, the BSP was certainly no stranger to sharp debate and internal conflict, but it remained a united organization incorporating the old Social-Democratic values and traditions, which gave a significant role to "strong" forms of radical democracy.

This unity was shattered by the war, and the polarization of the British Social-Democratic tradition was continued by the effects of the Bolshevik seizure of power. Thus, the BSP, having "bought" the notion of soviet democracy wholesale in spite of the doubts cast by Fairchild and Alexander in 1919, evolved into the founding core of the British Communist Party, while the remainder, who eventually reverted to the old Social-Democrat name, proved to be the element of the Left most persistently hostile to Bolshevism and all its work — not excepting such "right-wing" organs (in socialist terms) as the *New Statesman*. Meanwhile, conflicts over the reality, or otherwise, of soviet democracy in Russia, as well as the issue of how to relate to the new Communist Party and the Third International, beset the guild socialist movement and contributed significantly to its decline, with many of its most active members being recruited into the new party.

To begin with, at least, for many on the British Left the dictatorship of the proletariat meant nothing more than a situation in which, given a political structure founded on the workplace, "bourgeois" elements would be automatically excluded from representation, a plight they could quickly end by taking up socially useful work. Pankhurst's early campaign for the inclusion of "housewives" in the soviet resolutions passed at Leeds was aimed at the inclusion of many whose socially desirable and necessary work was in danger of being disregarded. But, for some time, the very vagueness and ambiguity of the phrase "dictatorship of the proletariat" helped to obscure what was really at issue. More and more, for those en route to orthodox Communism, the phrase came to be interpreted in terms of the imposed rule of the Communist Party, seen as the vanguard of the working class.

For those who did come to accept the Communist version of soviet democracy, the sense that by joining the Communist Party one was actually becoming an active participant in the ongoing world socialist revolution must have helped to stifle doubts. The "ultra-Left" groups could not offer this sense except in a much fainter and more abstract way. The problem for orthodox Communists was to make a transition from early beliefs in soviet democracy in a "pure" form to the notion of a vanguard party leading the working class, without actually explicitly abandoning the original idea. In the orthodox Communist version, which largely ignored their actual origins, the soviets quickly became a specialized form of working-class organization to be called into being only when the party decreed that a revolution was imminent and then to be led to victory by that party.[100]

Before 1914, what can be slightly anachronistically termed the "Left" of the British socialist movement — at the time, the term was only rarely used in this sense — espoused, and indeed was largely defined by, radical views on "real democracy." This was recognized by the Fabians in their *Report on Fabian Policy* of 1896 and again ten years later in their Special Committee report. The latter characterized the division of opinion as a "gulf" that "cuts the Labour movement right down the middle."[101] Fabians had no sympathy with the SDF, whose program included demands for "direct democracy," or the campaigns of Blatchford's *Clarion* for the referendum and initiative or other manifestations of belief in "primitive democracy." Fabian democracy — with the resolutely anti-democratic Shaw as an outrider — steered a much more modest and cautious course towards universal suffrage and a vision of democracy as a matter of consent rather than of active participation. The influence of syndicalism and guild socialism added to the mix the new — or revived — ingredient of demands for a democracy based, wholly or partially, on the workplace.

Taken in all its variations, commitment to radical democracy was widespread on the British Left. But how deep was it? How firmly rooted were such ideas? Although the phrase "real democracy" was frequently invoked, there was relatively little development of detailed proposals or analysis of possible problems and objections. Sometimes the cry for "real democracy" seems to have been little more than a convenient stick with which to beat the "bureaucratic" Fabians or the politically ambitious "leaders" — Hardie, MacDonald and Snowden — of the ILP.

Even the most committed exponents of "real democracy" sometimes expressed reservations. One example is the doubt expressed in *Justice* at the time of the South African war as to whether, despite its "abstract justice," universal suffrage was wise, given the way existing voters were "susceptible to outbursts of jingo feeling."[102] And in spite of writing three *Clarion* pamphlets advocating the referendum and initiative, Alex Thompson insisted in 1910 that foreign policy and defence issues should be left to "permanent officials unaffected by the fluctuations of party," with the referendum used only for matters "directly pertaining to the people's lives and needs."[103] Strangely, when one considers what the impact of war just a few years later would be, these matters did not include, for Thompson, foreign affairs or military issues.

As for the newer strains of radical democracy, old-style Social-Democrats had been wary of syndicalism, suspecting an underlying authoritarianism in its advocacy of "direct action." S.G. Hobson's enthusiasm for the building of the Panama canal by the US military was noted near the outset of this book, and, as we saw earlier in this chapter, Kevin Morgan has called attention to the way so many guild socialists, including G.D.H. Cole, were drawn towards Bolshevism, whether or not this included (as it did in many cases) actual enlistment in the Communist ranks. The fragility of many democratic commitments is something that has to be taken into account when we attempt to understand how the "depoliticized" version of soviet democracy came to prevail not only among Communists but considerably beyond their ranks in a conventionally rightward direction, as epitomized by the popularity of the Webbs' *Soviet Communism* in wider left-wing circles during the 1930s.

Not that the "Bolshevik" convictions that replaced radical social-democracy, syndicalism, or guild socialism necessarily proved any less fragile than the democratic convictions of the pre-Leninist Left. One has only to consider the trajectories of two leading lights of early British communism. One was J.T. Murphy. As I noted in the introduction, Ralph Darlington has characterized Murphy's passage as one "from syndicalism to communism to left reformism to popular frontism to anti-Marxism." [104] There are similarities here with the evolution of that other J.T. — J.T. Walton Newbold. In 1935, in the penultimate chapter of *Social-Democracy in Great Britain,* Archbold took evident delight in tracing the path of this "brilliant but unstable research man" from a Quaker background, through pacifism, the ILP, the BSP, and the Communist Party, to the 1922 British general election, in which he was the only successful Communist parliamentary candidate. He continued:

> It became evident, however, that the time was not ripe for the appearance of a British "Lenin," and so the research worker and financial

journalist in him overcame the revolutionary. Another *volte face,* and he became a very definite "Right Winger," and the protégé of Ramsay MacDonald, J.H. Thomas and Philip Snowden.

Before this, Newbold had joined the re-formed SDF and for a period edited its surviving publication, the *Social-Democrat.* This came to an "abrupt end," after which he served on the Macmillan Committee on Finance and Industry, set up in 1929. He had been scheduled to speak on the second day of the SDF's 1931 conference but failed to appear and was soon "in full cry as a supporter of the National Government." formed by Ramsay MacDonald that same year.[105]

It is important to be aware of such inconsistencies and changes of opinion in order to avoid overly schematic accounts of the Left, in which individuals sometimes appear to have played a much more stable role than was actually the case when their full trajectory is taken into account. Perhaps we can do no more than conclude — with respect both to the sometime proponents of pre-Bolshevik currents of radical socialist democracy and to those who were drawn, at least temporarily, by the magnetic attraction of Bolshevism — that early-twentieth-century British socialists were no more consistent than the rest of us.

Those on the far Left who remained committed to "council communism" found themselves in an increasingly isolated position, cut off from mainstream Labour by their anti-parliamentarism while at the same time cutting themselves off from what seemed for so many to be the only viable alternative, the CPGB. But, as politically insignificant minorities, they struggled on for as long as they could.[106] It is perhaps not surprising that, as Shipway has shown, those who had always been the least likely to be pulled into the Bolshevik orbit — the anarchist supporters of soviet democracy — seem to have been most resilient, with one of their most prominent figures, Guy Aldred, still actively engaged in promoting the idea of "anti-parliamentary communism" until his death in 1963.[107] For them and other supporters of "real" soviets uncontaminated by Communist manipulation and domination, soviet democracy would, in the final words of Israel Getzler's history of the Kronstadt soviet, "remain but an unfulfilled promise of the Russian revolution."[108]

To grasp the importance of the myth of soviet democracy it is only necessary to consider what the effect on the Left in Britain and elsewhere would have been had the Bolsheviks seized power *without* claiming to be installing soviet democracy. In Russia, the claim that "all power" had been taken by the soviets provided the vital camouflage for the October Revolution. In Britain, it enlisted the support of wide sections of the Left, particularly those most critical of the shortcomings of "bourgeois" democracy and especially those sympathetic to the syndicalist and guild socialist insistence on the primacy of the workplace. The myth of soviet democracy was crucial in establishing a sense of the legitimacy of Communist rule.

Broad-based support for Bolshevism eventually began to fall away — as the case of the ILP in 1920 and 1921 demonstrates — but, in hindsight, it took a surprisingly long time in doing so. And even among those who rejected the USSR as a model for the future of Britain, there often remained more than a few vestiges of the feeling that however unrealistic, inappropriate, and undesirable the Communist version of soviet democracy might be at home, it was perhaps real, worthwhile, and necessary *there*.

For those on the Left who rejected the Communist dictatorship, giving their wholehearted support to a Labour Party, albeit one that had little time for radical ideas of extending or deepening democracy, must have seemed the only viable and thus sensible alternative. This would have been particularly so after the ILP disaffiliation from Labour in 1932 began the marginalization of that relatively large constituency, which had become a sort of residuary legatee of pre-Bolshevik radical democracy. Such ideas increasingly found themselves almost squeezed out between the cautious and conservative "parliamentary socialism" of the Labour Party and a CPGB, in whose early appeal the notion of soviet democracy had been a key ingredient. And, in its depoliticized form, soviet democracy would remain central to a utopian vision of the "new civilization" being built in the USSR.

NOTES

Introduction

1   See C.B. Macpherson, *Possessive Individualism: From Hobbes to Locke* (Oxford: Clarendon Press, 1962).

2   See C.B. Macpherson, *The Real World of Democracy: The Massey Lectures*, 12–22, especially 12, 14, 16–18, and 22.

3   "Parliament *versus* Soviet," *New Statesman*, 6 March 1920.

4   For more on the Left's pursuit of "real" democracy and its distrust of "leaders," see Logie Barrow and Ian Bullock, *Democratic Ideas and the British Labour Movement, 1880–1914*; Ian Bullock, "Socialists and Democratic Form: Positions and Debates"; and Ian Bullock, "Sylvia Pankhurst and the Russian Revolution: The Making of a 'Left-Wing' Communist."

5   For a discussion of "weak" democracy, see Barrow and Bullock, *Democratic Ideas and the British Labour Movement*, especially 292–94.

6   On Shaw, see A.M. Mcbriar, *Fabian Socialism and English Politics, 1884–1916*, 85; and Barrow and Bullock, *Democratic Ideas and the British Labour Movement*, 176.

7   See Kevin Morgan, "English Guild Socialists and the Exemplar of the Panama Canal."

8   Robert Service, *The Bolshevik Party in Revolution: A Study in Organised Change, 1917–1923*, 211; Arthur Ransome, *Six Weeks in Russia in 1919*, vi.

9   Chushichi Tsuzuki, *H.M. Hyndman and British Socialism*, 268.

10 Michael Rustin, "What Happened to Socialism?" 208.

11 Tony Judt, *Ill Fares the Land: A Treatise on Our Present Discontents*, 142.

12 More precisely, it was the Social-Democratic *Party* (SDP) writ large. The SDF had changed its name from "Federation" to "Party" in 1907, a few years before the formation of the BSP.

13 For changes in Pankhurst's organizations, see Ian Bullock, "Sylvia Pankhurst and the Russian Revolution."

14 J.T. Murphy, *The Workers' Committee: An Outline of Its Principles and Structure*, 14–15.

15 J.T. Murphy, *Preparing for Power: A Critical Study of the History of the British Working-Class Movement*, 97, 141, 146.

16 Ralph Darlington, *The Political Trajectory of J.T. Murphy*, 261.

17 Kendall's *The Revolutionary Movement in Britain, 1900–21: The Origins of British Communism* appeared in 1969. See also L.J. Macfarlane, *The British Communist Party: Its Origin and Development Until 1929* (1966); James Hinton, *The First Shop-Stewards' Movement* (1973); and Bob Holton, *British Syndicalism, 1900–1914* (1976).

18 L.J.W. Barrow, "The Socialism of Robert Blatchford and the 'Clarion' Newspaper, 1889–1918." On the pre-war period, see also Barrow and Bullock, *Democratic Ideas and the British Labour Movement*; Bullock, "Socialists and Democratic Form"; and Ian Bullock and Sián Reynolds, "Direct Legislation and Socialism: How British and French Socialists Viewed the Referendum in the 1890s," *History Workshop Journal* 24 (Autumn 1987): 62–81.

19 Andrew Thorpe, *The British Communist Party and Moscow, 1920–45* (2000); Kevin Morgan, *Harry Pollitt* (1993); and Morgan, *Bolshevism and the British Left*, vol. 1,

Labour Legends and Russian Gold, (2006); vol. 2, *The Webbs and Soviet Communism* (2006); and vol. 3, *Workers of All Countries? Syndicalism, Internationalism and the Lost World of A A. Purcell* (forthcoming).

20   Sheila Rowbotham, *Edward Carpenter: A Life of Liberty and Love* (London: Verso, 2008). For David Howell's work, see, especially, *A Lost Left: Three Studies in Socialism and Nationalism* (1986); "Traditions, Myths and Legacies: The ILP and the Labour Left," in *The ILP on Clydeside, 1893–1932: From Foundation to Disintegration,* ed. Alan McKinlay and R.J. Morris (Manchester and New York: Manchester University Press, 1991); and *MacDonald's Party: Labour Identities 1922–31* (2002).

21   Gidon Cohen, *The Failure of a Dream: The Independent Labour Party from Disaffiliation to World War II.*

22   Karen Hunt, *Equivocal Feminists: The Social Democratic Federation and the Woman Question, 1884–1911* (Cambridge: Cambridge University Press, 1996).

CHAPTER 1
Well-Prepared Ground: The British Left on the Eve of the Russian Revolution

1   "The I.L.P. and the Labour Party: What Is the Difference?" Bristol ILP leaflet, 1919 (ILP Archives, London School of Economics, British Library of Political and Economic Science).

2   Gidon Cohen, *The Failure of a Dream: The Independent Labour Party from Disaffiliation to World War II,* 1.

3   Walter Kendall, *The Revolutionary Movement in Britain, 1900–21: The Origins of British Communism,* 269.

4   Ibid., Appendix 1, 303.

5   Kendall attributes the term "impossibilist" to Theodore Rothstein, who will figure prominently later in this book (especially in chapter 5). A year after the formation of the SLP, another "impossibilist" organization, the Socialist Party of Great Britain, was formed by SDF dissidents. It began with about a hundred members. (See Kendall, *The Revolutionary Movement in Britain,* chap. 1.) The SPGB never viewed itself, nor was it viewed, as a possible constitutent of a British communist party and so falls beyond the scope of the "far left" considered in this book. But it survived, and indeed still exists today.

6   Ibid., Appendix 5, 314.

7   *New Statesman,* 18 September 1920.

8   *The Herald,* 27 January 1917.

9   *The Herald,* 28 July 1917.

10   *Report on Fabian Policy and Resolutions Presented to the Fabian Society to the International Socialist Workers' and Trade Union Congress, London, 1896.* Fabian Tract No. 70 (London: Fabian Society, 1896), 6.

11   *Report of the Special Committee Appointed in February 1906, to Consider Measures for Increasing the Scope, Influence, Income, and Activities of the Society, Together with the Executive Committee's Report and Resolutions Thereon,* Fabian Society, November 1906, 38–39.

12 *Justice*, 25 October 1884.

13 *Justice*, 5 August 1893.

14 On the *Clarion* federation, see A.M. Thompson, *Hail Referendum! The Shortest Way to Democracy*, Clarion pamphlet no. 7 (1895); *The Referendum and Initiative in Practice*, Clarion pamphlet no. 31 (1899); and *The Only Way to Democracy*, Clarion pamphlet no. 35 (1900).

15 See Logie Barrow and Ian Bullock, *Democratic Ideas and the British Labour Movement, 1880–1914*, chap. 6.

16 *The Call*, 21 September 1916.

17 *Justice*, 9 January (Robertson) and 13 February 1919 (Hyndman).

18 *Woman's Dreadnought*, 3 February 1917.

19 Program of the London Labour Council for Adult Suffrage conference, 17 February 1917, in the Estelle Sylvia Pankhurst Papers, inventory no. 234, International Institute of Social History, Amsterdam. See also *Labour Leader*, 15 February 1917.

20 *Woman's Dreadnought*, 2 June 1917.

21 *Woman's Dreadnought*, 16 June and 21 July 1917.

22 *Woman's Dreadnought*, 21 July 1917.

23 *The Herald*, 25 August 1917.

24 *Woman's Dreadnought*, 15 September 1917.

25 *Workers' Dreadnought*, 17 November 1917.

26 *Workers' Dreadnought*, 19 January and 26 January 1918.

27 *Workers' Dreadnought*, 20 April (Watson) and 9 March 1918 (Pankhurst).

28 *Workers' Dreadnought*, 4 May 1918.

29 *The Call*, 2 May 1918. Pankhurst's argument was similar to the position that Alex Thompson eventually arrived at in the late 1890s, in his series of pamphlets on the referendum and initiative. See Barrow and Bullock, *Democratic Ideas and the British Labour Movement*, 50–56.

30 *Workers' Dreadnought*, 27 April 1918.

31 *Labour Leader*, 1 January 1920.

32 *The Call*, 8 January 1920.

33 James Hinton, *The First Shop-Stewards' Movement*, 298; Kendall, *The Revolutionary Movement in Britain*, 278.

34 *The Guildsman*, January 1917.

35 J.T. Murphy, *The Workers' Committee: An Outline of Its Principles and Structure*, 3.

36 *Solidarity*, October 1917.

37 *Justice*, 13 December 1917.

38 Murphy, *The Workers' Committee*, 19.

39 Ibid., 20–21.

40 Ibid., 21–23. Trades councils were composed of union branches, rather than being based on individual workplaces.

41 Ibid., 26.

42 Kendall, *The Revolutionary Movement in Britain*, 153.

43 *Labour Leader*, 18 January 1917.

44 Wartime restrictions on the availability of newsprint meant that *The Herald* had

been unable to continue as a daily and was now published weekly. The first part of Hobson's series appeared on 17 February 1917, and the series continued on a weekly basis, with the odd interruption caused in part by the need to give space to the events in Russia.

45 *The Herald,* 11 August 1917. The "never-ending audacity of elected persons" was a quotation from Walt Whitman popularized in British socialist circles by Robert Blatchford many years before.

46 *Labour Leader,* 22 March 1917.

47 *Labour Leader,* 16 October 1919.

48 *Daily Herald,* 18 August 1920.

49 G.D.H. Cole, "Beatrice Webb as an Economist," 275.

50 Lisanne Radice, *Beatrice and Sydney Webb: Fabian Socialists,* 223.

51 *Workers' Dreadnought,* 17 May 1924.

52 See Kendall's *The Revolutionary Movement in Britain,* chap. 1, for the "split," and chap. 4, for the evolution of the SLP.

53 Letter from R.C. Mitchell, of Govan, *The Socialist,* March 1918.

54 Kendall, *The Revolutionary Movement in Britain,* 69.

55 Ibid., 67, quoting Daniel De Leon, *Socialist Reconstruction of Society,* 3–4, published in Glasgow, probably in 1905.

56 *The Socialist,* April 1908, quoted in Raymond Challinor, *The Origins of British Bolshevism,* 52–53.

57 Kendall, *The Revolutionary Movement in Britain,* 133. Kendall quotes from Tom Bell's *Pioneering Days,* 149–51.

58 On delegation and the survival of trends towards "direct democracy" in trade unions in a wider context, see Anthony Carew, *Democracy and Government in European Trade Unions* (London: Allen and Unwin, 1976).

59 For NIGFTLU, see Barrow and Bullock, *Democratic Ideas and the British Labour Movement,* 88–135 (chaps. 5 and 6); for the views of the influential socialist journalist Robert Blatchford on leaders, see 45–50; on anti-leadership attitudes in the trade unions, see 89–92.

60 *The Clarion,* 25 June 1898.

61 J.T. Murphy, *The Workers' Committee,* 14.

CHAPTER 2
Initial Responses to the Russian Revolution: The British Left in 1917 and the Leeds "Soviet" Convention

1 *The Herald,* 24 March 1917 (Lansbury); *Woman's Dreadnought,* 31 March 1917 (Pankhurst).

2 See Keith Laybourn, *Philip Snowden: A Biography, 1864–1937,* 76. Laybourn corrects Snowden's own account, in his autobiography, which has his wife starting the Women's Peace Crusade much later, in November rather than August or September (*An Autobiography,* vol. 1, *1864–1919,* 438–40).

3 *Justice,* 22 March and 5 April 1917.

4   *Labour Leader,* 29 March and 5 April 1917.

5   *The Herald,* 7 April and 12 May 1917.

6   Maurice B. Reckitt, *As It Happened: An Autobiography,* 152; Raymond Postgate, *The Life of George Lansbury,* 165.

7   Original poster for the event, in the author's possession.

8   *Brighton Herald,* 19 May 1917; *Brighton Gazette,* 19 and 26 May 1917. See also Ian Bullock, "Sylvia Pankhurst and the Russian Revolution: The Making of a 'Left-Wing' Communist," 129.

9   *Labour Leader,* 26 April 1917. Chernov would briefly chair the ill-fated Constituent Assembly. No one on the British Left at that time would have given the least credence to Richard Pipes's dismissal of the Petrograd Soviet as "a private body, irregularly constituted and directed by representatives of socialist parties who no one had elected" (*The Russian Revolution, 1899–1919,* 297).

10 *Labour Leader,* 5 April 1917.

11 *Labour Leader,* 12 April 1917.

12 *Woman's Dreadnought,* 24 March 1917.

13 *The Herald,* 12 May 1917.

14 "Open Letter to Lenin," *The Socialist,* 3 February 1921. On Leeds, see also Stephen White, "Soviets in Britain: The Leeds Convention of 1917."

15 Walter Kendall, *The Revolutionary Movement in Britain, 1900–21: The Origins of British Communism,* 174.

16 *The Herald,* 19 May 1917; *The Call,* 24 May 1917.

17 *The Herald,* 19 May 1917.

18 *The Call,* 31 May 1917. Lansbury corrected the spelling in his autobiography when he referred to the "Magna Carta," whose demands he thought had stood the test of time (*My Life,* 188).

19 *Labour Leader,* 17 May 1917.

20 *Labour Leader,* 24 May 1917.

21 *The Herald,* 9 June 1917. For Fairchild's background, see Kendall, *The Revolutionary Movement in Britain,* 227, n. 36.

22 *Labour Leader,* 31 May 1917.

23 *The Herald,* 26 May 1917.

24 *Woman's Dreadnought,* 2 June 1917.

25 *Justice,* 2 June 1917.

26 *The Herald,* 24 March 1917.

27 Ken Coates, introduction to *British Labour and the Russian Revolution: The Leeds Convention—A Report from the Daily Herald,* 8–9. In addition to Coates's introduction, this volume contains a facsimile edition of *What Happened at Leeds: Report Published by the Council of Workers' and Soldiers' Delegates* (London: Pelican Press, June 1917), prepared from reports in the *Daily Herald.* The quotations are from Montefiore's *From a Victorian to a Modern,* 194, and Malleson's *After Ten Years,* 113–14.

Dora Montefiore (1851–1933) is chiefly remembered as a campaigner for women's suffrage and women's rights more generally, both in Britain and Australia. For Montefiore, see, especially, the work of Karen Hunt, such as "Gendering the

Politics of the Working Woman's Home," in *Women and the Making of Built Space in England, 1870–1950*, ed. Elizabeth Darling and Lesley Whitworth (Aldershot, Hampshire, UK: Ashgate, 2007), 107–22. Constance Malleson (1895–1975) was an actress whose stage name was Colette O'Niel, as well as the author of two novels and other books. Married to the actor Miles Malleson until their divorce in 1923, she was a pacifist during World War I and Bertrand Russell's lover. Nearly half a century later, Russell briefly recalled attending at Leeds "a great meeting of sympathisers" with what he called the "Kerensky Revolution." The meeting, he said, was also attended by "Colette and her husband" (*The Autobiography of Bertrand Russell*, vol. 2, *1914–1944*, 31).

28 See the reports in *The Call*, 7 June 1917, and in *The Herald*, 9 June 1917.

29 *Justice*, 7 June 1917.

30 Snowden, *An Autobiography*, vol. 1, 450–51.

31 Ibid., 451 and 450.

32 Ibid., 453.

33 *Labour Leader*, 7 June 1917; *The Call*, 7 June 1917.

34 *The Herald*, 9 June 1917.

35 *The Herald*, 2 June 1917.

36 *Woman's Dreadnought*, 9 June 1917. The WSF had put forward a very large number of amendments, including the ones quoted in the previous chapter. Given the limited time available at the conference, it is impossible to see how they could all have been debated, even if no other participants had followed suit with amendments of their own.

37 *The Call*, 7 June 1917.

38 *Labour Leader*, 7 June 1917.

39 *The Call*, 7 June 1917.

40 *The Herald*, 9 June 1917.

41 *The Call*, 7 June 1917.

42 J.T. Walton Newbold did use the phrase in an article that appeared in the 12 July 1917 issue of *The Call*, but this was, of course, after Williams had begun to popularize the expression in left-wing circles.

43 See *The Communist*, 30 April 1921. This particular "Black Friday"— 15 April 1921 — was so called because of the perceived betrayal of the miners by their "Triple Alliance" trade union partners, the National Union of Railwaymen and the National Transport Workers' Federation. The mines (like the railways) had been state controlled during the war, and this remained the case until the end of March 1921, when the mine owners, now back in charge, imposed wage reductions. When the miners refused to accept these, they were locked out, and their rail and transport allies were widely expected to strike in solidarity. But the NUR and NTWF decided against this, provoking much criticism and resentment, much of it directed at the secretaries of the two organizations, J.H. Thomas and Robert Williams. The "Triple Alliance" union, formed in 1910, took its name from the international diplomatic alliance between Germany, Austria-Hungary, and Italy.

44 *Labour Leader*, 7 June 1917.

45 *The Herald,* 2 June 1917.

46 *Woman's Dreadnought,* 9 June 1917. For the proposed change of terminology from "Workmen" to "Workers," see, for instance, *What Happened at Leeds,* in Coates, ed., *British Labour and the Russian Revolution,* 17, 18, 29. *The Call* was inconsistent in its nomenclature. For example, on 20 June 1918, an article titled "The International" refers to "Workmen's," while on 11 July, in "Litvinoff Answers Kerensky," the term used is "Workers'," and then, in a piece by Lenin the following week, it is "Workmen's" again.

47 See James Hinton, *The First Shop-Stewards' Movement,* 241; Ralph Miliband, *Parliamentary Socialism: A Study in the Politics of Labour,* 55; Fenner Brockway, *Socialism over Sixty Years: The Life of Jowett of Bradford,* 153; Laurence Thompson, *The Enthusiasts: A Biography of John and Katharine Bruce Glasier,* 225–26; and Bill Jones, *The Russia Complex: The British Labour Party and the Soviet Union,* 1.

48 Keith Laybourn, *Philip Snowden: A Biography, 1864–1937,* 78; Colin Cross, *Philip Snowden,* 157.

49 David Marquand, *Ramsay MacDonald,* 208–9; L.J. Macfarlane, *The British Communist Party: Its Origin and Development Until 1929,* 21.

50 Ken Coates, introduction to *British Labour and the Russian Revolution,* 15.

51 *The Herald,* 9 June 1917.

52 *Labour Leader,* 7 June 1917.

53 *Justice,* 7 June 1917.

54 *Justice,* 14 June 1917.

55 Kendall, *The Revolutionary Movement in Britain,* 129.

56 *The Call,* 14 June 1917.

57 *The Call,* 21 June 1917.

58 *The Herald,* 23 June 1917.

59 *The Call,* 28 June 1917.

60 *Labour Leader,* 7 June 1917.

61 *The Herald,* 14 July 1917.

62 *The Call,* 19 July 1917.

63 *The Call,* 7 August 1917. The Black Hundreds were extreme right-wing, anti-revolutionary, and anti-semitic organizations, which in some ways anticipated fascism, that were set up in early twentieth-century Russia, especially during and after the failed revolution of 1905.

64 *The Herald,* 4 August 1917.

65 *The Call,* 16 August 1917.

66 *The Call,* 23 August 1917.

67 Hinton, *The First Shop-Stewards' Movement,* 240.

68 *The Herald,* 8 September 1917.

69 *The Guildsman,* September 1917.

70 *The Call,* 4 October 1917. According to Hinton (*The First Shop-Stewards' Movement,* 240), who cites Ministry of Munitions records, there were attempts to set up local committees in "at least eight areas": London, Tyneside, Glasgow, Sheffield,

Norwich, Leicester, Bristol, and Swansea. There is no mention of the efforts to hold meetings for Manchester or the Southern Counties.

71   *The Call*, 25 October 1917. See also *The Herald*, 27 October 1917. Inkpin's report now listed delegates for twelve districts, who included two women: Mrs. C.A. Findlay, representing Lancashire, Cheshire, and North Wales, and Pankhurst.

72   J.T. Murphy, *Preparing for Power*, 97, 141, 146.

73   *Labour Leader*, 7 June 1917.

74   *The Call*, 28 December 1917.

75   *The Herald*, 26 January 1918.

76   *Workers' Dreadnought*, 9 February 1918. For Pankhurst's later reflections on the national Workers' and Soldiers' Council, which seems to have met only four times, see Ian Bullock, "Sylvia Pankhurst and the Russian Revolution," 130–31.

77   It is difficult to agree with Raymond Postgate that "soviet was a word only slowly assimilated" (*The Life of George Lansbury*, 165).

78   See Kendall, *The Revolutionary Movement in Britain*, 157–64.

79   *The Herald*, 25 August 1917.

CHAPTER 3
The Bolsheviks and the British Left: The October Revolution and the Suppression of the Constituent Assembly

1   *Workers' Dreadnought*, 19 July and 6 September 1919.

2   *The Call*, 17 July 1919. Rothstein wrote as John Bryan.

3   Walter Kendall, *The Revolutionary Movement in Britain, 1900–21: The Origins of British Communism*, 79.

4   *The Call*, 27 July 1916 (Luxemburg), and 23 March, 29 June, 3 August, and 16 November 1916 (Liebknecht).

5   *The Call*, 13 December 1916.

6   *The Call*, 12 April 1917. There had been a letter from George Tchitcherine, as he then spelled his name, on 13 July 1916. Chicherin was at this time a member of the Kentish Town Branch of the BSP. See Kendall, *The Revolutionary Movement*, 82.

7   *The Herald*, 24 March 1917.

8   *The Call*, 30 November 1916 and 1 March 1917.

9   *Justice*, 26 April 1917.

10   See Ian Bullock, "Sylvia Pankhurst and the Russian Revolution: The Making of a 'Left-Wing' Communist," 127–29.

11   *Woman's Dreadnought*, 23 June 1917; *Labour Leader*, 14 June 1917.

12   *Woman's Dreadnought*, 30 June 1917.

13   *The Herald*, 28 July 1917.

14   *The Call*, 7 August 1917.

15   *The Herald*, 1 September 1917.

16   *The Herald*, 8 September 1917.

17   *Justice*, 13 September 1917.

18   *The Call*, 4 October, 27 September, and 18 October 1917.

19 *The Call,* 1 November 1917. The "October Revolution" began on 25 October in the Julian calendar, which was still in use in Russia, but on 7 November in the Gregorian calendar.

20 *Justice,* 8 November 1917.

21 *The Call,* 15 November 1917.

22 *The Call,* 29 November and 6 December 1917.

23 *The Call,* 20 December 1917 and 10 January 1918 (Fairchild).

24 Keith Laybourn, *Philip Snowden: A Biography, 1864–1937,* 68–69. Snowden had been a regular contributor to *Labour Leader* in 1916 and 1917.

25 *The Socialist,* December 1917.

26 *The Herald,* 17 November 1917.

27 *Labour Leader,* 22 November 1917.

28 *The Herald,* 24 November 1917.

29 *The Herald,* 1 December 1917. F. M. Leventhal notes the way Lansbury distanced himself from Brailsford as regards Russian developments (*The Last Dissenter: H.N. Brailsford and His World,* 142).

30 *The Herald,* 29 December 1917.

31 *Labour Leader,* 6 December 1917.

32 *The Herald,* 29 December 1917. By "Revolutionary Socialists," Brailsford is referring to the Social Revolutionary Party.

33 *New Statesman,* 8 December 1917, "The Bolshevik Revolution — Smolny Nights." (The full text is available on the *New Statesman* website.) Much earlier, in its issue of 30 June, *The Herald* had questioned the "exquisitely ludicrous situation" whereby "the representation of British Socialism in Russia seems to have devolved entirely upon Mr Julius West." He was, the paper said, delegated by the Fabian Society, "a small though influential body which probably does not contain five hundred manual workers in all," and might at most represent about two thousand people. West, the twenty-six-year-old son of a Russian émigré and a member of the Fabian Society executive, had, according to the same source, been invited to Russia by the "Council of Soldiers and Workers' Councils." He died the following year of pneumonia, and his *History of the Chartist Movement* was published posthumously in 1920.

34 *The Call,* 22 March 1917.

35 *The Call,* 29 March 1917.

36 *Woman's Dreadnought,* 23 and 30 June 1917.

37 *Workers' Dreadnought,* 29 September 1917.

38 *Workers' Dreadnought,* 17 November 1917.

39 *The Call,* 6 December and 13 December 1917.

40 *Workers' Dreadnought,* 15 December 1917.

41 "Electing the Constituent Assembly," *New Statesman,* 19 January 1918.

42 *The Herald,* 5 January 1918. Farbman dedicated his book *Russia and the Struggle for Peace* (London: Allen and Unwin, 1918) to Maxim Gorky.

43 *The Herald,* 12 January 1918.

44 *Justice,* 17 January 1918.

45 *Labour Leader,* 24 January 1918.

46 *The Herald,* 9 February 1918.

47 *The Herald,* 23 February and 2 March 1918.

48 *The Herald,* 9 March 1918.

49 *The Herald,* 9 February 1918.

50 *The Herald,* 2 March 1918.

51 *Workers' Dreadnought,* 26 January 1918.

52 *The Call,* 31 January 1918.

53 *Justice,* 24 January 1918.

54 *Report of the Eighteenth Annual Conference of the Labour Party,* 35.

55 Ibid., 59.

56 *New Statesman,* 26 January 1918.

57 *Justice,* 31 January 1918.

58 *Labour Leader,* 24 January 1918. J.T. Murphy, a leading shop steward in 1918, recalled some sixteen years later "the tremendous reception given to Litvinoff" (*Preparing for Power: A Critical Study of the History of the British Working-Class Movement,* 154).

59 *The Herald,* 26 January 1918.

60 *Workers' Dreadnought,* 6 July 1918.

61 *The Herald,* 6 July 1918.

62 *Labour Leader,* 2 and 9 January 1919. For earlier Snowden comments sympathetic to the Bolsheviks, see, for example, *Labour Leader,* 23 May 1918.

63 *Labour Leader,* 6 March 1919.

64 Philip Viscount Snowden, *An Autobiography,* vol. 1, *1864–1919,* 480.

65 *Labour Leader,* 31 January 1918.

66 *Justice,* 22 August 1918.

67 *Justice,* 5 September 1918.

68 *The Call,* 30 May 1918. On the left-wing husband-and-wife team of Eden and Cedar Paul, see Kevin Morgan, *The Webbs and Soviet Communism,* vol. 2 of *Bolshevism and the British Left,* 154–59.

69 *Workers' Dreadnought,* 8 June 1918.

70 *Workers' Dreadnought,* 30 November 1918. The Spartacist League (*Spartakusbund*) had been founded by left-wing German socialists, notably Rosa Luxemberg and Karl Liebknecht, in opposition to the SPD majority, which supported the war. It became the German Communist Party in December 1918.

71 "Free Russia Greets the German Workers," *Workers' Dreadnought,* 14 December 1918.

72 *The Socialist,* 30 January 1919.

73 *Workers' Dreadnought,* 12 April 1919.

74 *The Call,* 18 July 1918.

75 *Workers' Dreadnought,* 20 December 1919.

76 Quoted in *The Communist,* 5 November 1921.

77 *The Call,* 4 July 1918.

78 *Workers' Dreadnought,* 21 June 1921.

79 *The Guildsman,* June 1920 ("Hussein," quoting Lenin's *The Proletarian Revolution*).

CHAPTER 4

The Myth Established: The Positive View of Soviet Democracy

1 "What Are the Soviets?" by N. [sic] Lenin, "President of the Council of People's Commissaries of the Russian Socialist Republic," *The Call*, 18 July 1918.

2 *The Call*, 14 February ("Learn to Speak Russian") and 1 August 1918.

3 *The Call*, 13 November 1919. Willis here refers to reactionary elements as "the Black International."

4 For contrasting views on the issue of delegation versus representation in the British socialist movement prior to World War I, see Logie Barrow and Ian Bullock, *Democratic Ideas Ideas and the British Labour Movement, 1880–1914*, especially chap. 2.

5 *Workers' Dreadnought*, 28 December 1918.

6 *The Call*, 1 July 1920.

7 *The Call*, 21 February 1918.

8 *The Call*, 18 March 1920.

9 *The Call*, 27 May 1920.

10 *Workers' Dreadnought*, 26 January 1918.

11 *Workers' Dreadnought*, 10 May 1919.

12 *Workers' Dreadnought*, 28 December 1918.

13 *Workers' Dreadnought*, 5 April 1919.

14 *The Socialist*, 29 April 1920. The translator was "Miss N Capoldi."

15 *The Communist*, 19 August 1920.

16 See *The Call*, 29 August 1918, and *Labour Leader*, 22 January 1920, for two examples.

17 *Labour Leader*, 30 May 1918.

18 *The Call*, 29 August 1918.

19 *New Statesman*, 6 March 1920.

20 *The Call*, 25 July 1918.

21 *Solidarity*, August 1918 and September 1918.

22 *The Herald*, 3 August 1918.

23 *The Call*, 6 November 1919.

24 *Workers' Dreadnought*, 29 January 1921.

25 *Workers' Dreadnought*, 28 December 1918.

26 *New Statesman*, 4 May 1918.

27 *The Call*, 13 November 1919.

28 Charles Read, *From Tsar to Soviets: The Russian People and Their Revolution, 1917–21*, 64.

29 Richard Pipes, *The Russian Revolution, 1899–1919*, 295.

30 See Diane Koenker, *Moscow Workers and the 1917 Revolution*, 144–86.

31 *The Call*, 18 July and 28 November 1918.

32 *Solidarity*, August 1918.

33 *Workers' Dreadnought*, 24 August 1918.

34 *Justice*, 13 June 1918.

35 See, for example, *Justice*, 19 September 1918.

36 *Workers' Dreadnought*, 30 April 1921.

37 Arthur Ransome, *The Autobiography of Arthur Ransome*, 220.

38 *New Statesman*, 12 July 1919.

39 "How a City Soviet Is Elected," *Workers' Dreadnought*, 11 October 1919, which cites the 7, 10, 11, 12, 13, and 29 April 1918 issues of *Pravda*.

40 See Orlando Figes, *A People's Tragedy: The Russian Revolution, 1891–1924*, 626.

41 Ibid.

42 *Workers' Dreadnought*, 12 June 1920.

43 *The Socialist*, 29 July 1920.

44 *The Communist*, 19 November 1921.

45 *The Socialist*, 15 January 1920.

46 *Workers' Dreadnought*, 21 December 1918.

47 *Labour Leader*, 16 May 1918.

48 *Labour Leader*, 30 May 1918.

49 *Labour Leader*, 29 May 1919. For other instances of the paper perceiving Russian events as "an experiment," see, for example, *Labour Leader*, 30 April and 1 May 1919; 29 January, 12 February, 24 June, and 16 and 28 September 1920; and 31 March 1921. For the continued use in British Labour circles of the notion that the USSR was an "experiment," see Andrew Williams, *Labour and Russia: The Attitude of the Labour Party to the USSR, 1924–34*. There was at least one book published during the interwar years that used this idea as a title — Arthur Feiler and H.J. Stenning's *The Russian Experiment* (1930).

50 *New Statesman*, 21 and 28 December 1918.

51 *New Statesman*, 4 January 1919.

52 *New Statesman*, 11 January 1919.

53 *New Statesman*, 26 July 1919.

54 *New Statesman*, 24 January 1920. The notion that the Communist system was "democratic in essence if not in form" does seem to anticipate C.B. Macpherson's formulation decades later — quoted in the introduction — that it was democratic in "the broader sense."

55 *New Statesman*, 24 and 31 January 1920, "Letters" section.

56 *New Statesman*, 13 March 1920.

57 *The Guildsman*, June 1920.

58 *New Statesman*, 3 April 1920.

59 *New Statesman*, 6 March 1920.

60 *New Statesman*, 5 March 1921.

61 *New Statesman*, 23 July 1921.

62 *New Statesman*, 5 November 1921. On famine relief, see the 13 August issue.

63 *New Statesman*, 26 June 1920. See also the 11 December 1920 issue.

CHAPTER 5
Polarized Social-Democrats: Denunciation and Debate

1 H.W. Lee and E. Archbold, *Social-Democracy in Britain: Fifty Years of the Socialist Movement* (London: Social-Democratic Federation, 1935), 240–41.

2 *Justice*, 20 June 1918.

3 *Justice*, 6 June and 8 August 1918.

4 *Justice*, 21 November 1918.

5 *Justice*, 15 August 1918. Shammes's first name appears in some sources as "Lewis" or "Leo."

6 *Justice*, 27 June 1918.

7 *Justice*, 22 August 1918.

8 *Justice*, 7 November 1918.

9 *Justice*, 12 December 1918; *The Call*, 14 November 1918.

10 *Justice*, 2 January 1919.

11 *Justice*, 20 March 1919.

12 L.E. (Lorenzo or "Len") Edward Quelch (1862–1937) was the brother of the prominent SDFer and long-time editor of *Justice*, Harry Quelch. The fact that Tom Quelch, of the pro-Bolshevik BSP, was Harry's son and Len's nephew serves to illustrate that the wartime split in the BSP had a strong generational aspect. See Walter Kendall, *The Revolutionary Movement in Britain, 1900–21: The Origins of British Communism*, chap. 1, n. 4, and chap. 6, nn. 82 and 114. The latest volume of the *Dictionary of Labour Biography* has a very comprehensive account of the life of Len Quelch, written by John S. Partington. See the *Dictionary of Labour Biography*, vol. 13, ed. Keith Gildart and David Howell (Basingstoke: Palgrave Macmillan, 2010), 319–34.

13 *Justice*, 14 March 1918.

14 *Justice*, 19 September 1918.

15 *Justice*, 10 October 1918.

16 *Justice*, 17 October 1918.

17 *Justice*, 26 September 1918.

18 *Justice*, 14 November 1918.

19 *Justice*, 10 and 17 April 1919.

20 *Justice*, 19 June 1919.

21 *Justice*, 29 November 1918.

22 *Justice*, 2 and 9 January 1919.

23 See Logie Barrow and Ian Bullock, *Democratic Ideas and the British Labour Movement, 1880–1914*, 19, 42.

24 *Justice*, 13 February 1919.

25 *Justice*, 10 October 1918.

26 *Justice*, 7 November 1918.

27 *Justice*, 2 January 1919.

28 *Justice*, 12 June 1919. "T.D.H."— the author of the letter, mentioned in chapter 2, arguing that the "soviet" resolution at the Leeds convention wasn't "seriousoly intended"— was a fairly regular contributor to *Justice*.

29 *Justice*, 12 June 1919.

30 For biographical details, see Kendall, *The Revolutionary Movement in Britain*, including 323, n. 66. See also David Burke, "Theodore Rothstein: Russian Emigré and British Socialist," in *From the Other Shore: Russian Political Emigrants in Britain, 1880–1917*, ed. John Slatter (London: Cass, 1984), 81–99.

31 *The Call*, 5 June 1919.

32 *The Call*, 12 June 1919.

33 *The Call*, 21 August 1919.

34 *The Call*, 19 June 1919.

35 *The Call*, 26 June 1919.

36 *The Call*, 3 July (Lowe) and 17 July 1919 (Hodgson).

37 See *The Call*, 24 July 1919, for Montefiore, and, for McLaine and Carney, 14 August 1919.

38 *The Call*, 31 July (Adshead) and 7 August 1919 (Ryde).

39 *The Call*, 28 August 1919.

40 Kendall, *The Revolutionary Movement in Britain*, 406, n. 64.

41 *The Call*, 4 September 1919.

42 *The Call*, 11 September 1919.

43 Kendall, *The Revolutionary Movement in Britain*, 245.

44 *The Call*, 25 September 1919.

45 *The Call*, 16 October 1919.

46 James Hinton, *The First Shop-Stewards' Movement*, 303.

CHAPTER 6
Equivocal Reformists: The Independent Labour Party, the Guild Socialists, and the Reaction to Kautsky

1 *Labour Leader*, 7 March 1918.

2 See A. Fenner Brockway, *Bermondsey Story: The Life of Alfred Salter*, 72–73. As Brockway's title suggests, Salter's chosen field of political activity was very much a local one, though this eventually included representing West Bermondsey as its MP. His outlook was anything but parochial, however. When he visited the USSR in 1931 with a group of medical experts to investigate Soviet health provision, he found things to admire. But the view he had first expressed in 1919 remained. According to Brockway, as a "democratically-minded man," Salter was appalled by the "absolute and ruthless suppression of all views contrary to those held by the Government clique" and by the way "dissentients," even among "prominent Communist leaders," simply "disappeared." Brockway concluded that Salter was "one of the first visitors to draw attention so clearly to what are now recognised as the fundamental characteristics of the regime — the consecration of industrial advance and the conservation of political dictatorship" (161).

3 *Labour Leader*, 4 July 1918.

4 *Labour Leader*, 15 August 1918.

5 *Labour Leader*, 8 August 1918.

6 *Labour Leader*, 17 July 1919.

7 *Labour Leader*, 11 September 1919.

8 *Justice*, 25 May and 10 July 1919. In the May issue, Hyndman repeated what he had originally revealed in January of that year. He had, very typically, conducted a "long correspondence" with the British government at the beginning of 1918,

in which he had urged that Russian forces in Britain, "acting in harmony with Russian democrats," should be sent to defend or restore the Constituent Assembly. A year later, he found it ironic that "His Majesty's Government declares in January that it is pledged not to intervene in internal Russian affairs for the purpose of upholding the Constituent Assembly whose members are friends of Great Britain, *even with Russian troops.* Shortly afterwards intervention is begun and carried out *by British troops* and money, for and on behalf of men whose sole desire is to re-establish Tsardom or a military dictatorship" (*Justice,* 9 January 1919).

9   *Labour Leader,* 17 July 1919.

10   H.J. Stenning, born Heinrich Strobel, translated a wide range of works, including *The Resurrection of the Dead,* by the Swiss theologian Karl Barth.

11   *Labour Leader,* 15 January 1920.

12   *Labour Leader,* 22 January 1920.

13   See G.D.H. Cole, "Political Action and the N.G.L.," *The Guildsman,* January and February 1919.

14   *The Guild Socialist,* April 1921.

15   *The Guildsman,* November 1919.

16   *The Guildsman,* June 1918.

17   *The Guildsman,* July 1918.

18   *The Guildsman,* August 1918. On the importance of white-collar workers, see also the January 1919 issue, which welcomed "the tendency of brain workers to join the Labour Party" and commented: "We congratulate the Labour Party on welcoming them." Under a subheading, "The Salariat," the paper announced that there was "every indication that clerks and typists are at last beginning to see the folly of regarding themselves as members of the ruling class."

19   *The Guildsman,* September 1918.

20   *The Guildsman,* February 1919.

21   *The Herald,* 4 January 1917.

22   See James Hinton, *The First Shop Stewards' Movement,* 44–48. Hinton's first chapter is titled "The Servile State." For the pre-war discussion of Belloc's *The Servile State* in the British socialist press, see Logie Barrow and Ian Bullock, *Democratic Ideas and the British Labour Movement, 1880–1914,* 261–64.

23   *The Guildsman,* January 1921. It was the issue of September 1919 that referred to "Chesterbelloc" as "friendly critics," ones whose "wide community of outlook . . . on many points transcends our differences. Mr Belloc and Mr Chesterton both believe profoundly in human freedom and see clearly that economic freedom is the key to other sorts of freedom." Their answer to the "Servile State" was promoted by the Distributist League, partly on the basis of Catholic social doctrine, which urged the virtues of a society comprised of small property owners. It is interesting that, during the 2010 British general election campaign, when the Conservative leader, David Cameron, was promoting the idea of the "Big Society" as an alternative to an allegedly over-large state, Jonathon Rabin traced the inspiration of Phillip Blond's *Red Tory* — for whose ideas, Rabin said, Cameron was a "mouthpiece"

— to Chesterton and Belloc's distributism. See *The Guardian*, Review section, 24 April 2010.

24 *The Guildsman*, April 1920. In his autobiography, *As It Happened*, Reckitt remembered John (or J.M.) Paton as a "the finest propagandist the National Guilds League ever had" (167). This John Paton should not be confused with the John Paton of *Left Turn!* who was to play a memorable role in the 1921 ILP conference debate on affiliation to the Comintern and later became secretary of that party.

25 *The Guildsman*, January 1918.

26 *The Guildsman*, July 1918.

27 *The Guildsman*, October 1918.

28 *The Guildsman*, July–August 1919. The voting figures given were 78 to 39. The vote by local group rejected the proposed change even more decisively, by 10 to 50.

29 *The Guildsman*, April 1920.

30 Penty, by profession an architect, later became a Distributist. He is mainly remembered for his 1906 book, *The Restoration of the Guild System,* and as a contributor, during the pre-war period, to A. R. Orage's *The New Age*.

31 *The Guildsman*, May 1920.

32 *The Guildsman*, June 1920.

33 *The Guildsman*, September 1920.

34 *The Guildsman*, May 1919.

35 *Labour Leader*, 29 January 1920.

36 Walter Kendall, *The Revolutionary Movement in Britain, 1900–21: The Origins of British Communism*, x.

37 *Labour Leader*, 29 January 1920.

38 See John H. Kautsky's introduction to the paperback edition of Stenning's translation of *The Dictatorship of the Proletariat* (Ann Arbor: University of Michigan Press, 1964), xv.

39 *New Statesman*, 13 March 1920. The other two books reviewed in the same article were Colonel Malone, MP, *The Russian Republic,* and W.T. Goode, MA, *Bolshevism at Work*.

40 *The Socialist*, 30 January 1919. "Comrade Martoff," that is, Julius Martov (1873–1923), was one of the preeminent leaders of the Mensheviks.

41 *The Socialist*, 12 February 1920.

42 *The Call,* 22 April 1920.

43 Karl Kautsky, *The Dictatorship of the Proletariat*, 42.

44 *Workers' Dreadnought*, 8 May 1920. The spelling of Kautsky's name in the "Letter" was erratic; in other places, he appeared as "Kautzki."

45 *The Communist*, 23 December 1920.

46 *The Communist*, 12 February 1921.

47 *New Statesman*, 18 December 1920. Regarding Russell, the reviewer claimed: "What shocks Russell is the religious nature of Bolshevism as a result of which they show contempt of democracy, freedom of speech and of the Press."

48 *The Communist*, 6 August 1921.

CHAPTER 7
The Dictatorship of the Proletariat

1 Karl Kautsky, *The Dictatorship of the Proletariat*, 43.

2 *Justice*, 8 December 1913.

3 *The Call*, 12 and 29 July 1917.

4 *Workers' Dreadnought*, 24 August 1918.

5 *Workers' Dreadnought*, 14 June 1919.

6 *The Socialist*, December 1918.

7 *Workers' Dreadnought*, 17 May 1919.

8 *The Call*, 30 October 1919.

9 *The Socialist*, 28 October 1920. Gregory Zinoviev (1883–1936) was a prominent Bolshevik, who chaired the executive committee of the Third International. In 1936, he became one of the "Old Bolshevik" victims of Stalin's first show trial.

10 *The Call*, 4 April 1918.

11 Walter Kendall, *The Revolutionary Movement in Britain, 1900–21: The Origins of British Communism*, 406, n. 59. Andrew Rothstein, Theodore's son, told Kendall that his father had used this pseudonym during 1918.

12 *The Call*, 26 September 1918.

13 *The Socialist*, 24 December 1919.

14 *The Call*, 24 October 1918.

15 *Workers' Dreadnought*, 8 February 1919. Lenin's "A Letter to American Workingmen" first appeared in *Pravda*, on 22 August 1918.

16 *The Communist*, 12 August 1920.

17 *The Communist*, 2 December 1920.

18 *Workers' Dreadnought*, 17 May 1919.

19 *Workers' Dreadnought*, 1 March 1919.

20 *Workers' Dreadnought*, 3 August 1918.

21 *The Call*, 13 February 1919.

22 Charles Roden Buxton (1875–1942) was a former Liberal MP who had come to the ILP via the Union of Democratic Control. In 1920, he would be one of the secretaries of the Labour Party/TUC delegation that visited Russia. He was later a parliamentary adviser to the Labour Party and, for two quite brief periods (1922–23 and 1929–31), a Labour MP.

23 *Labour Leader*, 15 May 1919.

24 *Workers' Dreadnought*, 8 November 1919.

25 *Workers' Dreadnought*, 3 May 1919.

26 *The Call*, 19 February 1920.

27 *Workers' Dreadnought*, 17 July 1920.

28 *The Communist*, 29 April and 13 May 1922.

29 *The Call*, 22 July 1920. See also the previous week's issue (15 July), in which the "Theses of the Executive Committee of the Communist International" denounced as "a surrender to those views of syndicalism, industrialism which are in essence reactionary" the declaration of the German Left Communists at their founding

conference that they were not creating a party in the "usual, traditional sense of the word (*Keine Partei im überlieferten Sinne*)."

30   *The Guildsman*, October 1919.

31   *The Guildsman*, November 1919 (Reckitt) and December 1919 (Dutt).

32   *Justice*, 12 June 1919.

33   *Workers' Dreadnought*, 12 April 1919.

34   *The Call*, 13 November 1919.

35   *The Call*, 22 April 1920.

36   *The Socialist* 15 January 1920.

37   *Workers' Dreadnought*, 3 July 1920.

38   *Workers' Dreadnought*, 24 and 31 July 1920.

39   *New Statesman*, 26 February 1921.

40   Bertrand Russell, *The Practice and Theory of Communism*, 27–28.

CHAPTER 8
The Independent Labour Party and the Third International: A Crucial Test for Belief in Soviet Democracy

1   For membership estimates, see Walter Kendall, *The Revolutionary Movement in Britain, 1900–21: The Origins of British Communism*, 269; and Philip Viscount Snowden, *Autobiography*, vol. 1, *1864–1919*, 484–85.

2   Laurence Thompson, *The Enthusiasts: A Biography of John and Katharine Bruce Glasier*, 230.

3   Keith Laybourn, *Philip Snowden: A Biography, 1864–1937*, 68–69.

4   *Labour Leader*, 22 May 1919.

5   *Labour Leader*, 14 August (MacDonald) and 28 August 1919 (Longden).

6   *Labour Leader*, 4 September (MacDonald) and 11 September 1919 (Longden). Described by David Howell as "an old-style ILP propagandist," Fred Longdon had been imprisoned as a conscientious objector during the war. In the 1920s, he became a full-time lecturer in the Workers' Educational Association, an adult education movement that has survived into the twenty-first century, and was a Labour MP for a Birmingham constituency in 1929–31 and 1945–52. See David Howell, *MacDonald's Party: Labour Identities and Crisis, 1922–1931*, 244.

7   *Labour Leader*, 16 October 1919.

8   David Marquand, *Ramsay MacDonald*, 257.

9   J. Ramsay MacDonald, *Parliament and Revolution*, 50–54.

10   Arthur Marwick, *Clifford Allen: The Open Conspirator*, 195–96.

11   *Labour Leader*, 1 April 1920.

12   *Labour Leader*, 11 December 1919.

13   *Labour Leader*, 18 December 1919.

14   *Labour Leader*, 1 January (Johnson) and 5 February 1920 (Cole).

15   *Labour Leader*, 29 January 1920.

16   *Labour Leader*, 12 February 1920.

17   *Labour Leader*, 8 January 1920.

18 *Labour Leader,* 12 February 1920.

19 Ibid.

20 *Labour Leader,* 19 February 1920. For Fred Jowett's pre-war advocacy of the "Bradford Resolution" and the replacement of the cabinet with a committee system, see Logie Barrow and Ian Bullock, *Democratic Ideas and the British Labour Movement, 1880–1914,* especially chap. 10.

21 *Labour Leader,* 15 January 1920.

22 *The Socialist,* 24 January 1920.

23 For the earliest such occasions, see Barrow and Bullock, *Democratic Ideas and the British Labour Movement,* 81.

24 *Labour Leader,* 26 February 1920.

25 *Labour Leader,* 15 April 1920.

26 *Labour Leader,* 25 March 1920.

27 *Labour Leader,* 8 April 1920. All quotations are from *Labour Leader's* report on the conference, by "Our Special Correspondent," who paraphrased many of the arguments made by the spearkers. Herron, the mover of the affiliation motion, is described in the report simply as "Herron (Preston)," but his first initial was probably "W."

28 A. Fenner Brockway, *Inside the Left: Thirty Years of Platform, Press, Prison and Parliament,* 138.

29 *Labour Leader,* 8 April 1920.

30 *Labour Leader,* 15 April 1920.

31 See Stephen White, *Britain and the Bolshevik Revolution: A Study in the Politics of Diplomacy, 1920–1924,* 13–14.

32 George Lansbury, *What I Saw in Russia,* xiv. According to Jonathan Schneer, Lansbury's book counteracted the prevalent anti-revolutionary propaganda and "stimulated greater pro-Russia feeling" (*George Lansbury,* 92).

33 *Labour Leader,* 1 April 1920.

34 See John Saville, "The British Labour Delegation to Russia, 1920." 257.

35 See Stephen Richards Graubard, *British Labour and the Russian Revolution, 1917–1924,* 214.

36 *Labour Leader,* 13 May 1920.

37 *Labour Leader,* 17 June 1920. Ben Turner (1863–1942), eventually Sir Ben Turner, was a leading trade unionist and later a Labour MP.

38 Saville, "The British Labour Delegation to Russia, 1920" 259. For the reaction of the government, see White, *Britain and the Bolshevik Revolution,* 15.

39 *Labour Leader,* 8 July 1920. A.A. Purcell (1872–1935) had chaired the first meeting of the Industrial Syndicalist League in 1910 (Kendall, *The Revolutionary Movement in Britain,* 144). *Workers of All Countries? Syndicalism, Internationalism and the Lost World of A.A. Purcell,* the final volume of Kevin Morgan's *Bolshevism and the British Left* trilogy, focuses on Purcell's life and activities. The advance notice for the volume states: "At different times in his life Purcell was a marxist local councillor, a syndicalist, a trade union officer, a Communist, a guild socialist and a Labour MP. He was part of a tradition of indiscriminate militancy which looked on Bolshevism as merely its boldest manifestation."

40 *Daily Herald,* 12 July 1920.

41 *Labour Leader,* 22 July 1920.

42 *Daily Herald,* 7 July 1920.

43 *Daily Herald,* 12 July 1920. Bertrand Russell had this to say of Willams: "Robert Williams, I found, was very happy in Russia, and was the only one of our party who made speeches pleasing to the Soviet Government. He always told them that a revolution was imminent in England, and they made much of him. I told Lenin he was not to be trusted, and the very next year, on Black Friday, he ratted" (*The Autobiography of Bertrand Russell,* vol. 2, *1914–1944,* 102). On Williams's role in "Black Friday," see n. 43 to chapter 2.

44 *Labour Leader,* 22 July and 19 August 1920.

45 *The Socialist,* 12 August 1920.

46 *Labour Leader,* 16 September 1920.

47 *Daily Herald,* 7 July 1920.

48 *Labour Leader,* 1 July 1920. L. Haden Guest had been joint secretary, with Charles Roden Buxton, of the delegation visiting Russia.

49 *Labour Leader,* 15 July 1920.

50 *Daily Herald,* 2 July 1920.

51 *Daily Herald,* 17 September 1920.

52 *Daily Herald,* 22 September 1920. Posterity has not been much kinder to Ethel Snowden's book, though F.M. Leventhal did judge that it "mingled insight and inanity in equal measure." See F.M. Leventhal "Seeing the Future: British Left Wing Travellers to the Soviet Union, 1919–32," in *The Political Culture of Modern Britain: Studies in Memory of Stephen Koss,* ed. J.M.W. Bean (London: Hamish Hamilton, 1987), 214.

53 Laybourn, *Philip Snowden,* 86.

54 *The Socialist,* 13 May 1920.

55 *Labour Leader,* 6 May 1920; for Rogers's letter, see the issue of 22 April.

56 *Labour Leader,* 2 December (Snowden) and 23 December 1920 (Parker).

57 *Labour Leader,* 10 February and 31 March 1921.

58 *The Socialist,* 9 December 1920.

59 *Labour Leader,* 3 March 1921.

60 *Labour Leader,* 10 March 1921.

61 *Labour Leader,* 17 March 1921.

62 *The Socialist,* June 1918.

63 *Labour Leader,* 13 January 1921.

64 *The Socialist,* 13 January 1921.

65 *Labour Leader,* 31 March 1921. Note that the report used "(Hear, hear)" to indicate that a particular statement provoked vocal support from the audience.

66 John Paton, *Left Turn! The Autobiography of John Paton,* 86. The irony, Paton went on to explain, was that he was already "at this time extremely critical of MacDonald."

67 *Labour Leader,* 31 March 1921.

68 *The Communist,* 2 April 1921.

69 Kendall, *The Revolutionary Movement in Britain,* 276.

70 *Labour Leader,* 22 April 1921.

71 David Marquand, *Ramsay MacDonald*, 256.

72 Labour Leader, 13 January 1921.

73 F.S. Northedge and Audrey Wells, *Britain and Soviet Communism: The Impact of a Revolution*, 184.

CHAPTER 9
"An Infantile Disorder": Communist Unity and the Brief Life of the Communist Party (British Section of the Third International)

1   See Logie Barrow and Ian Bullock, *Democratic Ideas and the British Labour Movement, 1880–1914*, chaps. 1, 4, 10, and 12.

2   Walter Kendall, *The Revolutionary Movement in Britain, 1900–21: The Origins of British Communism*, 197.

3   *Workers' Dreadnought*, 7 December 1918.

4   *Workers' Dreadnought*, 14 December 1918.

5   *Workers' Dreadnought*, 2 November 1918.

6   *Workers' Dreadnought*, 21 September 1918.

7   *Workers' Dreadnought*, 29 March and 12 April 1919 (editorial by Sylvia Pankhurst, "The Soviets Reach Bavaria").

8   *Workers' Dreadnought*, 26 July and 23 August 1919.

9   *Workers' Dreadnought*, 27 March 1920.

10 *Workers' Dreadnought*, 7 August 1920.

11 *Workers' Dreadnought*, 26 June 1920.

12 *Workers' Dreadnought*, 14 and 21 June 1919.

13 See Mary Davis, *Sylvia Pankhurst: A Life in Radical Politics*, 72; Kevin Morgan, *Labour Legends and Russian Gold*, vol. 1 of *Bolshevism and the British Left*, 35, 100.

14 See Barbara Winslow, *Sylvia Pankhurst, Sexual Politics and Political Activism*, 145–46.

15 *Workers' Dreadnought*, 26 April 1919.

16 *Workers' Dreadnought*, 21 February 1920.

17 See Davis, *Sylvia Pankhurst*, 77–79.

18 *The Socialist*, 15 January 1920.

19 *The Call*, 22 January 1920.

20 *The Call*, 5 February and 22 April 1920.

21 For the Pauls' support of Pankhurst's views, see *The Call*, 4 March 1920. For their argument regarding her letter, see *Solidarity*, February 1920.

22 Gallacher's letter appeared in the 21 February 1920 issue of the *Dreadnought*. It was this letter that Lenin quoted at length in *"Left-Wing" Communism*, patronizingly commending it for the "temper and point of view of the young Communists, or of rank-and-file workers who are only just coming to Communism." (Gallacher was thirty-eight at the time.) In Lenin's view, Gallacher's letter revealed "the rudiments of *all* the mistakes that are being made by the German 'Left' Communists and were made by the Russian 'Left' Bolsheviks in 1908 and 1918." See V.I. Lenin, *"Left-Wing" Communism: An Infantile Disorder*, 79–80.

23 *The Call*, 4 March 1920.

24 See Kendall, *The Revolutionary Movement in Britain*, 209–13.

25 *Workers' Dreadnought*, 8 May 1920. For a more complete version of the statement of the Amsterdam Sub-Bureau, see Kendall, *The Revolutionary Movement in Britain*, 210.

26 See Kendall, *The Revolutionary Movement in Britain*, 209–10.

27 *Workers' Dreadnought*, 22 May 1920.

28 See *The Call*, 3 June 1920, and Kendall, *The Revolutionary Movement in Britain*, 211–12 (quotation on 212).

29 *The Call*, 10 June 1920.

30 *Workers' Dreadnought*, 12 June 1920.

31 These are the organizations mentioned in the 12 June issue of the *Dreadnought*. Mark Shipway has "Holt" rather than "Hull" but otherwise provides the same list, as well as furnishing details about some of these very small groups. See Shipway, *Anti-Parliamentary Communism: The Movement for Workers' Councils in Britain, 1917–45*, 11–12.

32 The South Wales Socialist Society (SWSS) seems to have become a branch of the SLP about this time. See Kendall, *The Revolutionary Movement*, 385, n. 1, and also Raymond Challinor, according to whom the South Wales organization had decided to "dissolve into the SLP" (*The Origins of British Bolshevism*, 240). See also A.E. Cook's claim, in *The Communist*, 30 September 1920, that former SWSS members held a conference that was addressed by Edgar Whitehead, the secretary of the CP (BSTI). So the precise fate of the SWSS remains unclear.

33 *Workers' Dreadnought*, 26 June 1920. The August unity conference, which took place in London, officially opened on 31 July.

34 Shipway, *Anti-Parliamentary Communism*, 14.

35 Ibid., 12.

36 *Workers' Dreadnought*, 3 July 1920.

37 *The Call*, 8 July 1920.

38 *The Call*, 22 July 1920.

39 Gallacher makes no mention of Pankhurst in *Revolt on the Clyde* (1936), although he does say that Lenin made him "an outstanding example of 'Left' sectarianism in *"Left-Wing" Communism*" (251). But in his later book, *The Rolling of the Thunder* (1947), he offers an account of how the offending letter found its way into Pankhurst's paper.

40 *The Communist*, 16 September 1920.

41 *Solidarity*, August 1920. See *The Socialist*, 1 July 1920, for its attack on Pankhurst.

42 *Workers' Dreadnought*, 25 September 1920. The letter, which spanned two issues, was concluded the following week, in the 2 October edition.

43 *New Statesman*, 11 December 1920.

44 *Workers' Dreadnought*, 4 September 1920.

45 A.J.P. Taylor, *English History 1914–1945*, 193.

46 *Workers' Dreadnought*, 11 September 1920.

47 Ibid.

48 *The Communist*, 30 September 1920.

49 *Workers' Dreadnought*, 25 September 1920.

50 See Kendall, *The Revolutionary Movement in Britain*, 256–57.

51 *Workers' Dreadnought*, 2 October 1920.

52 *Workers' Dreadnought*, 28 August 1920.

53 *Workers' Dreadnought*, 2 October 1920.

54 *Workers' Dreadnought*, 16 October 1920.

55 *Workers' Dreadnought*, 23 October 1920.

56 *Workers' Dreadnought*, 20 November 1920.

57 *Workers' Dreadnought*, 27 November 1920.

58 Kendall, *The Revolutionary Movement in Britain*, 265.

59 *Workers' Dreadnought*, 11 December 1920.

60 *Workers' Dreadnought*, 25 December 1920.

61 *Workers' Dreadnought*, 1 January 1921.

62 *Workers' Dreadnought*, 8 January 1921.

63 *Workers' Dreadnought*, 15 January 1921.

64 *Workers' Dreadnought*, 22 January 1921 ("Branch Notes").

65 *Workers' Dreadnought*, 15 January 1921.

66 *Workers' Dreadnought*, 15 January 1921. The "Appeal" is attributed to a William Leslie. As we saw earlier, in reporting on the Cardiff conference, Whitehead credited the dramatic speech that helped to secure the party's participation in the unity process simply to a "Comrade Leslie." Although Kendall refers to a John Leslie, it seems rather unlikely that there were two Leslies simultaneously so active in the CP (BSTI).

67 *Workers' Dreadnought*, 5 February 1921.

CHAPTER 10
British Bolsheviks? The Socialist Labour Party

1 Raymond Challinor, *The Origins of British Bolshevism*, 206.

2 *The Socialist*, 24 December 1919.

3 See Challinor, *The Origins of British Bolshevism*, 215–24. For the identification of the SLP as Britain's "Bolshevik" party, see 188, 192, 212, and 242.

4 *The Socialist*, May 1915.

5 *The Socialist*, 17 February 1921.

6 For Morris's article, see *The Socialist*, March 1917. See also the issues of March 1916 and March 1918, which explicitly linked "Paris, March 1871" with "Russia 1917." On 13 March 1919, the William Morris piece was once again given front-page treatment.

7 See *The Socialist*, 1 July, 22 July, and 5 August 1920, on Douglas, Tawney, and Postgate, respectively.

8 *The Socialist*, 8 July 1920.

9 *The Socialist*, 17 and 24 November 1921.

10 *The Socialist*, 28 April 1921.

11 *The Socialist*, April 1918.

12 *The Socialist*, 22 June 1922.

13 *The Socialist*, 12 May 1921. Walter Citrine (1887–1983) was to be the general secretary of the Trades Union Congress for more than twenty years, covering such crucial

periods as the General Strike of 1926 and World War II. His *A.B.C. of Chairmanship* — known to many simply as "Citrine" — became the established authority on the subject throughout the British Labour movement and more widely.

14　*The Socialist*, February 1917, on London, and July 1923, on Eliot.

15　*The Socialist*, 8 July 1920 (Hen) and 10 March 1921 (Anderson).

16　See, for example, the editorial titled "Dawn of the Servile State," in the May 1915 issue; A.E. Cook, "The Servile State or Freeland," December 15; and the editorial "Why the SLP?" in the issue of 8 September 1921.

17　*The Socialist*, July 1915. If the account in the paper the previous month is to be believed, Holliday's prime offence — which earned him, before the appeal, three months' imprisonment with hard labour — was to mention in passing the German origins of the royal family. Sadly, he died the following year at the age of only forty-six. See *The Socialist*, June 1916.

18　Challinor, *The Origins of British Bolshevism*, 251. See also, for example, *The Socialist*, 2 September 1920 and 13 January 1921.

19　*The Socialist*, 24 February 1921.

20　Challinor, *The Origins of British Bolshevism*, 273.

21　See *The Socialist*, May 1923 and June 1923.

22　*The Socialist*, 11 August and 22 September 1921.

23　For the "Children's Corner," see *The Socialist*, 18 and 25 May and 8 June to 10 August 1922.

24　*The Socialist*, May 1915 (Stoker) and May 1918 ("Hero Worship").

25　*The Clarion*, 25 June 1898. On NIGFTLU, see Logie Barrow and Ian Bullock, *Democratic Ideas and the British Labour Movement, 1880–1914*, 112.

26　*The Socialist*, 24 March 1921.

27　*The Socialist*, 14 April 1921.

28　*The Socialist*, 22 September 1921. A "Bobby" was a policeman — the paper's point being that if someone in the police force were trying to get ahead by investigating the party's revolutionary activities, all they would need to do is ask for information.

29　See Challinor, *The Origins of British Bolshevism*, 266–67.

30　*The Socialist*, November 1918.

31　*The Socialist*, 30 January and 6 February 1919.

32　*The Socialist*, 11 March 1920 (and see also the issue of 1 May 1919).

33　*The Socialist*, 25 March 1920.

34　*The Socialist*, 15 April 1920.

35　*The Socialist*, 22 April and 6 and 13 May 1920.

36　*The Socialist*, 6 May 1920.

37　*The Socialist*, 1 July 1920.

38　*The Socialist*, 10 February 1921.

39　*The Socialist*, 25 August 1921.

40　See *The Socialist*, 18 August to 27 October. Some decades later, in the 1950s, James Clunie (1889–1972) would become a Labour MP.

41　*The Socialist*, 20 October 1921.

42　*The Socialist*, 27 October 1921.

43   *The Socialist,* January 1923. For Henderson on Lenin's speech, see the issue of March 1923.

44   *The Socialist,* 17 April 1919.

45   *The Socialist,* 20 November 1919.

46   *The Socialist,* 26 August 1920.

47   *The Socialist,* 10 March 1921.

48   *The Socialist,* 19 January 1922.

49   *The Socialist,* 9 February 1922.

50   *The Socialist,* January 1923.

51   See Challinor, *The Origins of British Bolshevism,* 49–53.

52   Ibid., 271.

53   *The Socialist,* 13 October, 10 November, and 8 December 1921.

54   For Henderson's critique, see *The Socialist,* 8 December 1921. The Sheffield announcement appeared in the issue of 19 January 1922.

55   *The Socialist,* 12 January 1922.

56   *The Socialist,* 12 January 1922.

57   *The Socialist,* 2 February 1922.

58   *The Socialist,* 8 December 1921.

59   *The Socialist,* 15 December 1921 (editorial note) and 23 February 1922 (Leslie).

60   *The Socialist,* 25 May 1922.

61   *The Socialist,* 16 February 1922.

62   *The Socialist,* 19 January 1922.

63   *The Socialist,* 25 August 1921.

64   *The Socialist,* 28 July 1921.

65   *The Socialist,* 4 and 11 August 1921.

66   *The Socialist,* 29 September 1921.

67   Raymond Challinor is withering about Campbell's the lack of any real qualifications for this role (*The Origins of British Bolshevism,* 271). J.R. Campbell (1894–1969) came to national prominence in 1924, in the "Campbell Case," when, as editor of the CPGB's *Workers' Weekly,* he was charged under the Incitement to Mutiny Act. The handling, or mishandling, of the case contributed to the demise of the first (minority) Labour government. Campbell remained a leading Communist for the rest of his life.

68   *The Socialist,* 9 February 1922.

69   *The Socialist,* 5 October 1922.

70   *The Socialist,* 3 April 1919.

71   *The Socialist,* 3 July 1919.

72   *The Socialist,* 8 April and 26 August 1920.

73   *The Socialist,* 3 February 1921.

74   *The Socialist,* 2 June 1921.

75   *The Socialist,* 15 September 1921, on Lusty and the Coventry branch, and 20 July 1922, on the defence of Sunday schools.

76   *The Socialist,* 1 and 8 September 1921.

77   *The Socialist,* 17 November 1921 and 5 January 1922.

78   *The Socialist,* 18 June 1922.

CHAPTER 11
Pankhurst's *Dreadnought* and the (Original) Fourth International:
"Left Communism" and Soviet Democracy

1   *Workers' Dreadnought,* 2 and 16 April 1921.
2   *Workers' Dreadnought,* 28 January 1922 and 10 February 1923.
3   *Workers' Dreadnought,* 16 May and 16 July 1921.
4   *Workers' Dreadnought,* 30 April 1921.
5   *Workers' Dreadnought,* 2 April and 29 October 1921.
6   The first part of Gorter's article appeared in the *Dreadnought* on 12 March and the final one on 21 May, but instalments were published somewhat sporadically in between, rather than at regular weekly intervals.
7   *Workers' Dreadnought,* 30 July 1921.
8   *Workers' Dreadnought,* 13 August 1921.
9   *Workers' Dreadnought,* 27 August 1921.
10 *Workers' Dreadnought,* 3 September 1921. Early in July, the *Dreadnought* had adopted "Sovrussia" to refer to Soviet Russia, but the term did not survive for long.
11 For Pankhurst's complete account of her expulsion, see the *Workers' Dreadnought,* 17 September 1921.
12 See *The Communist,* 17 September and 8 October 1921.
13 *Workers' Dreadnought,* 24 September 1921.
14 *Workers' Dreadnought,* 12 November 1921.
15 *Workers' Dreadnought,* 30 April and 7 May 1921.
16 *Workers' Dreadnought,* 17 September 1921.
17 *Workers' Dreadnought,* 8 October 1921.
18 Marcel van der Linden, "On Council Communism," 29.
19 *Workers' Dreadnought,* 8 and 15 October 1921.
20 *Workers' Dreadnought,* 10 December 1921.
21 *Workers' Dreadnought,* 11 February 1922.
22 *Workers' Dreadnought,* 11 March 1922.
23 *Workers' Dreadnought,* 1 April 1922.
24 *Workers' Dreadnought,* 3 June 1922.
25 *Workers' Dreadnought,* 17 June 1922.
26 *Workers' Dreadnought,* 15 July 1922.
27 *Workers' Dreadnought,* 4 November 1922.
28 *Workers' Dreadnought,* 7 October 1922.
29 *Workers' Dreadnought,* 27 October and 1 December 1923.
30 *Workers' Dreadnought,* 5 January 1924.
31 *Workers' Dreadnought,* 10 May 1924.
32 *Workers' Dreadnought,* 12 April 1924.
33 *Workers' Dreadnought,* 26 November and 3 December 1921.
34 *Workers' Dreadnought,* 28 January 1922. On 10 March, Pankhurst again attacked Zinoviev's thesis about the appropriate time to establish soviets.

35 *Workers' Dreadnought*, 7 July 1923.

36 *Workers' Dreadnought*, 21 July 1923.

37 *Workers' Dreadnought*, 19 December 1921.

38 *Workers' Dreadnought*, 24 December 1921. Pankhurst reiterated her views in, for example, "What Socialism Is Not," which appeared in the paper's 11 August 1923 edition.

39 *The Workers' Dreadnought*, 4 February 1922. Later, the establishment of workers' councils in Austria by the Social-Democrats was seen as supporting the view that even "capitalists find them useful" and as another instance "of the fact that workers' management of industry is not the impractical dream some 'Socialists' and 'Communists' would have us believe" (*Workers' Dreadnought*, 25 March 1922).

40 *The Workers' Dreadnought*, 10 June 1922.

41 *Workers' Dreadnought*, 15 July 1922.

42 *Workers' Dreadnought*, 10 May 1924.

43 *Workers' Dreadnought*, 7 and 28 January 1922.

44 *Workers' Dreadnought*, 1 April 1922.

45 *Workers' Dreadnought*, 11 March 1922.

46 *Workers' Dreadnought*, 18 November 1922.

47 *Workers' Dreadnought*, 24 February 1923.

48 *Workers' Dreadnought*, 28 April 1923.

49 *Workers' Dreadnought*, 27 October 1922.

50 *Workers' Dreadnought*, 2 February 1924.

51 *Workers' Dreadnought*, 24 March 1924.

52 *Workers' Dreadnought*, 7 January 1922.

53 *Workers' Dreadnought*, 4 February 1922.

54 *Workers' Dreadnought*, 4 March 1922.

55 *Workers' Dreadnought*, 25 March 1922.

56 *Workers' Dreadnought*, 20 May 1922.

57 *Workers' Dreadnought*, 15 July 1922.

58 *Workers' Dreadnought*, 26 August and 4 November 1922.

59 *Workers' Dreadnought*, 10 May 1924.

60 *Workers' Dreadnought*, 29 July 1922.

61 *Workers' Dreadnought*, 19 August 1922.

62 *Workers' Dreadnought*, 9 September 1922.

63 *Workers' Dreadnought*, 17 February 1923.

64 *Workers' Dreadnought*, 1 September 1923.

65 *Workers' Dreadnought*, 18 February, 25 March, and 27 May 1922.

66 *Workers' Dreadnought*, 9 June 1923.

67 *Workers' Dreadnought*, 3 and 17 May 1924.

68 *Workers' Dreadnought*, 7 July 1923.

69 *Workers' Dreadnought*, 2 and 9 February 1924.

70 *Workers' Dreadnought*, 15 March 1924.

71 *Workers' Dreadnought*, 6 October 1923 and 5 April 1924.

72 *Workers' Dreadnought*, 6 October 1923.

CHAPTER 12
The Early British Communist Party: Soviet Democracy Deferred and Redefined

1   *The Call*, 27 May 1920.

2   See *The Communist*, 1 July and 2 September 1922. Before this, the *Dreadnought* had concluded that the trial "smacks too much of political juggling to be anything but offensive to disinterested persons" (*Workers' Dreadnought*, 24 June 1922). The trial has since been seen as the forerunner of Stalin's "show trials": see Marc Jansen, *A Show Trial Under Lenin: The Trial of the Socialist Revolutionaries, Moscow 1922*.

3   *The Communist*, 19 August 1922.

4   *Workers' Dreadnought*, 2 August 1919. Reviewing M. Philips Price's *Reminiscences of the Russian Revolution* in 1921, the *New Statesman* noted that "he is not only on the side of the Bolsheviks, he has even taken service under the Soviet Government and at one moment he offered himself as a volunteer for the Red Army" (*New Statesman*, 11 June 1921). Morgan Philips Price was the "Squire of Tibberton" and director of Price, Walker and Co. See M. Philips Price, "Blue Blood and Bolshevism: An Open Letter to the Workers of Gloucester, and One of Interest to Workers Everywhere. Received by the Chairman of Gloucester Branch I.L.P. and read at a public meeting at Gloucester, and subsequently published in full in the local press," Gloucester ILP, 1920, (ILP Archives, London School of Economics, British Library of Political and Economic Science).

5   *Workers' Dreadnought*, 17 May 1919.

6   A rare use of the term *ergatocracy* appeared in the *Workers' Dreadnought* in 1923. The context was the coup in Bulgaria, facilitated, the paper argued, by the failure to democratize the army and police "on soviet lines": "In passing it may be said that Army and Police Forces are inevitably the negation of democracy, even of what some people call ergatocracy."

7   *The Call*, 5 February 1920.

8   *The Communist*, 12 August 1920.

9   Willie Thompson, *The Good Old Cause: British Communism, 1920–1991*, 38.

10 *The Call*, 12 July 1917.

11 *The Call*, 24 October 1918.

12 *The Communist*, 9 September 1920.

13 *The Communist*, 26 August 1920.

14 *The Communist*, 5 November 1921.

15 *Workers' Weekly*, 17 February 1923.

16 *Daily Herald*, 15 July 1920; *The Call*, 22 July 1920.

17 *The Communist*, 5 August 1920. George Young's article, from which Montefiore was quoting, appeared in *The Observer* on 11 July 1920.

18 *The Communist*, 19 August 1920.

19 *The Communist*, 14 October 1920.

20 *The Communist*, 30 April 1921. Not so very unusually, William Mellor (1888–1942) had a varied career in left-wing politics. An Oxford graduate, he worked on Lansbury's *Herald*, which he later edited, served as secretary of the Fabian Research Department in 1913–14, and was a founding member of the NGL and later of the

Guild Communist group. A conscientious objector during World War I, he was also a founding member of the CPGB but left the party in 1924. In the late 1930s, he would be the first editor of *Tribune.*

21 *The Communist,* 8 October 1921. Bell had a series of three articles published in *The Communist* at this time: "Party Organisation" (17 September), "Propaganda and Agitation" (1 October), and "On Party Organisation" (8 October).

22 Kevin Morgan, *Labour Legends and Russian Gold,* vol. 1 of *Bolshevism and the British Left,* 41–53. See also his earlier *Harry Pollitt,* 26.

23 *The Communist,* 25 March 1922.

24 *The Communist,* 8 April 1922.

25 *The Communist,* 7 and 14 October 1922.

26 *The Communist,* 6 January 1923.

27 *The Socialist,* 15 January 1920.

28 *The Socialist,* 29 April 1920.

29 *The Socialist,* 6 May 1920.

30 *Workers' Dreadnought,* 20 November 1920.

31 *Workers' Dreadnought,* 27 November 1920.

32 *Workers' Dreadnought,* 31 December 1921. For "Are We Realists?" see *The Communist,* 24 December 1921.

33 *The Communist,* 22 July 1922.

34 William Morris, *News from Nowhere, or an Epoch of Rest: Being Some Chapters from a Utopian Romance* (1890), ed. Krishan Kumar, Cambridge Texts in the History of Political Thought (Cambridge: Cambridge University Press, 1995), 87, 90.

35 Kevin Morgan, *The Webbs and Soviet Communism,* vol. 2 of *Bolshevism and the British Left,* 115.

36 *Workers' Dreadnought,* 2 August 1919.

37 *Solidarity,* January 1920 and February 1920.

38 *Solidarity,* 29 April 1921.

39 Ralph Darlington, *The Political Trajectory of J.T. Murphy,* 85.

40 *The Communist,* 6 May 1922.

41 Pat Sloan, *Soviet Democracy,* 9. Beatrice Webb wrote a preface to Sloan's *Russia Without Illusions,* which appeared the following year. See also Peter Beilharz, *Labour's Utopias: Bolshevism, Fabianism, Social Democracy,* 49. As Beilharz says: "The Bolshevik utopia exercised an extraordinary influence over socialist thinking." (18).

42 Sloan, *Soviet Democracy,* 11, 13–14.

43 Ibid., 222–23.

44 Ibid., 141–42 and 216.

45 *The Call,* 4 July 1918.

46 Sloan, *Soviet Democracy,* 242.

47 See Morgan, *The Webbs and Soviet Communism,* 11.

48 Ibid., 219, 220, 225. The references for the Webb quotations are *Soviet Communism: A New Civilisation,* 2nd ed., 342 and 1130, and Sidney Webb. "The Steel Frame of Soviet Society," *Political Quarterly* 4, no. 1 (January 1933): 1–15.

49 Morgan, *The Webbs and Soviet Communism,* 224.

CHAPTER 13
Endings and Conclusions

1 *Labour Leader*, 17 March 1921.

2 *Labour Leader*, 10 March 1921; *The Communist*, 12 March 1921.

3 Israel Getzler, *Kronstadt, 1917–21: The Fate of a Soviet Democracy*, 205.

4 Ibid., 249–50.

5 See Charles Read, *From Tsar to Soviets: The Russian People and Their Revolution, 1917–21*, 276.

6 *The Socialist*, 17 March 1921.

7 *The Socialist*, 2 and 9 June 1921.

8 *The Socialist*, 7 July 1921.

9 *Workers' Dreadnought*, 16 April 1922.

10 Raymond Postgate, *The Life of George Lansbury*, 203.

11 *Workers' Dreadnought*, 30 December 1922. Alexander Berkman (1870–1936) had been deported from the United States to Russia early in 1917, together with his partner and collaborator Emma Goldman (1869–1940) and over two hundred others.

12 *Workers' Dreadnought*, 9 February 1924.

13 *Workers' Dreadnought*, 23 February 1924. The first part of Gorter's article (9 February 1924) was prefaced by "Translated from German," which may explain why the city is referred to as "Petersburg" rather than the more usual (at that time) "Petrograd."

14 *Workers' Dreadnought*, 9 June 1923.

15 *Workers' Dreadnought*, 24 March 1923 and 26 January 1924.

16 *Workers' Dreadnought*, 2 February 1924.

17 John McIlroy and Alan Campbell, " 'Nina Ponomareva's Hats': The New Revisionism, the Communist International, and the Communist Party of Great Britain, 1920–30," 169.

18 See John McIlroy, "Rehabilitating Communist History: The Communist International, the Communist Party of Great Britain and Some Revisionist Historians," and Walter Kendall, "The Communist International and the Turn from 'Social Fascism' to the Popular Front" (and see also Kendall, *The Revolutionary Movement in Britain, 1900–21: The Origins of British Communism*, 152–56). Kendall's essay is an extract from his unpublished manuscript "World Revolution and the Communist International, 1898–1935," which is available in the library of Nuffield College, Oxford.

19 See, especially, Andrew Thorpe, "Comintern 'Control' of the Communist Party of Great Britain, 1920–43," and *The British Communist Party and Moscow, 1920–45*; and Kevin Morgan, *Labour Legends and Russian Gold*, vol. 1 of *Bolshevism and the British Left*.

20 L.J. Macfarlane, *The British Communist Party: Its Origin and Development Until 1929*, 27. For reactions of readers to Moscow's offer of £75,000, see the *Daily Herald*, 11 and 14 September 1920.

21 Kendall, *The Revolutionary Movement in Britain*, 299–300.

22 McIlroy and Campbell, "Nina Ponomareva's Hats," 153. For a full account of the role of Moscow gold in the CPGB's finances, see Morgan, *Labour Legends and Russian Gold*.

23 *Solidarity*, 13 May 1921.

24 G.D.H. Cole, "Beatrice Webb as an Economist," 286.

25 Kevin Morgan, *The Webbs and Soviet Communism*, vol. 2 of *Bolshevism and the British Left*, 49. Morgan cites Maurice Reckitt, *As It Happened*, 146–47. The list overlaps with the "study circle" that met at the Coles' home starting in May 1919, the members of which are listed in John S. Peart-Binns, *Maurice B. Reckitt: A Life*, 48. Common to both groups are Page Arnot, A.L. Bacharach, Ivor Brown, Raymond Postgate, and the Coles themselves.

26 Reckitt, *As It Happened*, 181.

27 See W.H. Greenleaf, *The British Political Tradition*, vol. 2, *The Ideological Heritage* (London and New York: Methuen, 1985), 437; Kendall, *The Revolutionary Movement in Britain*, 282–83; and Peart-Binns, *Maurice B. Reckitt*, 62.

28 *The Guildsman*, 9 June 1920.

29 *The Guild Socialist*, June 1922.

30 I am grateful to my friend Anthony Carew for this reference. For rival attempts, in the 1930s, to revive guild socialism by Cole, Mellor, Hobson, and others, see David Blaazer, "Guild Socialists After Guild Socialism: The Workers' Control Group and the House of Industry League," *Twentieth-Century British History* 11, no. 2 (2000): 135–55.

31 *The Socialist*, 11 August and 1 December 1921.

32 *The Socialist*, 5 January, 2 February, and 22 June 1922.

33 See *The Socialist*, 10 August (the Glasgow branch won a book) and 5 October 1922. In its October announcement, the paper said that it looked forward to resuming weekly publication at some future date. It also pointed out, encouragingly, that the monthly edition offered good value — sixteen pages for only tuppence.

34 *Workers' Dreadnought*, 7 October 1922 and 10 March 1923.

35 *Workers' Dreadnought*, 24 March 1923.

36 *Workers' Dreadnought*, 28 April and 5 May 1923.

37 *Workers' Dreadnought*, 4 August and 1 December 1923.

38 *Workers' Dreadnought*, 27 October 1923. Gondor is probably best known for his work in child psychology, first in Europe and, later, in the United States.

39 *Workers' Dreadnought*, 19 April 1924.

40 The 21 October 1922 issue of the *Dreadnought* seems to be the first in which "Printed by S. Corio" appeared.

41 *Workers' Dreadnought*, 9 September 1922.

42 *Workers' Dreadnought*, 4 November and 16 December 1922. The *Herald*'s attitude towards fascism was again under attack in the issue of 20 January 1923.

43 *Workers' Dreadnought*, 3 February and 31 March 1923.

44 *Workers' Dreadnought*, 24 February, 17 and 24 March, and 26 May 1923.

45 *Workers' Dreadnought*, 1 December 1923.

46   *Workers' Dreadnought,* 5 January and 2 February 1924.

47   *Workers' Dreadnought,* 3 May 1924.

48   See Richard Pankhurst, "Sylvia and the *New Times and Ethiopia News,*" in *Sylvia Pankhurst: From Artist to Anti-Fascist,* ed. Ian Bullock and Richard Pankhurst (Basingstoke and London: Macmillan, 1992), 149–91.

49   *Justice,* 1 and 22 January 1925.

50   H.W. Lee and E. Archbold, *Social-Democracy in Britain: Fifty Years of the Socialist Movement,* 263.

51   Ibid., 266.

52   Ibid., 270.

53   *Labour Leader,* 17 July 1919.

54   *Labour Leader,* 25 November 1920.

55   Laurence Thompson, *The Enthusiasts: A Biography of John and Katharine Bruce Glasier,* 231–32.

56   *Labour Leader,* 2 December 1920.

57   *Labour Leader,* 2 and 9 December 1920.

58   *Labour Leader,* 2 December 1920.

59   *Labour Leader,* 30 December 1920.

60   *Labour Leader,* 13 January 1921.

61   *Labour Leader,* 31 March, 14 April, and 7 July 1921.

62   *Labour Leader,* 16 June 1921.

63   See Thompson, *The Enthusiasts,* 233–43.

64   Philip Viscount Snowden, *An Autobiography,* vol. 2, *1919–1934,* 537–38.

65   A. Fenner Brockway, *Inside the Left: Thirty Years of Platform, Press, Prison and Parliament,* 142.

66   Arthur Marwick, *Clifford Allen: The Open Conspirator,* 77.

67   David Marquand, *Ramsay MacDonald,* 277.

68   Marwick, *Clifford Allen,* 79.

69   Brockway, *Inside the Left,* 145.

70   Robert E. Dowse, *Left in the Centre: The Independent Labour Party, 1893–1940,* 83.

71   Brockway, *Inside the Left,* 143. For Brailsford's salary, see Marquand, *Ramsay MacDonald,* 277; for Glasier's, see Thompson, *The Enthusiasts,* 230.

72   *Workers' Dreadnought,* 7 April 1923.

73   Marwick, *Clifford Allen,* 79–80.

74   Dowse, *Left in the Centre,* 71.

75   Kendall, *The Revolutionary Movement in Britain,* 300.

76   Ralph Darlington, *The Political Trajectory of J.T. Murphy,* 24.

77   On the "president/chairman" issue in the ILP, see Logie Barrow and Ian Bullock, *Democratic Ideas and the British Labour Movement, 1880–1914,* 79–81; on the *Clarion* federation, see ibid., chaps. 5 and 6.

78   For SDF opposition to "Fabianistic caesarim," see ibid., 38–43.

79   *Justice,* 15 March 1884.

80   See *Justice,* 24 and 31 January 1903, and 23 and 30 June 1906.

81   On Hyndman being censored and his "dominance" of the SDF, see Barrow and

Bullock, *Democratic Ideas and the British Labour Movement*, 12, 15–20, 26–28.

82 John Charles Cowley, "The Life and Writings of Ernest Belfort Bax: A Critical Analysis," 307.

83 Bax's "Democracy and the Word of Command" was originally published in *The Social-Democrat*, May 1898, and was later included in his *Essays in Socialism: Old and New* (London: Grant Richards, 1907).

84 *Justice*, 9 March 1901.

85 *Workers' Dreadnought*, 24 November 1917.

86 *Workers' Dreadnought*, 8 February 1919.

87 *The Call*, 19 June (Willis) and 6 November 1919 (Dell).

88 *Daily Herald*, 7 September 1920.

89 *The Call*, 8 April 1920.

90 *The Call*, 3 June 1920.

91 *The Communist*, 2 December 1920.

92 *Daily Herald*, 7 July 1920; *New Statesman*, 24 January 1920.

93 Adrian Smith, *The New Statesman: Portrait of a Political Weekly, 1913–1931*, 131.

94 *New Statesman*, 19 June 1920. Shaw had compared Lenin and Churchill some time before this. See the *Workers' Dreadnought*, 7 February 1920, and *The Call*, 12 February 1920, for reports on Shaw's lecture, "Socialism and the Labour Party," at the Kingsway Hall, under the headlines "Bernard Shaw Applauds Lenin" and "Bernard Shaw on Bolshevism," respectively.

95 *New Statesman*, 13 March 1920.

96 *The Communist*, 14 October 1922. For the full quotation, see chapter 12 at note 25.

97 See Morgan, *Labour Legends and Russian Gold*, for a full account of the role of the latter commodity in the CPGB's finances.

98 *The Socialist*, 10 February 1921.

99 *The Communist*, 10 December 1921; *The Socialist*, 5 January 1922.

100 On the unclear and mixed origins of soviets in 1905, see Madhavan K. Palat, "Police Socialism in Tsarist Russia, 1900–1905."

101 See Barrow and Bullock, *Democratic Ideas and the British Labour Movement*, 30–43 and 165–66; the 1906 Special Committee report is quoted at greater length on 165.

102 *Justice*, 22 June and 7 September 1901.

103 *The Clarion*, 16 and 23 December 1910.

104 Darlington, *The Political Trajectory of J.T. Murphy*, 261.

105 Lee and Archbold, *Social-Democracy in Britain*, 262–63.

106 The term *council communism* appears to have been in use from 1921 (see Marcel van der Linden, "On Council Communism," 27), but Pankhurst and the *Dreadnought* do not seemed to have used the expression.

107 Mark Shipway, *Anti-Parliamentary Communism: The Movement for Workers' Councils in Britain, 1917–45*, 201.

108 Getzler, *Kronstadt, 1917–21*, 258.

BIBLIOGRAPHY

Contemporary British Newspapers and Journals

NOTE: When a paper had a recognized organizational affiliation, this is indicated in parentheses. Other papers were independent publications.

The Call (later The Communist, then the Workers' Weekly) (CPGB)
The Clarion
The Communist (formerly The Call, later the Workers' Weekly) (CPGB)
Daily Herald (during the war, The Herald)
The Guildsman (later The Guild Socialist) (NGL)
The Guild Socialist (formerly The Guildsman) (NGL)
The Herald (a weekly, the wartime Daily Herald)
Justice (SDF/NSP)
Labour Leader (later the New Leader) (ILP)
The New Age
New Leader (formerly Labour Leader) (ILP)
New Statesman
Plebs (Plebs League)
The Socialist (SLP)
Solidarity (shop stewards' movement)
Woman's Dreadnought (later the Workers' Dreadnought) (WSF)
The Worker (shop stewards' movement)
Workers' Dreadnought (formerly the Woman's Dreadnought) (WSF, CP [BSTI], CWP)
Workers' Weekly (formerly The Communist and, before that, The Call) (CPGB)

Other Contemporary Writings

NOTE: I have regarded anything published before World War II as contemporary.

Bechofer, C.E., and M.B. Reckitt. The Meaning of the National Guilds. London: Palmer and Haywood, 1919.

Belloc, Hilaire. The Servile State. London: T.N. Foulis, 1912.

Brailsford, Henry Noel. The Russian Workers' Republic. London: Allen and Unwin, 1921.

Clayton, Joseph. The Rise and Decline of Socialism in Great Britain 1882–1924. London: Faber and Gwyer, 1924.

Coates, Ken, ed. British Labour and the Russian Revolution: The Leeds Convention — A Report from the Daily Herald. With an introduction by Ken Coates. Nottingham: Bertrand Russell Peace Foundation/ Spokesman Books, 1978.

Cohen, Gidon. The Failure of a Dream: The Independent Labour Party from Disaffiliation to World War II. London and New York: Tauris, 2007.

Cole, G.D.H. Guild Socialism Restated. With an introduction by Richard Vernon. London: Leonard Parsons, 1920.

Farbman, Michael. Russia and the Struggle for Peace. London: Allen and Unwin, 1918.

Feiler, Arthur, and H.J. Stenning. The Russian Experiment. New York: Harcourt Brace & Co., 1930.

Glasier, J. Bruce. *The Meaning of Socialism*. Manchester: National Labour Press, 1919.

Hobson, S.G. *National Guilds: An Inquiry into the Wage System and the Way Out.* London: G. Bell and Sons, 1914.

———. *National Guilds and the State.* London: Macmillan, 1920.

Hyndman, H.M. *The Evolution of Revolution.* London: Hyndman Literary Trust, 1920.

Hyndman, R.C. *The Last Years of H.M. Hyndman.* London: Grant Richards, 1923.

Kautsky, Karl. *The Dictatorship of the Proletariat.* Translated by H.J. Stenning. Repr. Ann Arbor: University of Michigan Press, 1964. Originally published 1919.

Lansbury, George. *What I Saw in Russia.* London: Leonard Parsons, 1920.

Lee, H.W., and E. Archbold. *Social-Democracy in Britain: Fifty Years of the Socialist Movement.* London: Social-Democratic Federation, 1935.

Lenin, V.I. *"Left-Wing" Communism: An Infantile Disorder.* Peking [Beijing]: Foreign Languages Press, 1965. Reprinted from V.I. Lenin, *Selected Works,* vol. 2, part 2 (Moscow: Foreign Languages Publishing House, 1952). Originally published 1920.

MacDonald, J. Ramsay. *Parliament and Revolution.* Manchester: National Labour Press, 1919.

Morris, William. *News from Nowhere, or an Epoch of Rest: Being Some Chapters from a Utopian Romance.* Edited by Krishan Kumar. Cambridge Texts in the History of Political Thought. Cambridge: Cambridge University Press, 1995. Originally published 1890.

Moscow's Reply to the I.L.P. Glasgow: The Left Wing Group of the I.L.P., n.d. [1920].

Murphy, J.T. *Preparing for Power: A Critical Study of the History of the British Working-Class Movement.* Reprint, London: Pluto Press, 1972. Originally published 1934.

———. *The Workers' Committee: An Outline of Its Principles and Structure.* Sheffield: Sheffield Workers' Committee, 1917. Reprinted for the IS [International Socialists] History Group, Reprints in Labour History, no. 1. London: Pluto Press, 1972.

Pankhurst, E. Sylvia. *Soviet Russia as I Saw It.* London: Dreadnought Publications, 1922.

Paul, Eden, and Cedar Paul. *Creative Revolution: A Study of Communist Ergatocracy.* London: Plebs League, 1921. Originally published 1920.

Ransome, Arthur. *Six Weeks in Russia in 1919.* London: Allen and Unwin, 1919.

Report of the Eighteenth Annual Conference of the Labour Party. London: Labour Party, 1918.

Russell, Bertrand. *The Practice and Theory of Communism.* London: Allen and Unwin, 1920.

———. *Roads to Freedom: Socialism, Anarchism, and Syndicalism.* London: Allen and Unwin, 1920.

Sloan, Pat. *Russia Without Illusions.* London: Frederick Muller, 1938.

———. *Soviet Democracy.* London: Gollancz, 1937.

Webb, Sidney, and Beatrice Webb. *Constitution for the Socialist Commonwealth of Great Britain.* London: Longmans, Green and Co., 1920.

———. *Soviet Communism: A New Civilisation.* 2nd ed. London: Longman's, 1937.

Autobiographies and Memoirs

Angell, Norman. *After All: The Autobioigraphy of Norman Angell.* London: Hamish Hamilton, 1951.

Bax, E. Belfort. *Reminiscences and Reflections of a Mid and Late Victorian.* London: Allen and Unwin, 1918.

Bell, Thomas. *Pioneering Days.* London: Lawrence and Wishart, 1941.

Brockway, A. Fenner. *Inside the Left: Thirty Years of Platform, Press, Prison and Parliament.* London: Allen and Unwin, 1942.

———. *Outside the Right.* London: Allen and Unwin, 1963.

———. *Towards Tomorrow: The Autobiography of Fenner Brockway.* London: Hart-Davis, MacGibbon, 1977.

Clynes, J.R. *Memoirs, 1869–1924.* London: Hutchinson, 1937.

Cole, Margaret. *Growing Up into Revolution.* London: Longmans, 1949.

Dalton, Hugh. *Call Back Yesterday.* London: Friederich Muller, 1953.

Elton, Godrey. *England Arise! A Study of the Pioneering Days of the Labour Movement.* London: Jonathan Cape, 1931.

Gallacher, William. *Revolt on the Clyde.* London: Lawrence and Wishart, 1936.

———. *The Rolling of the Thunder.* London: Lawrence and Wishart, 1947.

Hobson, S.G. *Pilgrim to the Left: Memoirs of a Modern Revolutionist.* London: Edward Arnold, 1938.

Jackson, T.A. *Solo Trumpet: Some Memoirs of Socialist Agitation and Propaganda.* London: Lawrence and Wishart, 1953.

Kirkwood, David. *My Life of Revolt.* London: George Harrap, 1935.

Lansbury, George. *Looking Backwards — and Forwards.* London: Blackie and Son Limited, 1935.

———. *My Life.* London: Constable, 1928.

Malleson, Constance. *After Ten Years.* London: Jonathan Cape, 1931.

Montefiore, Dora. *From a Victorian to a Modern.* London: E. Archer, 1927.

Pankhurst, E. Sylvia. *The Home Front: A Mirror to Life in England During the First World War.* London: Hutchinson, 1932.

Paton, John. *Left Turn! The Autobiography of John Paton.* London: Secker and Warburg, 1936.

Ransome, Arthur. *The Autobiography of Arthur Ransome.* Edited with prologue and epilogue by Rupert Hart-Davis. London: Jonathan Cape, 1976.

Reckitt, Maurice B. *As It Happened: An Autobiography.* London: Dent, 1941.

Redfern, Percy. *Journey into Understanding.* London: Allen and Unwin, 1946.

Russell, Bertrand. *The Autobiography of Bertrand Russell.* Vol. 2, *1914–1944.* London: Allen and Unwin, 1967.

Sanders, William. *Early Socialist Days.* London: Hogarth Press, 1927.

Shinwell, Emmanuel. *I've Lived Through It All.* London: Gollancz, 1973.

Snell, Harry. *Men, Movements and Myself.* London: Dent, 1936.

Snowden, Philip Viscount. *An Autobiography.* Vol. 1, *1864–1919.* London: Ivor Nicholson and Watson, 1934.

Turner, B. *About Myself, 1863–1930.* London: Toulmin, 1930.

Wicks, Harry. *Keeping My Head.* London: Socialist Platform, 1992.

Selected Secondary Sources

Barker, Bernard, ed. *Ramsay Macdonald's Political Writings*. London: Allen Lane, 1972.

Barrow, L.J.W. [Logie]."The Socialism of Robert Blatchford and the 'Clarion' Newspaper, 1889–1918." PhD dissertation, University of London, 1975.

Barrow, Logie, and Ian Bullock. *Democratic Ideas and the British Labour Movement, 1880–1914*. Cambridge: Cambridge University Press, 1996.

Beckett, Francis. *Enemy Within: The Rise and Fall of the British Communist Party*. London: John Murray, 1995.

Beilharz, Peter. *Labour's Utopias: Bolshevism, Fabianism, Social Democracy*. London: Routledge, 1992.

Berger, Stefan. *The British Labour Party and the German Social Democrats, 1900–1931*. Oxford: Oxford University Press, 1994.

Briggs, Asa, and John Saville, eds. *Essays in Labour History, 1886–1923*. London: Macmillan, 1971.

———. *Essays in Labour History, 1918–1939*. London: Croom Helm, 1977.

Brockway, A. Fenner. *Bermondsey Story: The Life of Alfred Salter*. London: Bermondsey Independent Labour Party Ltd./Allen and Unwin, 1949.

———. *Socialism over Sixty Years: The Life of Jowett of Bradford*. London: National Labour Press/Allen and Unwin, 1946.

Brogan, Hugh. *The Life of Arthur Ransome*. London: Jonathan Cape, 1984.

Broido, Vera. *Lenin and the Mensheviks: The Persecution of Socialists Under Bolshevism*. Aldershot, Hampshire, UK: Gower/Maurice Temple Smith, 1987.

Bullock, Ian. "Socialists and Democratic Form: Positions and Debates." PhD dissertation, University of Sussex, 1982.

———. "Sylvia Pankhurst and the Russian Revolution: The Making of a 'Left-Wing' Communist." In *Sylvia Pankhurst: From Artist to Anti-Fascist,* edited by Ian Bullock and Richard Pankhurst, 121–48. Basingstoke and London: Macmillan, 1992.

Callaghan, John. *Rajani Palme Dutt: A Study in British Stalinism*. London: Lawrence and Wishart, 1993.

Caute, David. *The Fellow Travellers: A Postscript to the Enlightenment*. London: Weidenfeld and Nicolson, 1973.

Challinor, Raymond. *The Origins of British Bolshevism*. London: Croom Helm, 1977.

Coates, David. *The Labour Party and the Struggle for Socialism*. Cambridge: Cambridge University Press, 1975.

Cole, G.D.H. "Beatrice Webb as an Economist." In *The Webbs and Their Work,* edited by Margaret Cole, 265–82. London: Muller, 1949.

———. *A History of the Labour Party from 1914*. London: Routledge and Kegan Paul, 1948.

Cowley, John Charles. "The Life and Writings of Ernest Belfort Bax: A Critical Analysis." PhD dissertation, University of London, 1969.

Cowling, Maurice. *The Impact of Labour, 1920–1924: The Beginning of Modern British Politics*. Cambridge: Cambridge University Press, 1971.

Cross, Colin. *Philip Snowden*. London: Barrie and Rockliff, 1966.

Darlington, Ralph. *The Political Trajectory of J.T. Murphy*. Liverpool: Liverpool University Press, 1998.

Davis, Mary. *Sylvia Pankhurst: A Life in Radical Politics*. London: Pluto Press, 1999.

Dodd, Kathryn, ed. *A Sylvia Pankhurst Reader*. Manchester and New York: Manchester University Press, 1993.

Dowse, Robert E. *Left in the Centre: The Independent Labour Party, 1893–1940*. London: Longmans, 1966.

Figes, Orlando. *A People's Tragedy: The Russian Revolution, 1891–1924*. London: Jonathan Cape, 1996. New edition, London: Pimlico Books, 1997.

Getzler, Israel. *Kronstadt, 1917–21: The Fate of a Soviet Democracy*. Cambridge: Cambridge University Press, 1983.

Glass, S.T. *The Responsible Society: The Ideas of Guild Socialism*. London: Longmans, 1966.

Graubard, Stephen Richards. *British Labour and the Russian Revolution, 1917–1924*, Cambridge, MA, and London: Harvard University Press, 1956.

Greenleaf, W.H. *The British Political Tradition*. Vol. 2, *The Ideological Inheritance*. London and New York: Methuen, 1985.

Hinton, James. *The First Shop-Stewards' Movement*. London: Allen and Unwin, 1973.

———. *Labour and Socialism: A History of the British Labour Movement, 1867–1974*. Brighton, East Sussex, UK: Wheatsheaf Books, 1983.

Holman, Bob. *Good Old George: The Life of George Lansbury*. Oxford: Lion Publishing, 1990.

Holton, Bob. *British Syndicalism, 1900–1914*. London: Pluto Press, 1976.

Howell, David. *A Lost Left: Three Studies in Socialism and Nationalism*. Manchester: Manchester University Press, 1986.

———. *MacDonald's Party: Labour Identities and Crisis, 1922–1931*. Oxford: Oxford University Press, 2002.

Hulse, James W. *The Forming of the Communist International*. Stanford, CA: Stanford University Press, 1964.

Jansen, Marc. *A Show Trial Under Lenin: The Trial of the Socialist Revolutionaries*. Studies in Social History, International Institute of Social History. Amsterdam, The Hague, and London: Martinus Nijhoff, 1982.

Jones, Bill J. *The Russia Complex: The British Labour Party and the Soviet Union*. Manchester: Manchester University Press, 1977.

Judt, Tony. *Ill Fares the Land: A Treatise on Our Present Discontents*. London: Allen Lane, 2010.

Kendall, Walter. "The Communist International and the Turn from 'Social Fascism' to the Popular Front." *Revolutionary History* 8, no. 1 (2001): 143–56.

———. *The Revolutionary Movement in Britain, 1900–21: The Origins of British Communism*. London: Weidenfeld and Nicolson, 1969.

Koenker, Diane. *Moscow Workers and the 1917 Revolution*. Princeton: Princeton University Press, 1981.

Laybourn, Keith. *Philip Snowden: A Biography, 1864–1937*. Aldershot, Hampshire, UK: Temple Smith, 1988.

Leventhal, F.M. *The Last Dissenter: H.N. Brailsford and His World*. Oxford: Clarendon Press, 1985.

Macfarlane, L.J. *The British Communist Party: Its Origin and Development Until 1929*. London: Macgibbon and Kee, 1966.

Macpherson, C.B. *The Real World of Democracy: The Massey Lectures*. Oxford: Clarendon Press, 1966.

Marquand, David. *Ramsay MacDonald*. London: Jonathan Cape, 1977.

Marwick, Arthur. *Clifford Allen: The Open Conspirator*. Edinburgh and London: Oliver, 1964.

Mcbriar, A.M. *Fabian Socialism and English Politics, 1884–1916*. Cambridge: Cambridge University Press, 1962.

McIlroy, John. "Rehabilitating Communist History: The Communist International, the Communist Party of Great Britain and Some Revisionist Historians." *Revolutionary History* 8, no. 1 (2001): 195–226.

McIlroy, John, and Alan Campbell. " 'Nina Ponomareva's Hats': The New Revisionism, the Communist International, and the Communist Party of Great Britain, 1920–30." *Labour/Le Travail* 49 (Spring/Printemps 2002): 147–87.

Miliband, Ralph. *Parliamentary Socialism: A Study in the Politics of Labour*. 2nd ed. London: Merlin Press, 1972.

Morgan, Kevin. *Bolshevism and the British Left. Vol. 1, Labour Legends and Russian Gold*. London: Lawrence and Wishart, 2006.

———. *Bolshevism and the British Left. Vol. 2, The Webbs and Soviet Communism*. London: Lawrence and Wishart, 2006.

———. *Bolshevism and the British Left. Vol. 3, Workers of All Countries? Syndicalism, Internationalism and the Lost World of A.A. Purcell*. London: Lawrence and Wishart, 2011 (forthcoming).

———. "English Guild Socialists and the Exemplar of the Panama Canal." *History of Political Thought* 28, no. 1 (Spring 2007): 120–57.

———. *Harry Pollitt*. Manchester: Manchester University Press, 1993.

Northedge, F.S., and Audrey Wells. *Britain and Soviet Communism: The Impact of a Revolution*. London and Basingstoke: Macmillan, 1982.

Palat, Madhavan K. "Police Socialism in Tsarist Russia, 1900–1905." *Studies in History* 2, no. 1 (n.s.) (February 1986): 71–136.

Peart-Binns, John S. *Maurice B. Reckitt: A Life*. Basingstoke: Bowerdean Press and Marshal Pickering, 1988.

Pelling, Henry. *The British Communist Party: A Historical Profile*. London: A. & C. Black, 1958.

———. *A Short History of the Labour Party*. 11th ed. Basingstoke: Macmillan, 1996.

———, ed. *The Challenge of Socialism*. London: A. & C. Black, 1968.

Pipes, Richard. *The Russian Revolution, 1899–1919*. London: Collins Harvill, 1997. Originally published 1990.

Postgate, Raymond. *The Life of George Lansbury*. London: Longmans, Green, 1951.

Radice, Lisanne. *Beatrice and Sydney Webb: Fabian Socialists*. London: Macmillan, 1984.

Read, Charles. *From Tsar to Soviets: The Russian People and Their Revolution, 1917–21*. London: UCL Press, 1996.

Rustin, Michael. "What Happened to Socialism?" *History Workshop Journal* 57 (Spring 2004): 202–15.

Saville, John. "The British Labour Delegation to Russia, 1920." Note following the entry on Sir Ben Turner, in *Dictionary of Labour Biography*, vol. 8, edited by Joyce M. Bellamy and John Saville, 257–61. London: Macmillan, 1987.

Schneer, Jonathan. *George Lansbury*. Manchester and New York: Manchester University Press, 1990.

Service, Robert. *The Bolshevik Party in Revolution: A Study in Organised Change, 1917–1923*. London: Macmillan, 1977.

———. *Lenin: A Biography*. London: Pan Books, 2002.

Shipway, Mark. *Anti-Parliamentary Communism: The Movement for Workers' Councils in Britain, 1917–45*. Basingstoke and London: Macmillan, 1988.

Smith, Adrian. *The New Statesman: Portrait of a Political Weekly, 1913–1931*. London: Frank Cass, 1996.

Taylor, A.J.P. *English History, 1914–1945*. Oxford: Clarendon Press, 1965. Repr. London: Penguin Books, 1970.

Thompson, Laurence. *The Enthusiasts: A Biography of John and Katharine Bruce Glasier*. London: Gollancz, 1971.

Thompson, Willie. *The Good Old Cause: British Communism, 1920–1991*. London: Pluto Press, 1992.

Thorpe, Andrew. *The British Communist Party and Moscow, 1920–45*. Manchester: Manchester University Press, 2000.

———. "Comintern 'Control' of the Communist Party of Great Britain, 1920–43." *English Historical Review* 113 (June 1998): 637–62.

———. *A History of the British Labour Party*. 3rd ed. Basingstoke: Palgrave Macmillan, 2008.

Tsuzuki, Chushichi. *H.M. Hyndman and British Socialism*. Oxford: Oxford University Press, 1961.

van der Linden, Marcel. "On Council Communism." *Historical Materialism* 12, no. 4 (2004): 27–50.

White, Stephen. *Britain and the Bolshevik Revolution: A Study in the Politics of Diplomacy, 1920–1924*. London and Basingstoke: Macmillan, 1979.

———. "Labour's Council of Action 1920." *Journal of Contemporary History* 9, no. 4 (1974): 99–122.

———. "Soviets in Britain: The Leeds Convention of 1917." *International Review of Social History* 19, no. 2 (1974): 165–93.

Williams, Andrew. *Labour and Russia: The Attitude of the Labour Party to the USSR, 1924–34*. Manchester: Manchester University Press, 1989.

Williams, Beryl. *The Russian Revolution, 1917–21*. Oxford and Cambridge, MA: Blackwell, 1987.

Winslow, Barbara. *Sylvia Pankhurst: Sexual Politics and Political Activism*. London: UCL Press, 1996.

INDEX

¶ This book was typeset in Bulmer MT, the modern edition of a face originally cut by William Martin of Birmingham in the late eighteenth century. The sans serif face is Mr Eaves, designed by Zuzana Licko.